The Æneid
Latin Dictionary

The Æneid Latin Dictionary

CHAPEL-EN-LE-FRITH
NIGEL GOURLAY

The DCC Aeneid Vocabulary List is based on Henry S. Frieze,
*Vergil's Aeneid Books I–XII, with an Introduction, Notes, and
Vocabulary,* revised by Walter Dennison (New York: American Book
Co., 1902). The frequency data derives from a human inspection
and analysis of every word in the Aeneid (Perret's text) carried
out by teams at the Laboratoire d'Analyse Statistique des Langues
Anciennes (LASLA) at the Université de Liège. The Frieze-Dennison
lexicon was revised and combined with the LASLA frequency data
in 2014 at Dickinson College. Lara Frymark edited the OCR of
Frieze-Dennison using ABBYY Finereader, and created a
spreadsheet in Excel. Tyler Denton created a preliminary match
between Frieze's headwords and those of LASLA. The interface
was built in Drupal by Ryan Burke. Christopher Francese edited
the whole vocabulary list.

This 2020 printed edition was edited, published, and typeset using
Meta Sans and Meta Serif by

Nigel Gourlay · Chapel-en-le-Frith

Notes and Abbreviations

The numbers within each dictionary definition are cross-references to the Æneid. For example, in the following definition:

Abaris, is *m* a Rutulian warrior, 9.344.

the number 9.344 refers to line 344 in book 9 of the Aeneid.

a. or act., active, -ly.
abbrev., abbreviated, -tion.
abl., ablative.
absol. or abs., absolute, -ly, i. e.
without case or adjunct.
abstr., abstract.
acc., accusative or according.
access., accessory.
ad loc. or ad h. l., ad locum or
ad hunc locum.
adj., adjective, -ly.
adv., adverb, -ial, -ially; or
adversus.
agric. or agricult., agricultural.
a. h. v., ad hanc vocem.
al., alii or alia, others or other.
amplif., amplificative.
analog., analogous, -ly.
antiq., antiquities.
ap., apud (in).
appel., appellative.
append. or app., appendix.

Arab., Arabic.
archit., architecture, -tural.
art., article.
aug., augmentative.
Aug., Augustan.
c., cum (with).
c. c., coupled with.
cf., confer (compare).
chh., church.
class., classic, -al.
Cod., Codex (MS).
collat., collateral.
collect., collective, -ly.
com., commonly, comicus,
comic, or in comedy.
comm. or c., common gender.
commentt., commentators.
comp., compare or comparative.
compd., compound.
concr., concrete.
conj., conjunction, conjunctive,
or conjugation.

constr., construed, -ction.

contr., contracted, contraction, or contrary.

corresp., corresponding.

dat., dative.

decl., declension.

demonstr. or dem., demonstrative.

dep., deponent.

deriv., derived, -ative, -ation.

diff., differs or different.

dim., diminutive.

dissyl., dissyllable, -abic.

distr., distributive.

dub., doubtful.

eccl., ecclesiastical.

ed., editio or editor.

e. g., exempli gratiâ.

ellipt., elliptical, -ly.

elsewh., elsewhere.

epic., epicene.

epit., epitaph.

equiv., equivalent.

esp., especially.

etc., et cetera.

etym. etymology, -ical.

euphon., euphonic, -ny.

ex., exs., example, examples.

expl., explanation, explained.

express., expression.

ext., externa.

extr., extremo (at the end).

f. or fem., feminine.

fig., figure, -ative, -atively.

finit., finite (opp. to infinitive).

foll., following.

fr., from.

Fr., French.

fragm., frgm., or fr., fragmenta.

freq. or fr., frequentative or frequent, -ly.

fut., future.

gen., genitive or general.

geog., geography, -ical.

Germ., German.

Goth., Gothic.

gr. or gram., grammar, -ian,

-atical, grammatici.

Gr. Greek.

h., hence.

h. l., hic locus (this passage).

h.v., h. vv., this word, these words.

Heb., Hebrew.

hibr., hybrid.

hist., history, -ian.

ib., ibidem.

id., idem.

i. e., id est.

i. q., idem quod.

imper., imperative.

imperf., imperfect.

impers., impersonal, -ly.

inanim., inanimate.

in bon. part., in bonam partem.

in mal. part., in malam partem.

inch., inchoative, inceptive.

indecl., indeclinable.

indef., indefinite.

indic., indicative.

inf., infinitive.

init., in., or ad init., at the beginning.

inscrr., inscriptions.

intens., intensive.

interrog., interrogative, -tion.

intr., intransitive.

Ital., Italian.

JCtus., juris consultus.

jurid., juridical.

kindr., kindred.

l., lege or lectio.

l. c. or l. l., loco citato or laudato, in the place already cited.

lang., language.

Lat., Latin.

leg., legit, legunt.

lex., lexicon.

lit., literal, in a literal sense.

Lith., Lithuanian.

m. or masc., masculine.

math., mathematics, -ical.

med., medio (in the middle).

medic., medical or medicine.

metaph., metaphorical, -ly.

meton., by metonymy.

mid. or med., medial; in a middle or reflexive sense.

milit., military, in military affairs.

MS., manuscript; MSS. manuscripts.

n. or neutr. neuter.

n. pr. or nom. propr., nomen proprium.

naut., nautical.

neg., negative, -ly.

no., numero.

nom., nominative.

num. or numer., numeral.

obj. or object., object, objective, -ly.

obl., oblique.

om., omit.

onomat., onomatopoeia.

orig., originally.

p., page.

P. a., participal adjective.

part., participle.

partit., partitive.

pass., passive, -ly, or passage.

patr., patronymic.

per., period.

perf., perfect.

perh., perhaps.

pers., personal, -ly.

philos., philosophy, -ical, -ically, -opher.

pl. or plur., plural.

pleon., pleonastically.

plqpf., plusquamperfectum.

plur. tant., used only in the plural.

poet., poetical, -ly.

polit., political, -ly.

posit. or pos., positive.

poss., possessive.

praef., praefatio.

praep., preposition.

preced., preceding.

pregn., pregnant, -ly.

prep., preposition.

pres., present.

prob., probably.

prol., prologus.

pron., pronoun.

prooem., prooemium.

prop., proper, -ly, in a proper sense.

prov. or proverb., proverbial, -ly.

qs., quasi.

q. v., quod videas.

rad., radical or root.

rar., rare, -ly.

ref., refer, -ence.

rel., relative or reliquiae.

respect., respectûs.

rhet., rhetoric, -al; in rhetoric.

Rom., Roman.

saep., saepe.

saepis., saepissime.

sc., scilicet.

s. h. v., sub hac voce.

signif., signifies, -cation.

simp., simple.

Span., Spanish.

specif., specifically.

sq., sequens; sqq., sequentes (and the following).

subj., subjunctive.

subject. or subj., subject, subjective. -ly.

subst., substantive, -ly.

suff., suffix.

sup., superlative or supine.

syll., syllable.

syn., synonym, -ymous.

sync., syncopated.

tab., tabula (table, plate).

temp. tense or temporal.

term., terminus.

trag., tragicus, tragic, or in tragedy.

trans., translated, -tion.

transf., transferred.

trisyl., trisyllable, -abic.

trop., in a tropical or figurative

sense.
t. t., technical term.
usu., usual, -ly.
v., verb, vide, or vox.
v. h. v., vide hanc vocem.

var. lect., varia lectio (different reading.
vb., verb.
voc., vocative.

ā, ab, abs *prep with abl* from, in relations of space, time, source, cause, and agency; from, 1.371; following a substantive directly, with ellipsis of participle, 1.160; at, on, to, 7.106; from the direction, on the side of, 5.19; in respect to, 11.174; according to, 9.235; from a period or point of time, 2.87; since, after, 1.730; (of persons), by, 2.429; **ā tergō** from the rear, behind, 1.186; **ab ūsque** as far as from, even from, 7.289. In composition, ab is unchanged before vowels and before i(= j), h, b, d, l, n, r, s; becomes abs before c, q, t, as before p; ā in āfui from absum; and au is used in auferō, from ab and ferō, and in aufugiō, from ab and fugiō.

Abaris, is *m* a Rutulian warrior, 9.344.

Abās, antis[1] *m* The twelfth king of Argos, grandson of Danaus, 3.286. .

Abās, antis[2] *m* A Trojan, follower of Aeneas, 1.121. .

Abās, antis[3] *m* An Etruscan, 10.427.

abdō, didī, ditus *3 v* to put away; *with the point or place where, in the abl alone or with a prep, the acc with prep, or the dative*; to hide, shut up, 1.60; to bury, plunge, thrust, 2.553.

abdūcō, dūxī, ductus *3 v* to lead away; remove, take away, 3.601; take away by force, 7.362; draw back, 5.428.

Abella, ae *f* Abella, a town in Campania, N.E. of Naples, 7.740.

abeō, īvī or **iī, itus, īre** *irreg v* to go away, depart, 2.675; go off, go aside, turn off, 5.162; pass into, sink into, 9.700; go forward, take the lead, 5.318; retreat, 2.382; change or be transformed.

abiciō, iēcī, iectus *3 v* to cast off, away or down, 10.736. (ab and iaciō).

abies, etis (often trisyllabbic in the oblique cases) *f* a fir tree; fir wood or fir timber, 2.16; *metonym* a ship, 8.91; a lance, 11.667.

abigō, ēgī, āctus *3 v* to drive off or away from, i.e. beyond (others in), 8.407; drive away, 11.261. (ab and agō).

abitus, ūs *m* a departure, 8.214; a passage, or outlet, 9.380. (abeō).

abiūrō, āvī, ātus *1 v* to swear off; deny upon oath; deny, disavow, 8.263.

abluō, luī, lūtus *3 v* to wash away, 9.818; cleanse, purify, wash, 2.720.

abnegō, āvī, ātus *1 v* to deny, refuse, *with acc and dat* 7.424, *with inf* 2.637; alone 2.654.

abnuō, nuī, nuitus or **nūtus** *3 v* to shake the head in dissent; refuse, *with acc* 4.108; reject, 5.531; forbid, *with acc and inf* 10.8.

aboleō, ēvī, itus *2 v* to cause to wane or waste; to destroy, 4.497; cleanse, efface,

wipe out, 11.789; obliterate
the memory of, 1.720.

abolēscō, olēvī, *2 v incomplete*
to decay, 7.232. (aboleō).

abripiō, ripuī, reptus *3 v*
to take away violently;
snatch, carry away, 1.108;
4.600. (ab and rapiō).

abrumpō, rūpī, ruptus *3 v* to
break off, away, or tear away
from, 9.118; tear asunder,
rend, 3.199; end suddenly
or abruptly, 4.388; put an
end to, 4.631; violate, 3.55;
part abruptus, a, um, having
burst, bursting, breaking
forth, *subst* abruptum, ī,
n, anything broken off; a
precipice; abyss, chasm, 3.422;
in abruptum, headlong, 12.687.

abscessus, ūs *m* a going
away, retreat, 10.445.
(abscēdō, to go away).

abscīdō, cīdī, cīsus *3 v* to cut
off, 12.511. (abs and caedō).

abscindō, scidī, scissus *3 v* to
tear off, away, from, 5.685;
separate, 3.418; tear, 4.590.

**abscondō, condī and condidī,
ditus** *3 v* to put out of
sight, hide, conceal; to
conceal, 4.337; lose sight
of, withdraw from, 3.291.

absēns, entis *adj* absent,
4.83. (absum).

absistō, abstitī *3 v* to stand off or
away from, *followed by the abl,
alone or with prep*; withdraw
from, 6.259; fly, dart from,
12.102; *with infin* desist, cease,
6.399; *alone* stop, cease, 1.192.

abstineō, uī, tentus *2 v* to hold
or keep off from, or abstain
from, *with abl* 7.618; *alone*
abstain, restrain one's self,
2.534. (abs and teneō).

abstrahō, trāxī, trāctus *3 v* to
drag or lead away, 8.263.

abstrūdō, trūsī, trūsus *3 v*
to push or thrust off; to
conceal, hide, 6.7.

absum, āfuī or **abfuī, āfutūrus**
or **abfutūrus, abesse** *irreg v* to
be away; to be absent, 2.620;
distant, 11.907; to be wanting,
missing, 1.584; *inf*, āfore, or
abfore, will be wanting, 8.147.

absūmō, sūmpsī, sūmptus *3 v*
to take away; of death, to end,
destroy, 3.654; exhaust, spend,
7.301; consume, devour,
3.257; cut off, end, 1.555.

abunde *adv* with *gen* (abundus),
sufficiently, enough, 7.552.

abundō, āvī, ātus *1 v* to overflow;
abound; abundāns, antis,
overflowing, 11.547.

Acamās, antis *m* Acamas, a son
of Theseus and Phaedra, 2.262.

acanthus, ī *m* the plant bear's-
foot; the acanthus, 1.649.

Acarnān, ānis *adj* of Acarnania,
a country between Epirus and
Aetolia; Acarnanian, 5.298.

Acca, ae *f* a companion
of Camilla, 11.820.

accēdō, cessī, cessus (*perf
ind*, accēstis for accessistis,
1.201) *3 v* to go or draw near
to; approach, *with acc alone*
1.307. (ad and cedo).

accelerō, āvī, ātus *1 v* to hasten; make haste, 5.675. (ad and celerō).

accendō, ī, cēnsus *3 v* to set fire to, light up, enkindle, 5.4; enrage, exasperate, incense, 1.29; incite, rouse, 4.232. (ad and candō, *rel to* candeō).

accessus, ūs *m* a going near to; an access, approach, 3.570. (accēdō).

accidō, cidī *3 v* to happen, 12.593. (ad and cadō).

accīdō, cīdī, cīsus *3 v* to cut into, or up; cut, 2.627; eat into, devour, consume, 7.125. (ad and caedō).

accingō, cīnxī, cīnctus (*pass inf*, accingier, 4.493) *3 v* to gird on; gird, 2.614; arm, equip, 6.184; make one's self ready; prepare, 1.210; resort to, 4.493. (ad and cingō).

acciō, cīvī, cītus *4 v* to summon, call, 11.235. (ad and cieō).

accipiō, cēpī, ceptus *3 v* to take to one's self; to receive, 1.304; take in or up, admit, receive, 1.123; 3.79; entertain, 3.353; see, 8.155; hear, attend, listen to, learn, 2.65; heed, regard, 4.611. (ad and capiō).

accipiter, tris *m* a hawk, 11.721.

accītus, ūs *m* a summons, call, 1.677; used only in *the abl sing* (acciō).

acclīnis, e leaning on or against, 10.835.

accola, ae, *c* a neighbor, 7.729. (accolō).

accolō, coluī, cultus *3 v* to dwell near or by. (ad and colō).

accommodō, āvī, ātus *1 v* to fit one thing to another; to buckle, gird, 2.393. (ad and commodō).

accommodus, a, um fit, suitable, 11.522. (ad and commodus).

accubō, uī, itus *1 v* to lie near or by, to recline, 6.606; bend over, project. (ad and cumbō).

accumbō, cubuī, cubitus *3 v* to lay one's self down, at or upon; recline, *with dat* 1.79. (accubō).

accumulō, āvī, ātus *1 v* to place heap on heap; heap up, load; honor, 6.885. (ad and cumulō).

accurrō, currī, *seldom* **cucurrī, cursus** *3 v* to run to; run, hasten up, 5.451. (ad and currō).

ācer, ācris, ācre *adj* sharp; *figuratively* bitter, pungent, 7.291; ardent, active, strong, 1.220; brave, valiant, 8.441; spirited, full of life, life-like, 5.254; elastic, springing, 7.164; swift, nimble, fiery, 1.444; fierce, furious, 2.414; keen, urgent, 1.362.

acerbō, *no perf*, ātus *1 v* to embitter; to aggravate, augment, 11.407. (acerbus).

acerbus, a, um harsh, bitter, in taste; *figuratively* cruel, fierce, 5.462; fatal, direful, sorrowful, sad, mournful, 5.49; 6.429; *pl* acerba, ōrum, *n* vengeful deeds, 12.500; *adv* acerba, harshly, savagely, fiercely, 9.794.

acernus, a, um of maple; maple-, 2.112. (acer, maple).

acerra, ae *f* an incense box; a censer, 5.745.

acervus, ī *m* a heap, pile, 4.402.

Acesta, ae *f* a town in Sicily, named after Acestes, 5.718.

Acestēs, ae *m* Acestes or Segestus, the son of Crimisus, a Sicilian river god, and Egesta or Segesta, a Trojan woman, 1.195.

Achaemenidēs, ae *m* Achaemenides, a companion of Ulysses, 3.614.

Achāicus (*poetic* **Achāius**), **a, um** of Achaia; Achaean; Greek, 2.462. (Achāia).

Achātēs, ae *m* Achates, a companion of Aeneas, 1.174 *et al.*

Acherōn, ontis *m* the Acheron, a river of Hades, 6.295; *metonym* the lower world, 5.99.

Achillēs, is (**eos** or **ī**) *m* the son of Peleus, king of Thessaly, and Thetis, daughter of Nereus, 1.468 *et al.*

Achillēus, a, um of Achilles; Achillean, 3.326.

Achīvī, ōrum or **um** the Greeks, the Achaeans 2.102.

Achīvus, a, um Achaean; Greek, 1.488; *pl subst* Achīvī, ōrum or um, the Greeks, 2.102.

Acīdalius, a, um pertaining to Venus; Acidalian, 1.720. (Acīdalia, an appellation of Venus, derived from the name of a fountain in Boeotia).

aciēs, ēī *f* a sharp edge or point; edge, 2.333; an arrowhead, 11.862; the sight of the eye, 6.200; the eye, 4.643; an army in line of battle; army, 10.408; the shock, of battle, 12.662; light; *pl* aciēs, the eyes, 12.558; squadrons, battalions, troops, 2.599; battles, 6.829; **aciēs īnferre**, to charge, 10.364.

aclys, ydis *f* a dart with a thong on its shaft, 7.730.

Acmōn, onis *m* a Trojan, 10.128.

Acoetēs, is *m* the armor-bearer of Evander, 11.30.

Aconteus, eī *m* a Latin warrior, 11.612.

Acragās, antis *m* Agrigentum, a city on the southern coast of Sicily, now Girgenti, 3.703.

Ācrisiōnēus, a, um pertaining to Acrisione or Danaë, daughter of Acrisius; Acrisonean, 7.410. (Ācrisiōnē).

Ācrisius, ī *m* a king of Argos, son of Abas, 7.372.

ācriter *adv* sharply, fiercely; *compar* ācrius, more vigorously.

Ācrōn, ōnis *m* a Greek warrior, 10.719.

acta, ae *f* the seashore; beach, shore, 5.613.

Actius, a, um *adj* (*poetic* for Actiacus, from Actium), pertaining to Actium, a promontory and town of Epirus, celebrated as the scene of the decisive victory of Augustus over

Antony and Cleopatra, in BC 31; Actian, 3.280.

Actor, oris *m* 1. The name of a Trojan, 9.500. 2. The name of an Auruncian, 12.94.

āctus, ūs *m* a driving or impelling; speed, swift descent, 12.687. (agō).

āctūtum *adv* promptly, immediately, 9.255. (āctus).

acuō, uī, ūtus *3 v* to make pointed; to sharpen, whet, 8.386; *figuratively* stimulate, provoke, 7.330; incite, rouse.

acus, ūs *f* a needle, 9.582. (acuō).

acūtus, a, um sharpened, pointed, sharp, 1.45. (acuō).

ad¹ (In relations of place) *prep followed by acc* to, towards, at, by, near, before, *frequently* present with, among, 6.481; .

ad² (Of time) *prep followed by acc* at, just at, about, by, 4.513 *et al.*; .

ad³ (In other relations) *prep followed by acc* in one's esteem, with, 12.648; **ad ūnum** even to a single one, to the last one, to a man, 5.687; **ad ūsque** as far as, 11.262 *et al.*

ad ūsque quite to, 11.262.

adamās, antis *m* that which cannot be overcome; the hardest iron, steel, adamant, 6.552.

Adamastus, ī *m* the father of Achaemenides, 3.614.

addēnseō, ēre, and **addēnsō, āre,** *v* to make compact; close up, 10.432.

addīcō, dīxī, dictus *3 v* to pronounce for; assign to; give up to, 3.653.

addō, didī, ditus *3 v* to put or lay near to or by, put on, 5.817; add, join, 9.765; erect on, 3.336; give, impart, 1.593; add, bestow, 5.249; addere sē, to join, 2.339.

addūcō, dūxī, ductus *3 v* to lead or draw to; lead on, 10.380; draw to, bend, draw tight, strain, of the muscles, 5.141; of a bow, etc., 5.507.

adedō, ēdī, ēsus *3 v* to eat up, devour, consume, 9.537.

adeō *adv* (ad + eō, *cf.* is), to this or that point; so far, to such a degree, so very, so much; *with correl.* ut following, 11.436 *et al.*; *explanatory of a preceding statement*, so much, so, 1.567 *et al.*; so, therefore, 4.533; added to this, besides, moreover; *frequently emphasizing a word or statement*, aye indeed, aye also, indeed, even, 3.203; 7.427; **iamque adeō** and **nunc adeō** and even now, now indeed, already, or moreover, 5.268; 9.156 *et al.*; **ūsque adeō** up to such a point, even so, so much; **vix adeō** hardly even, 6.498.

adeō, īvī or **iī, itus, īre** *irreg v* to go to, approach; visit, 4.56; reach, 4.322; encounter, undergo, 1.10.

adfābilis, e *adj* (adfor), that can be spoken to; easy to be approached, 3.621.

adfātus, ūs *m* a speaking to; address, 4.284. (adfor).

adfectō, āvī, ātus 1 *freq v* to strive after; grasp, seize, 3.670; seek. (adficiō).

adferō, attulī, allātus, adferre *irreg v* to bring, bear, or carry, convey to, 12.171; bring hither, 6.532; to present, 3.310; *passive* adferrī, to be brought to, *with acc* 7.217.

adficiō, fēcī, fectus 3 *v* to affect; reward, 12.352. (ad and faciō).

adfīgō, fīxī, fīxus 3 *v* to fasten to, put to, 9.536; *perf part pass*, clinging to, 5.852.

adflīctus, a, um dejected, desponding, 2.92; wretched, troubled, 1.452. (adflīgō, flīxī, flīctus 3 *v*).

adflō, āvī, ātus 1 *v* to blow upon; breathe upon, 5.739; blast, 2.649; inspire, 6.50; impart, 1.591.

adfluō, flūxī, flūxus 3 *v* to flow to; *figuratively* gather, flock together, assemble, 2.796.

adfor, fātus sum 1 *dep v* to speak to; address, 1.663; beseech, supplicate, 2.700; bid adieu, farewell to, 2.644.

adgnoscō, nōvī, nitus 3 *v* to recognize, 1.470.

adhibeō, uī, itus 2 *v* to hold or apply to, unite with, admit to, 8.56; to bring to, invite, 5.62; adhibēre animum or animōs, to give attention, 11.315. (ad and habeō).

adhūc *adv* to this place; to this time; hitherto, as yet, yet,

still, 1.547 *et al.*; neque adhūc, and not even yet, nor yet.

adiciō, iēcī, iectus 3 *v* to throw to or upon; add, join, 12.837. (ad and iaciō).

adigō, ēgī, āctus 3 *v* to drive, take, bring to, 9.601; thrust, 9.431; to strike down, hurl, 4.25; force, urge, impel, *with inf* 6.696; drive, 10.850. (ad and agō).

adimō, ēmī, ēmptus 3 *v* to take to one's self; take from or away, 4.244; pluck out, 3.658. (ad and emō).

aditus, ūs *m* a going to; an approach, avenue, access, passage, entrance, 2.494; *figuratively* approach, 4.423. (adeō).

adiungō, iūnxī, iūnctus 3 *v* to join to, moor, 9.69; associate with, 8.515; add, to ally, 7.238.

adiūrō, āvī, ātus 1 *v* to swear by, *with acc* of the thing sworn by, 12.816.

adiuvō, iūvī, iūtus 1 *v* to give aid to; to help, aid, support, 5.345; encourage, stimulate, incite further, 12.210.

adlābor, lāpsus sum 3 *dep v* to glide to; (*with dat* rarely *acc*), sail to, reach, 3.569; advance, glide (with *abl* of manner), 10.269; fly to, 9.474; descend, fall upon, 12.319.

adlacrimāns, antis weeping, 10.628. (*participle of obsol* adlacrimō, shed tears).

adligō, āvī, ātus 1 *v* to tie or bind to; hold fast, hold, 1.169; constrain, confine, 6.439.

adloquor, locūtus sum *3 dep v* to address, 1.229.

adlūdō, lūsī, lūsus *3 v* to speak playfully; sport, mock, jest, 7.117.

adluō, luī *3 v* to wash against, wash, 8.149.

admīror, ātus sum *1 dep v* to admire, 6.408; wonder, 2.797.

admisceō, miscuī, mixtus or **mistus** *2 v* to mingle with, *with dat*; to associate, unite, join, 7.579.

admittō, mīsī, missus (*pass inf* **admittier**, 9.231) *3 v* to allow to go to a place; to admit, 6.330.

admoneō, uī, itus *2 v* to put in mind; remind; admonish, warn, *with acc* 4.353; incite, urge on, 10.587; with interrogative clause, 10.153; remind, remonstrate, caution.

admoveō, mōvī, mōtus *2 v* to move, bring near to; to carry, convey to, 3.410; apply to, touch; admovēre ūbera, give suck, 4.367.

adnītor, nīsus or **nīxus sum** *3 dep v* to press upon; (*with dat*), lean against, 12.92; lean, rest upon, 4.690; *alone* make effort, strive, 5.226; ply the oars, 4.583.

adnō, nāvī, nātus *1 v* to swim to, sail toward or to, *with dat* 1.538.

adnuō, nuī (**ūtus, rare**) *3 v* to nod to; *with dat acc and dat* and *infin*; ascent, consent, 4.128; promise, 1.250; direct, permit, 11.20.

adoleō, oluī, ultus *2 v* to cause to increase; to magnify, honor, adore, worship, 1.704; burn in sacrifice, offer, 3.547; fire, kindle, 7.71.

adolescō, olēvī, ultus *3 inc v* to grow up, of animals or plants; become mature, ripen, 12.438; burn, blaze, 4.379; *part*, adultus, a, um, grown up; mature, 1.431. (adoleō).

adoperiō, operuī, opertus *4 v* to cover up, cover, 3.405.

adōreus, a, um *adj* (ador, spelt), of spelt or fine wheat, 7.109.

adorior, ortus sum *4 dep v* to rise toward or upon, to approach; to aim at, undertake, attempt, 6.397.

adōrō, āvī, ātus *1 v* to pray to; supplicate, worship, adore, 1.48.

adquīrō, quīsīvī, quīsītus *3 v* to seek in addition; gain, 4.175. (ad and quaerō).

Adrastus, ī *m* king of Argos, 6.480.

adsciō *4 v* to ally, adopt, 12.38.

adscīscō, scīvī, scītus *3 v* to call to one's aid; to ally, 11.308; to adopt, 11.472. (adsciō).

adsēnsus, ūs *m* an assenting; answering sound, response, echo, applause, 10.97. (adsentiō).

adsentiō, sēnsī, sēnsus *4 v* and, more frequently, adsentior, sēnsus sum *4 dep v* , to give consent; to assent, agree, 2.130.

adservō, āvī, ātus *1 v* to keep carefully; guard, watch, 2.763.

adsideō, sēdī, sessus *2 v* to sit by, besiege, 11.304. (ad and sedeō).

adsiduē *adv* (adsiduus), persistently, perpetually, constantly, 4.248.

adsiduus, a, um *adj* (adsideō), abiding by; persistent, constant, 4.447; perpetual, frequent, 9.245.

adsimilis, e *adj* like, similar to, 6.603.

adsimulō, āvī, ātus *1 v* to make like; to counterfeit, feign, 10.639; *passive* make one's self like, 12.224.

adsistō, adstitī *3 v* to stand at, by, or present; stand, 12.790.

adspīrō, āvī, ātus *1 v* to breathe to or upon, 5.607; breathe or emit fragrance, 1.694; *figuratively* inspire, 9.525; aid, favor, prosper, 2.385; aspire, 12.352.

adstō, stitī *1 v* to stand at, near, or upon; alight, 1.301; stand, 9.677; be present, 3.150; stand or be ready, 3.123; impend, 3.194.

adsuēscō, suēvī, suētus *3 v* to accustom to, make familiar, habituate to; *with dat acc and dat* and *infin*, to get or become accustomed, be wont, learn; *with abl* 7.746; adsuēscere bella animīs, instead of adsuēscere animōs bellīs, to cherish war in the heart, 6.832.

adsultus, ūs *m* a leaping upon; an assault, attack, 5.442. (ad and saliō).

adsum, adfuī, esse *irreg v* to be near or by; to be present, at hand, or here, 1.595; to have arrived, 2.132; to be with, attend, 2.701; aid, accompany, 10.547; be propitious, 3.116; to beset, 2.330; *inf*. adfore, to be about to come, destined to come, 7.270. (imp. subj., adforem, -ēs, -et, -ent).

adsurgō, surrēxī, surrēctus *3 v* to rise up; rise, 4.86; swell, fume, 10.95.

adulter, erī *m* an adulterer, 11.268.

adulterium, iī, *n* adultery, 6.612. (adulter).

advehō, vexī, vectus *3 v* to carry or convey to; *passive* advehī, sail to, 1.558; 3.108; foll. by *acc*, 8.136.

advēlō, āvī, ātus *1 v* to veil; wreathe, encircle, crown, 5.246.

advena, ae, *c* a new comer; a stranger, foreigner, 4.591; *adj*, foreign, 7.38. (adveniō).

adveniō, vēnī, ventus *4 v* to come to a place; to arrive, come, 7.803; arrive at, reach, 1.388.

adventō, āvī, ātus *1 intens v* to come rapidly nearer; to approach, draw near, 5.328; 6.258. (adveniō).

adventus, ūs *m* a coming, an arrival, 5.36; advance, 11.607. (advenio).

adversor, ātus sum *1 dep freq n* to be against; to oppose, 4.127. (advertō).

adversus (-um) *adv* opposite to , against , to , or toward a thing, in a friendly or hostile sense.

adversus, a, um turned toward or against; before, in front, opposite, 1.166; opposing, 3.38; against the wind, 12.370; contrary, 2.416; toward, to meet, 6.684; (subst.), adversus, ī, *m*, an enemy, 9.761; adversum, ī, *n*; in adversum, opposite, 8.237; *pl* adversa, ōrum, *n*, misfortunes, accidents, 9.172.

advertō, vertī, versus *3 v* to turn to or toward; turn, direct, 6.386; turn against, bring before, 12.555; of the mind, turn, direct, 8.440; attend, observe, mark, listen, 2.712; *passive* come to, arrive at, 5.34.

advocō, āvī, ātus *1 v* to call; summon, 5.44.

advolō, āvī, ātus *1 v* to fly to, fly, 10.511; hasten, run up, speed, 10.896.

advolvō, volvī, volūtus *3 v* to roll to; roll, 6.182.

adytum, ī, *n* the inaccessible; the innermost part of a temple, accessible only to the priest; a shrine, sanctuary, oracle, 2.115; the interior of a tomb, or shrine of the dead, 5.84.

Aeacidēs, ae *m* a son or descendant of Aeacus. 1. Achilles, as the grandson of Aeacus, 1.99. 2. Pyrrhus, the son of Achilles, 3.296. 3.

Perseus, their descendant, king of Macedon, 6.839.

Aeaeus, a, um *adj* of Aeaea, the island of Circe; Aeaean or Colchian, 3.386.

aedēs, is *f* in the *sing* a temple; *pl* a dwelling, palace, apartments, court, 2.487.512.

aedificō, āvī, ātus *1 v* to build; to construct, make, 2.16. (aedēs and faciō).

Aegaeōn, onis *m* Aegaean, a giant, also called Briareus, 10.565.

Aegaeus, a, um *adj* Aegaean; pertaining to the Aegaean, 3.74.

aeger, gra, grum *adj* indisposed; of the body, not well, suffering, sick, 5.651; wounded, 10.856; heavy, difficult, 5.432; feeble, 9.814; fainting, trembling, 5.468; wearied, exhausted, 2.566; of the mind, careworn, wretched, weary, sorrow-laden, 2.268; grieved, afflicted, desponding, oppressed, 1.208; heartbroken, 1.351; 4.389; of inanimate things, sickly, 3.142.

aeger, gra, grum *adj* indisposed; of the body, not well, suffering, sick, 5.651; wounded, 10.856; heavy, difficult, 5.432; feeble, 9.814; fainting, trembling, 5.468; wearied, exhausted, 2.566; of the mind, careworn, wretched, weary, sorrow-laden, 2.268; grieved, afflicted, desponding, oppressed, 1.208; heartbroken, 1.351; 4.389; of inanimate things, sickly, 3.142.

aegis, idis *f* the shield of Jupiter, carried also by Pallas; the aegis, 8.354.

aegrēscō *3 inc v* to become sick; grow worse, 12.46. (aegreō, to be sick).

Aegyptius, a, um *adj* (Aegyptos), Egyptian, 8.688.

Aegyptos (-tus), ī *f* Egypt.

aemulus, a, um *adj* striving to equal; competing, rivaling, 5.187; envious, 5.415; a rival for, aspiring, 10.371.

aemulus, a, um *adj* striving to equal; competing, rivaling, 5.187; envious, 5.415; a rival for, aspiring, 10.371.

Aeneadēs, ae *m* a son of Aeneas; *pl* Aeneadae, ārum, followers of Aeneas, the Trojans, 1.565; Aeneadae, 3.18.

Aenēās, ae *m* 1. A Trojan chief, son of Venus and Anchises, and hero of the Aeneid, 1.92. 2. Aenēās Silvius, one of the Alban kings, 6.769.

Aenēius, a, um *adj* (id.), of Aeneas, 7.1.

Aenīdēs, ae *m* a son of Aeneus or Aeneas; Iulus, 9.653. (Aeneus, a collat. form of Aenēās).

aēnus, a, um *adj* (aes), of bronze; brazen, 2.470; *subst* aēnum, ī, *n*, a bronze or brazen vessel; caldron, 1.213 *et al.*

aēnus, a, um *adj* (aes), of bronze; brazen, 2.470; *subst* aēnum, ī, *n*, a bronze or brazen vessel; caldron, 1.213 *et al.*

Aeolia, ae *f* Aeolia, an island near Sicily, the home of Aeolus, 1.52.

Aeolidēs, ae *m* a son or descendant of Aeolus. 1. Ulysses, 6.529. 2. Misenus, 6.164. 3. Clytius, 9.774.

Aeolius, a, um *adj* pertaining to Aeolus; Aeolian, 5.791.

Aeolus, ī *m* Aeolus. 1. The god who ruled over the winds, 1.52. 2. A follower of Aeneas from Lyrnesus, 12.542.

aequaevus, a, um *adj* (aequus and aevum), of equal age, 2.561.

aequālis, e *adj* (aequō), equal; of the same age, 10.194; fellow, companion; *subst c*, companion, 5.468.

aequālis, e *adj* (aequō), equal; of the same age, 10.194; fellow, companion; *subst c*, companion, 5.468.

aequē *adv* (aequus), equally; alike.

Aequīculus, a, um *adj* (Aequī), of the Aequi, a tribe adjacent to the Latins and Volscians, near Rome; Aequian, 7.747.

Aequīculus, a, um *adj* (Aequī), of the Aequi, a tribe adjacent to the Latins and Volscians, near Rome; Aequian, 7.747.

aequō, āvī, ātus *1 v* to make equal in size, number, weight, etc., 1.193; 5.419; to equalize, divide equally, 1.508; make equal in length, 9.338; in height, raise to, 4.89; to equal, be equal to; to be as high as, on a level with; keep pace with, 6.263; return equally, requite, 6.474; lift, exalt, 11.125; *part*, aequātus, a, um, made equal or even; steady, 4.587. (aequus).

aequor, oris, *n* an equal, horizontal, or level surface; the surface of the sea; the sea, 1.146; water, 6.355; wave, 3.197; a level field, plain, 5.456; low land, 12.524. (aequō).

aequum, ī, *n* that which is even; right, justice, 2.427; in aequum, to the open field, 9.68.

aequus, a, um *adj* plain, even; on a level with, leveled, *with dat* 12.569; equal, open, fair, 11.706; equal, adequate, prepared, 10.450; favorable, 1.479; impartial, equitable, just, 6.129; unprejudiced, unbiased, 9.234; aequō pede, with foot to foot, face to face, 12.465; aequum est, it is just, 12.20; aequius fuerat, it would have been more just, 11.115.

āēr, eris *m* (*acc* āera or āerem) the air or atmosphere, 1.300 *et al*.

aerātus, a, um *adj* (aes), furnished with copper, bronze; made of bronze, 2.481; bronze-covered; with brazen prow, 8.675; armed with bronze; armed, 7.703.

aereus, a, um *adj* (aes), made of copper or bronze; bronze, brazen (see *def* of aes), 1.448; brazen beaked, 5.198; of the copper or bronze plates or scales of a corselet, 10.313.

aeripēs, edis *adj* (aes and pēs), brazen- or bronze-footed, or hoofed, 6.802.

āerius, a, um *adj* pertaining to the air; airy, aërial, 5.520; rising into the air; towering, lofty, 3.291; air-cleaving, 9.803.

aes, aeris, *n* copper, bronze; brass, in one of the old English usages of that word, 1.449 *et al*.; anything made of copper or bronze; a trumpet, 3.240; cymbal; armor, 2.734; shield, 2.545; a bronze statue, 6.847; a track or course of bronze plates, 6.591; a ship's prow or beak, or a copper-bottomed ship, 1.35; *pl* aera, *n*, money, 11.329; aere nexus, bronze-bound, of bronze, 1.448.

aestās, ātis *f* the summer, 1.265 *et al*.; summer air, 6.707; a year.

aestuō, āvī, ātus *1 v* to glow, to be dried up or parched; boil up; heave, foam, 6.297; fume, 8.258; rage, seethe, 12.666. (aestus).

aestus, ūs *m* glowing heat; summer; a boiling; a billowy motion; waves of flame, flames, 2.706; wave, surge, 1.107; tide, sea, flood, 3.419; tide (of feeling), agitation, 4.532.

aetās, ātis *f* lifetime, age, 1.705; old age, 2.596; period, generation, age, 7.680; lapse of time; time, 8.200. (for aevitās, fr. aevum.)

aeternus, a, um *adj* (for aeviternus), lasting, through ages; eternal; immortal, 1.36; perpetual, 4.99; *adv* aeternum, for in aeternum, continually, eternally, 6.401; for ever, 11.98.

aethēr, eris *m* (*acc* **aethera** and **aetherem**) the upper air; ether, sky, heaven, 1.90; in a general sense, air, 1.587 *et al.*

aetherius, a, um *adj* (aethēr), pertaining to the upper air; ethereal, heavenly, 1.394 *et al.*; airy, 8.608.

Aethiops, opis *m* an Aethiopian.

Aethōn, onis *m* Aethon, one of the chariot horses of Pallas, 11.89.

aethra, ae *f* the cloudless air; serene sky; heaven, 3.585 *et al.*

Aetna, ae *f* a volcanic mountain on the eastern coast of Sicily, 3.579.

Aetnaeus, a, um *adj* (Aetna), of Aetna; Aetnaean, 3.678.

Aetōlus, a, um *adj* Aetolian, 11.428; Aetōla urbs, Arpi in Apulia, built by Diomedes, 11.239.

aevum, ī, *n* indefinite time; lapse of time, time, 3.415; age, 2.638; old age, 2.509; life, 10.582; immortality, 10.235.

Āfer, fra, frum *adj* African; (subst.), Āfrī, ōrum, *m*, Africans, 8.724.

Āfricus, ī *m* the southwest wind.

Agamemnonius, a, um *adj* pertaining to Agamemnon; Agamemnonian, Argive, Greek, 4.471.

Agathyrsī, ōrum *m* a Sythian tribe dwelling on the river Maros in what is now Hungary, remarkable for the practice of tattooing their bodies, 4.146.

age, agite (*imperat* of ago), onward! away! come on!.

Agēnor, oris *m* a son of Neptune and Lyba, king of Phoenicia and ancestor of Dido, 1.338.

ager, agrī *m* the land pertaining to a person or community; land under cultivation; a field, 2.306 *et al.*; land, 1.343 *et al.*

agger, eris *m* materials gathered to form an elevation; a heap of earth or stones, dike, embankment, bank, 1.112; 2.496; heap of earth, 9.567; top, summit, ridge, raised surface, 5.44.273; a rampart, 9.769 *et al.*; a height or rising ground, 12.446; aggerēs, mountains, mountain ramparts, 6.830. (aggerō).

aggerō, āvī, ātus *1 v* to pile up; *figuratively* increase, aggravate, 4.197. (agger).

aggerō, gessī, gestus *3 v* to bear to; heap upon, add to, 3.63. (ad and gerō).

agglomerō, āvī, ātus *1 v* to gather, assemble, crowd to, 2.341; sē agglomerāre, to join themselves to, 12.458. (ad and glomerō).

aggredior, gressus sum *3 dep v* attempt, dare, *with inf* 2.165; to advance toward; attempt, 3.38; attack, 9.325; assail, hew, 2.463; accost, address, 3.358. (ad and gradior).

Āgis, idis *m* a Lycian, follower of Aeneas, 10.751.

agitātor, ōris *m* one who drives; a charioteer, 2.476. (agitō).

agitō, **āvī**, **ātus** *1 intens v* to put in motion; drive; drive away; drive, pursue, 2.421; persecute, 6.68; harass, haunt, 3.331; stir up, arouse, 10.71; hasten, 2.640; move, animate, 6.727; excite to, 9.187; practice, exercise, 12.397; spend, pass; *passive* agitārī, to ride about, 11.694. (agō).

āgmen, **inis**, *n* that which is driven or moved; direction of movement; a train; gathering, winding; herd, flock, drove, 1.186; an army, on the march; battalion, squadron, 5.834; army, 11.60; troop, band, 5.549; company, multitude, throng, 5.378; assemblage, gathering, flood; motion, stroke, of oars, 5.211; stream, current, 2.782; course, 2.212; a leader, 10.561. (agō).

agna, **ae** *f* a ewe lamb, 5.772. (agnus).

agnus, **ī** *m* a lamb, 1.635.

agō, **ēgī**, **āctus** *3 v* to put in motion; to drive, 1.333; force, impel, 3.5; urge, incite, 7.393; advance, 9.505; move, turn, pursue, 10.540; drive away, dispel, lead, 4.546; send forth, raise, 6.873; rear by growth, 11.136; work, 3.695; work out, cut out, cleave, 10.514; convey, 1.391; bear onward, 3.512; bring, 9.18; do in general, 10.675; do, perform, 5.638; to be busy about, aim at, essay, try to accomplish, effect, gain, 11.227; treat, 1.574; derive, 12.530; consider, discuss, debate, 11.445; pass, spend, 5.51; *without an object*, to be at work, to work, perform, 12.429;

agere sē, to present one's self, appear, 6.337; *passive* agī, to move, hover, 12.336.

agrestis, **e** *adj* (ager), pertaining to the fields or country; country-, rustic, rural, 3.34; wild, 7.111; *subst* agrestis, is, *m*, a rustic, 7.504; husbandman.

agricola, **ae** *m* one who cultivates the land; a husbandman, 2.628. (ager and colō).

Agrippa, **ae** *m* Marcus Vipsanius Agrippa, one of the confidential counselors of Augustus, and his principal military commander, 8.682.

Agyllīnus, **a**, **um** *adj* of Agylla, a town in Etruria, afterwards called Caere, 7.652; *subst* Agyllīnī, ōrum, *m*, the people of Agylla, 12.281.

Aiāx, **ācis** *m* 1. Ajax, the son of Telamon. 2. Ajax, the son of Oileus, called also Ajax the Lesser, 1.41; 2.414.

āiō *4 def* to speak; to say yes; say, 1.142 *et al.*; sometimes pleonastic after fārī, etc., 5.551. (If the i in this verb is *followed by* a consonant, the a is short; as aīs, aīt; otherwise i coalesces with the following vowel; as āiō, pronounced ā-yō).

āla, **ae** *f* a wing, 1.301; the feather of an arrow, 9.578; the wing of an army; cavalry, 11.730; troop, battalion, 11.604; horsemen, mounted huntsmen, 4.121.

alacer (**alacris**, *m*, 5.380), **cris**, **cre** *adj* lively; active, eager;

bold, darting, exulting,
10.729; joyful, 5.380.

ālātus, a, um *adj* (āla),
winged, 4.259.

Alba, ae *f* Alba or Alba Longa,
a town on the Alban hills
in Latium, from which
Rome originated, 1.271.

Albānus, a, um *adj* (Alba),
pertaining to Alba; Alban,
1.7; *subst* Albānī, ōrum,
m, the Albans, 5.600.

albeō 2 *v* to be white,
12.36. (albus).

albēscō 3 *inc v* to grow
white, whiten; to brighten,
dawn, 4.586. (albeō).

Albula, ae *f* the Albula,
an ancient name of
the Tiber, 8.332.

Albunea, ae *f* Albunea, a fountain
at Tibur; also personified
as a nymph, 7.83. (albus).

albus, a, um *adj* white,
3.392; blank, undecorated,
9.548; *subst* album, ī,
n, whiteness, white.

Alcander, drī *m* a Trojan, 9.767.

Alcānor, oris *m* 1. Alcanor,
a Trojan hero, 9.672. 2.
A Rutulian, 10.338.

Alcathous, ī *m* a Trojan, 10.747.

Alcīdēs, ae. *m* a descendant of
Alceus; Hercules, 5.414 *et al.*

āles, itis (*gen pl sometimes*
alituum, 8.27) *adj* (āla),
winged, swift, 5.861
et al.; *subst c*, a bird,
1.394; an owl, 12.862.

Alētēs, is *m* a companion
of Aeneas, 1.121.

alga, ae *f* seaweed.

aliēnus, a, um *adj* (alius),
pertaining to another,
another's; strange; foreign,
4.311; intended for another,
10.781; not one's own.

āliger, era, erum *adj* (āla
and gerō), wing-bearing;
winged, 1.663.

ālipēs, edis *adj* (āla and pēs),
wing-footed, 12.484; *subst*
m, wing-footed horse.

aliquandō *adv* (alius
and quandō), at some
time; formerly, 8.602;
at length, 8.200.

aliquis, quid (*indef subst pron*),
some one, any one, something,
anything, in affirmative
sentences; some one, 6.864
et al.; some other, 2.48; *acc*,
aliquid, as to something, in
some respect, somewhat, in
some degree, 10.84; *adv* aliquā
(*sc* ratiōne or viā) (*abl*), in
some way. (alius and quis).

aliter *adv* in another manner;
otherwise, 1.399. (alius).

alius, a, ud (*gen* alīus, *dat* aliī)
(*adj* and *subst*), other, another;
repeated; alius — alius, one
— another; *pl* aliī — aliī, some
— others, 1.427.428; used once
for aliī— aliī, 4.593; *adv* aliō
(*old abl*), elsewhere, to another
place; aliās (acc. *pl* fem., sc.
vicēs), at another time.

Allēctō, ūs *f* Alecto, one of
the furies, 7.324 *et al.*

Allia, ae *f* the Allia, a small stream running into the Tiber, eleven miles above Rome, where the Romans were defeated by the Gauls, BC 389. 7.717.

Almō, ōnis *m* a Latin youth, son of Tyrrheus, 7.532.

almus, a, um *adj* (alō), giving nourishment; fostering, genial, blessing, blessed, benign, 1.306; fruitful; gracious, kind, kindly, propitious, 7.774.

alō, uī, altus or **alitus** 3 *v* to nourish, rear, 3.50; breed, 4.38; cherish, 4.2; animate, 6.726; encourage, 5.231.

Alōīdae, ārum *m* the stepsons of Aloeus, sons of Neptune and Iphemedia, named Otus and Ephialtes; giants who stormed Olympus and were slain by Apollo, 6.582.

Alpēs, ium *f* the Alps.

Alphēus, a, um *adj* of the Alpheus, Alphean, 10.179.

Alphēus, ī. *m* the Alpheus, a river in Elis, supposed to disappear under the sea, and rise again as the fountain of Arethusa, in the island of Ortygia, near Syracuse, 3.694 *et al.*

Alpīnus, a, um *adj* (Alpēs), pertaining to the Alps; Alpine, 4.442.

Alsus, ī *m* a Rutulian shepherd, 12.304.

altāria, ium, *n* the upper part of an altar; a high altar, 7.211; an altar, 2.515. (altus).

altē *adv* aloft, on high; high, 1.337; high up; deeply, deep; *compar* altius, higher. (altus).

alter, era, erum (*gen sing* **alterīus,** *dat* **alterī,** *in all genders*) *adj* (*rel to* alius), the other; one of two; the next; the second, 5.311; a single other; one- or another of the same class; another; any second one; with a neg., not one other, 1.544; alter — alter, the one — the other, 5.299; alter — alterīus, each — other's, 2.667.

alternō, āvī, ātus 1 *v* to do by turns; to alternate (attack) by turns; weigh or consider one thing after another, 4.287. (alternus).

alternus, a, um *adj* (alter), one after the other; alternating, 6.121; by turns, in succession, 5.376; every second, 12.233.

altrīx, īcis *f* a nurse; mother-, nurse-, native-, birth-, 3.273. (alō).

altum, ī, *n* the deep; the lofty; the deep sea, the main, the deep, 1.3; the sky, heaven, air, 1.297; from far, far-fetched, remote, 8.395. (altus).

altus, a, um raised high; high built, high, lofty, 5.489; on high, aloft, 11.837; high-born, noble, ancient, 4.230; renowned, 10.126; deep, deep or deeply, 12.357; *subst* altum, ī, *n,* the deep; the lofty; the deep sea, the main, the deep, 1.3; the sky, heaven, air, 1.297; from far, far-fetched, remote, 8.395; *pl* alta, ōrum, high places, heights of heaven, 6.787; heights, hills, 11.797;

battlements, 9.169; alta petere,
to aim high, 5.508; *compar*
altior, ius, higher, taller,
8.162; *superl*, altissimus,
a, um, very high, 8.234.
(alō, rear, cause to grow).

alumnus, ī *m* a foster-son,
11.33 *et al.* (alō).

alveus, ī *m* a cavity, hollow;
the hollow trunk of a tree;
metonym a boat, 6.412. (alvus).

alvus, ī *f* the abdomen, the belly;
waist, 12.273; body, 2.51.

amāns, antis (subst.) a lover;
loving, fond wife, 1.352.

amāracus, ī *m* marjoram, 1.693.

amārus, a, um *adj* bitter,
brackish, salt, briny;
figuratively bitter, 4.203;
biting, 11.337; cruel, 10.900.

Amasēnus, ī *m* the Amasenus,
a river of Latium, 11.547; the
river-god Amasenus, 7.685.

Amastrus, ī *m* a Trojan, 11.673.

Amāta, ae *f* the wife of
Latinus, 7.343 *et al.*

Amathūs, ūntis *f* a town
of Cyprus, 10.51.

Amāzōn, onis *f* an Amazon,
one of the race of female
warriors, said to have dwelt
on the Thermodon, in
Asia Minor, 11.648 *et al.*

Amāzonis, idis *f* an
Amazon, 1.490.

Amāzonius, a, um *adj* (Amāzōn),
Amazonian (such as the
Amazons used), 5.311.

ambāgēs, is *f* a going about;
a winding, 6.29; *figuratively*

details, particulars, story,
1.342; mysteries, 6.99. (in good
usage in *the abl sing* and all
cases of *pl*) (ambigō, go about).

ambedō, ēdī, ēsus 3 *v* to
eat round; to consume,
devour, eat, 3.257.

ambiguus, a, um *adj* (ambigō),
uncertain; doubtful,
undecided; 5.326; twofold,
3.180; dark, obscure, 2.99;
unreliable, treacherous,
1.661; hesitating, uncertain,
5.655; in suspense, 8.580.

ambiō, īvī or iī, ītus 4 *v* to go
round; encompass, 6.550;
figuratively approach, address,
4.283; entrap, circumvent,
7.333. (amb- and eō).

ambō, ae, ō *adj* both, 1.458.

ambrosia, ae *f* ambrosia,
the food of the gods.

ambrosius, a, um *adj*
(ambrosia), ambrosial,
heavenly, divine, 1.403.

ambūrō, ussī, ūstus 3 *v* to burn
round; *part*, ambūstus, a,
um, blazing, singed, 12.301.

āmēns, entis out of one's
mind or senses; amazed,
beside one's self, frantic,
mad, furious, 2.314; 4.203;
distracted, 3.307.

āmentum, ī, *n* a thong attached
to the shaft of a javelin or other
missile; *metonym* a javelin
with the amentum, 9.665.

amiciō, icuī or ixī, ictus 4 *v* to
throw around; veil, cover,
1.516. (am- and iaciō).

amīcitia, ae *f* friendship; *pl* friendly alliance, 11.321. (amīcus).

amictus, ūs *m* a veiling or draping of the person; an upper garment, covering; cloak, mantle, veil, 3.405; 5.421. (amiciō).

amīcus, a, um *adj* (amō), loving, friendly, kind, favorable, propitious, of persons, 2.735; of things, 2.255 *et al.; subst* amīcus, ī., *m,* a friend.

Amiternus, a, um *adj* (Amiternum), of Amiternum, a Sabine town near the source of the Aternus; Amiternian, 7.710.

āmittō, mīsī, missus *3 v* to send away; to let go, 5.853; 2.148; lose, 3.710; *part,* āmissus, a, um, missing 1.217; lost, 3.341; slain, 11.868.

amnis, is *m* flowing water; a river, *freq*; stream, 4.164; water, 12.417; amnis Eumenidum, the Cocytus, 6.374.

amō, āvī, ātus *1 v* to love, be fond of, like; *figuratively* to keep close to, hug the shore, 5.163; without an object, to be in love, to love, 4.101 *et al.*

amoenus, a, um *adj* charming; usually to the sight, delightful, pleasant, 6.638.

amor, ōris *m* love, affection, in all senses; the passion of love; love, affection, or esteem, in all human relations, as parental, filial, of friends, allies, etc., 4.624 *et al.;* of gods, 7.769; love, liking, fancy, fondness, preference, for things, 11.583 *et al.; frequently*

the hippomanes, or bunch of flesh supposed to appear on the forehead of a new-foaled colt, and instantly devoured by the dam, unless intercepted, and used as a love-charm, 4.516; personified, Amor, ōris, *m,* Cupid, Love, the god of love, 1.663; *pl* amōrēs, um, *m,* affections, love, 4.28; mutual love, 5.334. (amō).

āmoveō, mōvī, mōtus *2 v* to move away, take away, remove, 6.524.

Amphitryōniadēs, ae *m* Hercules, the son of Amphitryon (so called, though he was the son of Jupiter by the wife of Amphitryon), 8.103.

Amphrysius, a, um pertaining to the river Amphrysus; Amphrysian, an epithet of Apollo, who kept the flocks of Admetus on the Amphrysus; hence, of a priest or priestess of Apollo, 6.398.

amplector, amplexus sum *3 dep v* to embrace, clasp, 3.607; wind, pass around, 5.86; encircle, coil around, 2.214; *figuratively* comprehend, embrace, in description.

amplexus, ūs *m* an embrace, 1.687.(amplector).

amplus, a, um *adj* spacious, large, ample, 2.310; splendid, magnificent, glorious, 4.93; *compar* amplior, us, larger; *adv* amplius, more, longer, 1.683.

Ampsanctus, ī *m* Lake Amsanctus, in the country of the Hirpini, from its noxious exhalations supposed to be one of the entrances to Hades, 7.65.

Amyclae, ārum f a town of Latium, 10.564.

Amycus, ī m 1. Amycus, a son of Neptune, king of the Bebrycians, famous for his prowess in boxing, 5.373. 2. A companion of Aeneas, 1.221. 3. Another Trojan of the same name, 9.772.

an (conj, properly introducing the second member of a double question), or, 6.533; at the beginning of an interrogative sentence (the first member being suppressed), then, or rather, or perhaps, or even, 4.325.

Anagnia, ae f Anagnia, a town of the Hernici, 7.684.

anceps, cipitis adj (am- and caput), two-headed or two-edged, 7.525; figuratively twofold, 3.47; uncertain, wavering, doubtful, 5.654; 10.304; perplexed, perplexing, intricate, 5.589.

Anchemolus, ī m a Latin warrior, 10.389.

Anchīsēs, ae m son of Capys and Themis, and father of Aeneas by Venus, 2.687 et al.

Anchīsēus, a, um adj of Anchises, 5.761.

Anchīsiadēs, ae m son of Anchises; Aeneas, 5.407.

ancīle, is, n a small oval shield, 7.188; pl ancilia, ium, the sacred ancilia, made by the Romans in imitation of the ancile which came down from heaven, 8.664.

ancora, ae f an anchor, 1.169.

Ancus, ī m Ancus Martius, the fourth king of Rome, 6.815.

Androgeōs, eō, and **Androgeus, eī** m 1. Androgeus, a son of the Cretan king Minos, murdered by the Athenians, 6.20. 2. A Greek chief at Troy, 2.371.

Andromachē, ae f wife of Hector, 2.456.

anfrāctus, ūs m a breaking round; the winding of a way in and out, ravine, 11.522. (am- and frangō).

angō, ānxī, ānctus or **ānxus** 3 v to squeeze, compress, 8.260.

anguis, is m and f a snake of any kind, serpent, 2.379; hydra, 8.300.

Anguitia, ae f Anguitia or Angitia, a sister of Circe, worshiped by the Marsi, 7.759.

angustus, a, um adj (angō), strait, narrow, 3.411; straitened, perilous, 11.309; subst angustum, ī, n, a narrow place, passage, 2.332.

anhēlitus, ūs m hard-breathing; puffing, panting, 5.199. (anhēlō).

anhēlō, āvī, ātus 1 v to pant, 5.254; of a furnace, to puff, roar, 8.421. (am- and hālō).

anhēlus, a, um adj (anhēlō), panting, gasping, throbbing, 6.48.

anīlis, e *adj* (anus), of an old woman; an old woman's, 4.641.

anima, ae *f* a breeze or breath of air; the air; wind or blast of the bellows, 8.403; breath, 9.580; breath of life, the soul, spirit, life, 1.98; life-blood, 10.908; soul, 9.580; the soul of the dead, shade, manes, 5.81; the spirit or soul not yet inhabiting its destined body, 6.720.

animal, ālis, *n* a living being, animal, 3.147; a brute animal, beast, animal. (anima).

animōsus, a, um courageous, full of spirit, bold, 12.277. (animus).

animus, ī *m* the rational spirit or soul of man; *frequently* the mind, 1.464 *et al.*; design, intention, purpose, 4.639; mind, memory, 1.26; the heart; feeling, disposition, affection, inclination, 1.304 *et al.*; *pl* animī, ōrum, *m,* lofty spirit, heroism, 6.782; daring; courage, confidence, 2.617; strength; passion; anger, rage, 1.57; arrogance, pride, 11.366; fury, 10.357; of things, life, velocity, 7.383.

Aniō (Anien), ēnis or **ōnis** *m* the Anio, a branch of the Tiber, flowing from the Sabine Mountains through Latium, 7.683.

Anius, iī *m* a king of Delos and priest of Apollo, 3.80.

Anna, ae *f* a sister of Dido, 4.9.

annālis, e. *adj* (annus), pertaining to years, or lasting through a year; *subst* *m*, annalēs, ium, annals, records; story, history, 1.373.

annōsus, a, um *adj* (annus), full of years; aged, old, 4.441; hoary, 6.282.

annus, ī *m* a year, *freq*; a season, portion of the year; magnus annus, a complete year, or the great annual circuit of the sun, 3.284.

annuus, a, um *adj* (annus), annual, yearly, 5.46.

ānser, eris *m* a goose.

Antaeus, ī *m* a Latin, slain by Aeneas, 10.561.

Antandros (-us), ī *f* Antandrus, a coast town in Mysia, at the foot of Mount Ida, 3.6.

ante (*prep with acc*), in front of, before, 2.469 *et al.*; (of order or degree), before or beyond, 1.347; (of time), before, 4.328.

ante *adv* beforehand, 1.673; previously, past, 1.198; first, 12.680; *followed by* quam, = antequam.

anteeō, īvī or **iī, īre** *irreg v* to go before; surpass, 12.84.

anteferō, tulī, lātus, ferre *irreg v* to bear before; to prefer, 4.371.

Antemnae, ārum *f* Antemnae, a Sabine town on the Anio, 7.631.

antenna, ae *f* a sail yard, 3.549.

Antēnor, oris *m* Antenor, a Trojan prince, nephew of Priam, who fled from Troy, and settled in northern Italy at Patavium, shortly before the arrival of Aeneas in Latium, 1.242.

Antēnoridēs, ae *m* a son or descendant of Antenor; Antēnoridae, the three sons of Antenor, Polybus, Agenor, and Acamas, 6.484.

antequam (*or separated,* **ante quam**) *adv* before that; sooner than.

Antheus (*dissyl*), **eos** or **eī** *m* Antheus, a companion of Aeneas, 1.181.

Antiphatēs, ae *m* Antiphates, son of Sarpedon, slain by Turnus, 9.696.

antīquus, a, um *adj* (ante), done or existing before; pristine, of old, ancient, 1.12; aged, old, 2.714; former, 4.458; illustrious, noble, 12.529.

Antōnius, iī *m m* Antonius, the Triumvir, 8.685.

Antōrēs, ae *m* a Greek warrior, follower of Evander, 10.778.

antrum, ī, *n* a cave, cavern, grotto, 1.166.

Anūbis, is or **idis** *m* a god with the head of a dog, worshiped by the Egyptians, 8.698.

anus, ūs *f* an old woman, 7.419.

ānxius, a, um *adj* (angō), troubled or troubling, disquieting, 9.89.

Anxur, uris *m* Anxur, or Terracina, a town on the coast of Latium, 10.545; a Latin warrior, 10.545.

Anxurus, a, um *adj* (Anxur), of Anxur, 7.799.

aper, prī *m* a wild boar, 1.324 *et al.*

aperiō, uī, tus *4 v* to uncover, lay bare, 1.107; throw open, open, 2.60; disclose to the view, 3.206; disclose, reveal, 6.12; *passive* aperīrī, to appear, 8.681; *part*, apertus, a, um, opened, 8.585; unguarded, 11.748; *adj*, open, 1.155; clear, pure, 1.587. (ab and root par, whence pariō).

apex, icis *m* the point of anything; peak, top, summit, 4.246; pointed flame, 2.683; cone of a helmet, 10.270; a peaked cap, 8.664.

Aphidnus, ī *m* a Trojan, 9.702.

apis (-ēs), is *f* a bee, 1.430 *et al.*

Apollō, inis *m* Apollo, son of Jupiter and Latona; the god of prophecy, medicine, music, poetry, and archery, 2.430; met., a temple of Apollo, 3.275.

appāreō, uī, itus *2 v* to come into sight, appear, 2.622 *et al.*; be laid open, exposed to view, 8.241; attend, 12.850. (ad and pāreō).

apparō, āvī, ātus *1 v* to get ready, prepare; resolve, be ready; with *infin*, 11.117. (ad and parō).

appellō, āvī, ātus *1 v* to address; name, designate, call, 5.540. (1. appellō).

appellō, pulī, pulsus *3 v* to drive to; bring, convey to, 1.377; draw up to, moor on the shore, 7.39. (ad and pellō).

Appennīnicola, ae *m* a dweller in the Apennines, 11.700. (Appennīnus and colō).

Appennīnus, ī *m* the Apennines, the great mountain chain of Italy, 12.703.

appetō, īvī or **iī, ītus** *3 v* to push for; attack, assail, 11.277. (ad and petō).

applicō, āvī or **uī, ātus** or **itus** *1 v* to fold upon; join to; impel, drive to, 1.616; fasten, nail to, 12.303. (ad and plicō).

aprīcus, a, um *adj* (aperiō), open to the sun; sunny; sun-loving, 5.128.

aptō, āvī, ātus *1 v* to fit, join, or fasten to; *with acc and dat* 8.721; put on, 2.390; get ready, prepare, 10.259; fit out, prepare, 1.552; *with abl* of manner, 8.80. (aptus).

aptus, a, um *adj* (*obs* apō, lay hold), fixed, joined to; joined together; fitted with, studded, 4.482; fit, adapted, meet.

apud (*prep with acc*), near to; with, by, at, before, in presence of; near by, 5.261; among, 2.71; with, (in respect to the mind), 4.539; (with pronouns), at one's home, on one's ground.

aqua, ae *f* water, 1.105 *et al.*; a stream, river.

Aquīcolus, ī *m* a Rutulian, 9.684.

aquila, ae *f* an eagle, 11.752 *et al.*

Aquilō, ōnis *m* the north wind; wind in general, 1.391; wintry, tempestuous wind, 3.285; the north, 1.102.

aquōsus, a, um *adj* (aqua), abounding in water, bringing rain; watery, rainy, 4.52.

āra, ae *f* an altar, 2.514 *et al.*; funeral pile, 6.177; *pl* Ārae, ārum, the Altars, a reef in the Mediterranean Sea between Sicily and Africa, 1.109.

Arabs, abis *m* an Arabian, 8.706.

Arabus, ī *m* an Arabian, 7.605.

arātor, ōris *m* a plowman, 10.804. (arō).

arātrum, ī, *n* a plow, 5.755 *et al.* (arō).

Araxēs, is *m* the Araxes, a river of Armenia Major, 8.728.

arbor (-ōs), oris *f* a tree, *freq*; timber, wood, 5.504; an oar, 10.207.

arboreus, a, um *adj* (arbor), pertaining to a tree or trees; tree-like, massive, 12.888; branching, 1.190.

arbustum, ī, *n* a growth of trees; a grove; thicket, 10.363. (arbor).

arbuteus, a, um *adj* (arbutus), of the arbutus.

Arcadia, ae *f* the central country of Peloponnesus, 5.299.

Arcadius, a, um *adj* (Arcadia), of Arcadia.

arcānus, a, um *adj* (arca), hidden, secret, 4.422; *subst* arcānum, ī, *n*, a secret, 1.262.

Arcas, adis *m* an Arcadian, 10.452; *adj* 11.835.

Arcēns, entis *m* Arcens, a Sicilian, 9.581.

arceō, uī *2 v* to inclose, shut in; restrain, bind, 2.406; debar, keep off, repel, 1.435; protect, save from, 8.73.

arcessō, īvī, ītus *3 v* to cause to come; send for, summon, 5.746; hasten, provoke, 10.11; draw, derive; call up, bring, 6.119. (ar- for ad-, and cēdō).

Arcetius, iī *m* a Rutulian warrior, 12.459.

Archippus, ī *m* king of the Marsi, 7.752.

Arcitenēns, entis *adj* (arcus and tenēns), bow-bearing; *subst m*, the archer; Apollo, 3.75.

Arctos, ī *f* the constellation of the Great and Little Bear, or of the Great Bear alone; the north, 6.16.

Arctūrus, ī *m* the principal star in the constellation Boötes; Arcturus, 1.744 *et al.*

arcus, ūs *m* a bow, 5.500 *et al.*; the rainbow, 5.88.

Ārdea, ae *f* Ardea, the chief town of the Rutulians, 7.411.

ārdēns, entis burning, hot, sparkling, flaming, 5.637; bright, 4.482; impassioned, ardent, eager, 1.423; spirited, fiery, 1.472; glowing, lofty, 6.130; fierce, furious, 2.529; angry, 6.467. (ardeo).

ārdeō, ārsī, ārsus *2 v* to burn; to be on fire, or in flames, 2.311 *et al.*; be burned, 2.581; *figuratively* rage in combat, 1.491; burn with impatience, to long, 1.515; burn with love, 4.101; glow, 4.262.

ārdēscō, ārsī *3 inc v* to begin to burn; *figuratively* burn, 1.713; to increase, grow louder and louder, 11.607. (ārdeō).

ārdor, ōris *m* a burning; fire, flame, 11.786; heat, drought; ardor, zeal, fervor, 4.581. (ārdeō).

arduum, uī, *n* a high place; height, 5.695; 7.562.

arduus, a, um *adj* steep; erect, high, raised high, 2.475; 5.480; lofty, towering, 2.328; rearing, 11.638.

āreō *2 v* to be dry; wither, 3.142; *part*, ārēns, entis, dry; dried up, shallow, 3.350; dry, thirsty.

Arethūsa, ae *f* 1. Arethusa, a nymph; 2. A fountain near Syracuse, 3.696.

argenteus, a, um *adj* (argentum), silver-, silvery, white, 8.655.

argentum, ī, *n* silver, 1.359 *et al.*; articles of silver; plate, 1.640.

Argī, ōrum, *m,* and **Argos,** *n* Argos, the capital of Argolis, and a favorite abode of Juno, 1.24; Greece, 2.95. (nom. and *acc*).

Argīlētum, ī, *n* the Argiletum, a place in Rome at the foot of the Capitoline hill, 8.345. (argilla, clay; wrongly derived from Argī, lētum).

Argīvus, a, um *adj* (Argos), belonging to Argos; Argive; Greek, 2.254; *subst* Argivī, ōrum, Argives, Greeks, 1.40.

Argolicus, a, um *adj* of Argolis; Argolic; Greek, 2.55.

argūmentum, ī, *n* the means of making clear; subject, theme, story, 7.791. (arguō).

arguō, uī, ūtus 3 *v* to make clear; to manifest, show, betray, 4.13; prove, 9.282; accuse, 11.384.

Argus (Argos), ī *m* a guest of Evander, 8.346; Argus, the hundred-eyed keeper who was made the guard of Io, after she was changed into a heifer by Juno, 7.791.

argūtus, a, um clear; clear-sounding; melodious; whistling, rattling, whizzing, 7.14.

Argyripa, ae *f* Argyripa, afterwards Arpi, a town built by Diomedes in Apulia, 11.246.

Arīcia, ae *f* a nymph, mother of Virbius, 7.762.

āridus, a, um *adj* (āreō), dry, parched, 5.200; thirsty.

ariēs, ietis (*oblique cases often trisyll* **aryetis**, etc.) *m* a ram, *freq*; a military engine, a battering ram, 2.492.

arietō (*by synaeresis sometimes trisyll*), **āvī, ātus** 1 *v* to strike; to stumble; dash, 11.890. (ariēs).

Arisba, ae *f* a town in the Troad, 9.264.

arista, ae *f* the beard of wheat; a head of wheat.

arma, ōrum, *n* arms, defensive and offensive, *freq*; armor, 10.181; suits of armor, 8.565; *figuratively* or warlike exploits, 1.1; conflict, 12.844; implements, equipments, instruments, utensils, 1.183; sails, 5.15; rudder, helm, 6.353; military power, warlike command, 12.192; war, conflict, 12.6; means of injury, weapons, 2.99; arma movēre (of the lion), to prepare for battle, 12.6; arma colligere, shorten sail.

armātī, ōrum *m* armed men, warriors, 2.485. (armō).

armātus, a, um armed, charged, 12.857. (armō).

armentālis, e *adj* (armentum), of a drove; of the herd; unbroke, 11.571.

armentum, ī, *n* collective (arō), beasts used for plowing; cattle, 2.499 *et al.*; of all kinds of animals, a herd, drove; of deer, 1.185; of horses, 3.540.

armiger, erī *m* an armor bearer, 2.477; armiger Iovis, the eagle as the bearer of the thunderbolts of Jupiter; Jove's armor bearer, 9.564. (arma and gerō).

armipotēns, entis *adj* (arma and potēns), powerful in arms; valiant, brave, warlike, 2.425.

armisonus, a, um *adj* (arma and sonō), making arms to resound; with resounding arms, 3.544.

armō, āvī, ātus 1 *v* to equip with arms; arm, equip, 2.395 *et al.*; fit out, make ready, prepare, 4.299; *figuratively* imbue, charge, 9.773; *part*, armātus, a, um, armed, charged, 12.857; *subst* armātī, ōrum, *m*, armed men, warriors, 2.485. (arma).

armus, ī *m* the shoulder, strictly at the shoulder blade; of beasts, shoulder, 11.497; flank, side, 6.881; of men, the shoulder, 11.644.

arō, **āvī**, **ātus** *1 v* to plow;
till, cultivate, 4.212; of
navigation, to plow, 2.780;
of age, to furrow, 7.417.

Arpī, **ōrum** Argyripa, afterwards
Arpi, a town built by
Diomedes in Apulia, 11.246.

arrigō, **rēxī**, **rēctus** *3 v* to
raise up; erect; bristle up,
10.726; *figuratively* to excite,
rouse; *part*, arrēctus, a, um,
standing up, rising; erect,
5.426; bristling, 11.754;
attentive, 1.152; animated,
roused, encouraged, 1.579;
ardent, intent; intense,
5.138; in fearful expectation,
12.731. (ad and regō).

arripiō, **uī**, **reptus** *3 v* to seize
for one's self; seize, 9.561;
lay hold upon; surprise,
9.13; *figuratively* hasten to,
gain, 3.477. (ad and rapiō).

Arrūns, **untis** *m* Arruns or
Aruns, an Etruscan follower
of Tarchon, 11.759.

ars, **artis** *f* acquired skill;
dexterity, 5.521; art, 2.15;
warlike device, craft, 5.442;
skillful effort or toil, 5.270;
attainment, science, 7.772;
prophetic wisdom, 5.705;
aim, vocation, pursuit, 6.852;
avocation, craft, 12.519;
artifice, plot, stratagem,
intrigue, 1.657; craft, subtlety,
cunning, 2.152; skillful or
cunning workmanship, 5.359.

artifex, **icis** *m* an artist, 1.455;
artificis scelus, the iniquity of
the deceiver = the accursed
falsifier, 11.407; subtle
schemer, artful deviser,
2.125. (ars and faciō).

artus, **a**, **um** *adj* straitened,
narrow; close, tight, 1.293.

artus, **ūs** *m* a joint of the body
of man or beast, 5.422;
a limb, 2.173 *et al.*; part,
member, 6.726; frame, body,
9.490. (generally in the *pl*
except in later writers).

arundō, **inis** *f* a reed, arrow, 4.73.

arvīna, **ae** *f* grease, tallow, 7.627.

arvum, **ī**, *n* arable land; land;
a field, 1.246; soil; plain,
the ground, 12.237; the
shore, 2.209; *pl* arva, ōrum,
fields, lands, country;
waters, 8.695. (arō).

arx, **arcis** *f* a citadel, stronghold,
fortress, tower, 2.56 *et al.*;
high abode, heaven, 1.250;
a summit, height, 1.56;
mountain, hill, 6.783;
palace, 4.410. (arceō).

Asbytēs, **ae** *m* a Trojan, 12.362.

Ascanius, **lī** *m* Ascanius, son
of Aeneas, and traditional
founder of Alba Longa, 1.267.

ascendō, **scendī**, **scēnsus** *3 v* to
climb, mount, ascend, 1.419;
scale, 9.507. (ad and scandō).

ascēnsus, **ūs** *m* a climbing or
ascending, 2.303. (ascendō).

Āsia, **ae** *f* 1. Asia, a town of Lydia,
near the river Cayster. 2. Asia
Minor; Asia, 7.224 *et al.*

Asīlās, **ae** *m* 1. A Trojan warrior,
9.571. 2. An Etruscan chief
and soothsayer, 10.175.

Āsius, **a**, **um** *adj* (Āsia), of
Asia, a town near the
Cayster; Asian, 7.701.

Āsius, iī *m* a Trojan
warrior, 10.123.

aspargō, inis *f* a sprinkling
upon; spray, 3.534. (aspergō).

aspectō, āvī, ātus *1 intens v*
to look at or upon, behold,
10.4; survey earnestly, 6.186;
with admiration, 1.420; with
regret, 5.615. (ad and spectō).

aspectus, ūs *m* a looking at;
metonym that which is looked
at; a vision, 9.657; a view,
sight, 4.314; appearance,
presence, 1.613. (aspiciō).

asper, era, erum *adj* rough,
2.379; rugged, craggy, jagged,
6.360; chased, embossed,
5.267; *figuratively* of the
weather, stormy, 2.110; of
temperament, spirit, or
nature, barbarous, 5.730;
formidable, fierce, 1.14; full
of strife, warlike, 1.291; cruel,
stern, 6.882; angry, 1.279;
bitter, 2.96; displeased, 8.365.

aspergō, spersī, spersus
3 v to sprinkle upon, to
sprinkle. (ad and spargō).

aspernor, ātus sum *1 dep v*
to slight, despise, 11.106.
(ab and spernor).

asperō, āvī, ātus *1 v* to make
rough; raise, arouse, lift
up, 3.285. (asper).

aspiciō, spexī, spectus *3 v*
to look at; to behold, see,
1.393 *et al.*; *figuratively* to
consider, 1.526; regard, pity,
2.690. (ad and speciō, look).

Assaracus, ī *m* Assaracus, a king
of Phrygia, son of Tros, brother
of Ganymede and Ilus, and

grandfather of Anchises, 1.284;
Assaracī, ōrum *m* the Assaraci,
two Trojan heroes, 10.124.

astrum, ī, *n* a star, constellation;
pl astra, ōrum, heaven,
3.158; Tītānia astra, the
heavenly bodies; the sun,
moon, or stars, 6.725.

Astur, uris *m* Astur, an
Etruscan chief, 10.180.

astus, ūs *m* cunning; *abl* astū,
with cunning, craftily, 10.522.

Astyanax, actis *m* Astyanax,
the son of Hector and
Andromache, put to death
by Ulysses after the capture
of Troy, to prevent the
fulfillment of the prophecy
which said that Troy should
be restored by him, 2.457.

asylum, ī, *n* 1. A place of
refuge; an asylum; a temple,
sanctuary, 2.761. 2. The Asylum
established by Romulus
on the Capitoline, 8.342.

at and **ast** (*conj*, denoting
addition either with the
notion of difference, or of
decided opposition) but, 1.46;
yet, still, after conditional
propositions; in adding
new particulars, and in
transitions, but also, but, now,
4.1; denoting indignation,
with execration, 2.535.

atavus, ī *m* a great-great-great-
grandfather, or forefather of
the fifth previous generation;
forefather, 7.474.

āter, tra, trum *adj* black; dark,
gloomy, 1.60 *et al.*; smoky,
lurid, 7.456; 4.384; clotted,
dark, 3.622; soiled, blackened,

2.272; *figuratively* sad, fatal, 6.429; venomous, deadly; of the odor of smoke, 12.591.

Athesis, is *m* the Athesis, a river in the N.E. part of Upper Italy, 9.680.

Athōs (*acc* **on, ōna**) *m* a mountain in Macedonia on the Strymonian gulf, 12.701.

Atiī, ōrum *m* the Atii, a Roman gens, 5.568.

Ātīna, ae *f* a town of Latium, 7.630.

Atīnas, ātis *m* Atinas, a Latin chief, 12.661.

Atlantis, idis *f* a daughter or female descendant of Atlas; Electra, 8.135.

Atlās, antis *m* Atlas, a king of Mauretania, famed for his knowledge of the stars, and hence said to have borne the heavens on his head and shoulders, transformed, according to mythology, by Perseus with the Gorgon's head into the mountain that bears his name, 1.741 *et al.*

atque, or **ac** *conj*, and in addition, or and besides; and, as well, and indeed, and, 1.575; *freq*; even, 2.626; in comparisons, as, 4.90; than, 3.561; repeated, atque — atque, both — and.

Atrīdēs, ae *m* a son or descendant of Atreus; *pl* Atrīdae, ārum, the Atridae (Agamemnon and Menelaus), 2.104.

ātrium, iī, *n* a rectangular area in the middle of a dwelling, partly open to the sky; and often surrounded with a colonnade; the court or principal apartment of a dwelling; or, in a house containing more than one court, the forecourt or first hall; a court, hall, 2.483 *et al.*

atrox, ōcis *adj* (āter), cruel, fierce, relentless, 1.662.

attāctus, ūs (*only in the abl*, **attāctū**) *m* a touching; touch, 7.350. (attingō).

attingō, tigī, tāctus *3 v* to touch against; touch, grasp, 9.558; *figuratively* attain, reach, arrive at, 5.797; come upon, overtake, 4.568. (ad and tangō).

attollō *3 v* to lift or raise up, throw, cast up, 3.574; rear, build, 2.185; *figuratively* to rouse, excite, 2.381; with se, lift one's self or itself, 4.690; come into view, appear, 3.205; *figuratively* arise, be exalted, 4.49; *passive* attollī, to rise, 5.127. (ad and tollō).

attonō, uī, itus *1 v* to thunder at; *part*, attonitus, a, um, *figuratively* stunned; agitated, 7.580; amazed, astonished, 3.172; afflicted, overwhelmed, 12.610; spellbound, hushed, 6.53. (ad and tonō).

attorqueō *2 v* to swing or hurl, 9.52. (ad and torqueō).

attrahō, trāxī, trāctus *3 v* to draw or bring to, 11.250; fetch, bring up. (ad and trahō).

attrectō, āvī, ātus *1 v* to handle or touch, with the notion of violating, 2.719. (ad and tractō).

Atys, yos *m* a young comrade of Ascanius, 5.568.

auctor, ōris *m* one who increases, promotes, or produces; an originator, author, contriver, 2.150; founder, father, 4.365; adviser, counselor, guide, 5.17; favorer, patron, abettor, 12.159; messenger, 10.510; sender, 9.421. (augeō).

audāx, ācis *adj* (audeō), daring, bold, warlike, 4.615; rash, 12.786, *freq.*

audēns, entis venturing, daring, 2.347; bold, brave, 10.284; (compar.), audentior, bolder, more boldly, 6.95.

audeō, ausus sum, *semi-dep 2 v* to dare; *with inf freq;* dare, venture upon, attempt, *with acc* 10.811 *et al.;* to venture, 2.347; *part,* ausus, a, um, having dared, daring, 5.792.

audiō, īvī, ītus *4 v* to hear, *with acc* or *acc* and *infin, freq;* to listen to, hear of, 2.11; to heed, 4.612; *part,* audītus, a, um, heard of, known by report, 7.96; *part, subst* audītum, ī, *n,* a thing heard; report, 3.107.

auferō, abstulī, ablātus, auferre *irreg v* to carry, bear, or take away, 4.29 *et al.;* remove, cut off, 4.699; lay aside, leave off, 8.439; with se, withdraw, 4.389. (ab and ferō).

Aufidus, ī *m* the Aufidus, a river in Apulia, 11.405.

augeō, auxī, auctus *2 v* to cause to grow or increase; increase, 5.565; load, pile, 7.111; augment, 7.211; multiply, 9.407.

augur, uris, *m, and rarely f* a soothsayer, foretelling from any kind of sign; augur, diviner, prophet, 4.376.

augurium, iī, *n* the business of the augur; augury, divination, 1.392; an augury, omen, portent, 2.703; oracle, 3.89; presage, 5.523. (augur).

augurō, āvī, ātus *1 v* to divine, conjecture, 7.273. (augur).

augustus, a, um *adj* venerable, 7.153; the surname given to Octavius Caesar by the senate, BC 27, and, after him, to the emperors generally, 6.792.

aula, ae, archaic *gen* **āī** *f* a forecourt, atrium; court, peristyle (as surrounded with columns), hall, 3.354; palace, royal seat, 1.140.

aulaeum, ī, *n* a curtain, covering, hangings, embroidered stuff, tapestry, 1.697.

Aulestēs, is *m* an Etruscan chief, 10.207.

Aulis, idis *f* the port on the eastern shore of Greece, whence the Greek fleet sailed to the siege of Troy, 4.426.

Aunus, ī *m* an Italian chief, 11.700.

aura, ae *(archaic gen* **āī**) *f* the air in gentle motion; a breeze, 3.356 *et al.;* air, 4.278 *et al.;* a blast; ether, spirit, 6.747; splendor, brightness, 6.204; favor, applause, 6.816; *pl* air, 1.59.387; ad auras, to or into the air, on high, upward.

aurātus, a, um *adj* (aurum), gilded, golden, of gold, 12.163; embroidered with gold, 5.250.

aureus, a, um *adj* (aurum), of gold, golden, armed with gold, 11.490; gilded, 6.13; *figuratively* beautiful, fair, 10.16; perfectly pure and happy, golden, 6.792.

auricomus, a, um *adj* (aurum and coma), golden-haired; *figuratively* golden-leaved, *or with* golden sprays, 6.141.

aurīga, ae *m* a charioteer, 5.146; a groom, 12.85.

auris, is *f* the ear, 2.119 *et al.* (*rel to* audiō).

aurōra, ae *f* the dawn, morning, 3.521; personified, Aurora, the goddess of the dawn, who precedes the horses of the sun-god, 4.585; the east, 8.686; the sun, 6.535.

aurum, ī, *n* gold, 1.349 *et al.*; *metonym* a golden goblet, 7.245; golden bit, 7.279.

Auruncus, a, um *adj* (Aurunca), Auruncan, of Aurunca, an ancient town of Campania, 12.94.

Ausonia, ae *f* an ancient name of middle and lower Italy; Italy, in general, 3.496.

Ausonidēs, ae, *pl* **Ausonidae**, **ārum** *and* **ūm** *m* the Ausonians or primitive people of lower Italy; Italians, 10.564. (Auson, the eponymous father of the Ausonēs).

Ausonius, a, um *adj* (Auson), Ausonian; Italian, 4.349; *subst* Ausonii, ōrum, *m*, the Ausonians; Italians, 11.253.

auspex, **icis**, *c* one who divines by watching birds; a diviner; *figuratively* a leader, author, patron, guide, director, 3.20. (avis and speciō, look).

auspicium, īī, *n* an auspice; omen, token, sign, 3.499; power, authority, 4.103; will, 4.341; conduct, leadership, 11.347. (auspex).

Auster, **trī** *m* the southerly or south wind, opposite to Aquilo; wind in general, 3.70; *metonym* the south.

ausum, ī, *n* a daring deed; outrage, 2.535.

aut (*conj*, indicating an actual and positive alternative, and not, like vel, leaving the choice to the mind), or, 1.70 *et al.*; but sometimes used indifferently with vel, ve, sive, 1.379; repeated, aut — aut, either — or, 1.396 *et al.*

autem *conj*, but, yet, however, truly, indeed, now, moreover, denoting contrast, difference, addition, or transition, *freq*.

Automedōn, **ontis** *m* the charioteer of Achilles, and, after the death of Achilles, armor-bearer of Pyrrhus, 2.477.

autumnus, ī *m* the season of increase; autumn, 6.309 *et al.* (cf. augeō).

auxilium, īī, *n* that which promotes; assistance, help, relief, succor, 1.571; *pl* auxilia, ōrum, help, assistance, 2.163. (augeō).

avārus, a, um *adj* (aveō, desire), desirous of

gain; greedy; covetous, avaricious, 1.363; rapacious, devouring, *figuratively* of the land ruled over by an avaricious prince, 3.44.

āveho, vexī, vectus *3 v* to carry away, 2.179; *passive* āvectus esse, to have sailed away, departed, 2.43.

āvellō, vellī or **vulsī, vulsus** *3 v* to pluck, or tear off, or away from, *with acc* and *abl*, take away, steal, 2.165; to force away, 11.201; *part*, avulsus, a, um, torn from, 2.608; torn, rent, 3.575.

avēna, ae *f* oats; oat-, a straw, an oaten pipe; a Pan-pipe or syrinx.

Aventīnus, ī *m* the Aventine mount in Rome, 7.659; a Latin chief, 7.657.

Averna, ōrum, *n* Avernus, a lake near Naples, between Baiae and Cumae, in Campania, now Lago d' Averno. Near it was one of the entrances to Hades; hence, the lower world 3.442.5.732.

Avernus, a, um of Avernus (a lake near Naples, between Baiae and Cumae, in Campania, now Lago d' Averno. Near it was one of the entrances to Hades), Avernian, 4.512; 6.118.

Avernus, ī *m* Avernus, a lake near Naples, between Baiae and Cumae, in Campania, now Lago d' Averno. Near it was one of the entrances to Hades; hence, the lower world, Avernus, 6.126; portus Avernī, the harbor

of Cumae, near Avernus, 5.813. (αορνος, birdless).

āversus, a, um turned away, 1.482; with averted faces, 6.224; askance, 4.362; remote, 1.568; *figuratively* indignant, 7.618; displeased, 2.170.

āvertō, vertī, versus *3 v* to turn (anything) away from, *followed by an abl* with or without a *prep*, 1.38 *et al.*; turn or drive away, 1.472 *et al.*; transfer, *with acc* of place, 4.106; drive away, end, 4.547; neut. by omission of se, to turn away, 1.402; *passive* avertī, as middle or *dep, with acc* to be averse to; to shun, loathe.

avidus, a, um *adj* (aveō, desire), longing, eager, 1.514; eagerly, quickly, 6.210; with longing, 3.132; eager for destruction, devouring, destructive, baneful; with *infin*, 12.290; with *gen*, eagerly, desirous of, eager for, 9.661.

avis, is *f* a bird, 6.193 *et al.*

avītus, a, um *adj* (avus), of a grandfather; ancestral, ancient, 10.752.

āvius, a, um pathless, 2.736; devious, unapproachable, 12.480; that cannot be tracked, inaccessible, eluding pursuit, 11.810; *subst* āvium, iī, *n*, a devious, inaccessible place, or way, 9.58.

āvolō, āvī, ātus *1 v* to fly away, 11.712.

avunculus, ī *m* an uncle on the mother's side; uncle, 3.343. (avus).

avus, ī *m* a grandfather, grandsire, 2.457; sire, father, ancestor, 6.840.

axis, is *m* an axle; synecdoche, car, chariot, 5.820; the axis of the heavens, the sky, the heavens, 4.482; the pole; the north pole, the north.

bāca, ae *f* a berry, 3.649.

bācātus, a, um *adj* (bāca), set or studded with pearls; or made of beads, pearls, etc., 1.655.

bacchor, ātus sum *1 dep v* to perform the orgies of Bacchus; rage, rave, 6.78; rush or run madly or wildly, 4.301; fly wildly, 4.666; *part*, bacchātus, a, um, resounding with the revels of Bacchus, 3.125; filling with fury, spreading fury, 10.41. (Bacchus).

Bacchus, ī *m* Bacchus, the son of Jupiter and Semele, and god of wine, 1.734; wine, 1.215.

Bactra, ōrum, n, *pl* Bactra, the chief city of Bactria, 8.688.

Bāiae, ārum *f* Baiae, a town on the Bay of Naples, west of Puteoli, 9.710.

bālātus, ūs *m* a bleating, 9.565. (bālō).

bālō, āvī, ātus *1 v* to bleat; *subst* bālāns, antis (*sc* ovis), f.; *pl* bālantēs, ium or um, sheep.

balteus, ī (*gen dissyl,* 10.496) a belt, 5.313.

barathrum, ī, *n* an abyss, chasm, gulf, 3.421.

barba, ae *f* the beard, 3.593.

barbaricus, a, um *adj* foreign, barbaric, 2.504.

barbarus, a, um *adj* barbarian, savage, 1.539; foreign, barbaric, 11.777; *subst* barbarus, ī, *m*, a barbarian, mercenary stranger, or soldier.

Barcaeī, ōrum *m* the Barcaeans; people of Barce or Ptolemais, a town in Cyrenaica, 4.43.

Barcē, ēs *f* the nurse of Sychaeus, 4.632.

Batulum, ī, *n* a Samnite town in Campania, 7.739.

beātus, a, um blessed, happy, 1.94.

Bēbrycius, a, um *adj* Bebrycian, or Bithynian; of Bebrycia, a country in Asia Minor on the coast of Bithynia, 5.373.

Bēlīdēs, ae *m* a son or male descendant of Belus, 2.82.

bellātor, ōris *m* a warrior, 11.553; *adj*, warlike, 12.614. (bellō).

bellātrīx, īcis *f* a female warrior; *adj*, warring, a warlike heroine, 1.493. (bellō).

bellipotēns, entis *adj* (bellum and potēns), powerful in war; *subst m*, the god of war, 11.8.

bellō, āvī, ātus *1 v*, and **bellor,** *dep 1, n* to wage war; fight, 1.466; *dep*, 11.660; *subst* bellāns, antis, *c pl* bellantēs, ium or um, combatants, warriors, 1.466. (bellum).

Bellōna, ae *f* the goddess of war, sister of Mars, Bellona, 7.319. (bellum).

bellum, ī, *n* conflict; war, *freq*; a battle, 8.629; personified, Bellum, war, the demon of war, 1.294. (duellum, *cf.* duo).

bēlua, ae *f* a beast, large, monstrous, or hideous, 6.287.

Bēlus, ī *m* 1. Belus, king of Tyre and Sidon, and father of Dido, 1.621. 2. The founder of the line of kings from whom Dido was descended, 1.729.

Bēnācus, ī *m* a lake in Cisalpine Gaul, through which flows the Mincius, 10.205.

bene *adv* well, *freq*; pleasantly, sweetly; wisely, safely; compar., melius, better, more, 1.452. (bonus).

benīgnus, a, um *adj* of a kindly spirit; benevolent, friendly, favorable, hospitable, 1.304.

Berecyntius, a, um *adj* pertaining to Berecyntus, a mountain of Phrygia, sacred to Cybele, 6.784.

Beroē, ēs *f* Beroë, the wife of Doryclus, an Epirote follower of Aeneas, 5.620.

bibō, bibī *3 v* to drink, 1.473 *et al.*; *figuratively* take in, drink in, 1.749; of weapons, 11.804.

bibulus, a, um *adj* (bibō), drinking readily; absorbing quickly; dry, 6.227.

bicolor, ōris *adj* (bis and color), of two colors, 8.276; mottled, dappled, 5.566.

bicornis, e *adj* (bis and cornū), two-horned; of rivers, with reference to their divided mouths, 8.727.

bidēns, entis *adj* (bis and dēns), having two teeth or two complete rows of teeth; *subst* f. (*sc* victima), an animal suitable for the altar; a sheep with two conspicuous teeth supplanting two of the milk-teeth; a sheep, 4.57.

biforis, e *adj* having two doors or openings; twofold; double; of a double pipe with one mouth-piece, 9.618.

biförmis, is *adj* (bis and förma), of twofold shape or form, two-formed, 6.25.

bifröns, frontis *adj* two-faced, double-faced, 7.180.

bīgae, ārum *f pl* a team of two horses; a car or chariot drawn by two horses; a car, 2.272; bīgīs in albīs, in a chariot drawn by two white horses, 12.164. . (bis and iugum).

biiugus, a, um *adj* (bis and iugum), of a two-horse team or chariot; coupled, yoked, 10.253; chariot-, 5.144; *subst* biiugī, ōrum, *m*, a double team or two-horse chariot, 10.575.

biiugus, a, um *adj* (bis and iugum), of a two-horse team or chariot; coupled, yoked, 10.253; chariot-, 5.144; *subst* biiugī, ōrum, *m*, a double team or two-horse chariot, 10.575.

bilinguis, e *adj* (bis and lingua), double-tongued; *figuratively* deceitful, treacherous, 1.661.

bilīx, īcis *adj* two-threaded, double-plaited, 12.375. (bis and *cf.* licium, thread).

bimembris, is *adj* (bis and membrum), having two kinds of members; *subst* bimembrēs, ium, *m*, Centaurs, 8.293.

bīnī, ae, a (*adj num distrib.*), two by two; two to each, 5.61; (*poetic* as cardinal), two, 1.313 *et al.* (bis).

bipatēns, entis *adj* (bis and pateō), with twofold opening; with twofold or double doors, 2.330.

bipennis, e *adj* (bis and penna), two-winged; two-edged, 11.135; *subst f*, a two-edged ax, 2.627; a battle-ax, 2.479.

birēmis, is *f* a boat with two oars, or ship with two banks of oars; a galley or ship, 1.182. (bis and rēmus).

bis *adv* twice, 1.381. (in composition bi-).

Bitiās, ae *m* 1. Bitias, a Carthaginian nobleman, 1.738. 2. A Trojan, 9.672.

bivius, a, um *adj* (bis and via), leading two ways, 11.516; *subst* bivium, iī, *n*, the meeting of two roads; a crossway, 9.238.

blandus, a, um *adj* fondling; fawning; coaxing; persuasive, alluring, enticing, 1.670; grateful, calm, 5.827.

Bōla, ae *f* a town, of the Aequi in Latium, 6.775.

bonum, ī, *n* a good thing; good; blessing, happiness; *compar* melius, ōris, *n*, a better thing; melius est, it is better; in melius, for the better; to a better state, 11.426; meliōra, um, better things, 12.153.

bonus, a, um *adj* good, in every sense, *freq*; friendly, kind, 1.195; fit, valuable, proper, 5.483; skillful, expert, able, nimble, 5.430; auspicious, propitious, 1.734; *subst* bonum, ī, *n*, a good thing; good; blessing, happiness; *compar* melior, ius, better, *freq*; superior, 5.68; greater, 9.156; *subst* melius, ōris, *n*, a better thing; melius est, it is better; in melius, for the better; to a better state, 11.426; meliōra, um, better things, 12.153; *superl* optimus, a, um, best, *freq* For the *adv* melius, see bene.

Boreās, ae *m* the north wind, 3.687; the god of the north wind, Boreas, son of the river-god Strymon (others, the north), 10.350.

bōs, bovis, *c* an ox, 2.306; bull, 5.405; cow, 7.663; heifer, 7.790; *pl* cattle, 3.220.

bracchium, iī, *n* strictly, the forearm from the hand to the elbow; in general, the arm, 2.792 *et al.*; *figuratively* limb, branch, of a tree, 6.282; sail-yard, 5.829; of walls, 3.535.

bractea, ae *f* a thin plate of metal; gold-foil, -leaf, 6.209.

brevis, e *adj* short, of space, 3.507; shallow, 5.221; of time, brief, 10.467; *subst pl* brevia, ium, *n*, shoals, 1.111.

breviter *adv* briefly; in few words, 1.561. (brevis).

Briareus (*trisyll*) eī *m* Briareus, or Aegaeon, one of the three Uranids, or sons of Uranus, giant monsters with a hundred (i.e. very many) hands, 6.287.

Brontēs, ae *m* one of the Cyclops, in the forge of Vulcan, 8.425.

brūma, ae *f* the winter solstice; winter, 2.472.

brūmālis, e *adj* (brūma), of the winter; wintry, 6.205.

Brūtus, ī *m* a surname of the Junian gens, derived from Lucius Junius Brutus, the patrician leader who delivered Rome from the Tarquins, 6.818.

būbō, ōnis *m* an owl (f. only once in Virgil, 4.462).

būcina, ae *f* a trumpet, 7.519.

bulla, ae *f* something resembling a bubble; a boss, a stud, 9.359.

būstum, ī, *n* the mound where the dead have been burned; funeral pile, 11.201; tomb, 12.863. (cf. combūrō).

Būtēs, ae *m* 1. A descendant of Amycus, king of Bebrycia, 5.372. 2. A Trojan, attendant of Ascanius, 9.647. 3. A Trojan, 11.690.

Būthrōtum, ī, *n* a town of Epirus, opposite Corcyra, 3.293.

buxus, ī *f* the box tree; *metonym* a flute or pipe, 9.619.

Byrsa, ae *f* the citadel of Carthage, 1.367.

cacūmen, inis, *n* a point, peak; summit, 3.274.

Cācus, ī *m* Cacus, the giant of the Aventine, slain by Hercules, 8.194.

cadāver, eris, *n* a dead body, carcass, corpse, 8.264. (cadō).

cadō, cecidī, cāsus 3 *v* to fall, sink down, *freq*; set, of the sun and stars, 2.9; fall in battle, 2.368; in sacrifice, 1.334; of the wind, subside, cease; of the sea, subside, be hushed, 1.54; sink in death, die, 10.390; to fall out, happen, 2.709.

cadūcus, a, um *adj* (cadō), liable to fall; destined, doomed to fall, or die, 10.622; slain, 6.481.

cadus, ī *m* a jar; wine-jar, 1.195; an urn, 6.228.

Caeculus, ī *m* son of Vulcan, and mythical founder of Praeneste, 7.681.

caecus, a, um *adj* blind, *freq*; blinded mentally, reckless, 1.349; 11.781; with fury, mad, 2.357; of things which baffle or obstruct the sight or the mind, dark, 3.200; hidden, covered, 1.536; secret, private, 2.453; from behind, 10.733; uncertain or dim, 9.518; uncertain, 6.30; aimless, 4.209; blinding, 12.444; of uncertain origin, 12.617; of sound, indistinct, subdued, 10.98; obscure, 12.591.

caedēs, is *f* a cutting off or down; bloodshed, havoc, slaughter, 1.471 *et al.*; deadly blow, 2.526; bloody attack, assault, 3.256; blood, 9.818; *pl* caedēs, ium or um, slaughter, bloodshed, 11.648 *et al.* (caedō).

Caedicus, ī *m* Caedicus, an Etruscan chief, 9.362.

caedō, cecīdī, caesus 3 *v* to cut, *freq*; cut down, slay,

2.266; sacrifice, 5.96; strike, 10.404. (*rel to* scindō).

caelestis, e *adj* (caelum), belonging to the sky; celestial, 1.11; heaven-sent, divine, 6.379; *subst* caelestēs, ium or um, *c*, the gods of heaven, 1.387.

caelestis, e *adj* (caelum), belonging to the sky; celestial, 1.11; heaven-sent, divine, 6.379; *subst* caelestēs, ium or um, *c*, the gods of heaven, 1.387.

caelicola, ae, *c* an inhabitant of heaven; a god, 2.641 *et al.* (caelum and colō).

caelifer, era, erum *adj* (caelum *and* ferō), heaven-bearing, sky-bearing, 6.796.

caelō, āvī, ātus *1 v* to cut in relief; carve, engrave, chase, emboss, 1.640. (caelum, a chisel).

caelum, ī, *n* (*pl* caelī, ōrum, *m*) the sky, the firmament, the heavens; heaven, 1.225; region, 1.331; air, weather, 5.18; the upper world or abode of living men, as distinguished from Hades, 6.896; *personif,* Caelus, ī, *m,* the god Caelus, father of Saturn, 7.140.

Caeneus (*dissyl*), **eos** *m* 1. A Thessalian girl, formerly named Caenis, transformed by Neptune into a boy, 6.448. 2. A follower of Aeneas, 9.573.

caenum, ī, *n* dirt, mud, mire, slime, 6.296.

Caere, *n, indeclin* (*gen* **Caeritis** *f,* *abl* **Caerēte** *f*) Caere or Agylla, in the southern part of Etruria, now Cervetri, 8.597; 10.183.

caerulus, a, um *adj* dark blue, 2.381; sea-colored, azure, 5.819; dark; black, 3.64; *subst* caerula, ōrum, *n,* the dark blue waters; the sea, 3.208.

Caesar, aris *m* a surname of the Julian gens, esp. Gaius Iulius Caesar, dictator and founder of the Roman Empire. His name was inherited by his nephew and adopted son Octavius and his successors; Augustus Caesar, 1.286; 6.792.

caesariēs, ēī *f* the hair of the head, 1.590 *et al.*

caespes, itis *f* turf, sod, 3.304. (caedō).

caestus, ūs *m* a gauntlet for boxing; thongs or straps loaded with lead, and bound round the hand and arm, 5.69. (caedō).

caetra, ae *f* a short Spanish shield, 7.732.

Caīcus, ī *m* Caicus, commander of one of the ships of Aeneas, 1.183.

Cāiēta, ae *f* 1. The nurse of Aeneas, 7.2. 2. A town and haven of Latium, named after the nurse of Aeneas (now Gaëta), 6.900.

calamus, ī *m* a reed or cane; an arrow, 10.140.

calathus, ī *m* a wicker basket; workbasket, 7.805.

calcar, āris, *n* a spur, 6.881. (calx).

Calchās, antis *m* Calchas, a priest and prophet of the Greeks, at Troy, 2.100.

calcō, āvī, ātus *1 v* to put under the heel; trample upon; mix by trampling, 12.340. (calx).

calefaciō, fēcī, factus *3 v*; *passive* **calefīō, factus sum, fīerī** to make hot, glowing, 12.66; *figuratively* excite, arouse, 12.269. (caleō and faciō).

caleō, uī *2 v* to be warm; to glow, 1.417.

Calēs, ium *f* a town of Campania, 7.728.

calidus, a, um *adj* (caleō), warm, hot, 6.218; reeking, 10.486; of the spirit or disposition, hot, fiery.

cālīgō, āre *1 v* to be dark, darken, 2.606. (> cālīgō 1).

cālīgō, inis *f* mist, fog, 3.203; misty, obscurity; darkness, dimness, obscurity, 6.267; smoke, 11.187; cloud of dust, 9.36; blinding dust, 12.466.

Calliopē, ēs, and **Calliopēa, ae** *f* chief of the Muses, and mother of Orpheus, 9.525.

callis, is *m* a narrow, uneven footpath; path, 4.405.

calor, ōris *m* warmth, heat, vital heat, 4.705. (caleō).

calx, calcis *f*, and *rarely m* the heel, 5.324; the hoof of a horse, the fore foot, or hoof, 10.892; a spur, 11.714.

Calybē, ēs *f* an aged priestess of Juno, 7.419.

Calydōn, ōnis *f* a town of Aetolia, the abode of Meleager, 7.306.

Camarīna, ae *f* a Syracusan colony on the southwest coast of Sicily, 3.701.

Camers, ertis *m* Camertes or Camers, a follower of Turnus, 10.562.

Camilla, ae *f* a Volscian heroine, ally of Turnus, 7.803 *et al.*

Camillus, ī *m m* Furius Camillus, the conqueror of Veii, who expelled the Gauls from Rome after the capture of the city, BC 390.6.825.

camīnus, ī *m* a furnace; forge, 6.630; crevice, cavity, 3.580.

Campānus, a, um *adj* (Campānia), of Campania, the country lying on the bay of Naples; Campanian, 10.145.

campus, ī *m* a plain, field, 5.128 *et al.*; a race-course, 5.144; a field of combat, 12.116; *figuratively* of the surface of the sea, plain, 6.724; Mavortis Campus, the Campus Martius, or Field of Mars, on the left bank of the Tiber at Rome, 6.873.

candeō, uī *2 v* to be of pure whiteness; *part*, candēns, entis, white, 4.61; at white heat; glowing, 3.573; 12.91.

candidus, a, um *adj* (candeō), pure white; snow-white; white, 6.708; fair, 5.571.

candor, ōris *m* shining, brilliant whiteness; whiteness, 3.538. (candeō).

canis, is *c* a dog, *freq.*

canistra, ōrum, *n pl* a basket; baskets, 1.701.

cānitēs, **ēī** *f* hoariness, grayness; gray hair, 6.300; gray hairs, old age, 10.549. (cānus).

canō, **cecinī** *3 v* to make musical and rhythmical sounds with voice or instrument; to make melody, play, or sing, to sing, rehearse, celebrate in song or verse, 1.1; to speak in measure or rhythm; to proclaim, as prophet or priest, 2.176; reveal, 3.155; foretell, 2.124; rehearse, narrate, 4.14; explain, interpret, 5.524; warn, 12.28; forebode, croak, 11.399; sound, 7.513.

canōrus, **a**, **um** *adj* (canō), tuneful, harmonious, 6.120; resounding, 9.503.

cantus, **ūs** *m* a singing or playing; melody; song, 1.398; strain, sound, 6.165; incantation, charm, 7.754. (canō).

cānus, **a**, **um** *adj* white, of the hair and beard; whitened, hoary, of frost and cold; of the sea, foaming, hoary, 8.672; gray-haired, venerable; hoary, 1.292.

Capēnus, **a**, **um** *adj* (Capēna), of Capena, a town in the southern part of Tuscany, 7.697.

capessō, **īvī** or **iī**, **ītus** *3 intens v* to seize, 3.234; *figuratively* lay hold of, assume, 8.507; seek to reach, hasten to, 4.346; undertake, achieve, perform, 1.77. (capiō).

Caphēreus, **eī** *m* Caphareus, a promontory on the southern coast of Euboea, 11.260.

capillus, **i** *m* the hair of the head, the hair.

capiō, **cēpī**, **captus** *3 v* to take with the hand, *freq*; seize, 2.314; *figuratively* conquer, 9.267; occupy, 1.396; catch, captivate, deceive, charm, allure, receive, accept, 3.488; enter upon, celebrate, 7.403; contain, 7.466; confine, 9.644; *part*, *subst* captus, ī, *m*, a prisoner, captive, 2.64.

Capitōlium, **iī**, *n* the Capital, or national temple on the Capitoline hill at Rome, containing the shrines of Jupiter, Juno, and Minerva, 6.836; *pl* the Capitoline places, or buildings; the Capitoline, 8.653. (caput).

capra, **ae** *f* a she-goat; a goat. (caper).

caprea, **ae** *f* a kind of wild goat; a roe. (caper).

Capreae, **ārum** *f* Capreae, now Capri, an island in the Bay of Naples, 7.735. (caper).

caprigenus, **a**, **um** *adj* (caper and root gen-), pertaining to goats; of the goat kind, of goats, 3.221.

captīvus, **a**, **um** *adj* (capiō), taken in war; captured, captive, 2.765; of a captive or of captives, 10.520; *subst* captīvus, ī, *m*, a captive, 9.273.

captō, **āvī**, **ātus** *1 freq v* to lay hold upon vigorously, of the air, 3.514. (capiō).

capulus, **ī** *m* the handle; hilt, 2.553. (capiō),.

caput, **itis**, *n* the head of men or animals, *freq*; (by synecdoche), the person, being, life, 2.751 *et al.*; living body, life, 4.699; personal interest, welfare, fortune, life, 4.354; of plants, the head or flower, 9.437; of other objects, a captain, leader, chief, 11.399 *et al.*; author, instigator, source, cause, 11.361; chief town, capital, sovereign city, 10.203; a peak or summit, 6.360; point, end, of a bow, 11.861; of rivers, etc., fountain-head, source, spring; *pl* capita, in enumerating animals, head, 3.391; in caput, headlong, 1.116; suprā caput, overhead, above, 3.194; hōc caput, this person, myself, me, 8.570.

Capys, yos or **yis** *m* 1. The commander of one of the ships of Aeneas, 1.183. 2. The eighth king of Alba, 6.768.

carbaseus, a, um *adj* (carbasus), of linen, linen-, 11.776.

carbasus, ī *f* (*pl* **carbasa, ōrum,** *n*) linen, cloth or web of lawn, 8.34; canvas; a sail, 3.357.

carcer, eris *m* a dungeon, hold, prison, 1.54; carcer, or *pl* carcerēs, the stalls; the starting place or barrier in the circus or race-course, 5.145.

carchēsium, iī, *n* a large drinking vessel with two handles; bowl, beaker, 5.77.

cardō, inis *m* a hinge, pivot, 1.449; the socket in which the pivot plays, 2.493; *figuratively* a turning point, crisis, emergency, 1.672.

careō, uī, itus 2 *v* to be without, to be free from, 2.44; to be deprived of, 4.432.

Cārēs, Ium, *Gr acc,* **as** (*sing* **Cār, Cāris**) *m* the Carians, of Caria in the southwestern part of Asia Minor, 8.725. (Cāria).

carīna, ae *f* the keel of a ship, ship, 4.398; a boat, 6.391; frame, timber, 5.682.

Carīnae, ārum *f* the Carinae, a quarter of Rome between the Caelian and Esquiline, 8.361.

carmen, inis, *n* a song, hymn, ode or poem, *freq*; a line or verse, 3.287; a response, prophecy, 3.445; an incantation, charm, spell, 4.487; cry, moan, 4.462.

Carmentālis, e *adj* (Carmentis), of Carmentis, 8.338.

Carmentis, is *f* Carmentis, a prophetess, mother of King Evander, 8.336. (carmen.)

Carpathius, a, um *adj* of Carpathus, an island northeast of Crete; *subst* Carpathium, iī, *n*, the Carpathian Sea, 5.595.

carpo, carpsī, carptus 3 *v* to pluck or pull, crop, browse upon, eat, graze; cause to graze, pasture; gather, 6.146; *figuratively* catch, breathe, enjoy, 1.388; consume, 4.2; devour, waste, 4.32; carpere prāta, etc., to course over.

cārus, a, um *adj* dear, 4.91 *et al.*; *poetic*, active, loving, fond, 1.677; affectionate, tender, 11.215.

Casmilla, ae *f* the mother of Camilla, 11.543.

Casperia, ae *f* a town of the Sabines, 7.714.

Caspius, a, um *adj* of the Caspian Sea, Caspian; Asiatic, 6.798.

Cassandra, ae *f* a daughter of Priam, beloved of Apollo, and inspired by him with prophecy; but because she did not requite his love, condemned to foretell the destruction of Troy without being believed by her countrymen, 2.246.

cassida, ae, and **cassis, idis** *f* a helmet (of metal), 11.775.

cassus, a, um *adj* void; deprived of, 2.85; fruitless, vain, 12.780.

castellum, ī, *n* a fortress, stronghold, castle, 5.440. (castrum).

castīgō, āvī, ātus 1 *v* to chastise, punish; chide, reprove, rebuke, 5.387. (castus and agō).

Castor, oris *m* a Trojan warrior, 10.124.

castra, ōrum *n* a camp, 2.462; fleet, 4.604; naval camp, station, 3.519; hive, 12.589. (*sing* castrum, ī, *n*, castle, fort).

Castrum Inuī a town in Latium near Antium and Ardea, 6.775.

castus, a, um *adj* pure, 6.563; pious, 3.409; sacred, holy, 6.661.

cāsus, ūs *m* a falling; close; fall, destruction, 2.507; fortune, chance, fate, 1.615; event, 8.533; hardship, misfortune, 1.599; danger, peril, 2.563; juncture, crisis, 4.560; fate, death, 5.869. (cadō).

catēia, ae *f* a slender javelin, 7.741.

catēna, ae *f* a chain, fetter, 6.558.

caterva, ae *f* a troop, squadron, band, 2.370; crowd, throng, multitude, 2.40; flock, 11.456.

Catilīna, ae *m* L. Sergius Catiline, the conspirator, 8.668.

Catillus, ī *m* Catillus, with his brother, Tiburtus, founder of Tibur, 7.672.

Catō, ōnis *m* a family name in the Porcian gens. 1. *m* Porcius Cato, called the Censor and also Senex, 6.841. 2. *m* Porcius Cato the younger, who perished by his own hand at Utica; hence, called Uticensis, 8.670.

catulus, ī *m* a young dog; a whelp, the young of wild animals; a cub, whelp, 2.357.

Caucasus, ī *m* the Caucasus; the Caucasian Mountains, between the Caspian and Euxine, 4.367.

cauda, ae *f* the tail, 3.428 *et al.*

caulae, ārum *f* an opening, a passage; sheepfold, 9.60.

caulis, is *m* a stalk, 12.413.

Caulōn, ōnis *m* Caulon, or Caulonia, a town on the east coast of Bruttium, 3.553.

causa, ae *f* a cause, reason, 1.25; cause, occasion, 2.285; pretext, excuse, occasion, 4.51; a reason, an argument, 8.395; a cause (judicial), 6.849; with *infin*, 10.90.

cautēs, is *f* a craggy or pointed rock, or cliff; rock, crag, 3.534.

cautius *adv* comp. of cautē; more cautiously, 11.153.

cavea, ae *f* a hollow place; that part of the theater or circus which was occupied by the spectators, 8.636; a theater; natural amphitheater, 5.340. (cavus).

caveō, cāvī, cautus *2 v* to be on one's guard; to beware, *with subst* 11.293.

caverna, ae *f* a hollow; cavern, 2.53 *et al.* (cavus).

cavō, āvī, ātus *1 v* to hollow or scoop out; *part*, cavātus, a, um, hollowed out; vaulted, 1.310. (cavus).

cavus, a, um *adj* hollow, 1.81; concave, 8.599; arching, vaulted, 2.487; cavae manūs, the palms of the hands, 12.86.

Cēcropidēs, ae *m* a son or descendant of Cecrops; *pl* the Athenians, 6.21.

cēdō, cessī, cessus *3 v* to go, *frequently* go away, depart, 6.460; retire, withdraw, recede, 3.496; desist from, 9.620; give way, 7.636; abate, 9.126; draw back, 5.445; submit, yield, 2.704; fall to, come into one's possession, 3.297; to come behind, 3.484; result, turn out; turn out well, prosper, 12.148.

cedrus, ī *f* the cedar, 11.137; cedar wood, 7.178.

Celaenō, ūs *f* one of the Harpies, 3.211.

celebrō, āvī, ātus *1 v* to attend or be present in great numbers; to attend, honor, 1.735;

celebrate, 5.58; observe, 8.268. (celeber, frequented).

Celemna, ae *f* a town of Campania, 7.739.

celer, eris, ere *adj* fleet, rapid, active, nimble, swift, 4.180, et al; in a predicate, swiftly, 6.425.

celerō, āvī, ātus *1 v* to speed, hasten, 1.357 *et al.* (celer).

cella, ae *f* a storeroom, granary, wine-cellar; cell of the honeycomb, 1.433; shrine, of a temple.

cēlō, āvī, ātus *1 v* to hide, conceal, 1.351 *et al.*

celsus, a, um *adj* (cellō, rise), high, lofty, 1.56 *et al.*

Centaurus, ī *m* 1. A Centaur, a fabulous monster, with a human head and neck and the body of a horse, 6.286. 2. The name of a ship in the fleet of Aeneas (fem.), 5.122.

centēnus, a, um distr. *num adj* (centum); *pl* a hundred each, 9.162; *sing* (after the analogy of multus, many a), a unit repeated the hundredth time, render by the plural, a hundred, 10.207; as cardinal, a hundred, 10.566.

centum (*indecl num adj*), hundred, 6.625.

centumgeminus, a, um *adj* hundredfold; of the hundred- (or many-) handed Briareus, 6.287.

Ceraunia, ōrum, *n pl* the Ceraunian peaks, a range

of mountains on the coast of Epirus, 3.506.

Cerberus, ī *m* Cerberus, the three-headed watch-dog of Pluto, 6.417.

Cereālis, e *adj* (Cerēs), of Ceres; pertaining to Ceres or to grain; Cereālia arma, utensils for preparing grain or making bread; instruments of Ceres, 1.177.

cerebrum, ī, *n* the brain, 5.413 *et al.*

Cerēs, eris *f* daughter of Saturn and Ops, and goddess of agriculture; *metonym* corn, grain, 1.177; bread, 1.701; cake, loaf, 7.113; Cerēs labōrāta, bread, 8.181.

cēreus, a, um *adj* (cēra), waxen, 12.589.

cernō, crēvī, crētus *3 v* to distinguish; discern, perceive, see, behold, 1.413; *frequently* descry, 3.552; for dēcernere, to contend, decide, 12.709. (*rel to* κρίνω, decide).

cernuus, a, um *adj* with head or face prone downward; pitching, bending with the head to the ground, prostrate, 10.894.

certāmen, inis, *n* a striving, a struggle; effort, 5.197; combat, emulation, strife, 3.128; battle, war, 8.639; contest, game, 5.286. (certō).

certātim *adv* with striving or contention; emulously, vying one with another; with every blow, 2.628; emulously, 3.290;

impatiently, 11.486; as if in rivalry; fiercely, 11.209. (certō).

certē *adv* certainly, surely, at any rate, at least, 1.234 *et al.*

certō, āvī, ātus *1 v* to make certain by conflict; to contend, 2.30; struggle, strive, 3.668; *with dat* to struggle against, contend with, rival; *with infin,* 4.443; *impers,* certātur, it is fought; we fight; certātum est, we have fought, 11.313; certandum est, we must fight, 12.890. (certus).

certus, a, um determined; distinct; separate, peculiar; fixed, 2.350; 6.673; stated; direct, 2.212; resolved, 2.554; certain of, resolved on, 4.554; confident, stout, 9.249; unerring, 12.490; secure, 9.96; trustworthy, sure, faithful, 1.576; undoubted, true, 6.322; certum est, it is determined, I resolve, we resolve, 3.686; (aliquem) certum facere, to inform, 3.179; *adv* certē, certainly, surely, at any rate, at least, 1.234 *et al.* (cernō).

cerva, ae *f* a hind, 4.69; stag, 6.802. (cervus).

cervīx, īcis *f* the neck, including the back or nape of the neck, 1.477 *et al.*

cervus, ī *m* a stag, deer, 1.184 *et al.*

cessō, āvī, ātus *1 intens v* to remit action; stay, linger, rest; be inactive, 1.672; cease, 2.468; delay, 6.51; *impers,* cessātum est, delay has been made, has happened, 11.288. (cēdō).

cētera *adv* (n. *pl* of cēterus, a, um), in other respects, 3.594; as to the rest, henceforth, 9.656.

cēterus, a, um *adj* (nom. *sing* masc. not used), the other, 2.207; other; the rest of, 5.74, *freq*; *n pl* cētera, adverbially, in other respects, 3.594; as to the rest, henceforth, 9.656.

Cethēgus, ī *m* a Rutulian, 12.513.

cētus, ī, m; cētos, ī, n; *pl* cētē, κῆτος, whales, sharks, sea-monsters, 5.822.

ceu (*adv* and *conj*), as, just as, 5.88; as if, 2.438 *et al.* (ce-ve).

Chalcidicus, a, um *adj* of Chalcis, the chief town of Euboea; Chalcidian, 6.17.

Chalybes, um *m* a people of Pontus, skillful in making steel; the Chalybes; *metonym* masses of steel or iron, 8.421; metalla Chalybum, mines of iron, 10.174.

chalybs, ybis *m* steel, 8.446.

Chāōn, onis *m* a Trojan, brother of Helenus, 3.335.

Chāonia, ae *f* a country of Epirus, named after Chaon, 3.335.

Chāonius, a, um *adj* of Chaonia; Chaonian, 3.293.

Chaos (only in *nom* and *acc sing*), *n* 1. Void and boundless space. 2. Chaos, father of Night and Erebus, 4.510; placed among the infernal gods, 6.265.

Charōn, ōntis *m* son of Erebus and Night, and ferryman of the Styx, 6.299.

Charybdis, is *f* a whirlpool near the Sicilian coast, in the Straits of Messina, opposite the rock of Scylla; personified as a monster, 3.420.

Chimaera, ae *f* 1. A monster, said to have infested Lycia, having the head of a lion, the body of a goat, and the tail of a dragon, and breathing out fire, 6.288. 2. The name of one of the ships of Aeneas, 5.118.

chlamys, ydis *f* a mantle or cloak of woolen cloth, worn by the Greeks; a mantle, 3.484.

Chlōreus (*dissyll*), **eī** and **eos** *m* Chloreus, a Trojan, priest of Cybele, 11.768.

chorēa, ae *f* a circling dance, 10.224; a dance, 6.644.

chorus, ī *m* a dance in a circle; a dance; a company of singers or dancers, choir, train, 1.499; band, troop, 5.581; festival, 11.737.

Chromis, is *m* a Trojan, 11.675.

cieō, cīvī, citus *2 v* to cause, to move; stir, 2.419; agitate, move, 4.122; excite, kindle, rouse, 6.165; raise, 12.104; call upon, invoke, 3.68; call up, exhibit, 5.585; of tears, shed, 6.468.

Ciminus, ī *m* Lake Ciminus, in Etruria, 7.697.

cingō, cīnxī, cīnctus *3 v* to gird, 2.520; clothe, 8.282; surround, inclose, 1.112; encompass, envelop, 5.13; wreathe, crown, 5.71; involve, 1.673; fly around, 1.398.

cingulum, **ī**, *n* a girdle,
belt, 1.492. (cingō).

cinis, **eris** *m* ashes, embers,
5.743; ashes of the dead,
4.34; *metonym* tomb,
sepulcher, 4.633.

Cinyrus, **ī**, and **Cinyrās**, **ae** *m*
a Ligurian chief, 10.186.

circā *adv* around, 7.535; (*prep
with acc*), about, around.

Circaeus, **a**, **um** *adj* (Circē),
of Circe, 7.10.

Circē, **ēs** or **ae** *f* a sorceress,
daughter of Helios and Perse
or Perseis, 3.386 *et al.*

circēnsis, **e** *adj* (circus),
pertaining to the Circus
Maximus; Circensian, 8.636.

circuitus, **ūs** *m* a going round;
circuit, 3.413. (circumeō).

circulus, **ī** *m* a circle or orbit;
ring; chain, torques,
collar, 5.559. (circus).

circum *adv* about, around; (*prep
with acc*), around, about.

circumdō, **dedī**, **datus**, **dare** *1 v*
to put or throw around; (with
abl), to encircle, surround,
encompass, inclose with,
1.368; of dress, gird, 9.462;
adorn, 6.207; set, 1.593;
border, 4.137; (*with dat*), throw
around, 2.792; twine or coil
around, 2.219; put round, 2.510.

circumdūcō, **xi**, **ctum**,
3 v lead around.

circumeō, **īvī** or **iī**, **itus** *4 v*
to go about, circle round,
11.761. (circum and eō).

circumferō, **tulī**, **lātus**, **ferre**
irreg v to bear round; pass
around, sprinkle, purify
by sprinkling, 6.229;
cast about, 12.558.

circumflectō, **flexī**, **flexus**
3 v to bend around; turn
far round, 3.430.

circumfundō, **fūdī**, **fūsus**
3 v to pour around; to
encompass, surround;
passive circumfundor, fūsus
sum, (in middle signif.),
to rush around, surround,
2.383; *part*, circumfūsus,
a, um, surrounding, 1.586;
gathering around, 6.666.

circumligō, **āvī**, **ātus** *1 v* to tie
or bind round or to, 11.555.

circumsistō, **stetī** *3 v* to take
one's stand around; gather
round; assail, surround, 8.490.

circumsonō *1 v* to sound about;
raise a din around, 8.474.

circumspiciō, **spexī**, **spectus**
3 v to look around; cast a
glance round upon; survey,
2.68; look round and see,
12.896; observe, 3.517; look
round for, look out, seek.
(cīrcum and speciō, look).

circumstō, **stetī** *1 v* to stand
around; hem in; threaten,
beset, 10.905; encompass,
threaten, 2.559.

circumtextus, **a**, **um**
woven round, 1.649.
(circum and texō).

circumveniō, **vēnī**, **ventus** *4 v* to
come about; surround, 6.132.

circumvolō, **āvī**, **ātus** *1 v* to fly
around or surround in flying;

hover round, swoop round, 3.233; enshroud, cover, 2.360.

circumvolvō, *no perf*, **volūtus** 3 *v* to roll round; *passive* to complete, 3.284.

circus, **ī** *m* a circle, circuit, circular area, 5.289; surrounding multitude or throng of spectators, 5.109.

Cissēis, **idis** *f* the daughter of Cisseus; Hecuba, 7.320. (Cisseus).

Cisseus (*dissyll*), **eī** *m* 1. Cisseus, a king of Thrace, said by a late myth to have been the father of Hecuba, 5.537. 2. A Rutulian, 10.317.

citātus, **a**, **um** swiftly driven or swiftly running, 12.373. (cito -are).

Cithaerōn, **ōnis** *m* a mountain of Boeotia, where the orgies of Bacchus were celebrated, 4.303.

cithara, **ae** *f* the cithara, cithern, or lute, 1.740.

cito *adv* speedily; soon; *compar* citius, 5.242.

citus, **a**, **um** swiftly moved or driven; speedy, rapid, swift, 1.301; as an *adv*, 4.574. (cieo).

cīvīlis, **e** *adj* (cīvis), pertaining to the citizen; civil, civic, 6.772.

cīvis, **is**, *c* a citizen, 2.42 *et al.*; *pl* comrades, 5.196.

clādēs, **is** *f* destruction; slaughter, carnage, 2.361; scourge, destroyers, 6.843.

clam *adv* secretly, 1.350.

clāmō, **āvī**, **ātus** *1 v* to call, 12.600; call; call upon, 4.674; cry out or aloud, shout, 9.442. (*rel to* καλέω, call).

clāmor, **ōris** *m* a shout *et al.*; loud cry or shriek, 2.488; a call, 2.769; clamor, outcry, shouting, 1.87; sound, roaring sound, 3.566. (clāmō).

clangor, **ōris** *m* a clashing sound; braying, din, blast, 2.313; rushing sound, flapping, 3.226. (clangō, resound).

clārēscō, **claruī** 3 *inc v* to become clear to the ear or eye; grow loud, increase, 2.301.

Clārius, **a**, **um** *adj* of Claros, a town in Ionia, noted for one of the oracles of Apollo located there; Clarian, 3.360.

clārus, **a**, **um** *adj* clear, of sight or sound; clear, 1.588; shining, bright, lustrous, 9.582; making clear; fair, bright; shrill, loud, 3.519; *figuratively* renowned, 1.284; noble, illustrious, honored, 1.550.

Clārus, **ī** *m* Clarus, a Lycian follower of Aeneas, 10.126.

classicum, **ī**, *n* the sound of the trumpet; the trumpet, 7.637. (classis).

classis, **is** *f* a fleet, 1.39; a ship, 6.334; a troop or body of soldiers, 7.716; *pl* armies or hosts (coming in ships or fleets), 3.602. (*rel to* καλέω, call).

Claudius, **a**, **um** *adj* (Claudius), pertaining to the family of Claudius; Claudian, 7.708.

claudō, clausī, clausus *3 v*
to shut or close; *frequently*
shut up; shut up or close
against, 1.233; inclose, bound,
8.473; confine, 6.734; with
circum, surround, 1.311;
subst clausum, ī, *n*, a pen.

claudus, a, um *adj* lame,
limping, maimed, 5.278.

claustra, ōrum, *n pl*
fastenings; bolts, bars;
barriers, 1.56; narrows,
straits, 3.411. (claudō).

Clausus, ī *m* a chief of
the Sabines, 7.707.

clāva, ae *f* a club, 10.318.

clāvus, ī *m* a nail, a peg;
a helm, 5.177.

cliēns, entis *m* a client,
dependent, 6.609.
(cluō, to hear).

clipeātus, a, um *adj* (clipeus),
armed with a shield, or
shield-bearing, 7.793.

clipeus, ī, *m,* and **clipeum**
ī, *n* a round shield; a
shield, 2.227 *et al.*

Cloanthus, ī *m* commander
of one of the ships of
Aeneas, 1.222.

Cloelia, ae *f* the Roman heroine
who escaped with other
maiden hostages from the
camp of Porsena, and swam
across the Tiber to Rome, 8.651.

Clonius, iī *m* a Trojan, 9.574.

Clonus, ī *m* the name of a
Greek silversmith, 10.499.

Cluentius, iī *m* a Roman
gentile name, 5.123.

Clūsīnus, a, um *adj* (Clūsium),
of Clusium, 10.655.

Clūsium, iī, *n* one of the
chief cities of Etruria,
now Chiusi, 10.167.

Clytius, iī *m* the name of several
Trojans, 9.774; 10.129, etc.

Cnōsius, a, um *adj* (Cnōsus or
Gnōsus), of Knossos, a city in
Crete; Knossian, Cretan, 3.115.

Coclēs, itis *m* Horatius
Cocles, the Roman hero
who defended the bridge
against the Tuscans, 8.650.

Cōcytius, a, um *adj* of
Cocytus, 7.479.

Cōcytus, ī *m* the Cocytus, the
river of lamentation, in
the lower world, 6.132.

coeō, coīvī or **coiī, coitus, coīre**
irreg v to go or come together,
assemble, 7.582; come together
in conflict, join battle; of the
blood, stand still, congeal,
curdle, 3.30; come to terms,
form a compact, 7.317; coīre
in ūnum, to come to one
place, unite, concentrate,
combine, 9.801 *et al.*

coepiō, coepī, coeptus (*the
tenses of the stem of the present
are archaic*) *3 v* to begin, 1.521.

coeptum, ī, *n* a thing begun;
an undertaking, enterprise,
design, 4.642 *et al.* (coepiō).

coerceō, uī, itus *2 v* to keep in,
hem in, confine, restrain,
6.439; push on, lead on,
9.27. (com- and arceō).

coetus, ūs *m* a coming
together, an assembly, 5.43;

a flock, 1.398; banquet, feast, 1.735. (coeō).

Coeus, ī *m* one of the Titans, and father of Latona, 4.179.

cognātus, a, um *adj* near by birth; kindred, 3.502.

cognōmen, inis, *n* a name common to a family; a surname; name, 1.267.

cognōminis, e *adj* of the same, or his name, 6.383. (cognōmen).

cognōscō, nōvī, nitus *3 v* to get complete knowledge of; ascertain, trace out; know; learn, 2.10; for agnōscō, recognize, 6.340.

cōgō, coēgī, coāctus *3 v* to drive, lead, assemble together, 4.289; condense, 5.20; close up, 12.457; urge, impel, 9.463; force (of tears), feign, 2.196; compel, 1.563; with two accusatives, 3.56. (com- and agō).

cohibeō, uī, itus *2 v* to hold together, restrain, confine, 3.424; check, curb, repress, 12.314. (com- and habeō).

cohors, tis *f* a cohort, one of the divisions or regiments of a Roman legion; a cohort; a fleet or squadron, 3.563; a troop, 11.500.

Collātīnus, a, um *adj* (Collātia), of Collatia, a town of the Sabines near Rome; Collatine, 6.774.

colligō, lēgī, lēctus *3 v* to gather, collect, assemble, 1.143; gather up, fold up, 1.320; reef, 5.15; contract, 12.862; increase, 9.63; colligere sē in arma, to

gather one's self behind his shield, 10.412. (con and legō).

collis, is *m* a hill, *freq.*

collum, ī, *n* the neck of men and animals, 1.654 *et al.*; of a plant, 9.436; *pl* the neck, 11.692.

colō, uī, cultus, *v* to till, cultivate, 1.532; inhabit, live in, dwell in; *figuratively* care for, cherish, love, favor, 1.16; observe, 7.602; revere, honor, 4.458; worship, 5.63.

colōnus, ī *m* a cultivator or tiller; a husbandman, *freq*; settler, colonist, 1.12. (colō).

color, ōris *m* color, 4.701 *et al.*; complexion, hue, 4.558.

coluber, ubrī *m* a snake, serpent, 2.471.

columba, ae *f* a pigeon, dove, 2.516.

columna, ae *f* a column, pillar, 1.428; Proteī columnae, the pillars of Proteus; the northern extremities of Egypt, 11.262.

colus, ī and **ūs** *f* a distaff, 7.805; spinning, 8.409. (rarely *m*).

coma, ae *f* the hair, 1.319; mane, 10.726; *figuratively* foliage, leafy crown, 2.629; leaves, branches.

comāns, antis hairy, 3.468; crested, 2.391; leafy, 12.413. (como -are).

comes, itis, *c* a comrade; companion, 2.294; friend, follower, 2.796; attendant, 4.664; ally, confederate, 2.181; guide, 6.292; guardian, tutor, 9.649. (com- and eō).

cometēs (cometa), ae *m*
a comet, 10.273.

comitātus, ūs *m* an
accompanying or following;
a suite, train, retinue,
4.215. (comitor).

comitor, ātus sum, 1. *dep v* to
accompany, attend, follow,
3.660; *part*, comitātus, a,
um, attended, accompanied,
1.312 *et al.* (comes).

commendō, āvī, ātus 1 *v* to
commit, consign, intrust,
2.748. (com- and mandō).

commercium, iī, *n* trade;
negotiation, compact, 10.532.
(com- and merx, merchandise).

comminus *adv* hand to hand,
7.553.733; immediately; near
at hand. (com- and manus).

commisceō, uī, mixtus or
mistus 2 *v* to mix together,
freq; blend, mingle, 3.633.

commissum, ī, *n* an
offense, a fault, a crime,
1.136. (committō).

committō, mīsī, missus 3 *v*
to send or bring together;
join, unite, 3.428; engage
in, 5.69; join, begin battle,
11.589; perpetrate, commit
a crime, 1.231; begin, 7.542;
consign, intrust, 10.156;
manum committere, to engage
in conflict, to fight, 12.60.

commoveō, mōvī, mōtus 2 *v* to
move completely; move rapidly
in procession, 4.301; rouse,
start from cover, 7.494; shake,
stir, 5.217; disturb, move,
1.126; agitate, terrify 1.360.

commūnis, e *adj* shared together;
common, 2.573; public, 11.435.

cōmō, cōmpsī, cōmptus 3 *v*
to arrange; of the hair,
comb, dress, bind up, 6.48;
trim, 10.832; adorn, deck,
7.751. (com- and emō).

cōmō, cōmpsī, cōmptus 3 *v*
to arrange; of the hair,
comb, dress, bind up, 6.48;
trim, 10.832; adorn, deck,
7.751. (com- and emō).

compāgēs, is *f* a joining;
fastening, joint, 1.122.
(com- and pangō).

compellō, āvī, ātus 1 *v* to
address, accost, speak to,
1.581; greet, salute, 3.299;
chide, upbraid, 5.161.

compellō, pulī, pulsus 3 *v*
to drive together; compel
force, drive, 1.575.

compingō, pēgī, pāctus 3 *v* to
join together; *part*, compāctus,
a, um, close-jointed, 12.674.
(com- and pangō).

complector, plexus sum 3 *dep v*
to embrace; cover, 2.514; hold,
5.31; seize, grasp, 11.743.

compleō, ēvī, ētus 2 *v* to fill
up; fill, 2.20; complete,
5.46; fulfill, 9.108.

complexus, ūs *m* an embracing;
embrace, 1.715. (complector).

compōnō, posuī, positus (*part.
sometimes* **compostus**) 3 *v* to
put together; raise, build, 7.6;
found, 3.387; lay up, store,
8.317; put in order, arrange,
adjust; to regulate; close, 1.374;
put to rest in the tomb, bury,
1.249; end, 4.341; appease,

calm, 1.135; agree upon, form, 10.15; put side by side for comparison, to compare; bring together in society or in peace, 8.322; *passive* to be decided, to end, 12.109.

comportō, **āvī**, **ātus** *1 v* to bring together, carry away, 9.613.

compositō *adv* by compact, 2.129. (compono).

comprēndō, **prēndī**, **prēnsus** *3 v* to take hold of completely, seize, grasp, 2.793; inclose, include; catch, 7.73; to include in description, enumerate, describe, 6.626.

comprimō, **pressī**, **pressus** *3 v* to press together; repress, check, restrain, stay, 2.73. (com- and premō).

cōnātus, **ūs** *m* an effort, attempt, 12.910. (cōnor).

concavus, **a**, **um** *adj* completely hollow; hollow, concave, 5.677.

concēdō, **essī**, **essus** *3 v* to retire; come away, come, 2.523; go away, depart, 2.91; subside, come to an end, terminate, 8.41; allow, yield, grant, concede, 5.798; give up to, abandon, 7.305.

concha, **ae** *f* a shellfish; cockle shell, shell; a shell used as a trumpet; conch, 6.171; 10.209.

concidō, **cidī** *3 v* to fall completely; fall down, fall, 2.532. (com- and cadō).

conciēō, **īvī**, **itus** *2 v* to call together; incite, to stir up, arouse; enrage, fire, make furious, 9.694; hurl, shoot from, 12.921; disturb, 3.127;

passive to be impelled on, dart along, 11.744; hasten, speed, 12.902.

conciliō, **āvī**, **ātus** *1 v* to bring into accord; to win or gain over; procure, secure, 1.79. (concilium).

concilium, **iī**, *n* a body called together; assembly, council, 2.89; throng, company, 3.679. (com- and root cal-, call).

concipiō, **cēpī**, **ceptus** *3 v* to take completely; assume, 11.519; take in; conceive, 5.38; imagine, 4.502; to be possessed, filled with, 4.474; conceive, form, or express in words; form, draw up, 12.13. (com- and capiō).

concitō, **āvī**, **ātus** *1 intens v* to move with force; hurl, 11.784; spur, 11.742; (with sē), to speed, fly, 7.476.

conclāmō, **āvī**, **ātus** *1 v* to call out aloud; shout, cry, 3.523; call together, 7.504.

conclūdō, **clūsī**, **clūsus** *3 v* to shut completely; shut around, inclose, surround, 1.425. (com- and claudō).

concolor, **ōris** *adj* of the same color, 8.82.

concors, **cordis** *adj* (com- and cor), of one mind or spirit; harmonious, friendly, 6.827 *et al.*

concrēdō, **didī**, **ditus** *3 v* to trust, intrust, 10.286.

concrēscō, **crēvī**, **crētus** *3 v* to grow together; grow thick; stiffen, 12.905; *part*, concrētus, a, um, concreted, matted, 2.277; formed by natural growth, contracted, accumulated, 6.738.

concurrō, currī (*rarely* **cucurrī**), **cursus** *3 v* to run together or at once; crowd around, 12.297; rush, 2.315; rush to conflict, 7.224; rush against a foe; (*with dat*), engage, encounter, 1.493.

concursus, ūs *m* a running together; thronging, 6.318; concourse, multitude, throng, 5.611. (concurrō).

concutiō, cussī, cussus *3 v* to shake completely; shake, 2.629; push, 8.237; rouse, spur, 8.3; sift, examine, search, 7.338; agitate, strike with panic, terrify, 4.666; smite, afflict, 5.700. (com- and quatiō).

condēnsus, a, um *adj* thick, crowded, close together, 2.517.

condiciō, ōnis *f* terms, choice, 12.880. (condō).

conditor, ōris *m* a founder, 8.313. (condō).

condō, didī, ditus *3 v* to put or place together; found or build, 1.5; put together, devise, establish, 10.35; establish, restore, 6.792; put away, cover up, conceal, hide, with place in *abl* with or without in, or in *acc* with ad, 2.24 *et al.*; treasure up, keep, 3.388; consign to the tomb, bury, 3.68; *passive* sink or set, 7.719; sē condere, to go, hasten for protection, 9.39; confine, 9.32; plunge, 8.66; bury, conceal, 2.621.

condūcō, dūxī, ductus *3 v* lead, bring together; contract for, hire, rent, 12.520.

cōnectō, nexuī, nexus *3 v* to fasten together, connect; twist together, 8.437.

cōnferō, tulī, conlātus, ferre *irreg v* to bring together; cōnferre gradum, to walk side by side, accompany, 6.488; cōnferre manum or sīgna, to join battle, 11.517; 9.44; sē cōnferre, *with dat* to oppose, 10.735; cōnferre certāmina, to wage conflicts, 10.147.

cōnfertus, a, um crowded together, 2.347. (cōnferciō, crowd together).

cōnfestim *adv* immediately, forthwith, 9.231. (cōnferō).

cōnficiō, fēcī, fectus *3 v; passive* **cōnficior, cōnficī,** and **cōnfīō, fierī** to make completely, finish, accomplish, achieve, complete, 5.362; work out, wear out, waste, 3.590; exhaust, 4.599; destroy, 11.824; make infirm, 11.85; *passive* cōnfierī, to be accomplished, 4.116. (com- and faciō).

cōnfīdō, fīsus sum *3 v* to put entire trust in; to trust in, *with dat* or *abl*, 1.452 *et al.*

cōnfīgō, fīxī, fīxus *3 v* to fasten together or firmly; transfix, pierce, 2.429 *et al.*

cōnfiteor, fessus sum *2 dep v* to confess, acknowledge; manifest, reveal, 2.591. (com- and fateor).

cōnflīgō, flīxī, flīctus *3 v* to strike against; fight, contend, 2.417.

cōnfodiō, fōdī, fossus 3 v
to stab, wound, 9.445.

cōnfugiō, fūgī 3 v to flee for
refuge; flee, 8.493; resort;
flee, come for succor, 1.666.

cōnfundō, fūdī, fūsus 3 v
to pour together; mingle
with, 3.696; trouble,
confuse, 2.736; disturb,
interrupt, violate, 5.496.

cōnfūsus, a, um, mingled,
confused, promiscuous, 6.504;
bewildered, confounded,
12.665. (cōnfundō).

congeminō, āvī, ātus 1 v
to redouble, repeat,
12.714; multiply, multiply
blows with, 11.698.

congemō, uī 3 v to groan
deeply; send forth a sigh
or groan; *figuratively* to
creak or crash, 2.631.

congerō, gessī, gestus
3 v to bring together;
collect, heap up, 2.766;
construct, build, 6.178.

congredior, gressus sum 3
dep v to step, go together;
encounter, 1.475; join
battle; proceed to battle,
12.13. (com- and gradior).

congressus, ūs m a coming
together; conflict, assault,
12.514; *pl* an interview,
5.733. (congredior).

coniciō, iēcī, iectus 3 v to throw
together; pile up, 5.662;
throw, cast, hurl, 2.545; turn,
12.483. (com- and iaciō).

cōnifer, era, erum *adj* (cōnus and
ferō), cone-bearing, 3.680.

cōnītor, nīxus or **nīsus sum**
3 *dep v* to lean or brace
one's self against; struggle,
strive, put forth all one's
strength, 5.264; strain
every nerve, 9.769.

coniugium, iī, n a joining
together; marriage,
wedlock, 4.172; *metonym*
husband, wife, consort,
2.579; 3.296. (coniungō).

coniungō, iūnxī, iūnctus 3 v to
join together, clasp, 1.514;
fasten, moor, 10.653; unite,
ally, associate, 5.712.

coniūnx, iugis, c a consort;
husband, 1.343 *et al.*; wife,
2.597 *et al.*; betrothed,
3.331; spouse, bride,
9.138. (coniungō).

coniūrō, āvī, ātus 1 v to swear
together; conspire, unite, 8.5.

cōnlābor, lāpsus sum 3 *dep v*
to slip or fall together or
completely; sink down, 6.226;
swoon, faint, 4.391; fall, 4.664.

cōnloquium, iī, n a talking
together; discourse,
7.91. (conloquor).

cōnlūceō 2 v to be wholly
shining; shine on every
side; be lighted up; shine,
4.567; be refulgent, 10.539.

cōnlūstrō, āvī, ātus 1 v to
cast light upon; to look at,
inspect, survey, 3.651.

cōnor, ātus sum 1 *dep v*
to undertake, essay,
attempt, try, 2.792.

cōnsanguineus, a, um *adj* (com-
and sanguis), having common
blood; kindred, 12.40; *subst*

cōnsanguineus, ī, *m*, a brother, 6.278; kinsman, 5.771.

cōnsanguinitās, ātis *f* kinship, 2.86. (cōnsanguineus).

cōnscendō, scendī, scēnsus *3 v* to ascend, climb, 1.180; mount, 12.736; embark on, 1.381. (com- and scandō, climb).

cōnscius, a, um *adj* (com- and sciō), having complete knowledge; conscious, 5.455; conscious of, 2.141; conscious of guilt, guilty, 2.99; witnessing (w. *dat*), 4.167; having knowledge in common, or a mutual understanding; confederate, 2.267.

cōnsequor, secūtus sum *3 dep v* to follow closely, follow up, pursue, 2.409; overtake, 12.375.

cōnserō, seruī, sertus *3 v* to tie together; fasten, 3.594; arm, 11.771; cōnserere proelia, to join battle, engage in, fight, 2.398.

cōnserō, sēvī, situs or **satus** *3 v* to sow or plant.

cōnsessus, ūs *m* a sitting together; an assembly (others, place of assembly; others, tribunal or platform), 5.290; an assembly, 5.340. (cōnsīdō).

cōnsīdō, sēdī, sessus *3 v* to sit or settle down together or completely; sink, 2.624; sit, 4.573; sit in mourning, 11.350; take a seat, 5.136; alight, 3.245; settle, 10.780; dwell, 1.572; abide, rest, 11.915; to lie at anchor, to anchor, 3.378; to be moored, stationed, 7.431.

cōnsilium, iī, *n* counsel, advice, 5.728; plan, purpose, 1.281. (*rel to* cōnsulō).

cōnsistō, stitī, stitus *3 v* to stand still; stand, 1.226; halt, stop, 1.187; land, tread, 1.541; settle, 8.10; alight, rest, 4.253; to be quiet or at rest, 1.643.

cōnsonō, uī *1 v* to sound at once or together; sound loudly; resound, 5.149.

cōnsors, sortis *adj* having a common lot; participating, a companion, 10.906.

cōnspectus, ūs *m* a seeing or viewing; view, sight, 1.34; presence, 6.108; mediō in cōnspectū, in the midst of the gazing assembly. (cōnspiciō).

cōnspiciō, spexī, spectus *3 v* to have a complete view of; to look at, see, behold, 1.152; descry, discover, find, 6.508; *part*, cōnspectus, a, um, conspicuous. (com- and speciō, look).

cōnspīrō, āvī, ātus *1 v* to blow, sound together, 7.615.

cōnsternō, strāvī, strātus *3 v* to strew over; cover, strew, 4.444.

cōnstituō, uī, ūtus *3 v* to place, station, 5.130; erect, build, raise, 6.506; resolve, determine, 1.309. (com- and statuō).

cōnstō, stitī, stātus *1 v* to stand together; be or remain fixed; be settled, calm, 3.518; be determined, 5.748.

cōnstruō, strūxī, strūctus *3 v* to pile together, heap, gather, build up, 9.712.

cōnsuēscō (trisyllabic in poetry), **suēvī, suētus** 3 *inc v* to accustom, to acquire a habit or habitude; *part*, cōnsuētus, a, um, wonted, accustomed, familiar, 10.867.

cōnsul, ulis *m* one of the two coördinate chief magistrates of Rome; originally called praetors; a consul, 6.819.

cōnsulō, uī, tus 3 *v* to consult; advise, 11.344; inspect, 4.64; observe, 9.322.

cōnsultum, ī, *n* a thing deliberated upon; a decree; response, oracle, 6.151; deliberation, 11.410. (cōnsulō).

cōnsūmō, sūmpsī, sūmptus 3 *v* to take entirely; use up, devour, consume, 5.527; spend, 2.795.

cōnsurgō, surrēxī, surrēctus 3 *v* to rise together, rise up; rise at once, 8.110; rise, 5.20; rise or spring to the oars, ply, 10.299.

contāctus, ūs *m* a touching together or upon; touch, 3.227. (contingō).

contegō, tēxī, tēctus 3 *v* to cover, 12.885.

contemnō, tempsī, temptus 3 *v* to scorn, contemn, despise, set at naught, 8.364; defy, 3.77.

contemptor, ōris *m* a despiser, scorner, 7.648. (contemnō).

contendō, ī, tentus 3 *v* to stretch completely; stretch, strain; strain the bow, 12.815; level the arrow, 5.513; shoot, 5.520; endeavor, strive, 1.158; contend, 4.108;

hold, steer, 5.834; contend in skill of any kind.

contentus, a, um content, satisfied, 5.314. (contneō).

conterreō, uī, itus 2 *v* to frighten greatly; terrify, 3.597.

contexō, uī, tus 3 *v* to weave together; construct, build, 2.112.

conticēscō, ticuī 3 *inc v* to become still; be still, hushed, silent, 2.253. (com- and taceō).

contiguus, a, um *adj* (contingō), near, within reach, 10.457.

contineō, uī, tentus 2 *v* to hold together or in; keep together; hold, restrain, 2.593; check, stay, 3.598; confine; *part*, contentus, a, um, content, satisfied, 5.314. (com- and teneō).

contingō, tigī, tāctus 3 *v* to touch, 2.168; take hold of, touch, 2.168; strike, 2.649; attain, arrive at, reach, 5.18; fall to, fall to the lot of, 11.371; *impers*, contingit, it happens, falls to one's lot, chances, 1.96. (com- and tangō).

continuō *adv* immediately, straightway. (continuus).

contorqueō, torsī, tortus 2 *v* to turn round entirely, twist; turn, 3.562; hurl, cast, lance, 2.52; 9.705.

contrā (*prep* and *adv*; *prep with acc*), over against; opposite to, 1.13; against, 5.370; to, 9.280; on the contrary, 12.779; on the other hand, in reply, 1.76.

contrahō, trāxī, tractus *3 v* to
draw together, contract; bring
together, collect, assemble,
3.8; gather, assume, 12.891.

contrārius, a, um *adj* (contrā),
opposite; *figuratively*
contrary, opposed, opposing,
2.39; unfavorable, adverse,
1.239; *subst* contrāria,
ōrum, *n pl* opposite things,
different counsels, 12.487.

contremō, uī *3 v* to tremble, 7.515.

contrīstō, āvī, ātus *1 v* to make
sad, sadden, overcast, render
baneful or adverse; sadden,
10.275. (com- and trīstis).

contundō, tudī, tūnsus, or **tūsus**
3 v to pound thoroughly; beat,
bruise, pound; *figuratively*
subdue, conquer, 1.264.

contus, ī *m* a pole, 5.208.

cōnūbium (*sometimes trisyll*),
iī, *n* nuptials, marriage, 1.73;
wedlock, nuptial rite, 3.136;
marriage tie, nuptial bond,
3.319. (con- and nūbō, wed).

cōnus, ī *m* a cone; the
metallic point or apex
of a helmet, 3.468.

convallis, is *f* a valley
completely inclosed by
hills; a valley, vale, 6.139.

convectō *1 intens v* carry, bring
together; convey, 4.405.
(convehō, bring together).

convellō, vellī, vulsus *3 v* to pull
violently; pluck, tear, pull up,
3.24; wrench forth, 12.774; cut
off, 6.148; *part*, convulsus,
a, um, rent, shattered,
1.383; convulsed, 5.143.

conveniō, vēnī, ventus *4 v*
to come together; meet,
assemble, 1.361; (*impers*),
convenit, it is meet, proper,
fit; it is agreed, stipulated,
covenanted, 12.184.

conventus, ūs *m* an assembling;
assembly, 6.753. (conveniō).

convertō, ī, versus *3 v* to turn
completely; turn back, to
invert, reverse, 1.81; wheel
or turn against, 12.548; turn,
2.191; change, 2.73; *part*,
conversus, a, um, turned,
turning, 12.172; opposing,
12.716; returning, 7.543;
transformed, 12.623.

convexum, ī, *n* a convexity;
recess, 1.310; *pl* convexa,
ōrum, vault, arch, 4.451;
the concave vaulted sky or
heavens, 6.241; convexities,
sloping or hollow sides, 1.608.

convexus, a, um hollow,
11.515; concave.

convīvium, iī, *n* a banquet,
1.638. (com- and vīvō).

convolvō, volvī, volūtus *3 v* to roll
together; roll up, coil, 2.474.

coorior, ortus sum *4 dep v* to
arise completely, or at once;
break out, arise, 1.148.

cōpia, ae *f* complete supply;
abundance, plenty, force,
numbers, 2.564; host, 11.834;
ability, power, means, 5.100;
opportunity, 9.720; permission,
liberty, 1.520. (com- and ops).

coquō, coxī, coctus *3 v* to cook;
to cause to boil; to temper
(a spear) in fire, 11.553;
figuratively vex, fret, 7.345.

cor, cordis, *n* the heart, of the mind, feelings, spirit, passions; mind, heart, breast, 1.50; disposition, spirit, 1.303; pleasure, delight, 7.326.

Cora, ae *f* a town of the Volsci in Latium, 6.775.

cōram (*prep and adv; prep with abl*), in the presence of; before; *adv* in person, face to face, openly, in presence, 1.520.595.

Corās, ae *m* a hero of Tibur, 7.672.

Corinthus, ī *f* a city of the Peloponnesus, destroyed by Mummius, BC 146.6.836.

corneus, a, um *adj* (cornus), of cornel-wood, 3.22.

corneus, a, um *adj* (cornū), of horn, 6.894.

corniger, era, erum *adj* (cornū and gerō), horn-bearing; horned, 8.77.

cornipēs, edis *adj* (cornū and pēs), horn-hoofed, 6.591.

cornū, ūs, *n* a horn, 4.61; horny substance, horn; a trumpet or horn, 7.615; bow, 7.497; the knob or tip of the helmet in which the crest is inserted, 12.89; *pl* cornua, uum, the ends of sail yards, 3.549; horns of the moon, 3.645; in cornua surgere, to rise as to the horns; i.e., having high-branching horns, 10.725; īrāscī in cornua, to throw fury into the horns, 12.104.

cornum, ī, *n* the cornel cherry or cornel berry, 3.649.

cornus, ī *f* a cornel cherry tree; a spear shaft; a lance or javelin, shaft, 12.267.

Coroebus, ī *m* Coroebus, a Phrygian chief, son of Mygdon, lover of Cassandra, 2.341.

corōna, ae *f* a crown, 1.655; wreath, garland, 3.525; a crowd or throng; a circle of defenders on a rampart; a garrison, 9.508; a circle or crowd of assailants, 9.551.

corōnō, āvī, ātus *1 v* to encircle with a crown or garland; crown, wreathe, 4.506; encompass, surround, 9.380. (corōna).

corporeus, a, um *adj* (corpus), bodily, corporeal, 6.737.

corpus, oris, *n* the body, 1.484; body, form, frame, size, 3.427; mass, corporeal universe, 6.727; strength, 12.920; a ghost, shade, 6.303; summum corpus, the surface of the body, 12.376.

corripiō, ripuī, reptus *3 v* to take completely or eagerly; to grasp, snatch, seize, catch, 1.45; hurry away, 1.100; tear away; hasten on, take, 1.418; raise quickly, rouse, 4.572; sē corripere, to hasten away, 6.472. (com- and rapiō).

corrumpō, rūpī, ruptus *3 v* to burst completely, break up; destroy, ruin, spoil, injure, damage, 1.177; infect, 3.138. (com- and rumpō).

corruō, uī *3 v* to fall completely; fall down, 10.488. (com- and ruō).

cortex, icis *m* the bark, rind, 3.33.

cortīna, ae f a caldron; kettle; *figuratively* the tripod of Apollo, 3.92; an oracle, 6.347.

Cōrus, ī m Corus or Caurus, the northwest wind, 5.126.

coruscō 1 v to push with the horns; move quickly hither and thither; shake, brandish, wave, swing, 5.642; flash; glisten.

coruscus, a, um adj (coruscō), vibrating, tremulous, waving, 12.701; flashing, 1.164; gleaming, 2.172.

Corybantius, a, um adj of the Corybantes, priests of Cybele; Corybantian, 3.111.

Corynaeus, ī m 1. Corynaeus, a companion of Aeneas, 6.228; 12.298. 2. Another Trojan, 9.571.

Corythus, ī m an ancient city of Etruria, later, and now Cortona, 3.170.

cōs, cōtis f a whetstone, 7.627; a flint or jagged rock; cliff.

Cosa, ae, and **Cosae, ārum** f Cosa, a town in Etruria, 10.168.

Cossus, ī m a family name in the Cornelian gens; especially, A. Cornelius Cossus, who won the spolia opima from the king of Veii (BC 428), 6.841.

costa, ae f a rib, 1.211; side.

cothurnus, ī m the cothurnus; a triple soled shoe, or buskin, worn in tragedy; a kind of half-boot; hunting boot, buskin, 1.337.

crassus, a, um adj thick, gross, fat; clotted, 5.469.

crāstinus, a, um adj (crās, the morrow), pertaining to the morrow; tomorrow's, 4.118.

crātēr, ēris, m, acc sing **ēra**, pl **ēras** a large mixing bowl or urn; mixer; bowl, 1.724; jar, 6.225.

crātēs, is f a hurdle; wicker work, wattles; crātēs pectoris, the wattled covering of the breast; the ribs, 12.508.

creātrīx, īcis f she who brings forth; a mother, 6.367. (creō).

crēber, bra, brum adj repeated, frequent, 2.731; coming thick and fast, 11.611; blowing fresh; fresh, 5.764; abounding, in full of, 1.85.

crēbrēscō, crēbuī 3 inc v to become frequent, prevail, 12.222; to increase, swell, 12.407; blow fresh, 3.530. (crēber).

crēdō, didī, ditus 3 v to intrust, believe, *freq*; with dat acc and dat or with objective clause; trust to, 5.850; confide, 4.422; put faith in, 7.97; trust, 2.48; believe, think, 1.387; (with sē), to trust one's self to; risk, 5.383.

cremō, āvī, ātus 1 v to burn, 6.224 et al.

creō, āvī, ātus 1 v to bring forth, bear; produce, 7.283; *part*, creātus, a, um, born of; begotten by, 10.517.

crepīdō, inis f a base; a mound, bank; brow, edge (of a rock), 10.653.

crepitō 1 v to make a rattling noise; creak, crackle, murmur, rustle, 3.70; crack, crash, 5.436; rattle, 5.459; dash, 11.299. (crepō).

crepitus, ūs *m* a din; thunder clap, peal, 12.923. (crepō).

crepō, uī, itus *1 v* to rattle; creak, crack, 5.206; rustle, 11.775.

Crēs, ētis *m* a Cretan, 4.146.

crēscō, crēvī, crētus *3 inc v* to wax, grow; increase; *part*, crētus, a, um, sprung from, born of, 2.74. (creō).

Crēsius, a, um *adj* Cretan, 4.70.

Crēssa, ae *f* a Cretan woman, 5.285.

Crēta, ae *f* Crete, a large island south of the Aegean Sea, now Candia, 3.104.

Crētaeus, a, um *adj* (Crēta), of Crete; Cretan, 3.117.

Crētheus (*dissyll*), **eī** *m* 1. A Trojan warrior, 9.774. 2. A Greek ally of Aeneas, 2.538.

Creūsa, ae *f* the wife of Aeneas, and daughter of Priam, 2.562.

crīmen, inis, *n* an accusation, arraignment, charge, 2.98; imputation, 12.16; fault, crime, 2.65; infamy, 10.851; cause of woe, 10.183; guilty occasion, guilty instigator, 12.600; cause, 7.339. (cernō).

crīnālis, e *adj* (crīnis), of the hair, belonging to the hair, 11.576.

crīnis, is *m* the hair, 1.480; train of meteors, 5.528; (often in the *pl*), the hairs of the head, the hair.

Crīnīsus, ī *m* a river in the southwestern part of Sicily, 5.38.

crīnītus, a, um *adj* (crīnis), long-haired, 1.740.

crīspō, no perf, ātus *1 v* to crisp, curl; to vibrate, brandish, 1.313.

crista, ae *f* a crest, plume, 3.468; helmet, 7.185.

cristātus, a, um *adj* (crista), crested, plumed, 1.468.

croceus, a, um *adj* (crocus), of saffron; saffron-colored, yellow, 4.585.

crocus, ī *m* saffron; saffron color, 9.614.

crūdēlis, e *adj* (crūdus), unfeeling, ruthless, cruel, inhuman, 2.124; relentless, 1.547; unnatural, 6.24; mortal, deadly, 2.561; bloody, 1.355; bitter, 1.361.

crūdēliter *adv* cruelly, barbarously, 6.495. (crūdēlis).

crūdēscō, crūduī *3 inc v* to become harsh; to grow fierce, 7.788. (crūdus).

crūdus, a, um *adj* bloody, raw; of untanned hide, of raw hide, 5.69; covered with blood, bloody, 12.507; fresh, strong, vigorous, 6.304; rough, green, 9.743; deadly, cruel, fatal, 10.682.

cruentō, āvī, ātus *1 v* to make bloody, stain with blood, 10.731. (cruentus).

cruentus, a, um *adj* bloody, blood-stained, 1.296; covered with blood, 10.498.

cruor, ōris *m* shed blood; gore, 3.43; 4.455; blood.

crūs, crūris, *n* the leg, especially from the knee to the ankle.

crūstum, ī, *n* a crust, 7.115.

Crustumerī, ōrum *m* the people of Crustumerium, a town of the Sabines, or a town itself, 7.631.

cubīle, is, *n* a lair, bed, couch, 3.324. (cubō, lie down).

cubitum, ī, *n* the elbow, 4.690. (cubō, lie down).

culmen, inis, *n* a top, summit, height, 2.290; house top, ridge, roof, 2.458. (cf. columna).

culmus, ī *m* a stalk, stem; thatch; straw hut, 8.654.

culpa, ae *f* a wrong action; crime, fault, 2.140.

culpō, āvī, ātus *1 v* to blame; *part,* culpātus, a, um, at fault; blameable; the guilty cause, 2.602. (culpa).

culta, ōrum, *n* plowed fields; fields.

culter, trī *m* a plowshare; a knife, 6.248. (colō).

cultor, ōris *m* a husbandman, cultivator; inhabitant; worshiper, 11.788. (colō).

cultrīx, īcis *f* an inhabitant; protectress, 3.111. (colō).

cultus, ūs *m* a tilling; civilization, 8.316; dress, guise, appearance, 3.591; habits, mode of life, life, 5.730. (colō).

cum *adv* when, *freq*; and then, 3.10; vel cum, then again, 11.406; *conj*, whereas, while, when, though, since, because, *freq*.

cum (*prep* with *abl*), with, 1.74 *et al.* With personal pronouns mē, tē, sē, etc., it is suffixed; as mēcum, tēcum, etc.; and usually with the relative; as quōcum, quibuscum, etc. In composition the *archaic form* com- is employed instead of cum; remaining unchanged before b, m, p; changed to con- before l, cor- before r, co- generally before vowels, h, and gn; and before all other letters, con-.

Cūmae, ārum *f* Cumae, an ancient Greek town of Campania, west of Naples, 6.2.

Cūmaeus, a, um *adj* (Cūmae), Cumaean, 3.441.

cumulō, āvī, ātus *1 v* to heap up; load, 5.532; make greater, increase, 4.436. (cumulus).

cumulus, ī *m* a heap; flood, mass, 1.105.

cūnabula, ōrum, *n* a cradle; birthplace, 3.105. (cūnae, cradle).

cunctor, ātus sum *1 dep v* to delay, hesitate, linger, wait, 4.133; keep one's ground, stand at bay, 10.717.

cunctor, ātus sum *1 dep v* to delay, hesitate, linger, wait, 4.133; keep one's ground, stand at bay, 10.717.

cūnctus, a, um *adj* (coniūnctus), all taken together; all in a body; all, the whole, 1.154.

cuneus, ī *m* a wedge, 6.181; a wedge-shaped battalion; battalion, 12.269; dare cuneōs, to form battalions, 12.575; *pl* cuneī, ōrum, the seats of the theater; an assembly, 5.664.

Cupāvō, ōnis *m* a Ligurian ally of Aeneas, 10.186.

Cupencus, ī *m* a Rutulian, 12.539.

cupīdō, inis *f* ardent longing, desire; love, 7.189; ardor, thirst, 9.354; resolve, 2.349; personified, Cupīdō, inis, *m*, Cupid the son of Venus, and god of love, 1.658. (cupiō).

cupīdō, inis *f* ardent longing, desire; love, 7.189; ardor, thirst, 9.354; resolve, 2.349; personified, Cupīdō, inis, *m*, Cupid the son of Venus, and god of love, 1.658. (cupiō).

cupidus, a, um *adj* (cupiō), desirous, fond, fondly, 8.165.

cupiō, īvī or **iī, ītus** *3 v* to desire, be desirous; wish, 6.717; long, 4.394.

cupressus, ī *f* the cypress; a branch of cypress, 2.714.

cūr *adv* wherefore? for what reason? why? 1.408 *et al.* (for quārē).

cūra, ae *f* care, solicitude, anxiety, 1.261; toil; charge, duty, 1.704; love, passion, pang, 4.531; affection, love, 1.646; thought, 9.757; grief, anguish, 4.332; personified, Cūrae, Cares, 6.274.

Curēs, ium *m* a Sabine town east of Rome, 6.811.

Cūrētēs, um *m* the earliest inhabitants of Crete; Cretans, 3.131.

cūria, ae *f* one of the divisions of the Quirites of which the Comitia Curiata were composed; the place for the meeting of their senate; hence, a senate house, 7.174.

cūrō, āvī, ātus *1 v* to care for; have in charge; regard, attend to, 2.536; bring about, effect; to take care of, refresh with rest, food, and sleep, 3.511. (cūra).

curriculum, ī *n* career, course, 8.408. (currō).

currō, cucurrī, cursus *3 v* to run, *freq*; flow, 1.607; dart, shoot, 2.694; penetrate, thrill, 2.120; (with cogn. *acc*), traverse, sail over, 3.191.

currus, ūs *m* a chariot, car, 1.156; a chariot team, chariot horses, 7.163; *pl* for the *sing* 10.574. (currō).

cursus, ūs *m* a running; running, 12.890; hastening, hurrying to and fro, 4.672; speed, 5.67; way, passage, voyage, course, 1.157; career, onset, 12.489; pursuit, 9.559; hunting, the chase, 5.253; stream, current, channel, 6.313. (currō).

curvō, āvī, ātus *1 v* to bend, curve, 3.533; swell, 3.564; wind, 7.381. (curvus).

curvus, a, um *adj* curved, bent, bending, 2.51; winding, 2.748; crooked.

cuspis, idis *f* a spear point, 7.817; point, 5.208; spear, lance, javelin; a spear, 12.386; a spear or, perhaps, the shaft of a spear as a scepter, 1.81.

cūstōdia, ae *f* a watching, watch; guardianship, care; a watch, guard, 6.574. (cūstōs).

cūstōdiō, **īvī** or **iī**, **ītus** *4 v* to guard, 8.218. (cūstōs).

cūstōs, **ōdis**, *c* a guard; overseer, watchman, keeper, *freq*; guardian, governor, master, 5.546; collectively, a patrol, a guard, 1.564.

Cybelē, **ēs**, and **Cybēbē**, **ēs**, or **ae** *f* 1. Cybele, the principal goddess of Phrygia, corresponding to the Magna Mater of the Romans, and often identified with Rhea and Ops, 10.220. 2. A mountain in Phrygia sacred to Cybele, 3.111.

Cyclades, **um** *f* the Cyclades, the islands grouped around Delos in the Aegean Sea, 3.127.

Cyclōpius, **a**, **um** *adj* (Cyclōps), pertaining to the Cyclops; Cyclopean, 1.201.

Cyclōps, **ōpis** *m* a Cyclops, one of the Cyclopes, fabulous giants of Sicily, supposed to have a round eye in the middle of the forehead, 3.569.

cycnus, **ī** *m* a swan, 1.393.

Cycnus, **ī** *m* a king of the Ligurians, friend of Phaëthon, placed among the constellations, as the swan, 10.189.

Cydōn, **ōnis** *m* 1. A Cydonian or Cretan; of Cydonia, on the north coast of Crete, 12.858. 2. A Trojan warrior, 10.325.

Cyllēnē, **ēs** or **ae** *f* a mountain in the east of Arcadia, the birthplace of Mercury, 8.139.

Cyllēnius, **a**, **um** *adj* (Cyllēnē), of Cyllene; Cyllenian; *subst m*, the Cyllenian god; Mercury, 4.252.

cymba, **ae** *f* a boat, skiff, 6.303.

cymbium, **iī**, *n* a small, skiff-shaped drinking cup; cup, 3.66.

Cymodocē, **ēs**, and **Cymodocēa**, **ae** *f* Cymodoce, a Nereid, 5.826; 10.225.

Cymothoē, **ēs** *f* Cymothoe, a Nereid, 1.144.

Cynthus, **ī** *m* a mountain in Delos, birthplace of Apollo and Diana, 1.498.

cyparissus, **ī** *f* a cypress, 3.680.

Cyprus, **ī** *f* a large island in the Eastern Mediterranean, 1.622.

Cythēra, **ōrum**, *n* an island south of Laconia, near which Venus was said to have been born of the foam of the sea, 1.680.

Cythērēus, **a**, **um** *adj* (Cythēra), Cytherean; *subst* Cytherēa, ae, *f*, the Cytherean goddess; Venus, 1.257.

daedalus, **a**, **um** *adj* artificial, skillful, cunningly wrought; wily, artful, 7.282.

Daedalus, **ī** *m* Daedalus, the father of Greek sculpture; supposed to be of the time of Minos and Theseus; employed by Minos to build the Cretan Labyrinth, 6.14.

Dahae, **ārum** *m* the Dahae, a Scythian people beyond the Caspian, 8.728.

damnō, **āvī**, **ātus** *1 v* to inflict loss upon; to doom, condemn, consign, devote, *with dat*

4.699; to condemn, with *gen*, 6.430. (damnum, loss).

Danaē, **ēs** *f* daughter of Acrisius, and mother of Perseus, 7.410.

Danaī, **ōrum** *m* the Greeks, 2.327.

Danaus, **a**, **um** *adj* of Danaus, king of Argos; Greek, 3.602; *subst* Danaī, ōrum, *m*, the Greeks, 2.327.

daps, **dapis** *f* a feast, banquet, 1.210; food, viands, 1.706; flesh of sacrificial victims, 6.225; usually found in the *pl* but the *gen pl* is not used.

Dardania, **ae** *f* Troy, 2.281.

Dardanidēs, **ae** *m* a son or descendant of Dardanus; Aeneas, 10.545; *pl* Dardanidae, ārum (um), the Trojans, 1.560 *et al.*; *adj*, Dardanian, Trojan, 2.59.

Dardanis, **idis** *f* a daughter or descendant of Dardanus, 2.787.

Dardanius, **a**, **um** *adj* (Dardanus), Dardanian, Trojan, 5.711; *subst* Dardanius, ii, *m*, the Dardanian; the Trojan, 12.14.

Dardanus, **a**, **um** *adj* Trojan, 5.119; *subst* the Dardanian; Aeneas, 4.662; the Trojan, for the nation, 11.287.

Dardanus, **ī** *m* Dardanus, son of Jupiter and Electra, father of the Trojan line of kings, and thus progenitor of the Romans, 6.650 *et al.*

Darēs, **ētis** (*acc* **Darēta** and **Daren**) *m* Dares, a Trojan boxer, 5.369.

dator, **ōris** *m* a giver, 1.734. (1. dō).

Daucius, **a**, **um** *adj* (Daucus), of Daucus, a Rutulian; Daucian, 10.391.

Daunius, **a**, **um** *adj* (Daunus), pertaining to Daunus, father or ancestor of Turnus; Daunian, 12.785.

Daunus, **ī** *m* a mythic king of part of Apulia, father-in-law of Diomedes, and father of Turnus, 10.616.

dē (*prep with abl*), from, of place, time, source, material, etc., *freq*; out of; away from, 6.85; just from, on, 10.478; of 2.78; sprung from, 10.350; by, of, 4.327; according to, after, 1.318; over, upon, 6.502; concerning, for, about, 12.765.

dea, **ae** *f* a goddess, 1.17. (fem. of deus).

dēbellātor, **ōris** *m* a conqueror, 7.651. (dēbellō).

dēbellō, **āvī**, **ātus** *1 v* to war to the end; to put down by war; subdue, conquer, 5.731.

dēbeō, **uī**, **itus** *2 v* to owe, 10.853; secure, bind; *passive* dēbērī, to be due, meet, 2.538; decreed, 3.184; 6.714. (dē and habeō).

dēbilis, **e** *adj* (dē and habilis), disabled, maimed, crippled, 5.271; feeble, useless, 12.50.

dēbilitō, **āvī**, **ātus** *1 v* to weaken, abate, 9.611. (dēbilis).

dēcēdō, **cessī**, **cessus** *3 v* to withdraw, go away, depart from, 4.306; stand back, retire, 5.551.

decem (*num adj indecl*), ten, 2.198.

dēcernō, crēvī, crētus 3 *v* to decide, determine, resolve, 4.475; contend, combat, 7.525.

dēcerpō, sī, tus 3 *v* to pluck off; crop, pluck, 6.141. (dē and carpō).

decet, uit 2 *impers n* it is becoming; meet, proper, fitting, 4.597.

dēcidō, cidī 3 *v* to fall down; fall, 5.517. (dē and cadō).

dēcīdō, cīdī, cīsus 3 *v* to cut, lop off, 11.5. (dē and caedō).

Deciī, ōrum *m* several illustrious Romans of the Decian gens, especially the father and son Decius Mus, one killed in the battle of Vesuvius, BC 340, the other in the battle of Sentinum, BC 295.6.824.

decimus, a, um *adj* (decem), the tenth, 9.155.

dēcipiō, cēpī, ceptus 3 *v* to deceive; beguile, delude, mislead, 3.181. (dē and capiō).

dēclārō, āvī, ātus 1 *v* to make clear; to declare, proclaim, 5.246.

dēclīnō, āvī, ātus 1 *v* to turn down or away; of the eyes, to close in sleep, 4.185.

dēcolor, ōris *adj* of debased color; of baser metal; vitiated, corrupt, 8.326.

decorō, āvī, ātus 1 *v* to adorn, decorate, 6.217; honor, 11.25. (decus).

decōrus, a, um *adj* (decor), fit, proper, becoming, 5.343; graceful, beautiful, 1.589; adorned, 5.133; shining, 11.194.

dēcurrō, cucurrī or **currī, cursus** 3 *v* to run down, hasten down, 2.41; descend, 5.610; run completely round, 11.189; sail over, sweep over, 5.212.

dēcursus, ūs *m* a running down, descent, 12.523. (dēcurrō).

decus, oris, *n* that which is becoming; grace, ornament, decoration, 1.429; glory, honor, distinction, 2.89; pride, 10.858; beauty, 1.592; dignity, honor, 5.174; an honor, honorable gift, 12.83. (decet).

dēcutiō, cussī, cussus 3 *v* to shake off. (dē and quatiō).

dēdecus, oris, *n* dishonor, disgrace, shame, 10.681.

dēdīgnor, ātus sum 1 *dep v* to deem unworthy, disdain, scorn, refuse, 4.536.

dēdūcō, dūxī, ductus 3 *v* to lead, draw, bring down; of ships, to launch, 3.71; lead, conduct, 2.800; carry away, 6.397.

dēfendō, ī, fēnsus (*pass inf* **dēfendier,** 8.493) 3 *v* to ward off; forbid, avert, *with acc* 10.905; defend, guard, protect, 2.257. (dē and *obsol* fendō, strike).

dēfēnsor, ōris *m* a defender, protector; applied also to inanimate things, 2.521. (dēfendō).

dēferō, tulī, lātus, ferre *irreg v* to carry or bring down or away; bear, convey, 4.226; conduct, lead, 5.730; to report, 4.299.

defessus, -a, -um wearied, tired, fatigued, 1.157. (dēfetīscō).

dēficiō, fēcī, fectus, *pass* (**dē** and **faciō**), **dēfit, fierī** *3 v* to make off from; free one's self from; desert, leave, forsake, 6.196; fail, be wanting, 2.505; be exhausted, fail; give way, sink, 6.354; faint, 4.689; to be broken down, prostrated, sick at heart, 11.231; to be depressed, discouraged, 12.2; *passive* dēfit, fierī, to be wanting.

dēfīgō, fīxī, fīxus *3 v* to fasten or fix down or in; the object on or in which, in the *dat,* or in *the abl,* with or without a *prep;* fix, direct, 1.226; *part,* dēfīxus, downcast, 6.156.

dēflectō, flexī, flexus *3 v* to turn aside, 10.331.

dēfleō, flēvī, flētus *2 v* to weep much; weep over, bewail, bemoan, lament, 6.220.

dēfluō, fluxī, fluxus *3 v* to flow down; sail down, 8.549; alight, descend, 11.501; fall, descend, 1.404.

dēfodiō, fōdī, fossus *3 v* to dig down; sink deep; bury.

dēfōrmō, āvī, ātus *1 v* to disfigure, 10.844; clothe in mourning, sadden, darken, 12.805.

dēfringō, frēgī, frāctus *3 v* to break off, 11.748. (dē and frangō).

dēfungor, fūnctus sum *3 dep v* to complete, finish a duty, etc.; go through with, 6.83; to have done with, 6.306; used absolutely; to get through, fulfill one's destiny or course, 9.98.

dēgener, eris *adj* (dē and genus), degenerate, 2.549; of base descent, 4.13.

dēgō, dēgī *3 v* to pass, spend, 4.551. (dē and agō).

dēgustō, āvī, ātus *1 v* to taste of; touch, graze, 12.376.

dehinc (*often monosyll*) *adv* from this place; from this time; thereupon, then, 1.131.

dehīscō, hīvī *3 v* to gape, yawn, 1.106; stand open, open, 6.52.

dēiciō, iēcī, iectus *3 v* to cast down, 6.581; strike down, slay, 11.642; drive down, 4.152; shoot or bring down, 5.542; deprive of, 3.317; dēicere vultum, to cast down the eyes, 3.320; *passive* dēicī, to be disheartened, dismayed, 10.858. (dē and iaciō).

deinde (*often dissyll*) *adv* from that place (rarely) or time; then, thereupon, 5.321; now, immediately, 4.561; next, still, 9.781.

Dēiopēa, ae *f* a nymph in the train of Juno, 1.72.

Dēiphobē, ēs *f* a name of the Cumaean Sibyl, daughter of Glaucus and priestess of Apollo and Diana, 6.36.

Dēiphobus, ī *m* a son of Priam, who became the husband of Helen after the death of Paris, 6.495.

dēlābor, lāpsus sum *3 dep v* to glide, slip, or fall down; descend, 3.238; fall in with or upon, 2.377.

dēleō, ēvī, ētus *2 v* to destroy, 9.248; slaughter, 11.898.

dēlībō, āvī, ātus *1 v* to sip; kiss, 12.434.

dēligō, lēgī, lēctus *3 v* to choose from; choose, 2.18. (dē and legō).

dēlitēscō, dēlituī *3 inc v* to hide; lurk, lie hidden, 2.136. (dē and latēscō, be hidden).

Dēlius, a, um *adj* (Dēlos), of Delos; Delian, an epithet of Apollo, who was born in Delos, 3.162.

Dēlos, ī *f* an island in the midst of the Cyclades in the Aegean, where Latona gave birth to Apollo and Diana, 4.144.

delphīn, īnis, and **delphīnus, ī** *m* a dolphin, 3.428 *et al*.

dēlūbrum, ī, *n* the place for sacrificial cleansings; a shrine, temple, sanctuary, 2.225 *et al*. (dēluō, cleanse).

dēlūdō, lūsī, lūsus *3 v* to deceive, mock, delude, 6.344.

dēmēns, entis *adj* out of one's mind, insane, foolish, mad, blind, 4.107; *subst* fool, 11.399.

dēmentia, ae *f* madness, frenzy, folly, 5.465. (dēmēns).

dēmergō, mersī, mersus *3 v* to dip, plunge, 9.119.

dēmetō, messuī, messus *3 v* to reap; clip, break off, pluck, 11.68.

dēmissus, a, um let down; hanging down, 4.263; low, subdued, 3.320; downcast, 1.561. (dēmittō).

dēmittō, mīsī, missus *3 v* to send down, 1.297; shed, 6.455; let down into, receive, admit, (of the mind or the senses), 4.428; consign, condemn, 2.85; convey, conduct, 5.29; transmit, hand down, 1.288; dēmittere mentem, to lose heart, sink into despair, 12.609.

dēmō, dēmpsī, dēmptus *3 v* to take away, remove, 2.775. (dē and emō).

Dēmodocus, ī *m* an Arcadian follower of Pallas, 10.413.

Dēmoleos, ī *m* a Greek slain by Aeneas in battle, 5.260.

Dēmophoön, ontis *m* a Trojan slain by Camilla, 11.675.

dēmoror, ātus sum *1 dep v* to linger, protract, 2.648; detain, 3.481; wait for, await, 10.30.

dēmum *adv* at length, at last, 1.629; at least, indeed, especially. (dē with *n superl* ending -mum, hence, perhaps meaning downmost).

dēnī, ae, a (*adj num* distrib.), ten by ten; ten each; (as cardinal), ten, 1.381.

dēnique *adv* at last, at length, finally, 2.70.295.

dēns, dentis *m* a tooth, 3.664; the fluke of an anchor, 6.3.

dēnseō, ēre, and **dēnsō, āvī, ātus** *1 v* to make thick; thicken; close up, 12.264; cast thick, shower, 11.650; gather together, crowd, 7.794. (dēnsus).

dēnsus, a, um *adj* thick, dense, crowded, compact,

in close array, serried,
2.383; frequent, 5.459.

dēnūntiō, āvī, ātus 1 v to
announce emphatically;
declare, foretell, 3.366.

dēpāscō, pāvī, pāstus 3 v, and
dēpāscor, pāstus sum 3 dep v
to devour, consume, 2.215;
taste, 5.93; feed upon, graze.

dēpellō, pulī, pulsus 3 v to push,
drive from or away; drive away
from, with acc and abl, 5.727.

dēpendeō 2 v to hang
down; hang, 1.726.

dēpōnō, posuī, positus 3 v to
put down or aside; recline,
7.108; put off, from, put on
shore, 5.751; lay down, lay,
6.632; lay aside, dismiss,
banish, 2.76; (pass, of
sickness), to be laid down,
dying, despaired of, 12.395.

dēprecor, ātus sum 1 dep v to
avert by praying; deprecate;
beg for mercy, 12.931.

dēprēndō, prēndī, prēnsus 3 v
to catch, surprise, overtake,
5.52; intercept, 10.98.

dēprōmō, prōmpsī, prōmptus
3 v to draw forth, 5.501.

Dercennus, ī m an ancient
king of Laurentum, 11.850.

dērigēscō, riguī 3 inc v to
grow completely stiff; to be
cold, stiff; to be cold, stiff,
paralyzed with fear, 3.260;
stand staring, 7.447.

dērigō, rēxī, rēctus 3 v to
lay straight, bring into a
definite line; to aim, direct,
1.401 et al. (dē and regō).

dēripiō, ripuī, reptus 3 v to tear
away; cast off; loosen, 3.267;
haul down, launch, 4.593; cut
off, 10.414. (dē and rapiō).

dēsaeviō, iī 4 v to rage
furiously; rage, 4.52.

dēscendō, scendī, scēnsus
3 v go or come down; to
descend, 2.632; to stoop to,
5.782. (dē and scandō).

dēscēnsus, ūs m a going down;
descent, 6.126. (dēscendō).

dēscrībō, scrīpsī, scrīptus 3 v to
mark off; divide, distinguish,
describe, 6.850; write, 3.445.

dēsecō, uī, tus 1 v to
cut off, 8.438.

dēserō, uī, tus 3 v to disconnect,
loosen one's self; leave, 3.711;
forsake, abandon, desert,
4.323; leave behind, 5.220;
give up, break off, 9.694.

dēserta, ōrum, n desert, waste
places, 1.384; haunts, 7.404.

dēsertor, ōris m one who
has deserted; a renegade,
12.15. (dēserō).

dēsertus, a, um desolate;
abandoned, 12.664;
uninhabited, solitary,
lonely, 3.646.

dēsidia, ae f sloth. (dēsidō).

dēsīdō, sēdī 3 v to sink
down, 3.565.

dēsīgnō, āvī, ātus 1 v to mark
out, designate, 5.755.

dēsiliō, uī, sultus 4 v to leap
or spring down; alight from,
10.453. (dē and saliō).

dēsinō, sīvī or **īī, situs** 3 v
with infin to leave off, cease,
desist, 4.360; (with acc)
cease, end; n, forbear,
10.881; terminate, 10.211.

dēsistō, stitī, stitus 3 v to
cease, desist, with abl,
1.37; with dat 10.441.

dēsōlō, āvī, ātus 1 v to make
solitary, lay waste, 11.367; leave
without guidance, deprive of
commanders, leave in disorder,
11.870. (dē and sōlus).

dēspectō, āvī, ātus 1 intens
v to look down upon,
1.396. (dēspiciō).

dēspiciō, spexī, spectus
3 v to look down upon,
1.224; despise, reject, 4.36.
(dē and speciō, look).

dēstinō, āvī, ātus 1 v to place
apart; destine, doom, 2.129.

dēstruō, strūxī, strūctus 3 v to
destroy, tear down, 4.326.

**dēsuēscō (in poetry trisyll),
suēvī, suētus** 3 v to become
unaccustomed; part, dēsuētus,
a, um, unaccustomed, unused,
6.814; neglected, unfamiliar,
unpracticed, 2.509; unused
to love; dormant, 1.722.

dēsum, fuī, esse irreg v to be
absent, 7.678; to be wanting
or missing, 2.744; fail, be
wanting, lacking, 10.378.
(deest, deeram, deero,
etc., often pronounced and
sometimes spelled dest, etc.).

dēsuper adv from above;
above, 1.165.

dētegō, tēxī, tēctus 3 v to
uncover, 10.133; lay bare,
expose to view, 8.241.

dēterior, ius (comparative
adjective) worse; more
degenerate, 8.326.

dētineō, uī, tentus 2 v to hold
from or back; hold, detain,
2.788. (dē and teneō).

dētonō, tonuī 1 v to thunder
loudly, storm; thunder out,
cease to thunder, 10.809.

dētorqueō, torsī, tortus 2 v to
turn from; turn off, away, or
aside, 5.165; bend, turn, 4.196;
return, turn back, 5.832.

dētrahō, trāxī, trāctus 3 v to
draw from; take from, 5.260.

dētrūdō, trūsī, trūsus 3 v to
thrust down or away; push off
from, 1.145; drive from, thrust
out, 6.584; thrust down, 7.772.

dēturbō, āvī, ātus 1 v to
cast down, 5.175; strike
down, 10.555; drive
away, remove, 6.412.

deus, ī m a god, deity, 1.9 et al.;
in general, god the deity,
6.749; a goddess, 2.632; the god
Bacchus; metonym wine, 9.337.

dēveniō, vēnī, ventus 4 v to
come down; arrive at, reach,
with acc of place, 1.365 et al.

dēvexus, a, um adj (dēvehō),
inclined downwards;
descending; declining.

dēvinciō, vīnxī, vīnctus 4 v
to bind fast; bind, 8.394.

dēvincō, vīcī, victus 3 v to
conquer completely, to

vanquish, 9.264; wage
successfully, 10.370.

dēvolō, āvī, ātus *1 v* to
fly down, 4.702.

dēvolvō, volvī, volūtus
3 v to roll down; throw,
hurl down, 2.449.

dēvoveō, vōvī, vōtus *2 v* to set
apart by vows; devote, 12.234;
part, dēvōtus, a, um, devoted,
destined, doomed, 1.712.

dexter, tra, trum (-tera, -terum)
adj right, as opp. to left, 5.162;
on the right hand, 8.237; right
handed, adroit, dexterous,
9.769; fit, 4.294; favorable,
auspicious, propitious,
4.579; dextrā, on the right.

dextra (dextera), ae (*sc manus*)
f the right hand, 1.408; valor,
10.610; faith, a pledge, 7.366.

Diāna, ae *f* a goddess of the
Italians, and regarded by them
as one with the Greek Artemis,
daughter of Latona, and sister
of Apollo; called Luna, as
goddess of the moon; Hecate,
as an infernal deity, invoked in
magic rites, 4.511; and Diana,
as goddess of the chase, 1.499.
(*rel to* Iānus = Diānus).

diciō, ōnis *f* dominion, power,
sway, rule, 1.622. (only in
gen, *dat*, *acc*, and *abl sing*).

dicō, āvī, ātus *1 v* devote,
consecrate, 5.60; pronounce,
1.73. (*rel to* dīcō).

dīcō, dīxī, dictus *3 v* to say,
1.81; speak of, mention, 4.43;
celebrate; tell, rehearse,
relate, recount, 1.753; sing,
recite, 6.644; name, call,

1.277; pronounce, 6.231;
declare, 12.112; disclose,
portend, foretell, 3.362;
bid, 5.551; speak, say,
3.312; announce, 1.137.

Dictaeus, a, um *adj* (Dictē), of
Dicte, a mountain in Crete;
Dictaean, Cretan, 3.171.

dictamnus, ī *f*, **-um**, ī, *n*
dittany, an aromatic plant
found on Mount Dicte, in
Crete, 12.412. (Dicte).

dictum, ī, *n* a thing said;
word, 1.197; command,
precept, injunction, 1.695;
promise, 8.643. (dīcō).

dīdō, dīdidī, dīditus *3 v* to spread
abroad, disseminate, 7.144.

Dīdō, ūs or **ōnis** *f* Dido,
daughter of Belus, king of
Phoenicia, who fled from
her brother Pygmalion to
Africa, where she founded
the city of Carthage, 1.299.

dīdūcō, dūxī, ductus *3 v* to
lead or draw apart; separate,
sever, 3.419; distract, 5.720.

Didymāōn, onis *m* Didymaon,
an artist, mentioned
only by Virgil, 5.359.

diēs, ēī (*contracted form of gen*
diī, 1.636) *m and f* a day, the
diurnal period of twenty-four
hours, 1.732 *et al*.; a day, as
distinguished from night,
5.43 *et al*.; a fixed, definite, or
proper season, period, or time;
daylight, 1.88; an indefinite
period of time; time, 5.783;
6.745; length of time, 11.425.

differō, distulī, dīlātus, ferre
irreg v to carry apart; tear

asunder or in pieces, 8.643; stay, keep at bay, 9.135; put off, postpone, delay, 6.569.

difficilis, e *adj* (dis- and facilis), difficult; struggling, hard, 4.694; unyielding, stubborn, unfruitful; dangerous, 5.865.

diffīdō, fīsus sum 3 *v* to be distrustful; to distrust, 3.51.

diffindō, fidī, fissus 3 *v* to cleave asunder; split, pierce, 9.589.

diffugiō, fūgī 3 *v* to flee apart; run away, flee, 2.212.

diffundō, fūdī, fūsus 3 *v* to pour round about, pour out, 10.908; diffuse; spread, multiply, 7.708; to put in disorder, dishevel, 1.319; spread abroad, 4.195.

dīgerō, gessī, gestus 3 *v* to carry apart, separate one thing from another; arrange, dispose, lay in order, 3.446; explain, interpret, 2.182.

digitus, ī *m* a finger, 6.647; toe, 5.426.

dīgnor, ātus sum 1 *dep v* (w. *acc* and *abl*), to deem worthy of, 1.335; *with inf*, think, fit, deign, 4.192; *part*, dīgnātus, a, um, with *pass* meaning, deemed worthy of, honored by, 3.475. (dīgnus).

dīgnus, a, um (*adj, with abl*), deserving of, worthy of; with depend. clause or absol., fit, due, meet, worthy, 1.600 *et al*.; dīgna indīgna, worthy (and) unworthy; all fortunes, all things alike, 12.811.

dīgredior, gressus sum 3 *dep v* to walk or go apart,

aside, or away; depart, 3.410; separate, 4.80; come from, 2.718. (di- and gradior).

dīgressus, ūs *m* a going away; a departure, parting, 3.482.

dīlābor, lāpsus sum 3 *dep v* to slip, glide, fall apart; depart, pass away, 4.705.

dīligō, lēxī, lēctus 3 *v* to love, 8.590; *part*, dīlēctus, a, um, loved, dear, 1.344.

dīluvium, iī, *n* a washing away, flood, deluge, 12.205; desolation, destruction, 7.228. (dīluō, cleanse).

dīmētior, mēnsus sum 4 *dep v* to measure, mark out; lay out.

dīmittō, mīsī, missus 3 *v* to send apart or away, 1.571; dispatch, 1.577; dismiss, 10.46; give up, 11.706.

dīmoveō, mōvī, mōtus 2 *v* to move apart or away; remove, dispel, 3.589; divide, 5.839.

Dindyma, ōrum, *n*, and **Dindymus, ī** *m* Mount Dindymus or Dindyma, in Mysia, sacred to Cybele, 9.618.

dīnumerō, āvī, ātus 1 *v* to distinguish by number, enumerate, reckon, count, 6.691.

Diomēdēs, is *m* Diomedes, son of Tydeus, and king of Argos, distinguished among the Greeks at Troy, 1.752.

Diōnaeus, a, um *adj* (Diōnē), pertaining to Dione, mother of Venus; Dionaean, 3.19.

Diōrēs, is *m* a son of Priam and companion of Aeneas, 5.297.

Dioxippus, ī *m* a Trojan, 9.574.

Dīra, ae *f* a Fury, 12.869; *pl* Dīrae, ārum, the Furies, 4.473 *et al.*

dirimō, ēmī, ēmptus *3 v* to take asunder; to separate, 7.227; break off, end, 5.467; decide, 12.79. (dis- and emō).

dīripiō, ripuī, reptus *3 v* to tear apart or off; snatch, tear away, 3.227; plunder, pillage, sack, 2.563. See also dēripiō. (dis- and rapiō).

dīruō, uī, utus *3 v* to overthrow, tear apart or away from, 10.363.

dīrus, a, um *adj* accursed; portentous; fearful, dreadful, awful, dire, cruel, horrible, *freq*; accursed, 2.261; unhallowed, impious, 6.373; foul, carrion, 3.262; wild, furious, ardent, 9.185; *pl* dira *adv* fearfully, 10.572.

Dīs, ītis *m* Pluto, the ruler of Hades, 4.702 *et al.*

discēdō, cessī, cessus *3 v* to go apart or away, retire, withdraw, depart, 2.644; open, 9.20.

discernō, crēvī, crētus *3 v* to distinguish one thing from another; determine, distinguish, decide, 12.898; perceive, 3.201; mark, set off; work, embroider, 4.264.

discerpō, cerpsī, cerptus *3 v* to pluck asunder, to tear in pieces; disperse, 9.313. (dis- and carpō).

discessus, ūs *m* a departing, departure, 6.464. (discēdō).

discindō, scidī, scissus *3 v* to tear asunder, pull in pieces, rend, 12.602.

discingō, cīnxī, cīnctus *3 v* to ungird; *part*, discīnctus, a, um, loose-robed; indolent, effeminate, 8.724.

disclūdō, clūsī, clūsus *3 v* to open; loosen, 12.782. (dis- and claudō).

discō, didicī *3 v* to learn, *with acc*, 6.433; learn how, *with inf*, 5.222.

discolor, ōris *adj* of different color, 6.204.

discordia, ae *f* difference in feeling, or mind; dissension, strife; personified, Discord or Eris, 6.280. (discors).

discors, cordis *adj* (dis- and cor), disagreeing, 2.423; hostile, 9.688; opposing, contending, 10.356.

discrepō, uī *1 v* to be discordant in sound; *figuratively* to differ, 10.434.

discrīmen, inis, *n* a separating interval, space, 5.154; separation, division, 10.382; distance, 3.685; difference, distinction, 1.574; variation, division, of sound; note, 6.646; crisis, danger, peril, 1.204; *pl* difference, 10.529. (discernō).

discrīminō, āvī, ātus *1 v* to separate; to make distinct, with light; discover, illuminate, 11.144. (discrīmen).

discumbō, cubuī, cubitus *3 v* to recline separately; recline at table, 1.708;

discurrō ⋯⟩ dīva

(*impers*), discumbitur, they recline, 1.700.

discurrō, cucurrī, or **currī, cursus** 3 *v* to run apart; to ride in different directions, 5.580; to move in patrols, or hurry to and fro as patrols, 9.164; (*impers*), discurritur, they hurry in different directions, 11.468.

discutiō, cussī, cussus 3 *v* to shake off, strike off, 9.810; disperse, dissipate, dispel. (dis- and quatiō).

dīsiciō, iēcī, iectus 3 *v* to throw, cast asunder; overthrow, demolish, 8.355; scatter, disperse, 1.70; cleave, 12.308. (dis- and iaciō).

disiungō, iūnxī, iūnctus 3 *v* to disjoin, separate, drive away from, 1.252.

dispellō, pulī, pulsus 3 *v* to drive away; separate, scatter, disperse, 1.538; to part, 5.839.

dispendium, iī, *n* a weighing out; expense, cost; loss, 3.453. (dispendō, weigh out).

dispergō, spersī, spersus 3 *v* to sprinkle, shower around; disperse, scatter, 3.197; diffuse, dissolve, 11.617. (dis- and spargō).

dispiciō, spexī, spectus 3 *v* to see distinctly, descry, perceive, discern, 6.734. (dis- and speciō, look).

dispōnō, posuī, positus 3 *v* to put in order; arrange, distribute, 3.237.

dissēnsus, ūs *m* disagreement, dissent, 11.455. (dissentiō, disagree).

dissideō, sēdī, sessus 2 *v* to be situated apart, be separated, 7.370. (dis- and sedeō).

dissiliō, uī 4 *v* to spring apart; burst asunder; be rent asunder, 3.416; break in twain, 12.741. (dis- and saliō).

dissimilis, e *adj* unlike; inadequate, unfit, unequal, 9.282.

dissimulō, āvī, ātus 1 *v* to misrepresent the truth or reality; dissemble, hide, disguise; conceal, 4.291; remain disguised, or concealed (others, repress one's emotions), 1.516. (dissimilis).

dissultō 1 *v* to leap asunder; spring back or apart, 8.240; burst from, 12.923. (dis- and saltō).

distendō, tendī, tēnsus, or **tentus** 3 *v* to stretch apart or out; extend; distend; fill, 1.433.

distineō, uī, tentus 2 *v* to hold at bay, keep off, 11.381. (dis- and teneō).

distō 1 *v* to stand apart; be distant, 3.116.

distrahō, trāxī, trāctus 3 *v* to draw, tear asunder, 7.767.

distringō, strīnxī, strīctus 3 *v* to draw apart; draw, blind, stretch, 6.617.

diū *adv* long, for a long time, 1.351. (old *abl, cf.* diēs).

dīva, ae *f* a goddess, 1.632 *et al.*

dīvellō, vellī, vulsus 3 v to tear asunder; tear in pieces, 4.600; tear away, 8.568; separate, scatter (others, drive away), 2.434; loosen, uncoil, 2.220.

dīverberō, no perf, ātus 1 v to strike asunder, cleave, cut, 5.503.

dīversus, a, um opposite, contrary; away; ex dīversō, from different directions or from an opposite direction, 2.716; 3.232.

dīversus, a, um turned apart; opposite, contrary; away, 5.166; different, various, 2.298; distant, far remote, 3.4; pl apart, 9.623; in different directions, 1.70; different parts of, 5.676; in different places, 12.501; dīversa urbs, different parts of the city, 12.621; in dīversa, different or opposite ways; asunder, 8.642.

dīvertō, vertī, versus 3 v to turn one's self, turn or go apart.

dīves, itis, and **dīs, dīte** adj rich, wealthy; fertile, 7.262; with gen, rich in respect of, rich in, 1.14; with abl, rich in, abounding in, 4.38; superl, ditissimus, a, um, the richest, wealthiest, 1.343; very rich, opulent, 9.360.

dīvidō, vīsī, vīsus 3 v divide; cleave, 9.751; separate, 3.383; to divide by being inlaid; to be set in, 10.134; distribute, 1.197; open, break through, 2.234; of the mind, to turn, 4.285.

dīvīnus, a, um adj (dīvus), relating to the gods; heaven-descended, divine,

5.47; heavenly, 1.403; inspired, prophetic, 3.373.

dīvitiae, ārum f riches, wealth, 6.610. (dīves).

dīvortium, iī, n a separation; a parting, or crossway, 9.379. (dīvortō or dīvertō).

dīvus (dīus), a, um adj divine; godlike, 11.657; subst dīvus, ī, m, a god, freq; the image of a god, 12.286; dīva, ae, f, a goddess, 1.632 et al.

dīvus, ī m a god, freq; the image of a god, 12.286; dīva, ae, f, a goddess, 1.632 et al.

dō, dedī, datus, dare, v to give, freq; grant, 1.79; bestow, 12.394; offer, 8.106; show, betray, 12.69; present, make, render, effect, 9.323; consign, throw, cast, 2.566; yield, resign, 11.162; supply, 2.391; bring, 4.683; give forth, spread, 12.301; make, 11.385; form, 12.575; direct, 3.337; establish, ordain, 12.192; unfurl, 1.35; often with infin as object acc, 5.538; sē dare, to intrust one's self, venture upon, 9.56; to be given or afforded, 4.627; dare dēfēnsum, to defend completely, 12.437; dare poenās, to suffer punishment. Dare, with a substantive following, may often be translated by the verb kindred with the latter; as, dare complexūs, to embrace, 1.687; dare partū, to bring forth, bear, 1.274.

doceō, uī, tus 2 v to teach, instruct, 6.292; tell, inform, 1.332; describe, recount, 3.717; interpret, explain, 5.523; part,

doctus, a, um, well-informed; learned, wise, experienced, skillful, 10.225 *et al.*

doctus, a, um well-informed; learned, wise, experienced, skillful, 10.225 *et al.* (doceō).

Dōdōnaeus, a, um *adj* of, Dodona; Dodonaean, 3.466.

doleō, uī, itus 2 *v* to be in pain; to grieve, sorrow, mourn, *freq*; to endure grief, 4.434; to be displeased, angry, 1.9; to feel indignation, shame, disgrace, 11.732.

Dolichāōn, onis *m* a Trojan, 10.696.

dolō, ōnis *m* a staff or pole with an iron point; a pike, 7.664.

Dolōn, ōnis *m* a Trojan spy, 12.347.

Dolopes, um *m* the Dolopians, a warlike tribe of Thessaly, followers of Pyrrhus at Troy, 2.7.

dolor, ōris *m* pain, 4.693; grief, anguish, 4.474; resentment, 1.25; fury, vengeance, 2.594. (doleō).

dolus, ī *m* artifice, device, stratagem, 2.390; fraud, treachery, wile, 2.34; deception, craft, 1.684; secret or hidden crime, crafty misdeed, 6.567; *figuratively* maze, 5.590; treacherous work or fabric, 2.264.

domina, ae *f* mistress, queen, 3.438; goddess, 3.113. (dominus).

dominor, ātus sum (*pass inf*, **dominārier**, 7.70) 1 *dep v*

to be lord or master; rule, reign, be supreme, 2.363; foll. by *abl* with in, 2.327; by *abl* without in, 6.766; and in 1.285; take possession, overrun, prevail. (dominus).

dominus, ī *m* a master, owner, lord, ruler, 1.282 *et al.* (rel to domō).

domitō 1 *intens v* to tame; train, exercise, 7.163. (domō).

domitor, ōris *m* a tamer, 7.189; ruler, sovereign, 5.799. (domō).

domō, uī, itus 1 *v* to tame, train, vanquish, 2.198; subdue, 6.80; till, 9.608.

domus, ī *or* **ūs** *f* house, habitation, dwelling, palace, mansion, 1.637 *et al.*; home, 1.600; structure, building, 6.27; nest, 5.214; haunt, 3.647; abode, region, 6.534; family, house, race, posterity, country, lineage, 1.284 *et al.*; *pl* a palatial building with its several courts; palace, 2.445; *gen* as locat., domī, in the house, at home; *acc* domum, homeward, home.

dōnec *adv* as long as, while; until, till at length, *with* indic., 1.273; *with* subj., 11.860. (contract. fr. dōnicum, until).

dōnō, āvī, ātus 1 *v* to present; give, 5.262; reward, 5.268; *with acc* and *abl*, 5.361. (dōnum).

dōnum, ī, *n* a gift, present, 1.652; reward, prize, 5.266; sacrifice, offering, 3.301; 4.63; bounty, blessing, 2.269. (dō).

Donūsa, ae *f* an island between the Cyclades and Crete; one of the Sporades, 3.125.

Dōricus, a, um *adj* Doric; Greek, 2.27.

dorsum, ī, *n* the back, 11.577; a ridge, reef of rocks, 1.110; a bank, 10.303.

Doryclus, ī *m* Doryclus, a follower of Aeneas, 5.620.

dōs, dōtis *f* a marriage portion, dowry, 7.423. (dō).

dōtālis, e *adj* (dōs), pertaining to a dowry, dotal, 4.104.

dōtō, āvī, ātus *1 v* to endow, portion, 7.318. (dōs).

Dōtō, ūs *f* a sea nymph, 9.102.

dracō, ōnis *m* a dragon or fabulous kind of serpent, 4.484; a serpent, 2.225.

Drancēs, is *m* a Latin hero, 11.122 *et al.*

Drepanum, ī, *n* Drepanum, a town on the western coast of Sicily, now Trapani, 3.707.

Drūsus, ī *m* the family name of several distinguished Romans, 6.824.

Dryopē, ēs *f* a wood nymph, 10.551.

Dryopes, um *m* the Dryopes, a Pelasgian tribe, at first of Thessaly, later of Messene, 4.146.

Dryops, opis *m* Dryops, a Trojan follower of Aeneas, 10.346.

dubitō, āvī, ātus *1 v* to doubt, 3.170; hesitate, 6.806; fear, 8.614; to be in meditation, to ponder, 9.191; *part*, dubitandus, a, um, to be questioned, 3.170.

dubius, a, um *adj* uncertain, doubting, doubtful; active, 1.218; 4.55; passive, to be doubted, uncertain, doubtful, 2.359.

dūcō, dūxī, ductus *3 v* to lead, *freq*; draw; guide, direct, conduct, 1.401; draw, strain, draw, 11.860; draw, unsheath, 12.378; incline, 5.7; usher in, 2.802; draw over one's self, take on, 10.192; take (a wife), raise, build, 1.423; of metals, beat out, form, fashion, 7.634; mold, express, 6.848; choose by drawing lots; choose, 2.201; receive, 5.534; spend, protract, 6.539; draw out, prolong, 2.641; continue, 1.642; calculate, reckon, 6.690; deem, think, 10.669; derive, 5.568; *passive* dūcī, to be descended; to descend, spring from, 1.19.

ductor, ōris *m* a leader, 1.189; captain, commander, 5.133; prince, king, 9.691. (dūcō).

dūdum *adv* a while ago; some time ago; lately, not long ago; just now, 2.726 *et al.* (diū and dum).

dulcēdō, inis *f* sweetness; delight, joy, 11.538. (dulcis).

dulcis, e *adj* sweet, 1.433; pure, clear, pleasant, delightful, 1.694; dear, 2.777.

Dūlichium, iī, *n* Dulichium, an island southeast of Ithaca, belonging to the kingdom of Ulysses, 3.271.

dum *conj*, while, as long as,
1.607 *et al.*; even while (in
the act of), 6.586; until, till,
1.265; yet, as yet, 11.70; until,
while (of purpose), *with*
subj., 1.5; provided that, if
only, *with* subj., 11.792.

dūmus, ī *m* a bramble,
4.526; brake, thicket.

duo, ae, o (*num adj*),
two, 2.213 *et al.*

duplex, icis *adj* (duo and plicō),
twofold, double, 1.655; lying
over each other, lapping,
9.707; both, 1.93; twin, 12.198.

duplicō, āvī, ātus *1 v* to double;
double up, fold up or bend,
11.645; 12.927. (duplex).

dūrō, āvī, ātus *1 v* to make hard,
harden; to be enduring;
endure, persevere; be firm,
patient, bear up, 1.207;
continue, last. (dūrus).

dūrus, a, um *adj* hard, to
the touch; tough, stiff,
5.403; hardy, 5.730; sturdy,
7.504; strong, 2.479; harsh,
unpleasant; stern, cruel;
inexorable; insensible, 4.428;
difficult, 1.563; grievous, heavy,
4.488; rough, dangerous,
3.706; much enduring,
2.7; 4.247; much suffering,
tired with grief, 12.873.

dux, ducis, *c* a leader, guide,
head, 1.364; chief, captain,
commander, 2.261; groom
(others, a pilot), 3.470. (dūcō).

Dymās, antis *m* Dymas, a
Trojan warrior, 2.340.

ebur, oris, *n* ivory, 1.592.

eburnus, a, um *adj* (ebur),
of ivory; ivory, 6.647;
ivory-hilted, 11.11.

Ebusus, ī *m* a Latin
warrior, 12.299.

ecce (*interj*), see! lo! behold!
with a proposition,
5.793. (en and ce).

Echīonius, a, um of Echion,
one of the Theban ancestors,
produced from the dragon's
teeth; Echionian, Theban,
12.515. (Echīon).

ecquī, quae or **qua, quod**
(*adj* interr. *pron*, denoting
vehement feeling), whether
any? any? 3.341. (ec and qui).

ecquis, ecquid (subst. interr.
pron, denoting vehement
feeling), whether anybody?
anything, any one; anybody?
who, what, anything? *freq; adv*
ecquid, as to anything, in any
respect or degree? perchance?
at all? 3.342. (ec and quis).

edāx, ācis voracious; devouring,
consuming, 2.758. (edō).

ēdīcō, dīxī, dictus *3 v* to
speak forth; declare;
decree, order, *with* subj.
or *inf*, 3.235; announce,
order, charge, 11.463.

ēdisserō, uī, tus *3 v* to state; set
forth, declare, relate, 2.149.

ēdō, didī, ditus *3 v* to give
out, put forth, raise; bring
forth young; beget, 8.137;
produce, make, 9.527; utter,
5.693; *part*, ēditus, a, um,
exposed, raised up, elevated.

edō, ēdī, ēsus *3 v* to eat, 7.113;
to eat, waste, consume, 4.66;

pres., est, 4.66; *figuratively* fret, vex, torment, consume, 12.801.

ēdoceō, uī, tus 2 *v* to teach completely; communicate, declare, 5.748.

Ēdōnus, a, um *adj* pertaining to the Edoni, a people of southern Thrace; Edonian, Thracian, 12.365.

ēducō, āvī, ātus 1 *v* to train, breed, 10.518.

ēdūcō, dūxī, ductus 3 *v* to lead out, lead forth, 1.432; draw out, 10.744; bear, bring forth, 6.765; work out, forge, 6.630; erect, build, 2.186; rear, 2.461; bring up, maintain, 8.413.

efferō, extulī, ēlātus, ferre *irreg v* to bear, or bring out or forth, 2.297; bear away, rescue, 3.150; raise, elevate, lift up or high, 1.127; elate, puff up, 11.715; efferre gressum or pedem, walk, go, come forth, 2.753; efferre sē, arise, 3.215. (ex and ferō).

efferō, extulī, ēlātus, ferre *irreg v* to bear, or bring out or forth, 2.297; bear away, rescue, 3.150; raise, elevate, lift up or high, 1.127; elate, puff up, 11.715; efferre gressum or pedem, walk, go, come forth, 2.753; efferre sē, arise, 3.215. (ex and ferō).

efferus, a, um *adj* (ex and ferus, wild), extremely wild; savage, frantic, 4.642; fierce, 8.6; cruel, 8.484.

effētus, a, um *adj* (ex and fētus, productive), no longer producing; exhausted, 5.396; incapable (w. *gen*), 7.440.

efficiō, fēcī, fectus 3 *v* to make completely; form, make, 1.160; *with* subj. clause, cause. (ex and faciō).

effigiēs, ēī *f* something molded or fashioned; a figure, likeness, or image, 3.148. (effingō).

effingō, fīnxī, fīctus 3 *v* to mold out, shape forth; form, fashion; portray, represent, 6.32; counterfeit, imitate, 10.640. (ex and fingō).

efflāgitō, āvī, ātus 1 *v* to ask urgently; demand, 12.759. (ex and flagitō, demand).

efflō, āvī, ātus 1 *v* to blow or breathe out, 7.786. (ex and flō).

effodiō, fōdī, fossus 3 *v* to dig out, excavate, 1.427; dig up, 1.443; dig, thrust out, 3.663. (ex and fodiō).

effor, fātus sum 1 *dep v* to speak forth; speak, say, 6.560. (ex and for).

effringō, frēgī, frāctus 3 *v* to break out or open; crush, dash out, 5.480. (ex and frangō).

effugiō, fūgī 3 *v* to flee forth or away; glide away, 2.226; get off, escape; speed along, 5.151; pass swiftly from, flee from, escape from, 2.793; 3.272; escape, 3.653. (ex and fugiō).

effugium, iī, *n* a fleeing away; *pl* flight, escape, 2.140. (effugiō).

effulgeō, and effulgō, fulsī 2 and 3, *n* to shine forth or brightly; be effulgent, 2.616; 8.677; glitter, be distinguished, conspicuous, 5.133. (ex and fulgeō).

effultus, a, um propped up; supported, 7.94.

effundō, fūdī, fūsus 3 v to pour out or forth; shed, 2.271; throw, cast out, 7.780; cast, 6.339; overthrow, 11.485; bring out, 9.68; unbind, dishevel, 4.509; dissolve, 2.651; let loose, throw out, 5.818; spend, lose, waste, 5.446; of words, utter, 5.780; *passive* effundī, dart, 5.145; flow, 6.686. (ex and fundō).

effūsus, a, um poured forth; overflowing; thronging, 12.131. (effundō).

ēgelidus, a, um chilly, cold.

egēns, entis destitute, needy, necessitous, helpless, 4.373. (egeō).

egēnus, a, um *adj* (egeō), needy; in want, destitute, 1.599; distressed, straitened, imperiled, desperate, 10.367.

egeō, uī 2 v to be in want or need; (w. *abl* or *gen*), to want, need, 2.522; to be poor, destitute, 1.384; to feel the need of, be desirous of, 5.751.

Ēgeria, ae f a nymph of Roman mythology, instructress of Numa, 7.763.

egestās, ātis f poverty, destitution, penury, need, want; personified, 6.276. (egeō).

ego, meī, *pers pron; pl* **nōs, nostrī** or **nostrum** I, me, etc.; (*abl* with cum appended) **mēcum,** with me, 1.675 *et al.;* (*pl* often for the *sing*), I, me, etc.

ēgredior, gressus sum 3 *dep v* to step or walk forth; go out, 2.713; to disembark, land, 1.172. (ex and gradior).

ēgregius, a, um *adj* (ē and grex), apart from the herd; excellent, distinguished, 7.473; famous, renowned, 1.445; noble, 6.523; *with gen,* 11.417.

ei (*monosyll*) (*interj* expressive of grief), ah! alas! woe is me! 2.274 *et al.*

ēiciō, iēcī, iectus 3 v to cast out, forth, away; *part,* ēiectus, a, um, cast ashore, 1.578; banished, 8.646; stretched out at full length, thrust forth, 10.894. (ex and iaciō).

ēiectō, āvī, ātus 1 v to cast forth; vomit, 5.470. (ex and iactō).

ēlābor, lāpsus sum 3 *dep v* to slip or glide forth or away; escape from, 1.242; spring aside, dodge, 5.445.

Ēlectra, ae f one of the Pleiades (daughters of Atlas), and mother of Dardanus, 8.135.

ēlectrum, ī, n amber; a mixed metal of the color of amber, 8.402.

elephantus, ī m an elephant; *metonym* ivory, 3.464.

ēlīdō, līsī, līsus 3 v to dash forth, out, up, 3.567; suffocate, strangle, 8.289; force out, cause to start out, 8.261. (ex and laedō).

ēligō, lēgī, lēctus 3 v to select, choose, 7.274. (ē and legō).

Ēlis, idis *f* Elis, one of the countries of the Peloponnesus, west of Arcadia, 3.694.

Elissa ae *f* another name for Dido, 4.335.

ēloquium, ĭī, *n* eloquence; rant, 11.383. (ēloquor).

ēloquor, locūtus sum *3 dep v* to speak out; speak, 3.39.

ēlūdō, lūsī, lūsus *3 v* to play out; to mock, elude, 11.695; deceive, disappoint.

ēluō, uī, ūtus *3 v* to wash out or away, 6.742.

Ēlysium, ĭī, *n* Elysium, the Elysian fields, the dwelling place set apart for the blessed in the lower world.

Ēmathīōn, ōnis *m* a Trojan warrior, 9.571.

ēmētior, mēnsus sum *4 dep v* to measure out or off, 10.772; pass over, traverse, 5.628.

ēmicō, uī, ātus *1 v* to leap, spring forth, 6.5; to dart, bound, or spring upward, 2.175; run, rush, dart forward, 5.319.

ēmineō, uī *2 v* to stand out, project, rise up, 10.227.

ēminus *adv* from afar, at a distance, 10.346. (ē and manus).

ēmittō, mīsī, missus *3 v* to send forth, 6.898; hurl, throw, shoot, 11.676.

emō, ēmī, ēmptus *3 v* to buy, purchase, 10.503.

ēmoveō, mōvī, mōtus *2 v* to move off or away; throw off, start

from, 2.493; dispel, relieve, 6.382; tear away, shatter, 2.610.

ēmūniō, ĭī, ītus *4 v* to fortify; make strong, secure, 8.227.

ēn *(interj)*, lo! behold! with *nom*, 1.461; in indignation, 4.597.

ēnārrābilis, e *adj* (nārrō), that can be expressed or described, 8.625.

Enceladus, ī *m* Enceladus, a giant, son of Caelus and Terra, 3.578; 4.179.

enim causal *conj*, for, 1.198, et al; corroborative, truly, certainly, yes, aye, even, indeed; with *pers pron*, precisely, directly, 8.84; nec enim, nor indeed, 2.100; sed enim, but indeed, however, 1.19.

ēniteō, uī *2 v* to shine forth, 4.150; grow bright.

ēnītor, nīxus or **nīsus sum** *3 dep v* to struggle forth or upward; to bring forth, bear offspring, 3.327.

ēnō, āvī, ātus *1 v* to swim out or away, *figuratively* to fly away, 6.16.

ēnsis, is *m* a sword, 2.393 *et al*.; knife, 2.155.

Entellus, ī *m* a Sicilian boxer, 5.387.

ēnumerō, āvī, ātus *1 v* to count out or completely; enumerate, 4.334.

eō, īvī or **ĭī, itus, īre** *irreg v* to go; walk, come, 8.466; go forth, 2.578; depart, 2.111; issue, 4.130; advance, 12.903; move, appear, 4.149; ascend, 5.451; run down, flow, 9.434; hang,

5.558; enter upon, succeed to, inherit, 6.758; (w. cogn. *acc*), to pursue, 4.468; (*impers*), ītur, we, they, go, 9.641; *part*, iēns, euntis, going, etc., *freq*.

eōdem *adv* to the same place, 9.689. (idem).

eōus, a, um *adj* belonging to the dawn, eastern, 1.489.

Eōus, ī *m* Lucifer, the day star; the dawn, 3.588.

Epēos, ī *m* Epeius, a Greek architect, designer of the wooden horse, 2.264.

Ēpīros (Ēpīrus), ī *f* Epirus, the country on the Adriatic coast, west of Thessaly and Macedon, now Albania, 3.292.

epulae, ārum *f* a banquet, feast, 1.79; food, 1.216. (sing. epulum).

Epulō, ōnis *m* a Rutulian warrior, 12.459.

epulor, ātus sum *1 dep v* to banquet, feast, 4.207; *with abl*, to banquet, feast upon, 3.224; *with acc*, feast upon, 4.602. (epulae).

Ēpytidēs, ae *m* son of Epytus, a follower of Aeneas, and master of the equestrian games, 5.547.

Ēpytus, ī *m* a Trojan, 2.340.

equa, ae *f* a mare. (equus).

eques, itis *m* a horseman, 4.132; *pl* cavalry, 12.408; *sing* as collective, cavalry, 10.239. (equus).

equester, tris, tre *adj* (eques), pertaining to a horseman; equestrian, 5.667.

equidem *adv* indeed, at least, certainly, surely; *with* first person, for my part, 1.238. (demonstr. e or ec and quidem).

equīnus, a, um *adj* (equus), pertaining to horses; horse hair, 9.622.

equitātus, ūs *m* the horse, cavalry, 8.585. (equitō).

equitō, āvī, ātus *1 v* to be a horseman; to ride, 10.885. (eques).

equus, ī *m* a horse, 1.156 *et al*.

Eratō *f* the muse of love poetry; muse, in general, 7.37. (only in *nom*).

Erebus, ī *m* the god of darkness, son of Chaos and brother of Night, 6.247; darkness; the lower world, 4.26 *et al*.

Erētum, ī, *n* an ancient Sabine town, 7.711.

ergō *adv* therefore; *with gen* (like causā), for the sake of, on account of, 6.670; in a question, 6.456.

Ericētēs, ae *m* a Lycaonian follower of Aeneas, 10.749.

Ēridanus, ī *m* 1. A Greek name of the river Po. 2. The river in the lower world which flows forth and forms the Po in the upper world, 6.659.

ērigō, rēxī, rēctus *3 v* to raise up, rear, erect, 4.495; cast upward, 3.423. (ex and regō).

erīlis, e *adj* (erus), pertaining to an owner, master, or mistress; master's, 7.490.

Erīnys, yos *f* a fury, 2.337; pest, scourge, curse, 2.573.

Eriphȳlē, ēs *f* the wife of Amphiaraus, slain by her son Alcmaeon, for her treachery to her husband, 6.445.

ēripiō, uī, reptus 3 *v* to tear or pull away, *freq*; *with* the object from which in *abl*, *with prep* or without a *prep*; or in the *dat*; unsheath; draw, 4.579; snatch, 10.788; catch, 7.119; take away, 2.736; rescue, 1.596; bear safely, 2.665; hasten, 2.619; *imperat*, away! 3.560; *passive* ēripī, escape, 12.948; ēripere sē, hasten, fly, 12.917. (ex and rapiō).

errō, āvī, ātus 1 *v* to go astray, wander, 1.578; go to and fro, stray, 7.493; hover, 4.684; float, 3.76; to err, be uncertain, 7.498.

error, ōris *m* a wandering, 1.755; a winding maze, 5.591; mistake, error, 3.181; deception, 2.48. (errō).

ērubēscō, rubuī 3 *v* to redden; to blush; feel shame before; to revere, respect, 2.542.

ēructō, āvī, ātus 1 *v* to belch out; to vomit, throw forth or out, 3.632; discharge, 6.297.

ērudiō, īvī or **iī, ītus** 4 *v* to redeem from roughness; to teach, instruct, 9.203. (ē and rudiō).

Erulus, ī *m* king of Praeneste, and son of Feronia, said to have had three lives, and to have been killed by Evander, 8.563.

ērumpō, rūpī, ruptus 3 *v* to burst forth; burst, break through, 1.580; dash, dart forward, 10.890.

ēruō, ī, tus 3 *v* to cast out or up; to overthrow, 2.5.

erus, ī *m* an owner, householder, master, lord, 3.324.

Erycīnus, a, um *adj* (Eryx), pertaining to Eryx, Erycinian, 5.759.

Erymanthus, ī *m* a mountain in Arcadia, 5.448.

Erymās, antis *m* a Trojan slain by Turnus, 9.702.

Eryx, ycis *m* a mountain on the northwest coast of Sicily, 1.570. A Sicilian giant and king, son of Venus and Butes, and brother of Aeneas; slain by Hercules, 5.419.

ēsca, ae *f* food, bait. (edō).

et *conj*, and, *freq*; moreover, also, too, *freq*; and even, and indeed; and yet; and immediately, 9.22; et — et, both — and, *freq*.

etenim *conj*, for, indeed, truly, 7.390.

etiam *conj* (et emphasized by iam), and also, and besides; even, and even, *freq*; for praeterea, besides, moreover, 11.352; of time, still, yet, even now, 6.485.

Etrūria, ae *f* ancient Tuscany; Etruria.

Etrūscus, a, um *adj* (Etrūria), Etrurian, Tuscan, 8.503; *subst* Etrūscī, ōrum, *m*, the Etrurians, Tuscans, 9.150.

etsī *conj*, even if, although, though, 2.583.

Euander (-drus, 8.100; **Ēvander, -drus), drī** *m* Evander, an Arcadian prince, son of Carmentis, and king of Pallanteum on the Tiber, 8.52.

Euandrius, a, um of Evander, Evandrian, 10.394. (Euander).

Euanthēs, ae *m* a Trojan warrior, 10.702.

Euboicus, a, um *adj* of Euboea, an island on the eastern coast of Greece; Euboean, 6.2.

euhāns, antis, *part* crying Euhan! shrieking madly, celebrating, 6.517. (Evan or Euan, i.e. Bacchus).

euhoe (*dissyll*) (*interj*), a joyous Bacchanalian shout), evoe! joy! 7.389.

Eumēdēs, is *m* a Trojan, 12.346.

Eumēlus, ī *m* a Trojan, 5.665.

Eumenides, um *f* the well-disposed; a deprecatory title given by the Greeks to the Furies; the Eumenides, the Furies, 4.469.

Eunēus, ī *m* a Trojan slain by Camilla, 11.666.

Euphrātēs, is *m* the Euphrates.

Eurōpa, ae *f* 1. Europa, the daughter of Agenor, king of Phoenicia, borne by Jupiter over the sea to Crete. 2. Europe, 1.385.

Eurōtās, ae *m* the Eurotas; the river on which Sparta was situated, 1.498.

Eurōus, a, um *adj* (Eurus), pertaining to Eurus, the southeast wind; eastern, 3.533.

Eurus, ī *m* the southeast wind, 1.85 *et al.*; wind, 1.383 *et al.*

Euryalus, ī *m* a Trojan youth among the followers of Aeneas, 5.294.

Eurypylus, ī *m* a Thessalian prince, one of the Greek chiefs at Troy, 2.114.

Eurystheus (*trisyll*), **eī** *m* the king of Mycenae, who assigned to Hercules the twelve labors, 8.292.

Eurytidēs, ae *m* the son of Eurytus, 10.499. (Eurytus).

Eurytiōn, ōnis *m* brother of the Lycian archer Pandarus, and follower of Aeneas, 5.495.

Evadnē, ēs *f* Evadne, the wife of Capaneus, who cast herself on the funeral pile of her husband, 6.447.

ēvādō, vāsī, vāsus *3 v* to go out, forth, or up; ascend, 2.458; come in flight, 2.531; come forth from, *with* the idea of danger surmounted; (w. *acc*), to escape the dangers of, 2.731; escape, 5.689; 6.425; *with dat* 11.702; 9.99.

ēvalēscō, valuī *3 inc v* to grow strong; be able, can; 7.757.

ēvānēscō, vānuī *3 inc v* to disappear, vanish, 4.278.

ēvehō, vexī, vectus *3 v* to carry forth; carry up, raise, elevate, 6.130.

ēveniō, vēnī, ventus 4 v to come out; come to pass, happen, 2.778.

ēventus, ūs m an outcome, issue, result, event, fortune, 6.158. (ēveniō).

ēverberō, āvī, ātus 1 v to beat violently, strike, flap upon, 12.866.

ēversor, ōris m an over-thrower, destroyer, 12.545. (ēvertō).

ēvertō, vertī, versus 3 v to upturn, 1.43; overthrow, demolish, destroy, 2.603.

ēvinciō, vīnxī, vīnctus 4 v to bind round; crown, wreathe, 5.269; bind, 5.364.

ēvincō, vīcī, victus 3 v to conquer completely; overcome, 2.630; move, 4.548 et al.; bear down, sweep away, 2.497.

ēvīscerō, no perf, ātus 1 v to disembowel, 11.723. (ē and viscus).

ēvocō, āvī, ātus 1 v to call out or forth; summon, conjure, 4.242.

ēvolō, āvī, ātus 1 v to fly away, 9.477.

ēvolvō, volvī, volūtus 3 v to roll out or forth, 5.807; unroll a scroll or volume; hence, *figuratively* reveal, declare, 9.528.

ēvomō, uī, itus 3 v to vomit out or up, 8.253.

ex or **ē** (*prep with abl*), out of from; of place, 3.554, and freq; down from, 2.410; of source, material, of, 5.266; (partitive), of, 2.659; (of time), after, from, since, 1.623; (of transition from one condition to another), 10.221; (of correspondence), in, 1.456; according to, after, 5.244; with, 8.621; ex eō, illō, quō (tempore), from that, from which, what, time; since, 8.268.

exaestuō, āvī, ātus 1 v to boil up, foam up, rage, 3.577; to be agitated, to burn, 9.798.

exāmen, inis, n 1. A multitude; swarm, 7.67. 2. The tongue or indicator of the scales or balances; the index, 12.725. (ex and agō).

exanimis, e, and **exanimus, a, um** adj (ex and anima), breathless; lifeless, dead, 1.484; slain, 11.110; breathless with fear, terrified, 4.672.

exanimō, āvī, ātus 1 v to deprive of life; *part*, exanimātus, a, um, without breath, breathless; disheartened; terrified, 5.805. (ex and anima).

exārdēscō, ārsī, ārsus 3 *inc* v to begin to burn; *figuratively* to be roused to anger; kindle, burn, 2.575; 5.172.

exaudiō, īvī, or iī, ītus 4 v to hear distinctly; hear, 1.219; catch the sound, hear from afar, 7.15; listen to, heed, 11.157.

excēdō, cessī, cessus 3 v to go out or away; depart, 6.737; flee from, 1.357; withdraw from, 5.380; retire, 9.789.

excellēns, entis surpassing; beautiful, stately, 12.250.

excidium, iī, n a complete cutting or tearing down;

razing, demolition,
destruction. (exscindō).

excidō, cidī *3 v* to fall out; fall
from; drop, come from, 2.658;
come down, descend, 9.113;
depart, 1.26. (ex and cadō).

excīdō, cīdī, cīsus *3 v* to cut
out, 1.429; cut off, away,
or down, 2.481; destroy,
2.637. (ex and caedō).

exciō, cīvī or **ciī, ītus** *4 v*, and
excieō, itus *2 v* to rouse up
or forth; call forth, assemble,
5.107; arouse, excite, agitate,
4.301; stir, shake, 12.445.

excipiō, cēpī, ceptus *3 v* to take
out or up; except, exempt,
9.271; receive, receive in
turn, 1.276; receive, with
the notion of hospitality or
shelter or favor, 4.374; 5.41;
catch, take, surprise, fall
upon, 3.332; seize, 6.173;
overtake, 9.763; intercept,
11.517; befall, 3.318; hit, 12.507;
take up the conversation;
reply, answer, 4.114; catch
mentally; surmise, suspect,
detect, 4.297. (ex and capiō).

excitō, āvī, ātus *1 intens v* to
rouse up completely; excite,
awaken, arouse, 2.594;
alarm, 2.728; stimulate,
impel, 3.343. (exciō).

exclāmō, āvī, ātus *1 v* to
call or cry out, 2.733.

exclūdō, clūsī, clūsus *3 v* to shut
out, exclude. (ex and claudō).

excolō, uī, cultus *3 v* to till
completely; cultivate; refine,
perfect, polish, 6.663.

excubiae, ārum *f* a lying
out; watching; vigils,
watch, 4.201. (excubō).

excubō, uī, itus *1 v* to lie out; be
on guard, keep watch, 9.175.

excūdō, cūdī, cūsus *3 v* to
strike out, 1.174; beat
out, mold, 6.847.

excutiō, cussī, cussus *3 v*
to shake out or off, 2.224;
throw or cast down, 1.115;
cast out, 10.590; drive away,
3.200; expel, 7.299; shake
out, uncoil, 3.267; uncoil and
arrange (set the sails), 3.683;
deprive of, 6.353; throw aside,
break, 12.158; hurry forth, call
forth, 9.68. (ex and quatiō).

exedō, ēdī, ēsus *3 v* to eat
out, hollow out, devour;
consume, destroy, 5.785.

exemplum, ī, *n* example,
12.439. (eximō).

exeō, īvī or **iī, itus, īre**
irreg v to go out or forth,
1.306; come out, 5.492;
overflow, burst forth, 2.497;
avoid, elude, 5.438.

exerceō, uī, itus *2 v* to keep
in action or motion; hurry,
drive along, whip, 7.380;
exercise, carry on, pursue,
1.431; employ, 10.808; engage
in, cultivate, cherish, 4.110;
practice, 4.87; train, lead,
1.499; agitate, torment,
harass, 5.779; pursue,
4.623. (ex and arceō).

exercitus, ūs *m* an army,
2.415. (exerceō).

exhālō, āvī, ātus *1 v* to
breathe out, 2.562.

exhauriō, hausī, haustus *4 v*
to draw out, drain, exhaust,
toil through, achieve, 4.14;
undergo, 1.599; endure,
11.256; inflict, 9.356.

exhorrēscō, horruī *3 v* to shudder
greatly; shudder at, fear,
dread, 7.265. (exhorreō).

exhortor, ātus sum *1 dep v*
to encourage, rouse, 7.472;
advise, 8.510; to spur, 11.610.

exigō, ēgī, āctus *3 v* to drive
out or work out; drive
through, thrust, 10.682;
drive, 2.357; investigate,
examine, ascertain, 1.309;
weigh, consider, determine,
4.476; fulfill; finish,
complete, 6.637; of time,
spend, pass, 1.75; *part subst*
exācta, ōrum, discoveries,
1.309. (ex and agō).

exiguus, a, um *adj* (exigō),
minute, scanty, little;
insignificant, small,
4.212; few, 5.754; thin,
slender, feeble, 6.493.

eximius, a, um *adj* (eximō),
exceptional; choice, select;
distinguished, 7.496.

eximō, ēmī, ēmptus *3 v* to take
out; remove, 6.746; take away,
remove, 1.216. (ex and emō).

exinde (abbrev. **exin**) *adv*
from that place; thence, of
place; of time, thereafter;
thereupon, then, 6.743 *et al.*

exitiālis, e *adj* (exitium),
destructive, fatal, deadly, 2.31.

exitium, iī, *n* a going out; death;
hardship, 7.129; destruction,
downfall, ruin, 2.131. (exeō).

exitus, ūs *m* a going or coming
out; departure, exit, passage,
6.894; event, 5.523; end,
death, 2.554.(exeō).

exoptō, āvī, ātus *1 v* to choose
out; wish exceedingly, long
for, desire much, 2.138.

exōrdium, iī, *n* a beginning;
origin, 7.40; opening,
beginning, of discourse,
4.284. (exōrdior).

exorior, ortus sum *4 dep v* to
rise up; come forth, appear,
rise, 4.130; arise, 3.128;
spring up, arise, 4.625.

exōrō, āvī, ātus *1 v* to pray
effectually; entreat,
implore, 3.370.

exōrsum, ī, *n* a thing begun
or undertaken; enterprise,
action, 10.111. (exōrdior).

exōsus, a, um hating
much; usually *with* an
obj. *acc*; hostile, adverse
to, hating, 5.687.

expediō, īvī or **iī, ītus** *4 v* to make
the foot free; to extricate,
disentangle; bring forth,
get ready, 1.178; seize, use,
5.209; serve, 1.702; unfold,
describe, disclose, 3.379.460;
declare, 11.315; *pass* in middle
sig., make one's way out,
escape, 2.633. (ex and pēs).

expellō, pulī, pulsus *3 v* to drive
out; drive or carry up; banish,
1.620; repel, drive, 10.354.

expendō, pendī, pēnsus *3 v* to
weigh out; *figuratively* pay;
suffer, 6.740; expiate, 2.229.

experior, pertus sum *4 dep*
v to try thoroughly; try,

prove, resort to, 4.535; experience, encounter, know by experience, 1.202; employ, use; *with inf*, try; *part*, expertus, a, um, having tried, learned, 11.283; *part*, acquainted with, skilled in, tried in, *with gen*, 10.173.

expers, pertis *adj* (ex and pars), having no part in; *with gen*, free from, without, apart from, 4.550; destitute of, 10.752.

expleō, plēvī, plētus *2 v* to fill completely; fill up; gorge, 3.630; satisfy, 1.713; finish, complete, 1.270; *with gen*, satiate, glut, 2.586.

explicō, āvī or **uī, ātus** or **itus** *1 v* to unfold; deploy, draw out, extend; describe, tell, 2.362.

explōrātor, ōris *m* a scout, 11.512. (explōrō).

explōrō, āvī, ātus *1 v* to ascertain by calling out; investigate, search; reconnoiter, explore, examine, 1.307; observe, 3.514; find out, determine, 1.77.

expōnō, posuī, positus (**expostus**) *3 v* to put forth; plunge, 10.305; to land, 6.416; to put out or extend, 10.654; expose to, 10.694.

exposcō, poposcī *3 v* to ask importunately; to beg, entreat, seek, 3.261.

exprōmō, prōmpsī, prōmptus *3 v* to bring or draw out; to utter, 2.280.

expūgnō, āvī, ātus *1 v* to fight out; carry by storm, 9.532; win by assault, 10.92.

exquīrō, sīvī, sītus *3 v* to seek out, 3.96; discover, petition, pray for, implore, 4.57. (ex and quaerō).

exsanguis, e *adj* without blood; lifeless, 2.542; pale with terror, terrified, 2.212.

exsaturābilis, e *adj* (exsaturō), that can be satisfied, 5.781.

exsaturō, āvī, ātus *1, v* to satisfy, glut, 7.298.

exscindō, scidī, scissus *3 v* to tear out; tear down, destroy, 2.177; extirpate, 4.425.

exsecō, uī, tus *1 v* to cut out, 10.315.

exsecror, ātus sum *1 dep v* to curse bitterly; execrate, curse, 3.273. (ex and sacrō).

exsequiae, ārum *f* funeral rites, 7.5. (ex and sequor).

exsequor, secūtus sum *3 dep v* to follow out or throughout; to perform, conduct, 4.53; execute, 4.396; do, 4.421; pursue, treat of, describe.

exserō, uī, tus *3 v* to thrust out; expose, uncover; *part*, exsertus, a, um, stripped; naked, 1.492.

exsertō, āvī, ātus *1 intens v* to stretch or thrust forth, 3.425. (exserō).

exsilium, iī, *n* banishment, exile, 2.638; place of exile, 2.780. (exsul).

exsolvō, ī, solūtus *3 v* to loosen completely, *with acc and abl*; disengage, 11.829; set free, deliver, 4.652.

exsomnis, e *adj* (ex and somnus), sleepless, 6.556.

exsors, sortis *adj* without share, lot, or part; deprived of, 6.428; not provided or given by lot; unallotted, undesignated, 5.534; different from others; distinguished, 8.552.

exspectō, āvī, ātus *1 v* to look out for; to expect, wait for, 4.134; await, 6.614; tarry, linger, delay, 4.225; *part*, exspectātus, a, um, much looked for; much desired, 2.283; expected, trusted.

exspīrō, āvī, ātus *1 v* to breathe out, 1.44; to expire, die, 10.731.

extinguō, stīnxī, stīnctus *3 v* (*pluperf* **extīnxem**, *for* **extīnxissem**, 4.606) to extinguish, put out, quench, 8.267; blot out, extinguish, 6.527; extirpate, kill, destroy, 4.682; *part*, exstinctus, a, um, lost, 4.322.

exstō, āre, *n* to stand forth or out; rise above, 6.668.

exstruō, strūxī, strūctus *3 v* to build up; erect; raise, spread, 3.224; build, 4.267; *part*, exstrūctus, a, um, raised by, reclining on, 9.326. exstrūctum, ī, *n*, an elevated seat or tribunal, 5.290.

exsul, is, *c* an exile, 3.11.

exsulō, āvī, ātus *1 v* to be in exile, banished, or driven away, 11.263. (exsul).

exsultō, āvī, ātus *1 intens v* to spring; move with bold or exulting strides, 2.470; 10.643; advance proudly,

10.550; bound, 12.688; rise, surge in billows, swell, 3.557; bubble, 7.464; pant, 5.137; exult, rejoice, triumph, 2.386. (exsiliō).

exsuperō, āvī, ātus *1 v* to be completely above; mount upward, rise on high, 2.759; pass by, 3.698; pass over, 11.905; surpass, excel, 12.20; overrule, 7.591; surmount, 10.658; of wrath, boil over, 12.46.

exsurgō, surrēxī *3 v* to rise up; rise, 11.697; stand, 6.607.

exta, ōrum, *n pl* the inner parts of animals, esp. the upper portions, as distinguished from the lower intestines; entrails, 4.64.

extemplō *adv* immediately, forthwith, at once, directly, 6.210. (ex and tempus).

extendō, tendī, tentus or **tēnsus** *3 v* to stretch forth; stretch, extend, 5.374; continue, 12.909; magnify, advance, 6.806.

exter (**exterus**), **era, erum** *adj* (ex), on the outside; external, foreign, 4.350; *superl*, extrēmus (or extimus), a, um, outermost; outer, 12.925; last, most distant, farthest, 5.327; remotest, hindmost, last, 5.183; final, 3.714; consummating, finishing, 7.572; last in degree; extreme, basest, worst, 11.701; the instant of, verge of, 2.447; *subst* extrēma, ōrum, *pl n*, the most distant parts, 1.577; the last sufferings, death, 1.219; perils, 3.315; *adv*; extrēma, for the last time, one's last, 11.865.

externus, a, um *adj* (exter), external; pertaining to foreigners; foreign, 6.94; *subst* externus, ī, *m*, a stranger, 3.43.

exterreō, uī, itus 2 *v* to frighten; alarm, startle, terrify, 3.307; flutter in terror, 5.505; *part*, exterritus, a, um, startled; roused, 4.571.

extimēscō, timuī 3 *v* to be afraid, 8.129.

extollō 3 *v* to lift up; *figuratively* laud, extol, 11.401.

extorqueō, torsī, tortus 2 *v* to wrest out of, *with dat* 12.357.

extorris, e *adj* (ex and terra), out of one's country; exiled, *with abl*, 4.616.

extrā, *prep with acc* outside of, beyond, 6.796; out of; from, 2.672. (exterā, *abl* of exter).

extundō, tūdī, tūsus 3 *v* to beat out, emboss, 8.665.

exūberō, āvī, ātus 1 *v* to abound, overflow, 7.465.

exuō, uī, ūtus 3 *v* to put off; take off, lay aside, 1.690; unclasp, unbuckle, 9.303; put away, change, 4.319; divest; lay bare, strip, bare, 5.423; *with abl* of the thing from which, free from, 2.153 *et al.* (cf. induō).

exūrō, ussī, ūstus 3 *v* to burn out, consume with fire; burn up, 1.39; dry up, parch, 3.141; burn out, purge, 6.742.

exuviae, ārum *f* that which has been taken off; a garment, vestment, 4.496; armor, arms; spoils, 2.275; memorials, relics, 4.651; skin, 2.473; hide, 11.577. (exuō).

Fabaris, is *m* the Fabaris, a small branch of the Tiber, 7.715.

Fabius, iī *m* the name of a gens conspicuous in Roman history, of whom the most illustrious was Q. Fabius Maximus Verrucosus, who commanded the armies as dictator after the battle of Lake Trasimene, 6.845.

fabricātor, ōris *m* a constructor, contriver, framer, artificer, builder, 2.264. (fabricō).

Fabricius, iī *m* Fabricius, a Roman family name, esp. c Fabricius, consul, BC 281 and 278, conspicuous in the war with Pyrrhus, 6.844.

fabricō, āvī, ātus 1 *v*, and **fabricor, ātus sum** 1 *dep v* to construct, frame, build, 2.46. (fabrica, structure).

fabrīlis, e *adj* (faber, smith), pertaining to a smith; forging, 8.415.

facessō, cessī, cessītus 3 *intens v* to do effectively; perform, execute, 4.295. (faciō).

faciēs, ēī *f* the make or fashion of things; form, figure, 12.416; face, countenance, 1.658; image, specter, 7.448; aspect, 6.104; appearance, 3.310; form, kind, 6.560. (faciō).

facile *adv* easily.

facilis, e *adj* (faciō), that can be done; easy, 1.445; easily working, ready, skillful; of pliant, easy nature; good-natured; *superl*, facillimus, a, um, 11.761; *adv* facile, easily.

faciō, fēcī, factus 3 *v* to make or do, with or without an object; *freq*; constitute, render, make, 1.80; perform, execute, 1.302; do, 2.110; make or represent, in art, 8.710; compose, make; handle, manage, make, of sails or ropes, 5.281.830; suppose, grant, 4.540; to cause, make, *with inf*, 2.539; effect, cause that, take care, see, *with subj.*, 12.438; old *fut perf*; faxō, I will cause, will see to it, 9.154; *part*, factus, a, um, made, wrought, 10.527.

factum, ī, *n* a thing done; deed, action, achievement, 1.364.

Fādus, ī *m* a Rutulian, 9.344.

falcātus, a, um *adj* (falx), scythe-shaped; hooked, crooked, 7.732.

Faliscī, ōrum *m* the Falisci, a Tuscan people dwelling in Falerii; perhaps kindred with the Aequicoli, 7.695.

fallāx, ācis *adj* (fallō), prone to cheat; deceitful, treacherous, false, 5.850 *et al.*

fallō, fefellī, falsus 3 *v* to deceive, cheat, ensnare, beguile, 1.688; counterfeit, assume, 1.684; to be unobserved by, escape the notice of, 2.744; make useless or deceptive, 5.591; disappoint, 4.17; to violate an oath, 6.324; *passive* to deceive one's self, be mistaken, err, 5.49; (*impers*), fallit, it escapes one, is hid from or unknown to, 4.96.

falsus, a, um deceptive, misleading; delusive,

6.896; groundless, false, 2.83; pretended, feigned, 1.716; counterfeit, 3.302; longē fallēns, far-shooting (from a distant and unseen hand), 9.572. (fallō).

falx, falcis *f* a sickle, 4.513; a pruning hook or knife; scythe, 7.635.

fāma, ae *f* report, rumor, 1.532; tradition, 7.765; renown, name, fame, 1.463; glory, 9.195; fame, reputation, honor, 4.91; personified as a goddess, Fame, Rumor, 4.173. (cf. φήμη, report).

famēs, is *f* hunger, 1.216; famine, 3.256; greed, desire, 3.57; personified, Famine, Hunger, 6.276.

famula, ae *f* a female house slave; maidservant, 1.703. (famulus).

famulus, ī *m* pertaining to the house; a house servant or slave; manservant, 1.701; attendant, 5.95.

far, farris, *n* spelt, 4.402; grain or meal, 5.745.

fās, indecl *n* divine right or law; duty, justice, 3.55; privilege, 9.96; as predicate with esse, permitted, lawful, proper, incumbent, 1.77 *et al.* (rel to for).

fascis, is *m* a bundle; burden, *pl* fascēs, ium, the fasces or bundle of rods, a symbol of authority, borne by the lictors before the higher magistrates of Rome, 6.818; *metonym* civil honors.

fastīgium, iī, *n* that which is carried to a point or apex; the apex or point of a pediment; a gable, upper part of a house; roof, pinnacle, battlement, 2.444; slope of a trench; *figuratively* chief point, 1.342. (fastīgō).

fastus, ūs *m* haughtiness, pride, arrogance, 3.326.

fātālis, e *adj* (fātum), fated, 4.355; of fate or destiny, 2.165; sent by fate, 12.232; fraught with fate, destructive, calamitous, deadly, fatal, 12.919.

fateor, fassus sum 2 *dep v* to own, admit, acknowledge, confess, 2.134; tell, declare, 3.609; consent, 12.568. (*rel* to for).

fātidicus, a, um *adj* (fātum and dīcō), prophetic, soothsaying, 8.340.

fātifer, era, erum *adj* (fātum *and* ferō), fatal, deadly, 8.621.

fatīgō, āvī, ātus 1 *v* to weary, tire, 1.316; exhaust, 11.306; goad, 9.610; harass, vex, pursue, 6.533; infuriate, 9.63; rouse, 4.572; beat up, hunt, scour, 9.605; disturb, confound, 1.280; strike upon, beat, 10.304; demand with importunity, clamor for, 7.582.

fatīscō 3 *inc v* to come apart; to open, 1.123; gape open, 9.809.

fātum, ī, *n* that which is decreed; fate, lot, destiny, 1.299; a prophecy, an oracle, 1.382; misfortune, destruction, death, 4.20; natural destiny, a natural death, 4.696; the (usual) limits of life, 11.160. (for).

faucēs, ium *f* the jaws, throat, 2.358; *figuratively* mouth, entrance, jaws, 6.241; defiles, 11.516.

Faunus, ī *m* Faunus, the tutelary god of husbandmen, identified by the Romans with the Greek Pan, 7.254 *et al.* (faveō).

faveō, fāvī, fautus 2 *v* to be favorable to; befriend, favor, 1.735; applaud, 5.148; ore favēre, to keep reverent, religious, or solemn silence, 5.71.

favīlla, ae *f* ashes, embers, cinders, 3.573.

favor, ōris *m* good will, partiality, favor, 5.343. (faveō).

fax, facis *f* a torch; firebrand, 1.150; fire, 4.626; of a meteor, fiery train, 2.694.

fēcundus, a, um *adj* bringing forth; fruitful, productive, 6.598; teeming, 7.338.

fel, fellis, *n* the gall bladder; gall, bile; poison, 12.857; *figuratively* wrath, 8.220.

fēlix, īcis *adj* fruitful, 6.230; happy, lucky, fortunate, 3.493; successful, 11.196; skillful, 9.772; active, making happy; favorable, kind, propitious, 1.330.

fēmina, ae *f* a woman, 1.364.

fēmineus, a, um *adj* (fēmina), pertaining to women; female, 9.142; a woman's, of a woman, 2.584; of women, 4.667; fit for a woman, 12.53.

femur, oris, and (*from obsol* **femen**), **feminis,** *n* the thigh, 10.344; 788.

fenestra, ae *f* an opening for the admission of light; loop hole, window, 3.152; opening, gap, breach, 2.482. (*rel to* φαίνω, show).

fera, ae *f* a wild beast.

fērālis, e *adj* pertaining to the dead; funereal, funeral, 6.216; mournful, 4.462.

ferē *adv* almost, nearly, about; just, quite; generally, usually, for the most part; *freq*.

feretrum, ī, *n* a bier, 6.222. (ferō).

ferīnus, a, um *adj* (ferus), of wild beasts; of game; of animals, 11.571; *subst* ferīna (*sc* carō, flesh), ae, *f*, flesh, game, venison, 1.215.

feriō 4 *v* to smite or strike, 1.103; cut, 4.580; pierce, 12.304; slay, 10.315; strike or slay the covenant victim; hence, of a treaty, to make, 10.154.

feritās, ātis *f* fierceness, 11.568. (ferus).

ferō, tulī, lātus, ferre *irreg v* to bear, bring, carry, 1.702; bear away, 2.374; bring against, 12.465; carry, drive, 1.536; bear, bring forth, breed; produce, give, 1.605; conduct, lead, 6.295; offer, 3.19; aim, 12.299; cast, throw, 2.570; move, 3.490; induce, cause, attend, 5.356; suffer, allow, 2.94; take away, 2.555; destroy, 2.600; bring, afford, 1.463; grant, put, 3.145; render, make, 3.529; derive, have (others supply

sē with ferēbat), 11.341; bear, suffer, endure, 2.131; carry or lift, in praises, exalt, extol; bring tidings, report, 1.645; bring to light, disclose, 2.158; propose, 10.150; relate, tell, say, 2.230; call, 7.208; impel, prompt, direct, 2.34; require, 11.345; mē, tē, sē ferre, to bear, carry, present one's self; move, stalk, 8.199; return, 7.492; go, 2.456; appear, 1.503; rise, 6.241; rush, 2.672; boast, 5.373; *passive* ferrī, to be borne, carried, presented; to be rendered, to be, 4.110; rush, hurry, hasten, 2.337; ride, 5.587; march, 11.530; sail, 3.16; *part*, ferēns, of the wind, blowing; favoring, 4.430; sīgna ferre, to move the standards, move on to war, advance, 8.498; ferre manum, to engage in conflict, 5.403; ferre pedem, to come; return, go, 2.756.

Fērōnia, ae *f* an ancient Italian goddess, presiding over woods and orchards, 7.800.

ferōx, ōcis *adj* (ferus), wild; impetuous; ferocious, fiery, fierce, 5.277; warlike, martial; proud, 12.895.

ferrātus, a, um *adj* (ferrum), furnished or covered with iron; iron, 7.622; iron pointed, iron shod, 5.208; iron spurred, armed with the spur, 11.714.

ferreus, a, um *adj* (ferrum), of iron, iron-, 3.45; *figuratively* inflexible, stern, iron; of death, 10.745.

ferrūgineus, a, um *adj* (ferrūgō), of the color of iron rust; dusky, dark, 6.303.

ferrūgō, **inis** *f* iron rust; the color of iron rust; dusky or brown tint, 11.772; red or purple, 9.582. (ferrum).

ferrum, **ī**, *n* iron; an iron implement or weapon; battleax, ax, 2.55; sword, 1.350; arms; dart, arrow, 4.71; spear, javelin, 9.410; war, 10.10; iron point, 1.313; 9.633; curling iron, 12.100.

fertilis, **e** *adj* (ferō), productive, fertile, fruitful, 9.136.

ferus, **a**, **um** *adj* (rel to θήρ, wild beast), wild, untamed; fierce, 10.12; hard, cruel, 2.326; mad, frenzied, 6.49; of prey, carrion, 10.559.

ferus, **ī** *m* a wild beast; in *gen*, a brute; a beast, 2.51; courser, steed, 5.818; stag, 7.489.

ferveō, **ferbuī** *2 v*, and **fervō**, **fervī** *3 v* to boil; *figuratively* to blaze, be bright, 4.567; flash, 8.677; glow, 11.195; stir, be alive, teeming, 4.407; move, speed on, 1.436; rage, 9.693.

ferveō, **ferbuī** *2 v*, and **fervō**, **fervī** *3 v* to boil; *figuratively* to blaze, be bright, 4.567; flash, 8.677; glow, 11.195; stir, be alive, teeming, 4.407; move, speed on, 1.436; rage, 9.693.

fervidus, **a**, **um** *adj* (ferveō), glowing hot; glowing; fired, 9.736; furious, 7.397; boiling, 7.24; threatening, 12.894; eager, impetuous, 12.748.

fervor, **ōris** *m* fury, 10.578. (ferveō).

Fescennīnus, **a**, **um** *adj* (Fescennia), of Fescennia, a Tuscan city on the Tiber, 7.695.

fessus, **a**, **um** *adj* (rel to fatīscō), faint, wearied, tired; spent, exhausted, feeble, 2.596; languid; *figuratively* strained, sea-tossed, 1.168; afflicted, 3.145; wearied with, exhausted by, *with gen*, 1.178; *with abl*, 5.715.

festīnō, **āvī**, **ātus** *1 v* to make haste, hasten, 2.373; speed, quicken, hasten, 4.575.

festīnus, **a**, **um** *adj* (festīnō), hastening. 9.488.

fēstus, **a**, **um** *adj* festive, festal, 2.249.

fētus, **a**, **um** pregnant, with young; bearing; filled, full, teeming, 1.51; 2.238; having brought forth; fruitful.

fētus, **ūs** *m* a bearing or breeding; the young; the new swarm, 1.432; litter, 3.391; of vegetable products, growth, sprig, shoot, 6.207; fruit; product.

fibra, **ae** *f* a fiber, 6.600; root; entrail.

fībula, **ae** *f* a clasp, brooch, buckle, 5.313 *et al.* (figō).

fīctor, **ōris** *m* one who molds, or shapes; deviser, 9.602. (fingō).

fīctum, **ī**, *n* falsehood, 4.188. (fingo).

fīctus, **a**, **um** feigned, false, 2.107. (fingō).

fidēlis, **e** faithful, trusty, secure, 9.707. (fidēs).

Fīdēna, ae, and **Fīdēnae, ārum** *f*
Fidena, a town of the Sabines,
on the Tiber, five miles
northeast of Rome, 6.773.

fīdēns, entis *adj* trusting,
bold, confident, *with abl,
dat,* or *gen, freq* (fīdō).

fidēs, eī *f* a trusting; confidence,
faith, belief, reliance, trust,
3.69; confident hope, trust,
9.260; trustiness, faithfulness,
sincerity, fidelity, honor, 2.143;
4.597; an alliance, league,
10.71; truth, fact, 2.309;
certainty, assurance, 3.375;
personified as a goddess,
Faith, Fides, 1.292 *et al.* (fīdō).

fidēs, is, *mostly in the pl* **fidēs,
ium** *f* a lute string, string, or
stringed instrument, 6.120.

fīdō, fīsus sum *3 v* to confide,
trust, rely; *frequently with dat*
7.290; *with abl,* 5.398; *with
inf,* dare, 5.69; *part,* fīdēns,
entis, trusting, bold, confident,
with abl, dat, or *gen, freq*
(*rel to* πείθω, persuade).

fīdūcia, ae *f* confidence,
trust, reliance, assurance,
hope, 2.75 *et al.* (fīdō).

fīdus, a, um *adj* (fīdō),
trustworthy, faithful, trusty,
1.188; safe, secure, hospitable,
5.24; *with gen,* tuī fīdissima,
most faithful to thee, 12.659.

fīgō, fīxī, fīxus *3 v* to fix or
fasten; *frequently* the object
in or on which, in *the abl,*
1.212; *abl with prep,* 6.636; *acc
with prep,* 9.408; fasten up,
suspend from, 3.287; hang up,
1.248; set up, establish, make,
6.622; transfix, pierce, 5.516;

hurl (fix by hurling), 10.883;
wound, 10.343; inscribe, 11.84.

figūra, ae *f* a form, figure, shape,
12.862; sex, 6.449. (fingō).

fīlia, ae *f* a daughter, 7.52. (fīlius).

fīlius, iī *m* a son, 1.325.
(*rel to* fēmina).

fīlum, ī, *n* a thread, 6.30.

fimus, ī *m* mire, slime, 5.333.

findō, fidī, fissus *3 v* to
split, cleave, sever, crack;
separate, divide, 6.540.

fingō, fīnxī, fīctus *3 v* to
mold, shape, fashion, 8.726;
form; render, 2.80; arrange,
4.148; conceive, think out,
devise, invent, 3.18; feign,
11.406; imagine, suppose,
think, 4.338; of the will or
spirit, 6.80; *part,* fictus, a,
um, feigned; false, 2.107.

fīniō, īvī or **iī, ītus** *4 v* to end,
put an end to, 11.116. (fīnis).

fīnis, is, *m,* and *rarely f* a
boundary, limit, of space, time,
or action; term, end, 2.619;
1.241; a goal, 5.328; *pl* a starting
point or barrier, 5.139; borders,
1.339; a country, territories.

fīnitimus, a, um *adj* (fīnis),
pertaining to boundaries;
bordering upon, neighboring,
7.549; *subst* fīnitimus, ī,
m, a borderer; *pl* fīnitimī,
ōrum, neighboring
tribes, people, 5.106.

fīō, factus sum, fierī to be
made, done; sacrificed,
5.763; to become, 5.620.

firmō, āvī, ātus *3 v* to make firm
or strong; make steady, assure,

3.659; to establish, mature; confirm, 2.691; ratify, 12.212; encourage, 3.611, secure, guard, 11.466. (fīrmus).

fīrmus, a, um *adj* firm, strong, solid, 2.481; *figuratively* resolute, steadfast, 6.261.

fissilis, e *adj* (findō), easily split; fissile, 6.181.

flagellum, ī, *n* a scourge or whip, 5.579; thong, 7.731. (dim. of flagrum, a whip).

flāgitō, āvī, ātus *1 v* to ask importunately; demand, 2.124. (*rel to* flāgrō).

flāgrō, āvī, ātus *1 v* to be on fire or in flames; burn, blaze, 2.685; glow, 1.710; flash, 12.167; blush, 12.65; rage, 11.225.

flāmen, inis, *n* a blowing; blast, gale, breeze, wind, 4.241. (flō, blow).

flamma, ae *f* a blaze or flame; *frequently* fire, 6.6; torch, 6.518; signal fire, 2.256; funeral flame or fire, 5.4; lightning, 6.586; beam, 4.607; flaming brand, 2.478; burning rage; flame of wrath, wrath, revenge, 2.587; burning love, fire, passion, 1.673.

flammeus, a, um *adj* (flamma), like flame; fiery, flaming, 7.448.

flammō, āvī, ātus *1 v* to set in flames; *figuratively* inflame, enrage, 1.50. (flamma).

flātus, ūs *m* a blowing; wind; a blast, 4.442; breath, snorting, 11.911; *figuratively* boasting, pride, 11.346. (flō, blow).

flāveō, *no perf nor sup 2 v* to be yellow; *part,* flāvēns, entis, growing yellow, 10.324; *part,* yellow, golden, 4.590. (flāvus).

Flāvīnius, a, um *adj* (Flāvīnium), of Flavinium or Flavina, in Etruria; Flavinian, 7.696.

flāvus, a, um *adj* yellowish; yellow, 7.31; gold-tinted, golden, 1.592; 4.559; yellow-haired, golden-haired; pale green, 5.309.

flectō, flexī, flexus *3 v* to bend; make by twisting, weave, 7.632; turn, guide, 1.156; rein, manage, 9.606; influence, sway, bend, move; retain, check, 12.46.

fleō, flēvī, flētus *2 v* to shed tears; weep, 2.279; mourn; *v,* lament, bewail, weep for, 6.213 *et al.* (*rel to* fluō).

flētus, ūs *m* a weeping; tears, 3.599; a flood of tears, 2.271; lamentation, mourning, 4.463; tearful, sad message, 4.437. (fleō).

flexilis, e *adj* (flectō), flexible, pliant, 5.559.

flexus, a, um crooked, 5.500. (flectō).

flīctus, ūs *m* a striking, dashing, collision, stroke, 9.667. (flīgō).

flōreō, uī *2 v* to be in flower, bloom; to be adorned with flowers; *figuratively* blooming, decorated, 4.202; to be in the bloom, in the flower of age or life; to be prosperous, to flourish; to be bright, to flash, 11.433. (flōs).

flōreus, a, um *adj* (flōs), flowery, 1.430.

flōs, flōris *m* a blossom, flower, 6.708; flower, freshness, 7.162; down, 8.160; beauty, perfection, glory, flower, 8.500.

fluctuō, āvī, ātus *1 v* to wave, fluctuate; *figuratively* toss, 4.532; rage, boil, 12.527. (fluctus).

fluctus, ūs *m* a flowing; billow, surge, wave, 1.66; ocean, sea, 3.270; water, 5.182; *figuratively* of the mind, 12.831. (fluō).

fluentum, ī, *n* a stream, river, 4.143; current, water, 12.35. (fluō).

fluidus, a, um *adj* (fluō), flowing, fluid, running; dropping, 3.663.

fluitō, āvī, ātus *1 intens*, *n* to float, 5.867. (fluō).

flūmen, inis, *n* a stream, current, river, 3.389; torrent, flood, 2.305; water, 2.719; flood (of tears), 1.465; rēctō flūmine, by the direct stream, straight along the current or channel, 8.57. (fluō).

fluō, fluxī, fluxus *3 v* to flow; *frequently* run, stream, 5.200; drip, 5.179; pour forth, 12.444; flock, crowd, throng, 11.236; sink, fall, 11.828; ebb, droop, wane, 2.169; *part*, fluēns, entis, *figuratively* luxuriant; abounding with; *part*, fluxus, a, um, flowing away; perishing, waning, 10.88.

fluviālis, e *adj* (fluvius), pertaining to a river or brook, 4.635.

fluvius, iī *m* a stream; river, 1.607; water, fountains, abundant water; secundō fluviō, by the favoring stream, with or down the stream, 7.494. (fluō).

fluxus, a, um flowing away; perishing, waning, 10.88.

focus, ī *m* a fireplace, hearth, 5.660; home, 3.134; place where the funeral pyre has been consumed, place of burning, 11.212; fire, firebrand, 12.285.

fodiō, fōdī, fossus *3 v* to dig; pierce, 6.881.

foedē *adv* foully, basely, shamefully, 5.794. (foedus).

foedō, āvī, ātus *1 v* to make foul; defile, pollute, 3.227; *figuratively* disfigure, mutilate, 2.286; lacerate, wound, 12.871; break, tear in pieces, destroy, 2.55. (foedus).

foedus, a, um *adj* foul, filthy, loathsome, 3.216; malignant, 4.195; vile, base, 11.392.

foedus, eris, *n* a treaty, league, alliance, *frequently* truce, 5.496; side or party, 12.658; covenant, contract, 4.339; laws of hospitality, hospitality, 10.91; pledge, love, 4.520; law, term, condition, rule, 1.62. (*rel to* fīdō, trust).

folium, iī, *n* a leaf, 1.175.

follis is *m* a pair of bellows; the bellows, 8.449.

fōmes, itis *m* kindling stuff; fuel, 1.176. (foveō).

fōns, fontis *m* a spring, fountain, 1.244; water, 2.686; living water, 12.119; lake, 4.512.

for, fātus sum *1 dep v* to speak, report, say, 1.131.610; *ger.*, fandī; cōpia fandī, opportunity of speaking, 1.520; fandō, by report, 2.81; while speaking, 2.6; *part*, fandus, a, um; *subst* fandum, ī, *n*, that may be uttered; right, 1.543. (*rel to* φημί).

forceps, ipis *f* a pair of tongs, pincers, 8.453.

foris, is *f* a door; often in the *pl* with reference to double doors, 1.505; door or entrance. (*rel to* θύρα).

fōrma, ae *f* form, figure, shape, 1.72; beauty, 1.27; kind, species, sort (of penalty), 6.615; (of crime), 6.626.

formīca, ae *f* an ant, 4.402.

formīdō, āvī, ātus *1 v* to be in dread; to dread, fear; *part*, formīdātus, a, um, formidable, dreadful, 3.275.

formīdō, inis *f* dread, dismay, apprehension, terror, fear, 2.76; awe, 7.608; *personif*, Fear, Dismay, 12.335. (formīdō).

fōrmō, āvī, ātus *1 v* to form, fashion, train; build, 9.80. (fōrma).

fornāx, ācis *f* a furnace; forge, 7.636.

fornix, icis *m* an arch, vault, 6.631.

fors, fortis *f* chance, hazard, luck, hap, fortune, 1.377; *nom*, fors, as *adv* (for fors sit), haply, perchance, 2.139 *et al.*; *abl*, forte, by chance, perchance, haply, 1.375 *et al.* (*rel to* ferō).

forsan *adv* perhaps, 1.203. (for forsitan).

forsitan *adv* perchance, perhaps, 2.506. (fors sit an).

fortasse *adv* perhaps, 10.548.

forte by chance, perchance, haply, 1.375 *et al.*

fortis, e *adj* strong, physically, powerful, sturdy; strong in spirit; courageous, valiant, dauntless, bold, brave, 1.101; noble, 10.865.

fortūna, ae *f* fortune, destiny, lot, chance, fate, 1.628; success, 10.422; the proper moment, a chance, 12.920; misfortune, calamity, 12.593; personified, 3.53 *et al.* (fors).

fortūnātus, a, um *adj* (fortūna), befriended by fortune; fortunate, happy, blessed, prosperous, 1.437; *with gen*, 11.416.

Forulī, ōrum *m* a Sabine town, 7.714.

forum, ī, *n* a place of public assembly; market, exchange; forum, 5.758; Forum Rōmānum, the principal Roman forum or chief place of popular assemblies, situated nearly between the Capitol and the Palatine, 8.361.

forus, ī *m* a gangway between the rowing benches of a ship; the inferior, the hold or hatches of a ship or boat, 4.605; *pl* hatches, 6.412. (*rel to* forum).

fossa, ae *f* a ditch, trench, 7.157. (fodiō).

foveō, fōvī, fōtus 2 *v* to keep warm; *figuratively* foster, protect, cherish, 1.281; soothe, 12.420; caress, make love to, 1.718; rest, incline, 10.838; to toy away, enjoy, 4.193; cherish, hope, long, desire, 1.18.

frāgmen, inis, *n* a fracture; a piece broken off, fragment, 9.569. (frangō).

fragor, ōris *m* breaking, the noise of breaking; a crash; noise; a burst or clap of thunder, 2.692; roaring, uproar, 1.154; shout, 5.228; noise of lamentation, 11.214. (frangō).

fragōsus, a, um *adj* (fragor), crashing, clashing, roaring, noisy, 7.566.

frāgrō, 1 *m* to emit odor; be fragrant; *part*, frāgrāns, antis, fragrant, 1.436.

frangō, frēgī, frāctus 3 *v* to break, 1.104; crush, grind, 1.179; dishearten, discourage, 2.13; baffle; weaken, impair, ruin, destroy, 3.53.

frāter, frātris *m* a brother, 1.130.

frāternus, a, um pertaining to a brother; brother's, 4.21; fraternal, 5.24. (frāter).

fraudō, āvī, ātus 1 *v* to deprive of wrongfully; cheat, defraud (w. *abl* of the thing), 4.355. (fraus).

fraus, fraudis *f* fraud, deception, treachery, deceit, guile, 4.675; stratagem, ambuscade, 11.522; wickedness; fault, offense, 9.428; mischance, harm, 10.72;

hurt, harm, 11.708; treacherous nature, uncertainty, 9.397.

fraxineus, a, um *adj* (fraxinus), pertaining to the ash tree; of ash wood, ashen, ash, 6.181.

fraxinus, ī *f* an ash tree, 11.136.

fremitus, ūs *m* a murmuring, an uproar, din; tumult, shouting, 2.338 *et al.*; buzzing, humming; neighing, 11.607. (fremō).

fremō, uī, itus 3 *v* to make a murmuring noise; to roar, 1.56; whinny, neigh, 12.82; raise lamentations, 6.175; whiz, 12.922; resound, 4.668; rage, 5.19; to be fierce, furious, 4.229; fume, rave, 12.535; shout and sing, 4.146; *v*, rage, rave for, clamor for, 11.453 *et al.*; ore fremere, applaud, shout applause, 5.385; *part*, fremēns, entis, raging, 4.229.

fremor, ōris *m* a roaring, a murmur, 11.297. (fremō).

frēnō, āvī, ātus 1 *v* to bridle, 5.554; check, curb, restrain, 1.54.523. (frēnum).

frēnum, ī, *n*; **in the** *pl sometimes* **frēnī, ōrum** a bit, 4.135; bridle, reins, 3.542; *figuratively* 6.100.

frequēns, entis *adj* frequent; often present, often; in great numbers, thronging, 1.707; abounding in; plentiful.

frequentō, āvī, ātus 1 *v* to visit often; to visit or attend in great numbers; resort to, frequent, throng, inhabit, 6.478. (frequēns).

fretum, ī, *n* a frith or strait; water; the sea, 1.557.

frētus, a, um *adj* leaning on; *with abl* of the thing on which; relying on, confiding in, trusting to, 4.245.

frīgeō, frīxī 2 *v* to be cold, stiff with cold; stiffened, rigid with death, 6.219; to be benumbed, paralyzed, torpid, 5.396.

frīgidus, a, um *adj* (frīgeō), cold, 7.715; chilling, benumbing; chill, shuddering, 3.29; cool; *figuratively* without spirit, slow, *with dat* 11.338.

frīgus, oris, *n* cold, frost, 6.309; cold weather, a cold storm; coolness, cool breeze; frost; chilling, paralyzing fear, 1.92; the chill of death, 12.951. (*rel to* frīgeō).

frondeō 2 *v* to be leafy; to bear or put forth leaves; frondēns, leafy, 3.25; green; still bearing leaves, 4.399. (1. frōns).

frondēscō, fronduī 3 *inc v* to put forth leaves, 6.144. (frondeō).

frondeus, a, um formed of leaves; covered with leaves; leafy. (frōns).

frondōsus, a, um full of leaves, leafy; woody, 5.252. (frōns).

frōns, frondis *f* a leaf, 3.449; leafage, foliage; leafy spray, branch, twig, bough, 2.249; a leafy crown, a garland, wreath, 4.148.

frōns, frontis *f* the forehead, brow, 636; face, 11.238; 10.211; horns, 3.9.627; front, 1.166; prow, 5.158.

frūmentum, ī, *n* grain, corn; a grain, 4.406; growing wheat, blades of corn or wheat. (fruor).

fruor, frūctus and **fruitus sum** 3 *dep v* to enjoy, *with abl*, 3.352.

frūstrā *adv* in vain, to no purpose, 6.294 *et al.* (*rel to* fraus).

frūstror, ātus sum 1 *dep v* to render vain; frustrate, baffle, disappoint, 6.493. (frūstrā).

frūstum, ī, *n* a piece, 1.212.

frūx, frūgis *f* (found usually in the *pl* frūgēs, um) fruit, of the ground and of trees; fruit of the ground; corn, 1.178; wheaten meal, sacrificial grits, cake, 2.133; herbs, 6.420. (fruor).

Fūcinus, ī *m* a lake in the Apennines, east of Rome (now removed, or nearly so, by artificial drainage), 7.759.

fūcus, ī *m* the male bee; a drone, 1.435.

fuga, ae *f* a fleeing; a flight, 1.137; escape, 11.815; speed, 1.317; voyage, 3.190; *personif*, 9.719; ēripere, agitāre fugam, to hasten one's flight, 2.619.640; dare fugam, *with dat* to yield, i.e. take flight, 12.367. (fugiō).

fugāx, ācis *adj* (fugiō), swift in flight; fleet, 10.697; timid, 9.591.

fugiō, fūgī, fugitus 3 *v* to flee, fly, 2.528; recede, 6.61; run away from, outstrip, 10.266; flee back from, 11.405; escape, 2.156; shun, avoid; *with infin*, refuse, 9.200; *part*, fugiēns, entis, swift, flying, 11.654. (*rel to* φεύγω).

fugō, āvī, ātus *1 v* to put to
flight, drive, 6.312; make to
vanish, drive away, 3.521;
disperse, 1.143. (fugiō).

fulciō, fulsī, fultus *4 v* to sustain,
support, uphold, 4.247.

fulcrum, ī, *n* a support, prop,
post, foot, 6.604. (fulciō).

fulgēns, entis gleaming,
flashing, 2.749; glowing,
bright, 9.614. (fulgeō).

fulgeō, fulsī *2* and **fulgō** *3*
v to shine brightly; flash,
gleam, glance, 5.562.

fulgor, ōris *m* lightning,
flash of lightning, 8.431;
brilliancy, brightness,
splendor, 5.88. (fulgeō).

fulmen, inis, *n* lightning, 10.177;
thunderbolt, 2.649 *et al.*;
thunder, 1.230. (fulgeō).

fulmineus, a, um *adj*
(fulmen), like lightning;
gleaming, flashing, 4.580;
like lightning (with his
lightning darts), 9.812.

fulminō *1 v* to lighten, or
thunder, flash. (fulmen).

fulvus, a, um *adj* reddish or
tawny yellow; yellow, 5.374;
tawny, 2.722; brown, 11.751;
glowing, bright, 12.792.

fūmeus, a, um *adj* (fūmus),
smoky; smoking, 6.593.

fūmidus, a, um *adj* (fūmus),
smoking, 9.75; steaming, 7.465;
veiled with smoke, 7.76.

fūmifer, era, erum *adj*
(fūmus and ferō), smoke
bearing; smoky, 8.255.

fūmō, āvī, ātus *1 v* to smoke,
3.3 *et al.*; send up vapor;
fume, reek, 2.698; foam,
12.338. (fūmus).

fūmus, ī *m* smoke, 2.609 *et al.*

fūnālis, e *adj* (fūnis), made of or
pertaining to a rope, cord, or
wick; *subst* fūnāle, is, *n*, a wax
taper, candle, torch, 1.727.

funda, ae *f* a sling, 9.586.

fundāmentum, ī, *n* a foundation,
4.266. (1. fundō).

fundātor, ōris *m* a founder,
7.678. (1. fundō).

funditus *adv* completely,
utterly, entirely, 6.736.

fundō, āvī, ātus *1 v* to make or
lay the bottom of anything;
to found, erect, build, 4.260;
establish, render stable,
organize, 6.811; of ships,
hold to the bottom, fasten,
moor, hold, 6.4. (fundus).

fundō, fūdī, fūsus *3 v* to pour;
frequently pour in, 12.417;
pour forth, 2.329; discharge,
11.610; shed, 3.348; emit,
2.684; put forth, 12.207; bear,
8.139; disperse, rout, defeat,
2.421; prostrate, slay, 1.193;
utter, 3.344; *passive* fundī,
to spread, gather, crowd,
3.635; to assemble, swarm,
6.709; *part*, fūsus, a, um,
lying extended, stretched out;
expended, thrown away, 7.421;
flowing, 10.137; overspread,
10.838; fundī circum, to
encompass, encircle, 12.433.

fundus, ī *m* the bottom, 2.419;
depth, abyss, 6.581; the

ground; a farm; fundō, from
the foundation, 10.88.

fūnereus, **a**, **um** *adj* (fūnus), of
a funeral; funeral-, 4.507.

fūnestus, **a**, **um** *adj* (fūnus),
fatal, destructive, 7.322.

fungor, **fūnctus sum** *3 dep v* to
perform, fulfill, discharge,
pay, *with abl*, 6.885.

fūnis, **is** *m* a rope, 2.239 *et al.*;
cord, string, 5.488.

fūnus, **eris**, *n* a funeral;
frequently funeral rites,
4.308; death, carnage, 2.361;
corpse, dead body, 6.150;
deathbed, 9.491; funeral
pyre, 11.189; calamity, 1.232;
pl fūnera, um, a corpse
prepared for burial, 9.486.

furiae, **ārum** *f* rage, fury,
madness, frenzy, 1.41 *et al.*;
vengeance, 8.494; *personif*,
Furiae, ārum, the goddesses of
vengeance, the Furies, Allecto,
Megaera, and Tisiphone;
the Avengers, 3.331; for the
Harpies, 3.252. (furō).

furiālis, **e** *adj* (furiae),
raging, 7.375.

furibundus, **a**, **um** *adj* (furō),
filled with frenzy; raging,
raving, wild, frantic, 4.646.

furiō, **āvī**, **ātus** *1 v* to
madden, enrage, infuriate,
2.407. (furiae).

furō, **uī** *3 v* to be mad; *frequently*
to rave, be frantic, rage,
1.491; to be furious, burn,
storm (for war), 7.625; to be
burning or mad with love,
1.659; to be frenzied, in a
frenzy, 6.100; inspired, 2.345;

distracted with grief, 3.313;
plunge madly, 9.552; boil,
7.464; with cognate *acc*, give
vent to one's fury, 12.680.

fūror, **ātus sum** *1 dep v* to
steal, *with acc and dat*
5.845; *part*, fūrātus, a, um,
having stolen, *with dat* and
ellipsis of *acc*, 7.283. (fūr).

furor, **ōris** *m* rage, madness,
fury, 1.150 *et al.*; frenzy, 4.91;
love, desire; *personif as a*
deity, a Fury, 1.294. (furō).

fūrtim *adv* by stealth,
secretly, 2.18. (fūr).

fūrtīvus, **a**, **um** *adj* (fūrtum), of
the nature of stealing; stealthy,
secret, 4.171; *adv* fūrtīvum,
stealthily, in secret, 7.660.

fūrtum, **ī**, *n* that which is
stolen; *metonym* the act
of stealing; theft; secrecy,
concealment, 4.337; artifice,
deceit, fraud, deception, 6.24;
treacherous deed (adultery),
10.91; stealthy attack,
stratagem, 9.350; fūrta bellī,
an ambuscade, 11.515. (fūr).

fuscus, **a**, **um** *adj* dark,
dusky, 7.408.

futtilis, **e** *adj* (fundō), vain,
weak, foolish, 11.339; brittle,
treacherous, 12.740.

futūrum, **ī**, *n* the future, 4.508;
pl things to come, 6.12.

futūrus, **a**, **um** about to be;
future, 4.622. (sum).

Gabiī, **ōrum** *m* Gabii, a town
of Latium at the foot of
the Alban hills, 6.773.

Gabīnus, a, um *adj* (Gabii), of Gabii, Gabinian, 7.612.

gaesum, ī, *n* a Gallic javelin, long and heavy; a gaesum, 8.662.

Gaetūlus, a, um *adj* Gaetulian, African, 5.351.

Galaesus, ī *m* a Latin nobleman, 7.535.

Galatēa, ae *f* a sea-nymph, daughter of Nereus, 9.103.

galea, ae *f* a helmet, either of leather or of metal, 3.468 *et al.*

galērus, ī *m* a cap of fur or undressed skin; hat, cap, 7.688. (*rel to* galea).

Gallus, ī *m* a Gaul, 6.858; Gallī, ōrum, *m*, the Gauls, 8.656.

Gangēs, is *m* a river of India, 9.31.

Ganymēdēs, is *m* Ganymede, son of Tros, and cup-bearer of Jupiter, 1.28.

Garamantes, um (*acc pl* **-as**) *m* the Garamantes, a barbarian tribe of Northern Africa, in the modern Fezzan, 6.794. (Γαράμαντες).

Garamantis, idis *adj* f. (Garamas), Garamantian, 4.198.

Gargānus, ī *m* a mountain in Apulia, 11.247.

gaudeō, gāvīsus sum *2 v* to be affected with joy; foll. by *abl*, to rejoice in, *freq*; with *inf*, 2.239 *et al.*

gaudium, iī, *n* joyful feeling; delight, pleasure, joy, 1.502; *pl* joyful hope, 10.652; love, 10.325; *personif*, Gaudia, ōrum, Pleasures, 6.279. (gaudeō).

gāza, ae *f* strictly, the Persian royal treasure; in *gen*, riches, wealth, treasure, 1.119. (a Persian word, Greek form, γάζα).

Gela, ae *f* Gela, an ancient Greek town of Sicily on the river Gela, 3.702.

gelidus, a, um *adj* (gelū), frosty, ice-cold; cold, cool, icy, chilling, 2.120; chilled, 3.30.

Gelōnus, ī *m* a Gelonian, or Scythian; *pl* Gelōnī, ōrum, the Scythians, 8.725.

Gelōus, a, um *adj* (Gela), belonging to Gela; of Gela, 3.701.

gelū, ūs, *n* frost, cold, numbness, chilled blood, 8.508.

geminus, a, um *adj* twin, 1.274 *et al.*; twofold, 6.203; double, two, 4.470; *pl* geminī, ae, a, twin, 2.500; two, 1.162.

gemitus, ūs *m* a groaning; a groan, 3.39 *et al.*; sigh, 1.485; lamentation, 2.486; cry, 2.413; noise, roaring, 3.555. (gemō).

gemma, ae *f* a bud, precious stone, gem, 1.655 *et al.*

gemō, uī, itus *3 v* to groan, 7.501; sigh, 1.465; bemoan, bewail, lament, 1.221; of inanimate things, creak, 6.413.

gena, ae *f* the cheek, 4.644 *et al.*; eye, 6.686.

gener, erī *a* son-in-law, 2.344 *et al.*

generātor, ōris *m* one who begets; a breeder, 3.704. (generō).

generō, āvī, ātus *1 v* to beget,
with *abl* of source, 7.734;
produce; *part*, generātus,
a, um, descended, sprung
from, 5.61. (genus).

generōsus, a, um *adj*
(genus), of high lineage,
noble-blooded, generous,
renowned, famed, 10.174.

genetrīx, īcis *f* she who
brings forth; mother,
1.590 *et al.* (gignō).

geniālis, e *adj* (genius),
pertaining to, or sacred to
the birth-spirit, or guardian
genius; genial, joyous,
happy, festive, 6.603.

genitor, ōris *m* he who begets;
father, sire, 1.155 *et al.* (gignō).

genius, īī *m* the birth-spirit;
a tutelar deity, or guardian
genius, 5.95. (genō, gignō).

gēns, gentis *f* a family stock
or gens; a race; a clan or
tribe, 10.202; nation, 1.17;
people, 3.133; lineage, child,
offspring, descendant, 10.228;
descent, 11.331; *metonym* a
country, land, 1.533; 11.324;
pl gentēs, ium, nations;
the world. (genō, gignō).

genū, ūs *n* a knee, 1.320
et al. (γόνυ).

genus, eris *n* birth, origin,
lineage, descent, 1.132; noble
birth, nobility, 5.621; offspring,
progeny, 5.737, et al; a son,
descendant, 6.500; family,
4.365; tribe, people, nation,
race, 1.6 *et al.*; breed, 7.753;
sort, kind, 2.468 *et al.* (genō).

germānus, a, um *adj* of the same
parentage; particularly, of
the same father; own; *subst*
germānus, ī, *m*, own brother;
brother, 1.341 *et al.*; germāna,
ae, *f*, own sister; sister, 4.478.

gerō, gessī, gestus *3 v* to carry,
bear, 12.97 *et al.*; wear, 2.156;
assume, put on as a guise,
1.315; 12.472; bear, produce,
have, enjoy, 2.90; take, feel,
12.48; wage, carry on, 1.24;
achieve, manage, 7.444;
do (of conduct), 9.203.

Gēryon, onis, and **Gēryonēs,
ae** *m* Geryon, a giant with
three bodies, dwelling in
Gades, slain by Hercules,
who carried his herd of
cattle to Italy, 7.662; 8.202.

gestāmen, inis, *n* that which
is carried; equipment,
weapon, defense, 3.286;
crown, 7.246. (gestō).

gestō, āvī, ātus *1 v* to carry
habitually; bear, 1.336;
have, 1.567. (gerō).

Getae, ārum *m* the Getae, a
Thracian people dwelling
on the Danube.

Geticus, a, um *adj* (Getae),
pertaining to the Getae;
Getan, Thracian, 3.35.

gignō, genuī, genitus *3 v* beget,
10.848 *et al.*; bear, bring forth,
1.618 *et al.*; *part*, genitus,
a, um, *with abl* of source,
begotten of, born of, 9.642; son
of, 1.297. (γίγνομαι, become).

glaciālis, e *adj* (glaciēs),
of ice; icy, 3.285.

glaciēs, ēī *f* ice, 4.251 *et al.*

gladius, ī *m* a sword, 9.769 *et al.*

glaeba, ae *f* a lump of earth; a clod; soil, 1.531.

glāns, glandis *f* an acorn; a leaden ball or bullet, 7.686.

glaucus, a, um *adj* dark, 6.416; sea-green, 12.885. (γλαυκός, bluish gray).

Glaucus, ī *m* a fabled fisherman of Boeotia, one of the Argonauts, who was transformed into a sea-god, 5.823. 2. The father of Deiphobe, the Cumaean sibyl, 6.36. 3. A Lycian prince, allied with Priam, and slain by Ajax, son of Telamon, 6.483.

glīscō *3 inc v* to grow, swell; rise, increase, rage, 12.9.

globus, ī *m* any body of a spherical form; a globe, ball, 3.574; sphere, 6.725; phalanx, battalion, mass of assailants, 9.515; a mass of smoke or dust; a cloud, 9.36.

glomerō, āvī, atus *1 v* to gather into a ball or mass; roll, whirl, 3.577; collect; assemble, gather, 2.315; *passive* glomerārī, in mid. signif., to throng, gather; troop, flock, 1.500. (glomus, ball).

gloria, ae *f* glory, fame, renown, 2.83, et. al.; love of fame, ambition, 5.394.

Gorgō, onis the common name of the three daughters of Phorcus, terrible on account of their snaky hair; especially, the head of the Gorgon on the shield of Minerva, 2.616.

Gorgoneus, a, um *adj* (Gorgōn), pertaining to a Gorgon; Gorgonian, 7.341.

Gortynius, a, um *adj* of Gortyna, a town in Crete; Gortynian, Cretan.

gōrytus, ī *m* a quiver, 10.169.

Gracchus, ī *m* the name of a Roman family in the gens Sempronia, especially Tiberius and Gains, 6.842.

gracilis, e *adj* thin, slender.

gradior, gressus sum *3 dep v* to step, walk, go, 1.312; move, advance, 10.572.

Gradīvus, ī *m* the one who steps or marches; an epithet of Mars, 3.35. (gradior).

gradus, ūs *m* a step, footstep, pace, 3.598; step, stair, 1.448; cōnferre gradum, to walk side by side, 6.488. (gradior).

Graecia, ae *f* Greece.

Grāī (Grāiī) (*dissyll*), **ōrum** *m* the Greeks, 1.467 *et al.*

Grāiugena, ae (*quadrisyll*) *m* a native Greek; a Greek, 3.550. (Grāius and gignō).

Grāius, a, um (*dissyll*) *adj* Greek, Greek, 2.598; subs., Grāius, iī, *m*, a Greek, 3.594.

grāmen, inis, *n* grass, 3.537 *et al.*; a blade of grass or of grain, 7.809; plant; herb, 2.471; pasture, meadow; grassy field, plain, 7.655.

grāmineus, a, um *adj* (grāmen), of turf, grassy, 5.287 *et al.*

grandaevus, a, um *adj* (grandis and aevum), very aged; old, aged, 1.121.

grandis, e *adj* large, great; big, ponderous, 4.405.

grandō, inis *f* hail, 4.120 *et al.*

grātēs defect. (found only in *nom* and *acc pl*), f. (grātor), thanks, 1.600; in a bad sense, return, reward, 2.537.

grātia, ae *f* acceptableness, agreeableness; charm, delight, love, 6.653; gratefulness, gratitude, thankfulness, 4.539; regard, 7.402. (grātus).

grātor, ātus sum 1 *dep v* to wish joy to; *with dat* (the *acc* is doubtful), rejoice with; congratulate, 4.478; greet, welcome (perhaps *with* esse), 5.40. (grātus).

grātus, a, um *adj* acceptable, pleasing, agreeable, welcome, 2.269 *et al.*; dear, 10.158; thankful, grateful, 11.127.

gravidus, a, um *adj* (gravis), heavy, 7.507 *et al.*; with young, pregnant; *figuratively* pregnant, teeming with, 4.229.

gravis, e *adj* heavy, 1.728 *et al.*; pregnant, 1.274; ponderous, firm, 5.437; *figuratively* grave, venerable, 1.151; stern, grave (gravely), 5.387; cruel, 10.630; fierce, 10.755; weighed down with years or disease; infirm, enfeebled, 2.436; grievous, hard, 6.56; painful, deep, 4.1; offensive; *compar* graviōra, um, *subst n pl* greater hardships, sufferings, 1.199.

Graviscae, ārum *f* Graviscae or Gravisca, a Tuscan town, 10.184.

graviter *adv* heavily; deadly, 7.753; greatly, deeply, 1.126; heavily, mournfully, 2.288. (gravis).

gravō, āvī, ātus 1 *v* to weigh down, 9.437; oppress, burden, 2.708; *passive* to resist, yield reluctantly, 10.628. (gravis).

gremium, iī, *n* the lap, the bosom, 1.685 *et al.*; ante gremium suum, in front of or before one's self, 11.744.

gressus, ūs *m* a stepping; step, walk, course, way, 1.401; of a ship, 5.162; air, mien, gait, 5.649; ferre gressum, to walk, 6.677; efferre gressum, to go forth or out, 2.753; comprimere gressum, to stop, stay one's steps, 6.389. (gradior).

grex, gregis *m* a herd, 6.38; flock; litter; the young, 8.85.

grus, gruis *f* a crane.

Grynēus, a, um *adj* of Grynia, a town in Asia Minor, the seat of one of the oracles of Apollo; Gryneian, 4.345.

gubernāculum, ī, *n* a helm, 5.176. (gubernō, steer).

gubernātor, ōris *m* a helmsman, pilot, 3.269. (gubernō).

gurges, itis *m* a whirlpool, gulf, 3.421; flood, 2.497; wave, billow, 3.564; rolling, raging sea, abyss, 1.118; sea, ocean, 7.704.

gustō, āvī, ātus 1 *v* to taste, 1.473. (gustus, taste).

gutta, ae *f* a drop, 3.28.

guttur, uris, *n* the throat, 6.421.

Gyaros, ī *f* one of the Cyclades, between Tenos and Ceos, 3.76.

Gyās, ae *m* 1. Gyas, commander of one of the ships of Aeneas, 1.222. 2. A Latin slain by Aeneas, 10.318.

Gygēs, ae or **is** *m* a Trojan, 9.762.

Gylippus, ī *m* an Arcadian slain by Tolumnius, 12.272.

gyrus, ī *m* a circle, circular track, ring; circuit, 10.884; coil, 5.85.

habēna, ae *f* a rein, 1.63 *et al.*; strap, thong, 9.587; whip, 7.380; immissīs or laxīs habēnīs, with all the reins let out, without restraint, unchecked, 5.662; pressīs or adductīs habēnīs, with tightened reins, 12.622. (habeō).

habeō, uī, itus 2 *v* to have, in the most general sense, *freq*; hold, possess, 5.262; wield, use, 12.88; maintain, keep up, perpetuate; seize, inspire, possess, animate, 4.581; deem, esteem, reckon, regard, 2.102; designate, call, 12.134; hōc habet, he has got it, he is wounded, 12.296.

habilis, e *adj* (habeō), handy, wieldy, convenient, easily handled, light, 11.555; well formed, 1.318; well fitted for, adapted to, fit for; well fitted, 9.365.

habitō, āvī, ātus 1 *intens v* to have continually, have in possession; occupy, inhabit, 3.106; dwell, 3.110. (habeō).

habitus, ūs *m* the having itself or one's self; condition, habit; dress, attire, 1.315. (habeō).

hāc *adv* by this way or route, 8.203; this way, here, 1.467; on one side, 12.565.

hāctenus *adv* thus far, so far, of space and time; thus far (separated by tmesis), 5.603; 6.62.

Hādriacus, a, um *adj* (Hādria), pertaining to the Adriatic Sea; Adriatic, 11.405.

haedus, ī *m* a kid; Haedī, ōrum, *m*, the constellation of the Kids in the hand of Auriga, whose rising portends storms.

Haemōn, onis *m* a Rutulian, 9.685.

Haemonidēs, ae *m* a Latin slain by Aeneas, 10.537.

haereō, haesī, haesus 2 *v* to stick; foll. by *dat*, or by *abl with* or without a *prep*; hang, cling, adhere, cling to, 1.476 *et al.*; stop, stand fixed, 6.559; halt, 11.699; adhere to as companion, 10.780; stick to in the chase, 12.754; persist, 2.654; dwell, 4.4; pause, hesitate, 3.597; be fixed or decreed, 4.614.

Halaesus, ī *m* 1. An ally of Turnus, formerly companion of Agamemnon, 7.724. 2. Another ally of Turnus, 10.411.

hālitus, ūs *m* a breathing; breath, 4.684; exhalation, vapor, 6.240. (hālō).

Halius, iī *m* a Trojan, 9.767.

hālō, āvī, ātus *1 v* to breathe; exhale or emit odor; be fragrant or redolent, 1.417.

Halys, yos *m* a Trojan, 9.765.

Hammōn, ōnis *m* Jupiter, or Zeus Ammon, a god of Egypt and Libya, 4.198.

hāmus, ī *m* a hook, ring, 3.467.

harēna, ae *f* sand, 1.112; sandy shore, strand, 1.540; sandy ground, arena; space for races; an arena, 5.336.

harēnōsus, a, um *adj* (harēna), sandy, 4.257.

Harpalycē, ēs *f* a Thracian huntress, daughter of King Harpalycus, 1.317.

Harpalycus, ī *m* a Trojan warrior, 11.675.

Harpyia (*trisyll*), **ae** *f* a Harpy, a fabled monster, half woman and half bird, 3.112 *et al.*

harundineus, a, um *adj* (harundō), of reeds, reedy, 10.710.

haruspex, icis *m* an inspector of entrails; diviner, soothsayer, prophet, 8.498.

hasta, ae *f* a spear, 2.50, and *freq*; hasta pūra, a headless spear, 6.760; pampinea hasta, a thyrsus, 7.396.

hastīle, is, *n* the shaft of a spear; a spear, lance, javelin, 1.313 *et al.*; a spear-like sapling or branch; a shoot, 3.23. (hasta).

haud *adv* not at all; not, 1.387 *et al.*

haudquaquam not at all.

hauriō, hausī, haustus *4 v* to draw any fluid, 9.23; drink; drain, 1.738; draw blood with a weapon; devour, slay, 2.600; pierce, 10.314; take in with the eyes or ears; receive, 12.26; perceive, see, 4.661; hear, 4.359; strain, thrill, 5.137; suffer, 4.383; conceive, 10.648.

hebeō *2 v* to be blunt; *figuratively* to be sluggish, run slowly, 5.396.

hebetō, āvī, ātus *1 v* to make blunt; to make dull; to impair, dim, obscure, 2.605. (hebes, blunt).

Hēbrus, ī *m* a river of Thrace, 1.317 *et al.*; a Trojan slain by Mezentius, 10.696.

Hecatē, ēs *f* the sister of Latona; usually identified with Diana and Luna, and so represented with three heads, 4.511.

Hector, oris *m* son of Priam, and chief defender of Troy, 1.99 *et al.*

Hectoreus, a, um *adj* (Hector), of Hector, 2.543; Hectorean, Trojan, 1.273.

Hecuba, ae *f* daughter of Dymas and wife of Priam, 2.501 *et al.*

hēla (*interj*), up! come on! away! 4.569.

Helena, ae *f* Helen, daughter of Jupiter and Leda, sister of Clytemnestra and of Castor, and wife of Menelaus; on account of her flight with Paris to Troy, the immediate cause of the ten years' siege and destruction of that city; whence she was carried back by Menelaus to Sparta, 1.650 *et al.*

Helēnor, oris *m* a Lycian, follower of Aeneas, 9.545.

Helenus, ī *m* a prophet, son of Priam; carried away captive by Pyrrhus to Epirus, where he became the husband of Andromache and ruler of a small kingdom, 3.329 *et al.*

Helicōn, ōnis *m* a mountain in Boeotia, and favorite resort of Apollo and the Muses, 7.641 *et al.*

Helōrus, ī *m* a river on the S. E. coast of Sicily, 3.698.

Helymus, ī *m* a Sicilian Trojan, and friend of King Acestes, 5.73 *et al.*

herba, ae *f* any grassy or herbaceous growth; grass, turf, 1.214, et al; fodder; herb, plant, 3.650; grassy land, pasture, meadow, 3.221; a plant.

Herbēsus, ī *m* a Rutulian, 9.344.

Herculēs, is *m* the god of strength and labor, son of Jupiter and Alcmena, 5.410 *et al.*

Herculeus, a, um *adj* (Herculēs), of Hercules; Herculean, 3.551 *et al.*

hērēs, ēdis *m* an heir, 4.274.

Herminius, iī *m* a Tuscan, 11.642.

Hermionē, ēs *f* daughter of Menelaus and Helen, and wife of Orestes, 3.328.

Hermus, ī *m* a river in Aeolis, depositing gold, 7.721.

Hernicus, a, um *adj* (Hernicī), of the Hernici, an Italian tribe of Latium; Hernican, 7.684.

hērōs, ōis *m* a demigod; a hero, 6.192 *et al.*; an illustrious man, champion, hero, 5.453.

Hēsionē, ēs *f* daughter of Laomedon, saved from a sea monster by Hercules, and afterwards wife of Telamon, 8.157.

Hesperia, ae *f* the western land; Italy, 1.569 *et al.*

Hesperis, idis, *pl* **Hesperides, um** *f* the daughters of Hesperus, the Hesperides; called also daughters of Erebus and Nox, to whom was given the care of the fabled gardens of the Hesperides, in an island of the Atlantic west of Mount Atlas, 4.484; *adj*, Hesperian, Italian, 8.77.

Hesperius, a, um *adj* of Hesperus; western (as related to Asia and Greece); Hesperian, Italian, 3.418.

hesternus, a, um *adj* of yesterday, yesterday's, 8.543.

heu (*interj*), alas! ah! oh! 2.289 *et al.*

heus (*interj*), ho! hilloa! lo there! 1.321 *et al.*

hiātus, ūs *m* a gaping; throat, 6.576; opening, 11.680; cleft, chasm, vortex, abyss, 6.237. (hiō).

hīberna, ōrum, *n* winters, 1.266.

hībernus, a, um *adj* (*rel to* hiems), of winter; wintry (others, in winter), 4.143;

tempestuous, stormy, 4.309; *subst* hīberna, ōrum, *n*, winters, 1.266.

Hibērus, a, um *adj* Iberian, Spanish, 9.582; western, 11.913.

hīc *adv* here, there, 1.247, et al; of time, hereupon, thereupon, 1.728; now, then, here, 5.340; in this work, 10.73. (hīc).

hīc, haec, hōc (pron., referring to the first person), this; he, she, it; (*pl*), these, they; *frequently* (for meus), 9.205; (for is), 1.742; (repeated), hic — hīc, one — another, the one — the other, this — that; (*pl*), these — those, some — others; hīc — ille, the latter — the former; this — that, the one — the other; *freq.*

Hicetāonius, a, um *adj* (Hicetāon), of Hicetaon; the son of Hicetaon, 10.123.

hiems, hiemis *f* winter, 3.285; storm, tempest, 1.122; *personif*, 3.120.

Himella, ae *m* a river of the Sabine country, 7.714.

hinc *adv* from this place, from here, hence, 3.111; from that place, hence, thence, 3.707; from that or this time (others, from this thing), 2.97; henceforth, 2.148; for ab hōc or ab hīs, 9.763; then, thereupon, 1.194; hinc — hinc, on this side — on that, here — there, 4.40; hinc atque hinc, on both sides, on either side, 1.162. (hīc).

hiō *āvī, ātus 1 v* to yawn, gape; to distend or open the mouth, 6.493; *part*, hiāns, antis, with open mouth, 12.754.

Hippocoōn, ontis *m* companion of Aeneas, 5.492.

Hippolytē, ēs *f* an Amazon, captured by Theseus, 11.661.

Hippolytus, ī *m* son of Theseus and Hippolyte, 7.761.

Hippotadēs, ae *m* the son of Hippotas, Amastrus, 11.674.

hirsūtus, a, um *adj* rough, shaggy, hairy.

hirundō, inis *f* a swallow.

Hisbō, ōnis *m* a Rutulian, 10.384.

hīscō *3 v* to gape, open the mouth; speak in broken utterances, falter, 3.314. (hiō).

hispidus, a, um *adj* shaggy, hairy, 10.210.

hodiē *adv* today, 2.670, et *freq* (hōc and diē).

homō, inis, *c* man, a human being; *frequently* mortal, 1.328.

Homolē, ēs *f* a mountain near Tempe, in Thessaly, 7.675.

honestus, a, um *adj* (honōs), honorable, honored; good; fair, 12.155.

honōrō, āvī, ātus *1 v* to honor; keep, observe with honor, 5.50. (honōs).

honōs, ōris *m* honor, praise, renown, glory, 1.609 *et al.*; recompense, reward, 1.253; an honor, prize, 5.342; *metonym* sacrifice, offering, 1.49; luster, beauty, 1.591; celebration, game, ceremonial, festival, 5.601; libation, 3.178; a robe or mantle, 7.815.

hōra, ae *f* with the Romans, the twelfth part of the period from sunrise to sunset, an hour; in an indefinite sense, 4.679; *personif*, Hōrae, ārum, *f*, the Hours, 3.512.

horrendum *adv* frightfully, fearfully, 6.288. (horreō).

horrendus, a, um to be shuddered at; dreadful, fearful, 2.222; awe-inspiring, venerable, 6.10; strange, wonderful, 8.565; fierce, warlike, 11.507. (horreō).

horrēns, entis bristling, bristly, 1.634; rough, roughening, 1.165; fierce, 10.237. (horreō).

horreō 2 *v* to bristle up or be bristling, 6.419; to bristle, 11.602; *figuratively* to shudder, tremble, 2.12; shudder at, fear, dread, 4.209.

horrēscō, horruī 3 *v* to become rough; bristle, rise bristling, 7.526; *figuratively* to tremble, shudder, 2.204; dread, 3.394. (horreō).

horribilis, e *adj* (horreō), to be shuddered at; frightful, dreadful, horrible, fearful, 11.271.

horridus, a, um *adj* (horreō), rough, bristling, 3.23 *et al.*; bristling with arms; shaggy, grizzly, stiffened, 4.251; blustering, tempestuous, 9.670; terrible, fearful, 1.296.

horrifer, fera, ferum *adj* (horreō and ferō), fear-bringing; dreadful, 8.435.

horrificō, āvī, ātus 1 *v* to make rough; make to shudder; terrify, 4.465. (horrificus).

horrificus, a, um *adj* (horreō and faciō), occasioning horror; terrible, fearful, 3.225.

horrisonus, a, um *adj* (horreō and sonus), having or making a fearful sound; harsh-sounding, thundering, 6.573.

horror, ōris *m* a roughening or bristling; *figuratively* a shuddering; terror, dread, horror, dismay, 2.559; clashing din, 2.301. (horreō).

hortātor, ōris *m* one giving encouragement or inciting; an instigator, 6.529. (hortor).

hortor, ātus sum 1 *dep v* to encourage, urge, 2.74; advise, counsel, 2.33.

hospes, itis *m* one who either gives or receives the entertainment of a guest; a guest, 1.753 *et al.*; a visitor, stranger, 4.10; host, 11.105.

hospitium, iī, *n* the relation of host and guest; hospitality, 10.460; friendly reception, entertainment; protection, hospitality, welcome, 1.299; guest-land, ally, 3.15; refuge, 1.540; alliance, 11.114. (hospes).

hospitus, a, um *adj* (hospes), welcoming; friendly, hospitable; foreign, strange, 3.377; friendly, 3.539.

hostia, ae *f* a sacrificial animal; victim, 1.334 *et al.*

hostīlis, e *adj* (hostis), of an enemy, an enemy's, 10.847;

of the foe, 3.322; hostile, unpropitious, ominous, 3.407.

hostis, is, *c* a stranger; foreigner; an enemy, foe, 1.378, and *freq*.

hūc *adv* to this place; hither, here, 2.18, and *freq*; hūc — hūc, this way and this, or this way and that, 11.601; hūc — illūc, this way and that, in every direction, 12.764. (hīc).

hūmānus, a, um *adj* (cf. homō), of or pertaining to man; human, 1.542.

humilis, e *adj* (humus), near the ground; low down; low, 4.255; low-lying, 3.522; near the surface, shallow, 7.157; unpretentious, lowly.

humō, āvī, ātus *1 v* to lay earth on anything; inhume, inter, bury, 6.161. (humus).

humus, ī *f* the surface of the ground, the soil; the ground, 3.3 *et al.*; humī, locative, on the ground, upon the ground; to the earth, 1.193 *et al.*

hyacinthus, ī *m* a hyacinth.

Hyades, um *f* the Hyades, daughters of rain; the seven stars in the head of Taurus, whose rising, which occurs in the month of May, was thought to betoken rain, 1.744.

Hydaspēs, is *m* a Trojan, 10.747.

hydra, ae *f* a water-serpent; any serpent like the Lernaean Hydra, a monster with many heads, slain by Hercules, 6.576.

hydrus, ī *m* a water-serpent; snake, 7.447.

Hylaeus, ī *m* a centaur who assailed Atalanta.

Hyllus, ī *m* a Trojan warrior, 12.535.

Hymenaeus, ī *m* Hymen, the god of marriage, 4.127; *pl* Hymenaeī, ōrum, *metonym* marriage, 1.651.

Hypanis, is *m* a Trojan, 2.340.

Hyrcānus, a, um *adj* pertaining to the Hyrcani, a tribe on the Caspian; Hyrcanian, 4.367. (Hyrcānī).

Hyrtacidēs, ae *m* the son of Hyrtacus. 1. Hippocoön, 5.492. 2. Nisus, 9.177.

Hyrtacus, ī *m* the father of Nisus, 9.406.

iaceō, uī, itus *2 v* to be prostrate, lie, 1.99; extend, spread out; *part*, iacēns, entis, spread out, extended, 1.224; lying low, 3.689.

iaciō, iēcī, iactus *3 v* to throw, cast, hurl, 5.643; scatter, strew, 5.79; lay foundations, build, 5.631.

iactāns, antis arrogant, assuming, ambitious, 6.815. (iaciō).

iactō, āvī, ātus *1 freq v* to throw often or much; toss to and fro; toss, *freq*; hurl, cast, 2.459; thrust out, 5.376; aim, 5.433; *figuratively* throw out words, utter, say, 1.102; of the mind, revolve, meditate, 1.227; sē iactāre, boast, exalt one's self, rejoice, glory, 1.140; prae sē iactāre, to make pretense of, 9.134; *part*, iactāns,

antis, arrogant, assuming,
ambitious, 6.815. (iaciō).

iactūra, ae *f* a throwing away;
loss, 2.646. (iaciō).

iactus, ūs *m* a cast; leap; shot;
reach, 11.608. (iaciō).

iaculor, ātus sum *1 dep v* to hurl
the javelin; to dart; throw,
cast, hurl, 1.42. (iaculum).

iaculum, ī, *n* a thing hurled;
a spear, dart, or javelin,
3.46 *et al.* (iaciō).

Iaera, ae *f* a wood-nymph, wife
of Alcanor and mother of
Bitias and Pandarus, 9.673.

iam *adv* at that time, at this
time; even then, even now;
already, 1.437 *et al.*; with tum,
even, 1.18; *with imperat*, at
length, at once, 3.41 *et al.*;
soon, presently, immediately,
4.566; then, at length, 1.272;
marking a transition, now,
2.567 *et al.*; iam iam, emphatic,
now indeed, 4.371; now, now,
2.530; iam dūdum, iam prīdem,
already for some time, long,
1.580 *et al.*; iam inde, iam ab
illō tempore, even from then
or that time, 1.623; iam tum,
even then; iam — iam, at one
time, at another time, now
— now; nōn iam, no longer,
4.431; iamdūdum, at once.

iamprīdem *adv* some time
before or since; long ago,
long since, 2.647, *freq.*

Iāniculum, ī, *n* the Ianiculum; a
mount or high hill on the right
bank of the Tiber opposite
the Palatine, 8.358. (Iānus).

iānitor, ōris *m* a gate- or door-
keeper; porter, 6.400. (iānua).

iānua, ae *f* the outer door
or gate, 2.493; entrance,
way, 2.661. (Iānus).

Iānus, ī *m* an ancient divinity of
Latium, probably symbolizing
the sun, represented with
two faces, 7.180 *et al.*

Iāpyx, ygis *adj* Iapygian,
Apulian, 11.678; *subst*
(*sc* ventus), the wind
blowing from Iapygia;
the N.W. wind, 8.710.

Iāpyx, ygis *m* a son of Iasius and
physician of Aeneas, 12.391.

Iarbās, ae *m* a king of the
Mauretani in Numidia,
and suitor for the hand
of Dido, 4.36.

Iasidēs, ae *m* a son or
descendant of Iasius.
1. Palinurus, 5.843. 2.
Iapis, 12.392. (Iasius).

Iasius, iī *m* son of Jupiter and
Electra, brother of Dardanus,
and beloved by Ceres, 3.168.

iaspis, idis *f* a precious stone of
greenish hue; jasper, 4.261.

ibī *adv* in or at that place;
there; of time, thereupon,
then, 2.792 *et al.* (*rel to* is).

ibīdem *adv* in the same
place, 1.116.

Īcarus, ī *m* the son of
Daedalus, 6.31.

icō and **iciō** (*obsolete in the
present except in the forms* icit,
iciunt), **īcī, ictus** *3 v* to smite,
hit, strike, 6.180; of treaties or
leagues, make, ratify, 12.314.

ictus, ūs *m* a smiting; a stroke, blow, 5.198, and *freq*; shooting, 7.165; wound, 7.756; force, 2.544. (icō).

Īda, ae *f* 1. Mount Ida in Crete, where Jupiter was reared, 12.412. 2. A mountain in the Troad, where Ganymede was caught up by the eagle of Jupiter, 2.801. 3. A Nymph, 9.177.

Īdaeus, a, um *adj* of Mount Ida (either in Crete or in the Troad), Idaean, 3.105; 2.696 *et al.*; pertaining to Cybele, goddess of the Trojan Ida, 9.112.

Īdaeus, ī *m* Idaeus, the charioteer of Priam, 6.485.

Īdalia, ae *f*, and **Īdalium, iī**, *n* Idalia, a town and headland of Cyprus; one of the favorite resorts of Venus, 1.681.

Īdalius, a, um *adj* (Īdalia), of Idalia, Idalian, 5.760.

Īdās, ae *m* 1. A Trojan warrior, 9.575. 2. A Thracian of Ismara, 10.351.

idcircō *adv* on that account, therefore, 5.680. (id and circā).

īdem, eadem, idem, *pron* the same, 1.240; at the same time, at once, 3.80 *et al.* (is and -dem).

ideō *adv* on that account, therefore, for this end, for such a purpose, 4.228.

Īdmōn, onis *m* a follower of Turnus, 12.75.

Īdomeneus (*quadrisyll*), **eī** *m* Idomeneus, king of Crete, and conspicuous among the Greek chiefs at Troy, 3.122 *et al.*

iecur, oris or **iecinoris,** *n* the liver, 6.598.

igitur *conj*, therefore, then, accordingly, 4.537.

ignārus, a, um *adj* not knowing; *freq*; unaware, ignorant, 11.154; often *with gen*, ignorant of, 1.630; unsuspicious of, 2.106; unconscious, 9.345; not knowing the land; *passive* unknown, a stranger, 10.706.

ignāvia, ae *f* want of spirit, cowardice, 11.733. (ignāvus).

ignāvus, a, um *adj* inactive, idle, slothful, spiritless, cowardly, 12.12; of inanimate things, unoccupied, inactive.

īgnēscō 3 *inc v* to take fire; to be fired, inflamed, to burn, 9.66. (ignis).

īgneus, a, um *adj* (īgnis), of fire or fiery substance; fiery, 6.730; of lightning swiftness, 11.718.

īgnipotēns, entis *adj* (ignis and potēns), having power over fire; *subst* Īgnipotēns, the fire-god, Vulcan, 10.243.

īgnis, is *m* fire, 1.175, and *freq*; torch, 7.320; conflagration, 2.312; light, 3.585; lightning, 1.90; fiery spirit; wrath, rage, fury, 2.575; 7.577; fire of love, passion, 4.2; the beloved; one's flame, love, firebrand or fiery missile, 7.692; *pl* torches, 4.384.

ignōbilis, e *adj* unknown; obscure, 7.776; low, base, 1.149; undistinguished, bringing no renown, ignoble.

ignōrō, āvī, ātus *1 v* not to know; to be ignorant of, 5.849. (*rel to* ignārus).

ignōtus, a, um *adj* unknown, 1.359; strange, 5.795; not well known, but little known, 11.527.

īlex, icis *f* the holm-oak, scarlet oak, ilex, 6.180.

Īlia, ae *f* Ilia, a name assigned by the poets to Rhaea Silvia, the daughter of Numitor, 1.274.

īlia, ium, *n pl* the groin, flank, 7.499; belly, 10.778.

Īliacus, a, um *adj* belonging to Ilium; Ilian, Trojan, 1.97 *et al.*

Īlias, adis *f* a daughter of Ilium or Troy; *pl* Īliades, um, Trojan women, 1.480.

īlicet *adv* straightway, immediately, at once, instantly, 2.424. (īre and licet).

Īlionē, ēs *f* eldest daughter of Priam and Hecuba, 1.653.

Īlioneus (*quadrisyll.*), **eī** *m* (*acc.* **ēa** *instead of* ea, 1.611) commander of one of the ships of Aeneas, 1.120 *et al.*

Īlium, īī, *n* Troy, 1.68 *et al.*

Īlius, a, um *adj* (Īlium), of Ilium; Ilian, Trojan, 1.268.

ille, a, ud, *gen* **illīus** dem. *pron* (archaic, olle, 5.197 *et al.*), that, 6.760 *et al.*; that, well known, distinguished, great, 1.617; some formidable, some bold, 10.707; 11.809; as subs., he, she, it, they, *freq*; ille — hīc, the one — the other, 5.430; the former — the latter, 6.395; joined to an *adj* or partic.

for emphasis, 1.3 *et al.*; ex illō, from that time, 8.268.

illīc *adv* in that place; there, 1.206. (ille and -ce; *cf.* hīc).

illinc *adv* from that side, thence; on that side, 4.442.

illūc *adv* to that place, thither; that way, there, 4.285. (pron. illīc).

Illyricus, a, um *adj* (Illyria), pertaining to Illyria, the country north of Epirus; Illyrian, 1.243.

Īlus, ī *m* 1. Ilus, son of Tros and king of Troy, 6.650. 2. An earlier name of Ascanius or Iulus, 1.268. 3. Ilus, a Rutulian, 10.400.

Īlva, ae *f* an island near the coast of Etruria, now Elba, 10.173.

imāgō, inis *f* an image, form, 2.560 *et al.*; figure, statue, 7.179; apparition, 1.408; ghost, phantom, 1.353; idea, thought, 12.560; manifestation, example, 6.405; echo.

Imāōn, onis (*acc* **Imāona**) *m* a Latin warrior, 10.424.

imbellis, e not fit for war; unwarlike, effeminate, feeble, 2.544; timid.

imber, imbris *m* a rain-storm; shower, 1.743 *et al.*; rain-cloud, 3.194; of sea-water, flood, 1.123; hail, 8.429.

Imbrasidēs, ae *m* the son of Imbrasus; Asius, a Lycian follower of Aeneas, 10.123.

Imbrasus, ī *m* a Lycian, 12.343.

imbuō, uī, ūtus *3 v* to wet, moisten; stain, 7.554.

imitābilis, e *adj* (imitor), that can be imitated; imitable, 6.590.

imitor, ātus sum *1 dep v* to imitate, 6.586; substitute for, use for, literally, imitate with, 11.894.

immāne *adv* wildly, fiercely, 12.535.

immānis, e *adj* vast, huge, immense, 1.110; wild, savage, barbarous, 1.616; cruel, ruthless, 1.347; unnatural, monstrous, hideous, 6.624; *adv* immāne, wildly, fiercely, 12.535.

immātūrus, a, um *adj* untimely, 11.166.

immedicābilis, e *adj* incurable, deadly, 12.858.

immemor, oris *adj* not remembering, without memory, oblivious, 6.750; unconscious, 9.374; reckless, heedless, 2.244; often *with gen*, unmindful, forgetful of, 5.39.

immēnsus, a, um unmeasured; boundless; vast, immense, 2.204; mighty, 3.672; insatiate, unbounded, 6.823.

immergō, mersī, mersus *3 v* to plunge into, immerse in, *with acc and abl*, 3.605 *et al.*

immeritus, a, um *adj* undeserving; guiltless, 3.2.

immineō *2 v* to rest over; overhang, 1.165; to be at hand; approach, 9.515.

immisceō, miscuī, mixtus or **mistus** *2 v* to mingle with; usually *with dat* 2.396; blend with, vanish in, 4.570.

immītis, e *adj* not mellow; not mild; merciless, fierce, cruel, ruthless, 1.30.

immittō, mīsī, missus *3 v* to send upon or to; drive to, 6.312; bring upon, 4.488; let in, 2.495; let fly, go, loosen, 6.1; hurl, fling, cast, 11.562; (with sē), rush into, 6.262; *part,* immissus, a, um, of the reins of horses, let loose; hence, *figuratively* swiftly running, 5.146; unchecked, unbridled, 5.662; of the hair or beard, descending, left growing, neglected, long, 3.593.

immō yes indeed; nay rather, 1.753; but, 9.98.

immōbilis, e *adj* unmoved, 7.623; immovable, 9.448.

immolō, āvī, ātus *1 v* to sprinkle the sacred meal upon the victim; to immolate, sacrifice, 10.519; kill, 10.541. (in- and mola).

immortālis, e *adj* undying, immortal, unperishable, 6.598.

immōtus, a, um *adj* unmoved, motionless; immovable, 3.77; *figuratively* firm, fixed, steadfast, unchangeable, 1.257.

immūgiō, īvī or **iī, ītus** *4 v* to bellow within; roar, resound, 3.674.

immulgeō *2 v* to milk into, 11.572.

immundus, a, um *adj* unclean, uncleanly; filthy, foul, noisome, 3.228.

immūnis, e *adj* free from service; *with gen*, exempt, freed from, 12.559.

impār, aris *adj* unequal, in unequal combat, 1.475; unequally matched.

impāstus, a, um *adj* unfed; hungry, 9.339.

impatiēns, entis *adj* impatient, *with gen*, 11.639.

impavidus, a, um *adj* not afraid; fearless, intrepid, 10.717.

impediō, īvī or **iī, ītus** 4 *v* to hinder, 9.385; hamper, 10.553; involve, intersect, 5.585; combine, 8.449. (1. in and pēs).

impellō, pulī, pulsus 3 *v* to push, thrust, drive to or upon; push onward, impel, 5.242; push, open, 7.621; smite, 1.82; ply, 4.594; put in motion, urge on, 8.3; shoot, 12.856; move, disturb, 3.449; (w. *inf*), lead on, impel, induce, persuade, 2.55; force, compel, 1.11.

impēnsa, ae *f* (*sc* **pecūnia**) outlay, cost, expense, 11.228. (impendō).

impēnsē *adv compar* impēnsius, with unusual or much outlay; carefully, earnestly, 12.20. (impēnsa).

impēnsus, a, um ample, considerate, great, 4.54.

imperditus, a, um *adj* undestroyed, 10.430.

imperfectus, a, um *adj* unfinished, 8.428.

imperitō, āvī, ātus 1 *intens* *v* to command, govern, rule, 12.719. (imperō).

imperium, iī, *n* a command, 1.230; absolute command, sway, control, authority, power, 1.54; dominion, 1.138; empire, kingdom, 2.191. (imperō).

imperō, āvī, ātus 1 *v* to command, *with dat*; *with dat and inf* 7.36.

imperterritus, a, um *adj* undaunted, 10.770.

impetus, ūs *m* an attack; a strong impulsion; pressure, impulse, impetus, 5.219; vehemence, violence, 2.74. (impetō, attack).

impexus, a, um *adj* uncombed, untrimmed; shaggy, 7.667.

impiger, gra, grum *adj* not sluggish, not inactive; quick, not backward, 1.738.

impingō, pēgī, pāctus 3 *v* to fasten upon; drive, dash against, 5.805. (1. in and pangō).

impius, a, um undutiful in sacred relations; iniquitous, impious, 2.163; nefarious, detestable, perfidious, 4.496; with reference to civil war, 6.612; of actions, 4.596.

implācābilis, e *adj* inexorable, inflexible, 12.3.

implācātus, a, um *adj* unappeased; insatiable, 3.420.

impleō, plēvī, plētus 2 *v* to fill up; fill, 1.729; with sound, fill, 3.313; reach, 11.896; regale (w. *gen*), 1.215; satisfy, 1.716; inspire, 3.434.

implicō, āvī or **uī, ātus** or **itus** 1 *v*, to fold in; involve,

entangle, entwine, 2.215;
to wheel, 12.743; (w. *dat*),
bind to, 11.555; infuse, 1.660;
insinuate, mingle, 7.355; sē
implicāre, cling to, 2.724.

implōrō, āvī, ātus *1 v* to entreat,
implore, supplicate, 4.617.

**impōnō, posuī, positus (p.
impostus**, 9.716) *3 v* to put or
lay on, in, into, over, upon,
1.49; put, 2.619; place over
the dead, erect, build, 6.233;
lay down, prescribe, 6.852;
(*impers*), impositum est, it is
incumbent, a necessity, 8.410.

importūnus, a, um *adj* ill-timed,
unseasonable; of birds of ill
omen, ominous, inauspicious,
12.864; ill-advised, dangerous,
hazardous, 11.305.

imprecor, ātus sum *1 dep v*
to call down good or, more
usually, evil by prayer;
to invoke evil upon,
imprecate, invoke, 4.629.

imprīmīs *adv* especially,
chiefly, 1.303.

imprimō, pressī, pressus *3 v* to
press into, on, or upon, 4.659;
impress, mark; engrave, chase,
5.536. (1. in and premō).

improbus, a, um *adj* not good;
bad; malicious, wicked; cruel,
2.80; savage, 10.727; furiously
impelled, destructive,
12.687; unappeasable,
ravenous, rapacious, 12.250;
importunate, raging, 2.356; of
military devices, with warlike
craft, 11.512; with murderous
intent, 11.767; *subst m*,
shameless, impudent boaster,
braggart, 5.397; wretch, 4.386.

improperātus, a, um *adj*
unhastened; delayed,
delaying, 9.798.

imprōvidus, a, um *adj* not
looking before; improvident;
unsuspecting, blinded;
unprepared, 2.200.

imprōvīsō *adv*
unexpectedly, 8.524.

imprōvīsus, a, um *adj*
unforeseen; unlooked
for, unexpected, 1.595.

imprūdēns, entis *adj* not seeing
or knowing beforehand;
unconscious, 9.386; unwarned.

impūbēs, is or **eris** *adj* not
full grown; beardless,
9.751; youthful, 5.546.

impulsus, ūs *m* an
impelling; impulse,
shock, 8.239. (impellō).

impūne *adv* without punishment
or retribution; with impunity,
3.628; without harm, 12.559.
(impūnis, unpunished).

in (*prep with acc or abl*); with
acc, into, unto, to, toward,
1.587 *et al.*; against, 9.424
et al.; on, upon, 5.426 *et al.*; in
expressions of time, unto, to,
for; according to, by; denoting
purpose, 12.854 *et al.*; as, for,
11.771; in adversum, contrary,
against, opposite, 8.237; in
melius, for the better, 1.281;
in numerum, in time or order,
8.453; in ūnum, together; in
abruptum, headlong, 3.422;
with abl of situation, in, on,
over, upon, *freq*; in the midst
of, within, among, 1.109 *et al.*;
for, as, 5.537; on account

of, at, 10.446; in respect to, 2.541; after its noun, 6.58.

inaccessus, a, um *adj* difficult of approach, perilous to be approached; dangerous, 7.11; impervious, 8.195.

Īnachius, a, um *adj* (Īnachus), of Inachus, Inachian; Argive, Greek, 11.286.

Īnachus, ī *m* the first king of Argos, father of Io and Phoroneus, 7.372.

inamābilis, e *adj* unlovely; odious, abhorred, accursed, 6.438.

ināne, is, *n* void space, a void, 12.354.

inānis, e *adj* empty, void, 3.304; light; vain, idle, fruitless, 4.210; valueless, trivial; little, brief, 4.433; lifeless, unreal, 1.464; shadowy, 6.269; unsubstantial, shadowy, airy, phantom, 6.651; *subst* ināne, is, *n*, void space, a void, 12.354.

inārdēscō, ārsī *3 inc v* to take fire; become glowing, glow; be gilded, 8.623.

Īnarimē, ēs *f* an island at the entrance of the Bay of Naples, called also Aenaria and Pithecusa, now Ischia, 9.716.

inausus, a, um *adj* undared, unattempted, 7.308.

incānus, a, um *adj* covered over with gray; hoary, 6.809.

incassum *adv* in vain, 3.345.

incautus, a, um *adj* unguarded, heedless, 10.386; unsuspecting, 1.350.

incēdō, cessī, cessus *3 v* to step onward; walk, especially with pomp or dignity; advance, 1.497; move (for am), 1.46 *et al.*; march, proceed, 9.308.

incendium, iī, *n* a burning, conflagration; flame, fire, 2.706; desolation, 1.566; fiery material, firebrand, 9.71. (incendō).

incendō, cendī, cēnsus *3 v* to set fire to, burn, 2.353; kindle, 3.279; illuminate, 5.88; *figuratively* of the mind, fire, inflame, 1.660; arouse, rouse to action, 5.719; excite, irritate, enrage, madden, provoke, 4.360; disturb, rend, fill, 10.895.

inceptum, ī, *n* a beginning; deliberation, 11.469; undertaking, design, purpose, 1.37; measure, movement, 12.566. (incipiō).

incertus, a, um *adj* uncertain, 2.740; wavering; fickle, 2.39; doubtful, 3.7; undistinguished, base, 11.341.

incessō, cessīvī *3 intens v* to attack, assail, beleaguer, 12.596. (incēdō).

incessus, ūs *m* a walking or advancing; a manner of walking; walk, gait, 1.405. (incēdō).

incestō, āvī, ātus *1 v* to defile, pollute, 6.150. (incestus, unclean).

incidō, cidī, cāsus *3 v* to fall into; descend or fall, 2.305; encounter, meet, 11.699; inspire, 9.721. (1. in and cadō).

incīdō, cīdī, cīsus 3 v to cut into; cut upon; cut, 3.667. (1. in and caedō).

incingō, cīnxī, cīnctus 3 v to gird on, gird about, gird, array, clothe, 7.396.

incipiō, cēpī, ceptus 3 v to undertake; begin, 1.721; begin to speak, 2.348; cherish, 12.832.

incitus, a, um adj rapid, swift, 12.534.

inclēmentia, ae f unkindness; inclemency, cruelly, severity, 2.602. (inclēmēns, unkind).

inclīnō, āvī, ātus 1 v to bend; part, inclīnātus, a, um, bent; bending; declining, tottering, sinking, 12.59.

inclūdō, clūsī, clūsus 3 v to shut in, inclose, 6.680; secrete, 2.19; for interclūdō, stop, choke, 7.534; to mount, set, inlay, adorn, 12.211. (1. in and claudō).

inclutus, a, um adj famous, glorious, renowned, 2.82. (rel to clueō, to be heard of; κλύω, hear; κλυτός, renowned).

incognitus, a, um adj unknown, unnoticed, unperceived, 12.859; not understood, 1.515.

incohō, āvī, ātus 1 v to lay the foundation; begin, essay; to consecrate, 6.252.

incolō, uī 3 v to dwell; inhabit, 6.675.

incolumis, e adj uninjured; unharmed, safe, 2.88.

incomitātus, a, um adj unattended; alone, 2.456.

incommodum, ī, n detriment, misfortune, woe, 8.74. (incommodus, inconvenient).

inconcessus, a, um adj not allowed; unlawful, 1.651.

incōnsultus, a, um adj uninstructed, unadvised, without advice, 3.452.

incrēbrēscō, crēbruī 3 inc v to become frequent; increase more and more; be spread abroad, 8.14.

incrēdibilis, e adj not to be believed; incredible, strange, 3.294.

increpitō, āvī, ātus 1 intens v to make a great noise; to call or cry out to; chide, blame, reproach, 3.454; dare, challenge, 1.738; taunt, 10.900. (increpō).

increpō, uī, itus, rarely **āvī, ātus** 1 v to make a noise or din; resound, 8.527; clash, 12.332; snap, 12.755; figuratively chide, blame, reprimand, 6.387; taunt, 9.560; (w. cognate acc), utter, 9.504.

incrēscō, crēvī, crētus 3 v to grow in; grow up, 3.46; increase, with dat 9.688.

incubō, uī, itus 1 v to lie, recline upon, with abl or dat, 4.83; rest upon, 1.89.

incultus, a, um adj uncared for, neglected, unshorn, 6.300; wild; subst inculta, ōrum, n pl waste, desert regions, 1.308.

incumbō, cubuī, cubitus 3 v to lay one's self upon; lean or recline upon; (w. dat), lie on or stretch over, 2.205;

fall upon, 1.84; bend to, ply, 5.15; hasten, urge, press on, 2.653; overhang, 2.514; press or bend toward, 5.325; (w. ad and *acc*), lean, hang, incline, 8.236; absolute, bend to, urge on the work, 4.397.

incurrō, **currī** or **cucurrī, cursus** *3 v* to run into or against; rush upon, charge, 2.409; 11.759.

incurvō, āvī, ātus *1 v* to bend in; bend, 5.500.

incūs, ūdis *f* an anvil, 7.629. (incūdō, to beat).

incūsō, āvī, ātus *1 v* to bring a cause or case against any one; to accuse, reproach, blame, 2.745; without object, upbraid, complain, 1.410. (1. in and causa).

incutiō, cussī, cussus *3 v* to strike into or upon; add, put into, 1.69. (1. in and quatiō).

indāgō, inis *f* an inclosing or surrounding of the woods with the hunting nets; toils, the chase, 4.121.

inde *adv* from that place; of time, thence, thereupon, then, 1.275; thereupon, 2.434; afterwards; for ex hōc, ex hāc, etc., 3.663; for ab illō, from that quarter, from him, 10.54; iam inde, at once, forthwith, 6.385.

indēbitus, a, um *adj* not due; unassigned, unallotted, unpromised, 6.66.

indecor, oris, and **indecoris, e** *adj* disgraceful, bringing disgrace, 7.231; disgraced, infamous, 11.423; unhonored, 11.845.

indēfessus, a, um *adj* unwearied, 11.651.

indēprēnsus, a, um *adj* not overtaken; uncaught, undetected; untraced, intricate, 5.591.

Indī *adj* belonging to India, Indian, 12.67; *subst* Indus, ī, *m*, an Indian; *pl* Indī, ōrum, the Indians, 7.605.

indicium, iī, *n* a means of informing; a proof, sign, token, indication; evidence, charge, 2.84; trace, 8.211. (indicō).

indīcō, dīxī, dictus *3 v* to declare, 7.616; ordain, appoint, 5.758; order, summon, 11.737.

indictus, a, um *adj* unmentioned; unsung, unrecorded, 7.733.

indigena, ae (*adj* *m* f. *n*), born in the land; native, indigenous, 8.314. (indu-, an old form of in-, and genō).

indiges, etis *m* a hero worshiped as a god of his native land, 12.794. (indu-, an old form of in-, and genō).

indīgnor, ātus sum *1 dep v* to deem unworthy; to fret, chafe, be impatient, 1.55; resent, 2.93; scorn, 8.728; be angry, indignant, 11.831; *with inf*, 7.770.

indīgnus, a, um *adj* unworthy; unmeet, unjust, 10.74; disgraceful, shameful, revolting, cruel, 2.285; once with *gen*, 12.649; *n pl subst* indīgna, ōrum, indignities, 12.811.

indiscrētus, a, um
adj unseparated;
undistinguished, 10.392.

indocilis, e *adj* unteachable;
untaught, rude, 8.321.

indoles, is *f* that which is bred
within; natural disposition;
genius, nature, spirit, 10.826.
(indu-, an old form of in-,
and *cf.* olēscō, grow).

indomitus, a, um *adj*
untamed; unbridled, 2.594;
impetuous, fierce, 2.440.

indubitō, āvī, ātus *1 v* to doubt,
mistrust, *with dat* 8.404.

indūcō, dūxī, ductus *3 v* to
lead, bring into or to; lead
on, 11.620; draw, put on, *with
acc and dat* 5.379; put on,
clothe, *pass with acc and abl*,
8.457; *figuratively* influence,
induce, persuade, 5.399.

indulgeō, dulsī, dultus *2 v* to
be indulgent, kind, yielding,
give way to, 2.776; yield to,
indulge in, 4.51; favor, 8.512.

induō, uī, ūtus *3 v* to put into;
put on, assume, 1.684; clothe;
surround, crown, 3.526;
pierce, slay, 10.682; *(pass
as middle, with acc)* gird
one's self with, put on, 2.393;
induere in vultūs, transform
to the features, 7.20.

Indus, a, um *adj* belonging to
India, Indian, 12.67; *subst*
Indus, ī, *m*, an Indian; *pl* Indī,
ōrum, the Indians, 7.605.

inēluctābilis, e *adj* that
can not be averted by
struggling; inevitable,
2.324; resistless, 8.334.

ineō, īvī or iī, itus, īre *irreg v* to
go into; come upon; enter,
5.114; of a period of time,
open, commence, begin;
undertake, perform, 5.846.

inermis, e unarmed; helpless,
defenseless, 1.487 *et al.*

inermus, a, um unarmed, 10.425.

iners, inertis without ability;
without force; inactive,
inanimate, indolent; feeble,
timid, 9.730; helpless,
lifeless, 2.364; of the
voice, weak, 10.322.

inexcītus, a, um *adj* not roused,
dormant, quiet, 7.623.

inexhaustus, a, um
adj unexhausted;
inexhaustible, 10.174.

inexpertus, a, um (active)
unacquainted with
, inexperienced in,
unaccustomed to a thing;
(passive) unused, untried,
unproven, 4.415.

inexplētus, a, um *adj*
unsatisfied, insatiate, 8.559.

inextrīcābilis, e *adj*
inextricable, intricate, 6.27.

īnfabricātus, a, um *adj*
unwrought, unhewn, 4.400.

īnfandus, a, um *adj* not to
be uttered; unutterable,
inexpressible, unspeakable,
4.85; cruel, 1.525; dreadful,
horrible, 10.673; accursed,
perfidious, 4.613; fatal, 2.132;
neut., in exclamations,
īnfandum! O shame, O
woe unutterable! 1.251; *pl*
īnfanda, as *adv* 8.489.

īnfāns, antis *adj* not capable of speech; *subst* īnfāns, c, an infant, 6.427.

īnfaustus, a, um *adj* unfortunate, of ill omen, ill-starred, 5.635.

īnfectus, a, um not done; unworked, unwrought, 10.528; unfinished, unconsummated, 10.720; not actual; untrue, 4.190; of a covenant, not made, unmade, 12.243; broken, 12.286.

īnfēlix, īcis *adj* unlucky; unfortunate, luckless, unhappy, 1.475 *et al.*; sad, miserable, 2.772; of ill omen, ill-starred, ill-boding, fatal, 2.245; unfruitful.

īnfēnsus, a, um hostile, inimical, 5.587; fatal, destructive, 5.641; angry, furious, 2.72.

īnferiae, ārum *f* sacrifices to the Manes or powers below; funeral rites, 9.215. (inferī, the powers of the lower world).

īnfernus, a, um *adj* (inferus), that which is below; of Hades, infernal, 3.386.

īnferō, intulī, inlātus, ferre *irreg v* to bear into, upon, or to; convey to, 1.6; offer in sacrifice, 3.66; bring, make, wage war, 3.248; sē inferre, to betake, present one's self, appear, 5.622; move, advance, 1.439; *passive* inferrī, as middle, go against, pursue, 4.545.

īnferus, a, um *adj* below, lower; *compar* inferior, ius, lower; less distinguished, inferior, 6.170; *superl*, īnfimus or īmus, a, um, lowest, deepest, 2.419; inmost, 2.120; below, 4.387;

lowest part, bottom of, 3.39; ex īmō, from the foundation, 2.625; īma, ōrum, *n*, depths.

īnfestus, a, um infested; unsafe, hostile, inimical, 2.571; dangerous, mortal, 2.529; fatal, pernicious, destructive, 5.641.

īnficiō, fēcī, fectus 3 *v* to impart some foreign quality to an object; to taint, infect; poison; stain, 5.413; mix, tincture, 12.418; *part*, infectus, a, um, inwrought, contracted, 6.742; infected, filled, 7.341. (1. in and faciō).

īnfīgō, fīxī, fīxus 3 *v* to fasten in or upon, *with dat or abl*, 1.45, et al; thrust, 12.721; *part*, infixus, a, um, thrust deeply, deep, 4.689.

īnfindō, fidī, fissus 3 *v* to cut, cleave, of a ship's keel, 5.142.

īnfit, *irreg def* one begins; he begins to speak, 5.708 *et al.*

īnflammō, āvī, ātus 1 *v* to set on fire; *figuratively* to rouse, inflame, inspire, 4.54; infuriate, madden, 3.330.

īnflectō, flexī, flexus 3 *v* to bend, 3.631; *figuratively* move, sway, change, 4.22; *passive* to be bent or swayed, 12.800.

īnflētus, a, um *adj* unlamented, unwept, 11.372.

īnflīgō, flīxī, flīctus 3 *v* to strike, dash on or against, 10.303.

īnflō, āvī, ātus 1 *v* to blow into; fill, inflate, swell, 3.357.

īnfodiō, fōdī, fossus 3 *v* to dig in; bury, 11.205.

īnfōrmis, e shapeless; deprived of beauty, deformed, blank, waste; misshapen, hideous, 3.658; uncouth, foul, 6.416; unseemly, dishonored, 12.603.

īnfōrmō, āvī, ātus 1 v to impart form to; mold, forge, 8.447; mold, shape in the rough, 8.426.

īnfrā adv below, 8.149 et al. (īnferā, sc. parte).

īnfremō, uī 3 v to bellow; rage, storm, 10.711.

īnfrendeō 2 v, and **īnfrendō** 3 v to gnash, 3.664.

īnfrēnō, āvī, ātus 1 v to furnish with a bridle; to rein, harness, 12.287.

īnfrēnus, a, um; also, īnfrēnis, e unbridled; riding without bridle, 4.41.

īnfringō, frēgī, frāctus 3 v to break in; break, 12.387; figuratively to break down, subdue, 5.784; dishearten, paralyze, 9.499. (in and frangō).

īnfula, ae f a bandage, miter; a fillet of red and white wool, twisted together, worn by priests, 2.430.

īnfundō, fūdī, fūsus 3 v to pour into or upon, 6.254; pour down, 4.122; assemble, crowd together, 5.552; infuse, diffuse, 6.726; passive lie, repose, 8.406.

ingeminō, āvī, ātus 1 v v, repeat; redouble, multiply, increase, 7.578; name often, 2.770; n, shout again and again, 1.747; reëcho, 5.227; flash often

or continuously, 3.199; be redoubled, return, 4.531.

ingemō, uī, itus 3 v to sigh or groan, 1.93; (w. acc), groan for; lament, bewail.

ingēns, entis adj great, freq; huge, enormous, 2.400; monstrous, vast, 3.658; mighty, giant-, 1.99; immense, 5.423; great, massive, 1.640; ponderous, 6.222; vast, spacious, 6.81; lofty, towering, 4.89; stately, 1.446; exalted, great, 2.325; dread, 7.241; fearful, 5.523.

ingerō, gessī, gestus 3 v to carry, bring, throw, cast into, at, or upon, 9.763.

inglōrius, a, um adj without glory; unrenowned, inglorious, 10.52.

ingrātus, a, um adj not acceptable; disagreeable, unpleasing, 2.101; hateful, 12.144; subjective, ungrateful, thankless; unfeeling, cold, insensate, 6.213; with gen, 10.666.

ingravō, āvī, ātus 1 v to make heavy; aggravate, 11.220.

ingredior, gressus sum 3 dep v to walk into; with dat proceed to, take, 10.763; without a case foll., enter, land, 3.17; walk along, advance, 6.157; enter upon discourse; begin to speak, 4.107; with inf, attempt, 11.704. (1. in and gradior).

ingruō, uī 3 v to rush into; advance furiously, 11.899; assail, 8.535; rush upon the ear, resound, 2.301; descend, 12.284.

inguen, inguinis, *n* the groin, 10.589.

inhaereō, haesī, haesus 2 *v* to stick to; cling to, hang upon, fasten upon, 8.260; embrace, *with abl.* 10.845.

inhibeō, uī, itus 2 *v* to hold back, hold in, keep back, 12.693. (1. in and habeō).

inhiō, āvī, ātus 1 *v* to gape at or over; inspect, examine, 4.64; yawn; gape at, gaze at.

inhonestus, a, um dishonorable; ignominious, shameful, 6.497.

inhorreō, uī 2 *v* to be rough; of the sea, rise up, become rough, swell, 3.195; to cause to bristle, 10.711.

inhospitus, a, um *adj* unfriendly, inhospitable, *figuratively* 4.41.

inhumātus, a, um *adj* unburied, 4.620.

īniciō, iēcī, iectus 3 *v* to cast or throw into, or upon, 6.366; hurl, 2.726; lay on, of the hand of Fate, 10.419. (1. in and iaciō).

inimīcus, a, um unfriendly; inimical, hostile, 2.622; of one's foe, 10.795; adverse, 12.812; dangerous, 11.880; fatal, destructive, 1.123.

inīquus, a, um unequal; uneven in surface, rounding, 10.303; of the sun, torrid, 7.227; too narrow, dangerous, 5.203; treacherous, 11.531; morally, unfavorable, hard, inequitable, 4.618; unjust, cruel, 1.668 *et al.*

inlūria, ae *f* violation of human right; injustice, violence, wrong, injury, 4.354 *et al.*; affront, insult, 1.27. (2. in- and iūs).

iniussus, a, um *adj* not commanded; uncalled, unbidden, 6.375.

inlābor, lāpsus sum 3 *dep v* to glide or fall into, *with dat;* move into, 2.240; descend into, inspire, 3.89.

inlacrimō, āvī, ātus 1 *v,* and **inlacrimor, ātus sum** 1 *dep v* to weep.

inlaetābilis, e *adj* joyless; sad, mournful, 3.707.

inlīdō, līsī, līsus 3 *v* to dash upon, thrust, drive upon, 1.112; dash into, 5.480. (1. in and laedō).

inligō, āvī, ātus 1 *v* to bind on; attach to; impede, encumber (separated by tmesis), 10.794.

inlūdō, lūsī, lūsus 3 *v* to play upon; *with dat; figuratively* insult, mock, 2.64; set at naught, 4.591; injure, hurt; (w. *acc*), insult, 9.634.

inlūstris, e *adj* (in and lūstrō), illuminated; *figuratively* conspicuous, distinguished, illustrious, noble, 6.758.

inluviēs, ēī. *f* that which is deposited by washing; dirt, filth, 3.593. (cf. ēluō).

innectō, nexuī, nexus 3 *v* to bind, tie, 5.511; entwine, 7.353; link together; *figuratively* devise, 4.51.

innō, āvī, ātus 1 *v* to swim upon or over, 8.691; swim, 10.222; (w. *acc*), sail over, 6.134; swim, pass by swimming.

innocuus, a, um *adj* harmless, involving no danger to any one, 7.230; *passive* unharmed, safe, 10.302.

innoxius, a, um *adj* harmless, 2.683.

innumerus, a, um *adj* numberless, countless, 6.706.

innūptus, a, um *adj* not veiled; unmarried, virgin-, 2.31.

inoffēnsus, a, um *adj* unobstructed; unbroken, smooth, 10.292.

inolēscō, olēvī, olitus 3 *v* to grow into, upon, or in, *with dat*; fasten upon, be incorporated, be fixed by growth, without a case foll., 6.738.

inopīnus, a, um unexpected, 5.857.

inops, inopis *adj* without means; poor, needy; wretched (destitute of means to pay Charon), 6.325; of things, meager, mean, humble, 8.100; of the mind, *with gen*, bereft of, 4.300.

Īnōus, a, um *adj* (Īnō), pertaining to Ino, daughter of Cadmus and mother of Melicertes or Palaemon; Inoan, 5.823.

inquam, *n def* to say; always used after one or more words in a direct quotation, 1.321 *et al.*

inremeābilis, e *adj* that can not be gone over again; not to be repassed, or retraced, 6.425; inextricable, 5.591.

inreparābilis, e *adj* irrecoverable, irretrievable.

inrīdeō, rīsī, rīsus 2 *v* to laugh at; deride, 5.272; set at naught, insult, 4.534.

inrigō, āvī, ātus 1 *v* to water; *figuratively* diffuse, 1.692; pervade, 3.511.

inrītō, āvī, ātus 1 *v* to exasperate, provoke, 4.178.

inritus, a, um baffled in calculation or purpose; ineffectual, unavailing; useless, vain, 2.459. (2. in- and ratus).

inrumpō, rūpī, ruptus 3 *v* to burst; *with acc*, rush into, rush through, 11.879; *with dat* burst into, 6.528.

inruō, ruī 3 *v* to rush in, break in, 2.757; rush on, 2.383; rush, 9.555.

īnsalūtātus, a, um *adj* not saluted; without farewell greeting (separated by tmesis), 9.288.

īnsānia, ae *f* unsoundness; insanity, madness, folly, frenzy, 2.42; violence, fury, 7.461. (īnsānus).

īnsānus, a, um *adj* unsound; mad, insane, 6.135; inspired, 3.443.

īnscius, a, um not knowing; unaware, unwitting, ignorant, 1.718; amazed, bewildered, 2.307; *with gen*, ignorant of, 12.648.

īnscrībō, scrīpsī, scrīptus 3 *v* to work upon, mark, furrow, 1.478; inscribe.

īnsequor, secūtus sum 3 *dep v* to follow up, pursue,

follow, 5.321; press on, follow up; succeed, 1.87; persecute, pursue, 1.241; *with inf*, proceed, 3.32.

īnserō, uī, tus *3 v* to fasten or put in; insert, 3.152.

īnsertō *1 freq v* to put or thrust into; pass through, 2.672. (īnserō).

īnsideō, sēdī, sessus *2 v* to sit or be seated on; *with dat* rest, recline upon, 1.719; settle on, 8.480; *with acc*, occupy, hold, 2.616. (1. in and sedeō).

īnsidiae, ārum *f* a sitting down, or lying in ambuscade; an ambush, 11.783; snare, toil; plot, treachery, wile, 2.36; stealthy journey or enterprise, 9.237; artifice, stratagem, 2.421; *personif pl* Īnsidiae, ārum, Stratagem, 12.336. (īnsideō).

īnsidior, ātus sum *1 dep v* to lie in ambush; lie in wait, lurk for, *with dat* 9.59. (īnsidiae).

īnsīdō, sēdī, sessus *3 v* to sink, take a seat, or settle upon; (w. *dat*), alight upon, 6.708; to be stationed or secreted in, 11.531; (w. *acc*), settle upon, 10.59.

īnsīgne, is *n* a distinguishing mark; symbol, ensign, 10.188; trophy, 12.944; *pl* īnsīgnia, ium, distinctive arms, tokens, 2.339; royal ensigns or insignia, 8.506; trappings, 11.89.

īnsīgniō, īvī or **iī, ītus** *4 v* to decorate with a mark; adorn, mark, decorate, 7.790. (īnsīgne).

īnsīgnis, e beautiful, 3.468; splendid, adorned, 4.134;

conspicuous, 6.808; marked, renowned, distinguished, 1.10; illustrious, glorious, 10.450. (in and sīgnum).

īnsinuō, āvī, ātus *1 v* to embosom; to penetrate, 2.229.

īnsistō, stitī *3 v* to place one's self in or upon a thing; (w. *dat*), to tread or stand upon, (w. *acc*), to tread, 6.563; impress, 11.574; *figuratively* of the will, continue, persist, 4.533.

īnsomnis, e without sleep, wakeful, 9.167.

īnsomnium, iī, *n* that which comes in sleep; a dream, 4.9.

īnsonō, uī *1 v* to sound within; resound, snap, 5.579; (w. *acc*), sound, crack (as to, or with) the lash, 7.451.

īnsōns, sontis *adj* innocent, guiltless, unoffending, 2.84.

īnspērātus, a, um *adj* unhoped for, 3.278; unexpected, 8.247.

īnspiciō, spexī, spectus *3 v* to look into or overlook, 2.47. (1. in and speciō, look).

īnspīrō, āvī, ātus *1 v* to breathe into; inspire, impart, 1.688; instill, 7.351.

īnspoliātus, a, um *adj* not despoiled, upon; unstripped, 11.594.

īnstar, indecl, *n* an image; figure; noble or majestic form, majesty, 6.865; *with gen*, likeness; the size of, as large as, 2.15; like, 3.637. (1. in and stō).

īnstaurō, āvī, ātus *1 v* to build; perform, celebrate, 3.62; revive, resolve anew, 2.451; celebrate anew, 4.63; renew, 2.669; repay, requite, 6.530.

īnsternō, strāvī, strātus *3 v* to spread over; cover, 2.722; saddle, 7.277; extend over, 12.675.

īnstīgō, āvī, ātus *1 v* to goad on; incite, stimulate, encourage, 5.228.

īnstituō, uī, ūtus *3 v* to fix in a place; put down, plant, step with, 7.690; found, inaugurate, 6.70; *with inf*, ordain, 6.143; prepare, begin, 7.109; teach. (1. in and statuō).

īnstō, stitī *1 v* to stand on or upon; *with dat acc, inf*, or *alone; with dat* to stand on, 11.529; stand or hang over, 10.196; (w. *acc*), to work at, ply work upon, 8.834; (w. *inf*), urge on, press on, 1.423; persist, 10.118; *alone* to follow up, press on; pursue, 1.468; struggle, 12.783; be near at hand, approach, threaten, 12.916; to be urgent, important, incumbent, 4.115.

īnstō, stitī *1 v* to stand on or upon; *with dat acc, inf*, or *alone; with dat* to stand on, 11.529; stand or hang over, 10.196; (w. *acc*), to work at, ply work upon, 8.834; (w. *inf*), urge on, press on, 1.423; persist, 10.118; *alone* to follow up, press on; pursue, 1.468; struggle, 12.783; be near at hand, approach, threaten, 12.916; to be urgent, important, incumbent, 4.115.

īnstruō, strūxī, strūctus *3 v* to build upon; build up; arrange, draw up ships or troops, 2.254; 8.676; prepare, 1.638; furnish, equip, supply, 3.231; support, 6.831; instruct, train, 2.152.

īnsuētus, a, um (*trisyll*) *adj* unaccustomed; unused, unwonted, 6.16; (*pl n as adv*), īnsuēta, strangely; hideously, 8.248.

īnsula, ae *f* an island, 1.159.

īnsultō, āvī, ātus *1 v* (w. *dat*), to leap upon, bound upon, gallop over, trample on, 12.339; (w. *acc*), bound, dance, rush through, 7.581; absol., prance, 11.600; insult, be insolent, mock, 2.330; exult, 10.20. (insiliō, leap upon).

īnsum, fuī, esse *irreg v* to be in or on; be represented on, 6.26.

īnsuō, uī, ūtus *3 v* to sew or stitch in, into, or on, 5.405.

īnsuper *adv* above, over, upon, 1.61; moreover, 2.593; (*prep with abl*), besides, 9.274.

īnsuper *adv* above, over, upon, 1.61; moreover, 2.593; (*prep with abl*), besides, 9.274.

īnsuperābilis, e *adj* that can not be surmounted; invincible, 4.40.

īnsurgō, surrēxī, rēctus *3 v* to rise to; *with dat* 9.34; rise, spring to, ply, 3.207; (without case), lift or raise one's self, rise upward, 5.443.

intāctus, a, um *adj* untouched, unbroken, 11.419; unhurt, 10.504; untouched by

the yoke, unyoked, 6.38;
pure; a virgin, 1.345.

integer, gra, grum
undiminished; entire; healthy,
fresh, sound, *with gen*, 2.638.

intemerātus, a, um *adj* not
violated, inviolate, 2.143; pure,
holy, 3.178; a virgin, 11.584.

intempestus, a, um
unseasonable; unpleasant;
gloomy, dark, 3.587; of
unhealthy atmosphere
or climate, malarious,
unhealthy, 10.184.

intendō, ī, tentus or **tēnsus** *3 v*
to stretch to or towards; strain;
stretch strings or chords;
strain, aim, shoot, 9.590; tune,
9.776; extend, spread out,
swell, *with acc*, 5.33; bind, *with
acc* and *abl*, 5.403; festoon,
4.506; tie around, *with acc and
dat* 2.237; stretch to, 5.136.

intentātus, a, um *adj* untried,
unsolicited, 10.39.

intentō, āvī, ātus *1 intens v*
to stretch, hold out, 6.572;
threaten, 1.91. (intendō).

intentus, a, um earnestly
attentive, intent, 2.1;
expectant, 5.137. (intendō).

intepeō, uī *2 v* to become
warm, 10.570.

inter (*prep with acc*), between;
among, amid, in the midst of,
3.646 *et al.*; through, 2.782;
in, 4.70; (implying both to
and amid), 12.437; *with* sē
or sēsē, mutually, 4.193;
one with another, 2.455;
alternately, in turn, 5.433;

against each other, 6.828; on
or upon each other, 11.121.

intercipiō, cēpī, ceptus *3 v*
to catch a thing passing
along; intercept, 10.402.
(inter and capiō).

interclūdō, clūsī, clūsus *3 v* to
close the way; hinder, detain,
2.111. (inter and claudō).

interdum *adv* sometimes.

intereā *adv* amid these
things; meanwhile, in the
meantime, 1.418 *et al.*

interfor, fātus sum *1
dep v* to speak between;
interrupt, 1.386.

interfundō, fūdī, fūsus
3 v to pour between;
besprinkle; mark, 4.644;
pass as middle, pour itself,
flow between, 6.439.

interimō, ēmī, ēmptus *3 v* to
take from the midst; kill,
10.428. (inter and emō).

interior, ius *adj* inner, interior;
interior or inner part of,
1.637; on the inner side,
5.170; *superl*, intimus, a, um,
innermost, 1.243. (compar.
of obs interus, *rel to* inter).

interlūceō, lūxī *2 v* to give light
through; to open, 9.508.

interluō *3 v* to wash between;
flow between, 3.419.

internectō *3 v* to bind
together, bind up, 7.816.

interpres, etis, *c* an agent
between parties; a mediator,
messenger, 4.355; author,
4.608; prophet, 3.359.

interritus, a, um *adj*
unaffrighted; dauntless,
5.427; of inanimate things,
undisturbed; without
peril, secure, 5.863.

interrumpō, rūpī, ruptus 3 *v*
to break asunder; interrupt,
discontinue, suspend, 4.88;
of fire, extinguish, 9.239.

intersum, fuī, esse, irreg,
n to be in the midst; be
present at, share in, 11.62.

intertexō, uī, tus 3 *v* to
interweave, embroider, 8.167.

intervāllum, ī, *n* the space
between two stakes; an
interval, distance, 5.320.

intexō, uī, tus 3 *v* to weave into
or in; work in, inweave, 5.252;
festoon, wreathe, entwine,
cover, 6.216; frame, 2.16.

intonō, uī, ātus 1, *v* to thunder,
1.90; (*impers*), intonat,
it thunders, 2.693.

intōnsus, a, um *adj* unshaven,
unshorn, 9.181; leafy, 9.681.

intorqueō, torsī, tortus 2 *v* to
turn or hurl toward, or against,
2.231; shoot, dart, 9.534.

intrā (*prep with acc*, and
adv), on the inside; within,
2.33 *et al.*; for in, 7.168.

intrāctābilis, e *adj* that can
not be handled or managed;
indomitable, invincible, 1.339.

intrāctātus, a, um *adj*
unhandled, untried, 8.206.

intremō, uī 3 *v* to tremble,
5.505; quake, 3.581.

intrō, āvī, ātus 1 *v* to go into,
enter, 3.254; penetrate,
pierce, 8.390. (*rel to* inter).

intrōgredior, gressus sum 3
dep v to go within; enter,
1.520. (intrō and gradior).

intus *adv* within, 1.294 *et al.* (in).

inultus, a, um *adj*
unavenged, 2.670.

inumbrō, āvī, ātus 1 *v*
to cast a shade upon;
overshadow; shade, 11.66.

inundō, āvī, ātus 1 *v* to overflow,
v, 10.24; *n*, 11.382; of an army,
rush on, pour on, 12.280.

inūtilis, e *adj* useless, 2.510;
helpless, 10.794.

invādō, vāsī, vāsus 3 *v* to go
into; enter, 3.382; enter upon,
6.260; invade, violate, 6.623;
rush into, 12.712; attack, assail,
2.414; address, accost, 4.265;
undertake, adventure, 9.186.

invalidus, a, um *adj* not
strong; feeble, infirm,
5.716; timid, 12.262.

invehō, vexī, vectus 3 *v* to carry
into or forward; *passive*
invehī, to ride or drive,
1.155; sail, 5.122; *with acc*
of place, sail to, arrive at,
or in, 7.436; enter, 8.714.

inveniō, vēnī, ventus 4 *v*
to come upon; find out,
find, discover, 6.8 *et al.*

inventor, ōris *m* a finder;
contriver, 2.164. (inveniō).

invergō 3 *v* to cause to incline;
turn into, pour upon, 6.244.

invertō, vertī, versus *3 v* to turn over; invert, change, 11.202.

invictus, a, um *adj* unconquered; invincible, 6.365.

invideō, vīdī, vīsus *2 v* to look into; to look at with dislike; begrudge, envy, 4.234 *et al.*; withhold, deny.

invidia, ae *f* dislike, hatred, jealousy, envy, 2.90; invidia est, foll. by *inf* with *acc*, 4.340. (invideō).

invigilō, āvī, ātus *1 v* to be awake, watch, provide for; wake, or rise early for, or to, 9.605.

inviolābilis, e *adj* not to be violated, inviolable, certain, 11.363.

invīsō, vīsī, vīsus *3 v* to come, or go to see; visit, 4.144 *et al.*

invīsus, a, um hated, hateful, odious, 1.387; (act.), inimical, an enemy, hostile, 11.364.

invīsus, a, um unseen, 2.574.

invītō, āvī, ātus *1 v* to ask as a guest; to invite, 8.178; encourage, incite, 5.292.

invītus, a, um *adj* unwilling, 6.460; unfriendly, 2.402.

invius, a, um without a way; trackless, inaccessible, impassable, 1.537; difficult, 3.383.

invocō, āvī, ātus *1 v* to call upon; invoke, adore, 7.140.

involvō, volvī, volūtus *3 v* to roll on or in; cast upon, 12.292; roll along, carry, 12.689; cover up, obscure, 3.198; conceal, involve, 6.100.

Īō, ūs *f* Io, daughter of Inachus, changed into a cow, watched by Argus, and again restored to her own form, and worshiped by the Egyptians as Isis, 7.789.

iō! (*interj* of joy), ho, huzza! (of woe), oh! behold! woe is me! 7.400.

Iollās, ae *m* a Trojan, 11.640.

Īonius, a, um *adj* Ionian, 3.671; *subst* Īonium, iī, *n*, the Ionian sea, 3.211.

Iōpās, ae *m* a Carthaginian poet, 1.740.

Īphitus, ī *m* a Trojan warrior, 2.435.

ipse, a, um (*gen* ipsīus, dem. *pron*), self, used to emphasize substantives and pronouns expressed or understood; myself, thyself, himself, herself, itself, ourselves, etc., *freq*; sometimes equivalent to just, precisely, exactly, very, even, 5.767 *et al.*; denoting distinction or preëminence, 1.575 *et al.*; of one's self, spontaneously, 7.492 *et al.*; the whole as contrasted with the parts, 12.303.

īra, ae *f* anger, fury, wrath, *freq*; resentment, hatred, 1.251; revengeful, wrathful thought, 2.575; curse, wrathful intent, 11.443; vengeance, 12.946; *pl* angry passions, wrath, 1.4 *et al.*; *personif*, Īrae, ārum, *f*, the Demon of wrath, Wrath, 12.336.

īrāscor, īrātus sum *3 dep v* to be angry, furious; to show anger, 10.712; to collect rage, throw fury into, 12.104; to attack, 10.712. (īra).

Īris, idis *f, acc* **Īrim** Iris, the goddess of the rainbow, daughter of Thaumas and Electra, and messenger of the gods above, 4.694 *et al.*

is, ea, id, *gen* **ēius** dem. *pron* 1. *subst* (= 3d *pers pron*), he, she, it, they, 3.596 *et al.* 2. *adj* that, this, those, these, 2.103 *et al.*; such, 1.529 *et al.*

Ismara, ae *f* a city al the foot of Ismarus, a mountain in Thrace, 10.351.

Ismarus, ī *m* a Maeonian, follower of Aeneas, 10.139.

iste, ista, istud dem. *pron,* properly relating to the second person, that of which you speak, or which pertains to you; that, this; such, 2.521.

istīc *adv* there, in that place, where you are, 10.557. (iste).

istinc *adv* from there, thence, from where you are, 6.389. (iste).

ita *adv* thus, so, in such a manner, 4.533 *et al.*; in oaths, 9.208. (rel to is).

Italī, ōrum *m* the Italians, 1.109. (Ītalia).

Ītalia, ae (Ī by poetic (epic) license) *f* Italy, 1.2 *et al.*

Ītalides, um *f* Italian women; Italian nymphs, 11.657. (Italus).

Italus, a, um Italian, 3.440 *et al.*; *subst* Italī, ōrum, *m,* the Italians, 1.109. (Ītalia).

Italus, ī *m* the ancient king from whom Italy was supposed to have been named, 7.178.

iter, itineris, *n* a going; a journey, passage, voyage, 3.507 *et al.*; track, path, way, 1.370; course, 7.35. (eō).

iterum *adv* a second time, again, *freq*; iterumque iterumque, both again and again, again and again, 2.770.

Ithaca, ae *f* Ithaca, the island of Ulysses in the Ionian sea, 3.272.

Ithacus, a, um *adj* (Ithaca), of Ithaca, Ithacan; *subst* Ithacus, ī, *m,* the Ithacan, Ulysses, 2.104 *et al.*

Itys, yos (*acc* -ym) *m* a Trojan slain by Turnus, 9.574.

iuba, ae *f* the mane of a horse; of a serpent, 2.206; of a helmet, plume, crest, 2.412.

iubar, aris, *n* brightness, radiance, of the sun, or of a star; the sun, morning, 4.130.

iubeō, iussī (*fut perf* **iussō** for iusserō, 11.467), **iussus** 2 *v* to order, request, usually *with inf, freq*; bid, 2.3; ask, invite, 1.708; will, wish, desire, 3.261; direct, enjoin, admonish, 3.697; persuade, advise, 2.37; to clear by command, 10.444; *with subj.*, 10.53.

iūcundus, a, um *adj* pleasant, sweet, delightful, 6.363.

iūdex, icis, *c* a judge, 6.431 *et al.* (iūs and rt. dic, say).

iūdicium, iī, *n* a judgment, decision, 1.27 *et al.* (iūdex).

iugālis, e *adj* (iugum), pertaining to the yoke; yoked together; matrimonial, nuptial, 4.16; *subst* iugālēs, ium, *m*, yoked, or harnessed horses; a team, 7.280.

iūgerum, ī, *n* a Roman acre, about five eighths of the English acre; a iuger, an acre, 6.596; *pl* iūgera, um, acres, 6.596; fields, lands, ground. (*rel to* iungō *and* iugum).

iugō, āvī, ātus 1 *v* to yoke; *figuratively* join in marriage, unite, 1.345. (iugum).

iugulō, āvī, ātus 1 *v* to cut the throat; slay, slaughter, 11.199; immolate, 12.214. (iugulum).

iugulum, ī, *n* the joining part; the throat, 10.415 *et al.* (*rel to* iungō).

iugum, ī, *n* a yoke, 3.542 *et al.*; a span, team, horses, 5.147 *et al.*; cross-bench, seat, bench, 6.411; of hills or mountains, summit, top, ridge, 1.498; mount, 7.799; brow of a hill, 8.236; *figuratively* subjection, 10.78; *pl* iuga, ōrum, *metonym* car, chariot, 6.804; 10.594. (*rel to* iungō).

Iūlius, iī *m* Julius, the name of the Roman gens in which the family of Caesar was the most prominent, 6.789; applied to Augustus, 1.288.

Iūlus, ī *m* Iulus or Ascanius, son of Aeneas, 1.267, et *freq*.

iūnctūra, ae *f* a joining; joint, 2.464. (iungō).

iungō, iūnxī, iūnctus 3 *v* to join; unite, 1.73 *et al.*; clasp, 3.83; yoke, harness, 5.817; bind, tie, 8.485; connect, arrange, 3.451; ally, reconcile, 11.129; (w. sē understood), to join one's self to, reach, *with dat* 10.240; (with sibi), to join, 4.142; 11.145; *part*, iūnctus, a, um, joined, *freq*; close together, equal, 5.157.

Iūnō, ōnis *f* Juno, the Sabine and Roman name for the wife and sister of Jupiter, daughter of Saturn, 1.4 *et al.*; Iūnō īnferna, the Juno of the lower world, Proserpine, 6.138.

Iūnōnius, a, um *adj* (Iūnō), pertaining to Juno, under the influence of Juno; Juno's, 1.671.

Iuppiter, Iovis *m* Jupiter, son of Saturn and Rhea, and king of the gods, 1.223; Iuppiter Stygius, Pluto, 4.638.

iūre *adv* with right, justly, 9.642. (iūs, iūris, *n*).

iūrgium, iī, *n* a lawsuit; a quarrel; reproof, 11.406. (iūrgō, dispute).

iūrō, āvī, ātus 1 *v* to take an oath, 4.426; call to witness, swear by, *with prep* per, 6.458; *with acc alone* 6.351; *with acc* of thing and person, 12.197. (iūs).

iūs, iūris, *n* law, right, equity, justice, *freq*; obligation, 2.157; *pl* iūra, um, justice, 1.293; laws, courts, 1.426; rules, 1.731; dare iūra, to administer laws or justice; dispense laws, rule (perhaps also including the idea of enacting laws), 1.293.

iussum, ī, *n* a thing ordered; command, injunction, order, 1.77 *et al.* (iubeō).

iussus, ūs, *m, only in abl sing* (**lubeō**) by command, order, decree, 2.247.

iūstitia, ae *f* righteousness, justice, equity, 1.523 *et al.* (iūstus).

iūstus, a, um *adj* (iūs), righteous, just, 1.544 *et al.*; fair, equal, 1.508; *subst* iūstum, ī, *n*, that which is just, meet, proper, sufficient, enough.

Iūturna, ae *f* a Naiad, sister of Turnus, 12.154 *et al.*

iuvenālis, e *adj* (iuvenis), pertaining to youth; youthful, 2.518.

iuvencus, a, um *adj* (iuvenis), young; *subst* iuvencus, ī, *m*, a young bullock, 3.247 *et al.*; iuvenca, ae, *f*, a heifer, 8.208 *et al.*

iuvenis, e *adj* young; in the vigor or flower of life; young, youthful, *freq*; *subst* iuvenis, is, *c*, a young person, youth; young man, 1.321 *et al.*

iuventa, ae *f* youthfulness; the age of youth; youth, 1.590 *et al.* (iuvenis).

iuventās, ātis *f* youthfulness; the age of youth; youthful vigor, 5.398. (iuvenis).

iuventūs, ūtis *f* youthfulness; the age of youth; collective, young people, the youth; warriors, 1.467. (iuvenis).

iuvō, iūvī, iūtus 1 *v* to help, aid, assist, 1.571; delight; *impers*, iuvat, it is of use, it avails, helps, 10.56; pleases, delights, gratifies, 1.203.

iūxtā (*adv and prep with acc*), near, close, near by, 2.513; at the same time, 2.666; near to, 3.506.

Ixīōn, onis *m* the father of Pirithous, and king of the Lapithae, who was bound to an ever revolving wheel in Hades for offering violence to Juno, 6.601.

Karthāgō, inis *f* a city built by Phoenician adventurers on the northern coast of Africa, opposite Sicily, a short distance N.E. of the modern Tunis, 1.13 *et al.* (Καρχηδών, new city).

labefaciō, fecī, factus 3 *v, passive* **labefīō, fīerī, factus** (**labō** and **faciō**) to cause to totter or waver; *part*, labefactus, a, um, shaken, 4.395; yielding, melting, 8.390.

lābēs, is *f* a falling, sinking down; decline, beginning of evil or ruin, downward step, 2.97; corruption, stain, blemish, 6.746. (1. lābor).

Labīcī, ōrum *m* the Labici, or people of Labicum or Labici, a Latin town near the present Colonna, 7.796.

labō, āvī, ātus 1 *v* to give way, begin to yield; totter, 2.492; of the mind, waver, 4.22; falter, flag, despond, 12.223.

labor (**labōs**), **ōris** *m* labor, effort, toil, working, work, 1.431 *et al.*; care; task, 4.115; effort, activity, of man, 11.425; adventure, enterprise, 2.385; burden, 2.708; fatigue, difficulty, hardship, 1.330;

struggle, danger, distress, misfortune, calamity, woe, suffering, 1.10 *et al.*; hard fate, 12.727; an eclipse, 1.742; the product of work, workmanship, work, 1.455; *personif*, Labōs, Toil, 6.277.

lābor, lapsus sum *3 dep v* to slide, glide down, or slip, *freq*; fall down, 2.465; ebb, 11.628; pass away, 2.14; descend, 2.262; glide, sail, skim along, 8.91; flow, 3.281; fall, perish, 2.430; decline, 4.318; faint, 3.309.

labōrō, āvī, ātus *1 v* to toil, make effort; work out; prepare, knead, 8.181; fashion; embroider, 1.639. (2. labor).

labrum, ī, *n* a lip, 11.572.

lābrum, ī, *n* a vat or tub; a bowl, vase, vessel, 8.22.

Labyrinthus, ī *m* the Labyrinth, 5.588.

lac, lactis, *n* milk, 3.66 *et al.*; juice, 4.514.

Lacaena, ae, *adj f* Lacedaemonian or Spartan; *subst* the Spartan woman; Helen, 2.601.

Lacedaemōn, onis (*acc* **ona**) *f* Lacedaemon or Sparta, the capital of Laconia, 7.363.

Lacedaemonius, a, um *adj* Lacedaemonian, Spartan, 3.328.

lacer, era, erum *adj* torn, mangled, bruised, mutilated, 5.275.

lacerō, āvī, ātus *1 v* to tear, mutilate; wound, 3.41; rend, 12.98. (lacer).

lacertus, ī *m* the upper arm, from the shoulder to the elbow; the arm, 5.141 *et al.*

lacessō, cessīvī, cessītus *3 intens v* to provoke, rouse, irritate, incite, 5.429; call forth, summon, rouse, 10.10; challenge, attack, assail, 11.585; strike, smite, 7.527; slap with the hand, caress, cheer, 12.85.

Lacīnius, a, um *adj* (Lacinium), of Lacinium, a promontory near Croton, on the southern coast of Italy; Lacinian; Dīva Lacīnia, the Lacinian goddess; Juno, 3.552.

lacrima, ae *f* a tear, 1.228 *et al.*

lacrimābilis, e *adj* (lacrimō), that calls for tears; piteous, 3.39; causing tears; woeful, disastrous, 7.604.

lacrimō, āvī, ātus *1 v* to shed tears, weep, 1.459. (lacrima).

lacrimōsus, a, um *adj* (lacrima), tearful; sad, mournful, piteous, 11.274.

lacteus, a, um *adj* (lac), milky, full of milk; milk-white, 8.660.

lacus, ūs *m* a lake, pool, source, 8.74; fen, 2.135.

Ladēs, is *m* a Lycian follower of Aeneas, slain by Turnus, 12.343.

Lādōn, ōnis, *acc* **-ōna** *m* Ladon, a follower of Pallas, 10.413.

laedō, laesī, laesus *3 v* to strike violently; smite,

2.231; bruise, strike, hit, 7.809; hurt, injure, offend, thwart, 1.8; violate, 12.496.

laena, ae *f* an upper garment; cloak, mantle, 4.262.

Lāertius, a, um *adj* (Lāertēs), of Laertes, father of Ulysses; Laertian, 3.272.

laetitia, ae *f* joy, 1.514 *et al.* (laetus).

laetor, ātus sum 1 *dep v* to rejoice, *with abl, gen, infin,* or absolute, 1.393 *et al.* (laetus).

laetus, a, um *adj* joyful, joyous, glad, 4.418, et *freq;* delighting in (w. *abl*), 1.275.696; 2.417; springing, 10.643; sparkling, radiant, 1.591; happy, auspicious, 1.605; abounding, rich, full (w. *abl* or *gen*), 1.441; well fed, fat, 3.220; blissful, blessed, 6.744.

laeva *adv* on the left, 5.163.

laeva, ae *f* (*sc* **manus**) the left hand, 1.611; ab laevā, on the left side, 8.460.

laeva, ōrum, *n* the left-hand places; waters or waves on the left hand, 5.825.

laevum *adv* on the left, 2.693.

laevus, a, um *adj* the left, 10.495; (situated) on the left, 3.412; the left, 3.420; *figuratively* ill-starred, unpropitious, baleful, 10.275; infatuated, blind, 2.54.

Lagus, ī *m* a Rutulian, 10.381.

lambō, ī, itus 3 *v* to lick, 2.211; of flame, touch, lick, 3.574.

lāmenta, ōrum, *n* a wailing, cry of grief, lamentation, mourning, moaning, 4.667. (sing. not in good use).

lāmentābilis, e *adj* (lāmentor, deplore), deplorable; pitiable; to be deplored, 2.4.

lampas, adis *f* a light, torch, 6.587; firebrand, 9.535.

Lamus, ī *m* a Rutulian, 9.334.

Lamyrus, ī *m* a Rutulian, 9.334.

lancea, ae *f* a lance, light spear, javelin, 12.375.

langueō, uī 2 *v* to be faint, to languish, grow feeble; *part,* languēns, entis, of the sea, 10.289; of flowers, drooping, 11.69.

languēscō, languī 3 *inc v* to become faint, grow weak, droop, 9.436. (langueō).

languidus, a, um *adj* (langueō), languid, 12.908.

lāniger, era, erum *adj* (lāna, wool, and gerō), bearing wool; fleecy, 3.660.

laniō, āvī, ātus 1 *v* to lacerate, mangle, mutilate, 6.494.

lānūgo, inis *f* wooly substance, down.

lanx, lancis *f* a broad dish or plate; a charger, platter, 8.284; *pl* lancēs, the basins of weighing scales; scales, 12.725.

Lāocoön, ontis *m* a Trojan prince and priest of Apollo, 2.41; serving also as priest of Neptune, 2.201.

Lāodamīa, ae *f* daughter of Acastus and wife of Protesilaus, who killed herself after her husband was slain by Hector, 6.447.

Lāomedontēus, a, um *adj* (Lāomedon), pertaining to Laomedon, father of Priam; Laomedontean, Trojan, 4.542.

Lāomedontiadēs, ae *m* a son or descendant of Laomedon, 8.162; *pl* the Trojans, 3.248 *et al.* (Lāomedon).

lapidōsus, a, um *adj* (lapis), full of stones; hard as stone, stony, 3.649.

lapis, idis *m* a stone, rock, 12.906 *et al.*; marble.

Lapitha, ae, c one of the Lapithae; *pl* Lapithae, ārum (um, 7.305); the Lapithae, a race of Thessalians, who fought with the Centaurs at the marriage of Pirithous, king of the Lapithae, 6.601 *et al.*

lāpsō, āre, *freq n* to fall down; slip, 2.551. (1. lābor).

lāpsus, ūs *m* a slipping; gliding, 2.225; gliding movement, 2.225; turning, movement, 2.236; descent, flight, 3.225; course, 4.524. (1. lābor).

laquear, āris, *n* a ceiling with hollows or panels; a paneled or fretted ceiling, 1.726.

Lār, Laris *m* a fireside, hearth, or household god, 5.744; hesternum Larem, the household god of yesterday, 8.543; *metonym* household, property, home, dwelling.

largior, ītus sum 4 *dep* to give largely; bestow, grant, 10.494. (largus).

largus, a, um *adj* ample; spacious, expansive, 6.640; plentiful, copious, flowing, 1.465; bountiful, free, 10.619; *with gen,* lavish, 11.338.

Larīdēs, is *m* a Rutulian, son of Daucus, 10.391.

Larīna, ae *f* a follower of Camilla, 11.655.

Larīsaeus, a, um of Larissa, a Thessalian town, on the southern bank of the Peneus; Larissaean, 2.197. (Larissa).

lassus, a, um *adj* faint, tired, wearied, 2.739.

Latagus, ī *m* a Tyrrhenian, 10.697.

lātē *adv* widely; far and wide, 1.21; on all sides, far around, 1.163; all over, 12.308. (lātus).

latebra, ae *f* a hiding place; recess, lodgment, retreat, 12.389; usually in *pl* latebrae, ārum, an ambuscade; covert, retreat; cavern, 3.424; recess, cavity, 2.38; the hatches of a ship, the hold, 10.657. (lateō).

latebrōsus, a, um *adj* (latebra), full of lurking places or recesses; full of holes; porous, 5.214; secret, 8.713.

lateō, uī 2 *v* to be hidden, lie concealed, 2.48; to lurk; be sheltered, 10.805; be unknown to, escape the knowledge of, 1.130; *part,* latēns, entis, hidden, concealed, 3.237; hiding, lurking, 2.568.

latex, icis *m* a liquid; liquor; wine, 1.686; water, 4.512.

Latīnī, ōrum *m* the people of Latium; the Latins, 12.823 *et al.*

Latīnus, a, um *adj* (Latium), of Latium; Latin, 1.6 *et al.*; Latīna, ae, *f*, a Latin woman, 12.604.

Latīnus, ī *m* Latinus, a king of Latium, whose capital was Laurentum, and whose daughter, Lavinia, became the wife of Aeneas, 6.891 *et al.* (Latium).

Latium, iī, *n* a country of ancient Italy, extending from the left bank of the lower Tiber to Campania, 1.6; *metonym* for Latīnī, the Latins, people of Latium, 10.365 *et al.* (2. latus; Virgil, 8.323, derives it from lateō).

Lātōna, ae *f* the mother of Apollo and Diana, 1.502.

Lātōnia, ae *f* Diana, 11.534.

Lātōnius, a, um *adj* (Lātōna), of Latona, Latonian, 9.405 *et al.*; *subst* Lātōnia, ae, *f*, Diana, 11.534.

lātrātor, ōris *m* one who barks like a dog; a barker, the barking, 8.698. (lātrō).

lātrātus, ūs *m* a barking; baying, 5.257 *et al.* (lātrō).

lātrō, āvī, ātus *1 v* to bark, snarl, bay, 6.401 *et al.*; of waves, 7.588.

latrō, ōnis *m* a hired servant, mercenary soldier, huntsman, 12.7.

lātus, a, um *adj* wide, broad, 1.313; spacious, ample, large, 4.199; widespread, far-extending, 1.225.

latus, eris, *n* a side, 1.105 *et al.*; coast, 8.416; laterum

iūnctūrae, joinings of the sides of a belt, i.e, ends of a belt, 12.274.

laudō, āvī, ātus *1 v* to praise, 2.586; commend, 11.460. (laus).

Laurēns, entis *adj* (Laurentum), of Laurentum, the ancient capital of Latium; Laurentine, Laurentian, 5.797 *et al.*, *subst* Laurentēs, um, *pl m*, the Laurentians, 7.63 *et al.*

Laurentēs, um, *pl m* the people of Laurentum, the ancient capital of Latium, the Laurentians, 7.63 *et al.*

Laurentius, a, um *adj* (Laurentum), of Laurentum, the ancient capital of Latium; Laurentine, Laurentian, 10.709.

laurus, ī *f* the laurel or bay tree, 2.513; a laurel crown or wreath, 3.81.

laus, laudis *f* praise, 1.609 *et al.*; fame, glory, 2.584; praiseworthy conduct, prowess, heroism, virtue, merit, 1.461 *et al.*

Lausus, ī *m* an Etruscan chief, son of Mezentius, 7.649 *et al.*

lautus, a, um washed; neat, elegant; stately, magnificent, 8.361. (lavō).

Lāvīnia, ae *f* a Latin princess, daughter of King Latinus, 6.764 *et al.*

Lāvīnium, iī, *n* a city of Latium, built by Aeneas and named after his Latin wife, Lavinia, 1.270 *et al.* (Lāvīnia).

Lāvīnius, a, um and Lāvīnus, a, um, *adj* (Lāvīnium), of or belonging to Lavinium, 4.236.

lavō, lāvī, lautus, and **lōtus,** *1* and *3, v* to wash, bathe, 3.663; wet, sprinkle, 6.227; *part,* lautus, a, um, washed; neat, elegant; stately, magnificent, 8.361.

laxō, āvī, ātus *1 v* to loosen, slacken; unfasten, undo, open, 2.259; uncoil, let out, 3.267; open, clear, 6.412; of the body, relax, 5.836; of the mind, relieve, 9.225. (laxus).

laxus, a, um *adj* loose; disjointed, unfastened, gaping, open, 1.122; slack, loosened, free, 1.63; unbent, 11.874.

lebēs, ētis *m* a kettle or caldron, 3.466.

lēctus, a, um gathered, collected, 6.228; picked, culled; chosen, choice, 9.272 *et al.* (legō).

lēctus, ī *m* a gathering, as of boughs, leaves, straw, etc.; a couch, 4.496. (legō, to gather).

Lēda, ae *f* wife of Tyndarus, and mother of Castor and Pollux, and of Helen and Clytemnestra, 1.652.

Lēdaeus, a, um *adj* (Lēda), pertaining to Leda; Ledaean; daughter of Leda, 7.364; descendant of Leda, 3.328.

lēgātus, ī *m* a legate, envoy, ambassador, 8.143 *et al.* (lēgō, lēgāre, to delegate).

lēgifer, era, erum *adj* (lēx and ferō), law-bringing, law-giving, 4.58.

legiō, ōnis *f* a levy of troops; the original Roman army; then, a grand division of the army; a legion; host, 7.681; army, 8.605.(legō, to choose).

legō, lēgī, lēctus *3 v* to gather, collect, 5.209; cull, pick, gather; gather in, furl, 3.532; wind up, 10.815; select, elect, choose, 1.426; take to one's self, claim, 10.79; take in point after point in travel *or* with the eye, coast along, pass by, 3.292; trace, pursue, 9.393; traverse, 2.208; 12.481; read; survey, review, 6.755.

Leleges, um *m* Pelasgian tribes of Asia Minor and Greece, 8.725.

Lēmnius, a, um *adj* pertaining to Lemnos, an island in the Aegean Sea; the home of Vulcan; Lemnian, 8.454.

Lēnaeus, a, um *adj* pertaining to the wine press; Bacchic, Lenaean, 4.207.

lēniō, īvī or **iī, ītus** *4 v* to render mild; allay; soothe, 4.528; quiet, calm, 6.468; of inanimate things, 8.87. (lēnis).

lēnis, e *adj* mild, 3.70; gentle, quiet, 2.782.

lentō, āvī, ātus *1 v* to make flexible; of oars, bend, ply, 3.384. (lentus).

lentus, a, um *adj* adhesive, clammy, sticky, viscid; tough, 12.773; pliant, limber, 6.137; ductile, malleable, 7.634; slender, 3.31; 12.489; sluggish, creeping, 5.682; quiet, 7.28; inactive, 12.237.

leō, leōnis *m* a lion, 2.722 *et al.*

lepus, oris, *m,* and **epicene** a hare, 9.563 *et al.*

Lerna, ae *f* Lerna, a marshy forest near Argos, where the Lernaean hydra was slain by Hercules, 6.287 *et al.*

Lernaeus, a, um *adj* (Lerna), of Lerna, Lernaean, 8.300.

lētālis, e *adj* (lētum), deadly, fatal, mortal, 4.73; ominous of death, 12.877.

Lēthaeus, a, um *adj* of Lethe, the river of forgetfulness in Hades; oblivious, Lethean, 5.854 *et al.*

lētifer, era, erum *adj* (lētum *and* ferō), death-bringing; deadly, 3.139.

lētum, ī, *n* death, destruction, 2.134 *et al.* (cf. dēleō).

Leucaspis, is *m* Leucaspis, a companion of Aeneas, 6.334.

Leucātēs, ae *m* Leucata, a promontory of the island of Leucadia, off the coast of Acarnania, 3.274.

levāmen, inis, *n* an alleviation; relief, mitigation; solace, 3.709. (2. levō).

levis, e *adj* of little weight, light, 2.682 *et al.*; thin, slender, 10.817; delicate, tender, 12.207; light-armed, 11.868; fleeting, fleet, swift, flying, 1.147; flitting, airy, 10.663; sudden, 12.489; insignificant, small, 7.232; mean, 12.764.

lēvis, e *adj* smooth; slippery, 5.328; polished, 5.91.

levō, āvī, ātus *1 v* to render light; lighten; lift, aid, 1.145; raise, 4.690; *figuratively* ease,

relieve of (w. *abl*); support, rest, 10.834; reënforce, help, 2.452; mitigate, 3.36; allay, 7.495; cure, 7.755; relieve, 7.571. (2. levis).

lēvō, āvī, ātus *1 v* to make smooth, polish, 5.306. (1. lēvis).

lēx, lēgis *f* a bill proposed to the people for enactment; statute, law, decree, 1.507 *et al.*; *pl* lēgēs, um, government, 4.231; conditions, terms, 4.618.

lībāmen, inis, *n* a libation; sacrifice, offering, 6.246. (lībō).

libēns, entis *adj* willing; well-pleased, ready, gladly, freely, 3.438 *et al.*

liber, brī *m* the rind; inner bark of a tree.

līber, era, erum *adj* (rel to libet), acting at pleasure; free, unrestrained, 12.74; freeborn, *with abl,* set free, loosed from, loose, 11.493; *with gen,* 10.154; *adv* liberē, freely.

Līber, erī *m* Liber, the god of wine and hilarity, identified by the Romans with the Greek Bacchus, 6.805 *et al.*

lībertās, ātis *f* liberty, freedom, 6.821. (2. līber).

libet, uit or **libitum est,** *2 (impers),* it pleases, is agreeable to, is one's pleasure, will, mind.

lībō, āvī, ātus *1 v* to taste, sip; to touch lightly; kiss, 1.256; pour out as a drink offering, 1.736; make a libation, 3.354; (w. *acc* of the object on which the libation is poured), to pour libations on, 12.174.

lībrō, āvī, ātus *1 v* to balance, poise; of weapons, to aim, 5.479; to dart, 9.417. (lībra, a balance).

lībum, ī, *n* a cake of meal, oil, and honey, used in sacrifice. (lībō).

Liburnī, ōrum *m* the Liburni or Liburnians, a warlike people, inhabiting Liburnia, near the head of the Adriatic Sea on the Illyrian coast, 1.244.

Libya, ae *f* Libya; northern Africa; by poetic license, Africa, 1.22 *et al.*

Libycus, a, um *adj* Libyan, 1.339 *et al.*; *subst* Libycum, ī, *n*, the Libyan or African sea, 5.595.

Libystis, idis *adj* Libyan, 5.37.

licenter *adv* without restraint, freely, 7.557. (licēns), (comp. licentius).

licet (*conj*, as a concessive), though, albeit, although, 6.802 *et al.* (liceō).

licet, licuit or **licitum est** it is allowed; permitted, proper, lawful, right; one may, 5.82 *et al.* (liceō).

Lichās, ae *m* a Latin slain by Aeneas, 10.315.

licitus, a, um, allowed, allowable; free, 8.468. (liceō).

Licymnia, ae *f* Licymnia, a slave, 9.546.

Liger, erī *m* an Etruscan slain by Aeneas, 10.576 *et al.*

līgnum, ī, *n* wood; structure, frame, 2.45; tree, 12.767.

ligō, āvī, ātus *1 v* to tie, fasten, bind, 2.217; with in, encumber, 10.794.

Ligus, uris *m* a Ligurian; inhabitant of Liguria, the modern Piedmont; *pl* Ligurēs, um, the Ligurians, 10.185.

līlium, ī, *n* a lily, 6.709.

Lilybēius, a, um *adj* (Lilybaeum), of Lilybaeum, the western promontory of Sicily; Lilybaean, 3.706.

limbus, ī *m* a border, hem, fringe, 4.137.

līmen, inis, *n* a threshold, 2.242 *et al.*; *metonym* door, gate, portal, 2.480; a dwelling, abode, palace, 1.389; realm, 6.696; border, limit, 10.355; the line where the race begins or ends, the calx, the starting point, 5.316; in limine, near at hand, in sight, 7.598.

līmes, itis *m* a cross path bounding two fields; border, boundary, train, 2.697; track, passage, 10.514. (*rel to* limen).

līmōsus, a, um full of mud; miry, slimy, 2.135. (līmus).

līmus, ī *m* mud, mire, slime, 6.416.

līneus, a, um *adj* (linum), flaxen, 5.510.

lingua, ae *f* the tongue, 2.211 *et al.*; speech, 11.338; voice, note, 3.361.

linquō, līquī *3 v* to leave, 1.517, and *freq*; desert, abandon, flee from, 3.213; pass by, 3.705; depart from, leave, 3.124; of death, yield up, 3.140; give up or over, desist from, 3.160.

linteum, ī, *n* linen cloth; sailcloth; a sail, 3.686. (linum).

līnum, ī, *n* flax or hemp.

Liparē, ēs *f* Lipara or Lipare, one of the Aeolian Islands, N.E. of Sicily, 8.417.

liquefaciō, fēcī, factus *3 v, pass*; **liquefīō, fierī, factus sum** to render liquid; melt, liquefy, 3.576. (liqueō and faciō).

liqueō, liquī *2 v* to be fluid; *part*, liquēns, entis, liquid, fluid, 5.238.

liquēscō, licuī *3 inc v* to become fluid or liquid; melt, 8.446. (liqueō).

liquidus, a, um *adj* (liqueō), flowing, liquid, fluid, 5.217 *et al.*; clear, serene, 6.202.

līquor *3 dep v* to be in a liquid state; run, ooze, trickle, flow, 3.28; *part*, liquēns, entis, liquid, fluid, 1.432.

Līris, is *m* an Etruscan warrior, 11.670.

līs, lītis *f* a strife, contest, dispute, 12.898.

litō, āvī, ātus *1 v* to sacrifice auspiciously; atone, expiate, make atonement, 2.118; to offer in sacrifice, 4.50.

lītoreus, a, um *adj* (lītus), pertaining to the seashore; on the shore; very rarely, on the river bank, 3.390; of the shore, seashore, 12.248.

lītus, oris, *n* the seashore, beach, strand; shore, coast, 1.3 *et al.*; shore, 6.900.

lituus, ī *m* an augur's staff or wand, 7.187; a cornet, trumpet, clarion, 6.167.

līveō *2 v* to be bluish, pallid, livid, 7.687.

līvidus, a, um *adj* (liveō), lead-colored, livid, dusky, 6.320.

locō, āvī, ātus *1 v* to place, put, 1.213 *et al.*; lay, 1.428; found, 1.247. (locus).

Locrī, ōrum *m* the Locriam; inhabitants of Locris, in Greece; Locri Epizephyrii, in Bruttium, 3.399; the Opuntii, of Opus, in Locris, 11.265.

locus, ī, *m, pl* **loca,** *n*, and **locī** *m* a place, 1.159, and *freq*; site, 1.425; country, locality, region, 1.51; station, 2.30; way, 2.633; place, point, 2.322; lot, 5.492; room, opportunity, place, 4.319; space, course, 11.180.

longaevus, a, um *adj* (longus and aevum), of advanced age; aged, 2.525 *et al.*

longē *adv* at a long distance, far; far off, remote, 1.252; from afar, 3.556; far out, or forward, 11.606; in a long train, 11.94; longē esse, to be far away; *figuratively* to be unavailing, 12.52; *compar* longius, farther; too far, 5.461.

longinquus, a, um *adj* (longus), far distant, in space or time; distant, remote, long, 3.415.

longus, a, um *adj* long, 1.186, and *freq*; extended, far-extending, 3.383; distant,

2.780; far-receding, deep,
1.159; in time, long, protracted,
2.109; long-continued, 4.463;
many, 10.549; lingering,
8.488; abiding, lasting,
3.487; *superl*, very long,
1.641; ex longō, long, 9.64;
adv longum, for a long time,
long, 10.740; a long distance.

loquāx, ācis *adj* (loquor),
talkative; prattling, chirping,
12.475; noisy, 11.458.

loquēla, ae *f* a talking; speech;
a word, 5.842. (loquor).

loquor, locūtus sum 3 *dep v*
to speak, 1.614 *et al.*; tell,
6.266; say, 1.731; sing, 6.662.

lōrīca, ae *f* a leather corselet;
a corselet of any material; a
hauberk, cuirass, coat of mail,
3.467; 10.485 *et al.* (lōrum).

lōrum, ī, *n* a leather strap
or thong, 2.273; *pl* lōra,
ōrum, reins, 1.156 *et al.*;
harness, 9.318.

lūbricus, a, um *adj* smooth,
slippery, 2.474; *figuratively*
subtle, cunning, slippery,
11.716; *subst* lūbrica, ōrum,
n, a slippery place, 5.335.

lūbricus, a, um *adj* smooth,
slippery, 2.474; *figuratively*
subtle, cunning, slippery,
11.716; *subst* lūbrica, ōrum,
n, a slippery place, 5.335.

Lūcagus, ī *m* an Etruscan
slain by Aeneas, 10.575.

Lūcās, ae *m* a follower
of Turnus, 10.561.

lūceō, lūxī 2 *v* to shine,
beam, gleam, glisten,

10.137 *et al.*; to be exposed
to view, show, 11.693.

Lūcetius, iī *m* a Latin slain
by Ilioneus, 9.570.

lūcidus, a, um *adj* (lūceō),
bright, shining, gleaming,
glittering, 5.306; clear, 3.585.

Lūcifer, erī *m* the light bearer;
Lucifer; Venus as morning
star, 2.801 *et al.* (lūx and ferō).

lūctāmen, inis, *n* a striving;
toil, 8.89. (lūctor).

lūctificus, a, um *adj* (lūctus
and faciō), causing grief;
woe-bearing, 7.324.

lūctor, ātus sum 1 *dep v* to
struggle, strive, contend, 1.53;
wrestle, 6.643; *with inf*, 12.387.

lūctus, ūs *m* a mourning;
sorrow, grief, woe,
lamentation, 2.298, and *freq*;
personif, 6.274. (lūgeō).

lūcus, ī *m* a consecrated wood;
sacred grove, 6.259 *et al.*; in
general, a grove, wood, forest.

lūdibrium, iī, *n* a mocking;
mockery, sport, 6.75. (lūdō).

lūdicer, cra, crum *adj* (lūdus),
sportive; vain, trivial, 12.764.

lūdō, lūsī, lūsus 3 *v* to play,
frolic, sport, 1.397 *et al.*; play
with dice, 9.336; make sport of,
mock, delude, deceive, 1.352;
make one's sport, 11.427.

lūdus, ī *m* play, sport, pastime,
9.606; mirth; *pl* lūdī,
ōrum, games, public or
national, 3.280. (lūdō).

luēs, is *f* a pestilence, plague, contagion, blight, 3.139; disorder, infection, 7.354.

lūgeō, lūxī, lūctus *2 v* to mourn, 11.287; bewail, deplore, 2.85; *part*, lūgēns, entis, wailing, mourning; of mourning, 6.441.

lūgubrē *adv* mournful, mournfully, dismally, ominously, 10.273. (lūgubris, *adj* mournful).

lūmen, inis, *n* light, 2.683 *et al.*; a light; a luminary, star; a taper, candle, 8.411; fire, 9.189; daylight, dawn, day, 6.356; beam, ray, 8.69; the eye, 1.226 *et al.*; life, 2.85; air, 3.600; glow, brightness, beauty, luster, 1.590; *pl* emphatic for *sing* 12.63 *et al.*; lūmina ducum, splendid leaders, 11.349. (lūceō).

lūna, ae *f* the moon, 1.742 *et al.*; moonlight, 2.340 *et al.* (rel to lūceō).

lūnō, āvī, ātus *1 v* to shape like a half moon; *part*, lūnātus, a, um, shaped like the half moon; crescent-shaped, crescent-, 1.490.

luō, uī *3 v* to set free by atonement; pay for, atone for, expiate, 1.136 *et al.*; suffer, 11.849. (rel to λύω, loosen).

lupa, ae *f* a she-wolf, 1.275. (cf. lupus).

Lupercal, cālis, *n* the Lupercal, a cave on the Palatine at Rome, sacred to Lupercus or Pan, 8.343.

Lupercī, ōrum *m* priests of Lupercus or Lycean Pan, 8.663.

lupus, ī *m* a wolf, 3.428 *et al.*

lūstrālis, e *adj* (lūstrum), pertaining to the lustrum; expiatory, 8.183.

lūstrō, āvī, ātus *1 v* to purify by atonement, 3.279; go round the fields with the victims; hence to bless, ask for a blessing on; go or dance around an altar or the image of a god, 7.391; traverse, pass across, around, or over, 1.608; pass in review, parade before, 5.578; run through, 2.528; search, 1.577; observe, survey, 1.453; watch, mark, 11.763; of the sun, illuminate, 4.607. (lūstrum).

lustrum, ī, *n* bog, morass; den or haunt of wild beasts; a wood, forest.

lūstrum, ī, *n* a purifying atonement; the national lustrum or atoning sacrifice, the suovetaurilia, made at Rome every fifth year, at the taking of the census; the period of a lustrum, five years; an indefinite period; age, 1.283. (luō, to atone).

lūteus, a, um *adj* (lūtum, a plant yielding a yellow dye), yellowish; gold-colored, saffron-hued, 7.26.

lūx, lūcis *f* light, 1.306, and *freq*; day or hour, 2.668; life, 4.631; the upper world as opposed to Hades; flame, 12.115; mental light, 12.669; metaph., glory, light, 2.281; lūce, in the light, by day, 9.153. (cf. lūceō).

lūxuriō, āvī, ātus *1 v*, and **lūxurior, ātus sum** *1 dep v* to luxuriate, foll. by *ablat*;

to abound, be full; rejoice, 11.497. (lūxuria, abundance).

lūxus, ūs *m* excess, extravagance; luxury, sumptuousness, magnificence, 1.637; wanton pleasure, sensuality, 4.193.

Lyaeus, ī *m* the wine-god, Bacchus, 4.58.

Lycaeus, a, um of Lycaeus, a mountain in Arcadia noted for the worship of Zeus and Pan, Lycaean, 8.344.

Lycāōn, ōnis *m* a Gnossian or Cretan maker of arms, 9.304.

Lycāonius, a, um *adj* of Lycaonia, a country of Asia Minor, 10.749.

lychnus, ī *m* a lamp, light, 1.726.

Lycia, ae *f* a country on the S.W. coast of Asia Minor, 4.143.

Lyciī, ōrum *m* the Lycians, 1.113.

Lycius, a, um *adj* (Lycia), Lycian, 6.334 *et al.*; *pl* Lyciī, ōrum, *m*, the Lycians, 1.113.

Lyctius, a, um of Lyctus, a town in Crete; Lyctian, Cretan, 3.401.

Lycūrgus, ī *m* son of Dryas, and king of the Thracian Edoni, punished by Bacchus with madness, and driven to self-destruction, on account of his opposition to the Bacchanalian orgies, 3.14.

Lycus, ī *m* a companion of Aeneas, 1.222.

lympha, ae *f* clear spring water; water, 4.635 *et al.*; *pl* for *sing* 1.701 *et al.*

lymphō, āvī, ātus 1 *v* to dilute with water; to craze;

part, lymphātus, a, um, mad, distracted, frenzied, furious, 7.377. (lympha).

Lynceus (*dissyll*), **eī** *m* one of the companions of Aeneas, 9.768.

lynx, lyncis, *c* a lynx, 1.323 *et al.*

Lyrnēsius, a, um *adj* (Lyrnēsus), of Lyrnesus; Lyrnesian, 10.128.

Lyrnēsus, ī *f* Lyrnesus or Lyrnessus, a town in the Troad, 12.547.

Lydī, ōrum *m* the people of Lydia; the Lydians; Etruscans, descendants of the Lydians, 9.11. (from the *adj* Lydus, a, um, used as *subst*).

Lydius, a, um. (*adj*) of Lydia; Lydian, 8.479; also Etruscan or Tuscan (as the Etrusci were supposed to have sprung from the Lydians), 2.781 *et al.*

Machāōn, onis *m* a Greek prince, surgeon of the Greeks at Troy, and said to have been the son of Aesculapius, 2.263.

māchina, ae *f* a machine, fabric, engine, 2.46 *et al.*

maciēs, ēī *f* emaciation, leanness; ghastliness, 3.590.

māctō, āvī, ātus 1 *v* to magnify by worship; to sacrifice, immolate, 2.202; slay, slaughter, 8.294 *et al.*

māctus, a, um *adj* only used in *nom* and vocat., honored; voc., mācte, well done! go on! 9.641.

macula, ae *f* a spot, 5.566 *et al.*

maculō, āvī, ātus 1 *v* to spot; stain; defile, 3.29; *figuratively* 10.851. (macula).

maculōsus, a, um adj (macula), covered with spots; speckled, spotted, 1.323.

madefaciō, fēcī, factus 3 v; passive **madefīō, factus sum, fierī** to make wet, to wet, moisten, 5.330. (madeō and faciō).

madeō 2 v to be moist, wet; drenched, 12.691; part, madēns, entis, wet, moist; besmeared, perfumed, 4.216.

madēscō, maduī 3 inc v to become wet; drip, be drenched, 5.697. (madeō).

madidus, a, um adj (madeō), wet, dripping, drenched, 5.179.

Maeander, drī m a river of Ionia, famous for its windings; met., a winding; a waving or winding border, 5.251.

Maeōn, onis m Maeon, a Rutulian, 10.337.

Maeonia, ae f the ancient name of Lydia, the country in Asia Minor whence emigrated the Tyrrhenians or Etruscans to Italy; hence, for Etruria, 8.499.

Maeonidae, ārum m Maeonians or Lydians; people of Lydian descent; hence, Tyrrhenians or Etrurians, Etruscans, 11.759.

Maeonius, a, um adj of Maeonia; Maeonian, Lydian, 4.216 et al.

Maeōtius, a, um adj (Maeōtae), pertaining to the Maeotae, or Scythians on the Palus Maeotis, or Sea of Azof; Maeotian, 6.799.

maereō 2 v to be sorrowful, sad; mourn, grieve, 1.197 et al. (cf. miser).

maestus, a, um adj (maereō), sad, sorrowful, 2.270 et al.; melancholy, depressing, 1.202; gloomy, mournful, 3.64; betokening grief, 11.35.

māgālia, ium, n pl huts, dwellings, 1.421. (a Punic word).

magicus, a, um adj pertaining to magi, or magicians; magic, 4.493.

magis, and short form, **mage** adv in a greater measure; more, 5.94; 10.481; the more, 7.787; for potius, by preference, rather, 5.29; better, 4.452. (rel to māgnus).

magister, trī m master; governor, instructor, 5.669 et al.; leader, chief, 5.562; helmsman, pilot, 1.115; herdsman, 12.717. (rel to māgnus and μέγας, great).

magistra, ae f a mistress, directress; appositive, masterly, skill-giving, 8.442; teaching, instructive, 12.427. (magister).

magistrātus, ūs m magistracy; a civil officer, magistrate, 1.426. (magister).

māgnanimus, a, um adj (māgnus and animus), possessing a great soul; noble-minded; great, generous, noble, 5.17; brave, 10.139; mighty, 12.144; of animals, high-spirited, highbred, 3.704.

māgnum adv largely, widely, greatly, loudly, 9.705.

mägnus, a, um; compar., mäior, ius; *superl,* **mäximus, a, um** *adj (rel to* μέγας, *great),* great, 1.602, *and freq;* wide, vast, extended, expansive, 1.300; grand, stately, lofty, towering, 3.703; in number, 1.148; in weight, 5.248; in rank, power, character, 1.241; mighty, 5.414; venerable, 6.544; formidable, direful, 2.190; *compar* mäior, with or without nätū, the elder; mäximus, a, um, with or without nätū, eldest, 1.654 *et al.; subst* mägnum, ī, *n,* a great, noble, difficult, lofty thing, *freq;* mägna, ōrum, great things; great rewards, 2.161; *adv* mägnum, largely, widely, greatly, loudly, 9.705.

Magus, ī *m* a Rutulian, 10.521.

Mäia (*dissyll*), **ae** *f* one of the Pleiades or seven daughters of Atlas and Pleione, who became by Jupiter the mother of Mercury, 1.297.

mäiestās, ätis *f* greatness; majesty, dignity, authority, power, 12.820. (mägnus, mäius).

mäla, ae *f* the cheek bone, jaw, 5.436; *pl* mälae, cheeks, 9.751; teeth, 3.257.

male *adv* badly, ill, wrongly, wickedly; for parum, or nōn, not, un-, 2.23 *et al.;* 4.8. (malus).

Malea, ae *f* one of the southern promontories of Peloponnesus, 5.193.

malesuädus, a, um *adj* (male and suädeō), crime-impelling; desperate, 6.276.

mälifer, era, erum fruit-producing, fruitful, 7.740.

malīgnus, a, um *adj* (malus and genō), spiteful, malicious, malignant, 5.654; treacherous, 6.270; = inīquus, inadequate, confined, 11.525.

mälō, mäluī, mälle *irreg v* to wish rather or more; to prefer. (magis and volō).

malum, ī, *n* an evil, a misfortune, calamity, adversity; suffering, woe, misery, 1.198; misdeed, crime, sin, wickedness, 6.739; pest, curse, scourge, 4.174; mischief, poison, 7.375.

malus, a, um *adj* bad; noxious, baneful, poisonous, 2.471; morally, hostile, 3.398; evil, wicked, impious, 1.352; ill-boding; *subst* malus, ī, *m,* a wicked man or person; *pl* the wicked, 6.542; *compar* pēior, ius, worse.

mälus, ī *m* a standing pole; a mast, 5.487 *et al.*

mamma, ae *f* the breast, 1.492.

mandātum, ī, *n* a charge, order, command, 4.270 *et al.*

mandō, ävī, ätus *1 v* to give in hand or consign; *with acc alone* or *acc and dat* or *inf;* to commission, charge, bid, command, 4.222; place, deposit; commit, consign, confide, intrust, 3.50; of burial, to inter; order, *with inf* (manus and dō).

mandō, mandī, mänsus *3 v* to chew, bite, champ, 4.135; eat, devour, 3.627; of falling in battle, bite the dust, 11.669.

maneō, mānsī, mānsus *2 v* to stay, remain; abide, 3.409; last, continue, endure, 1.609; abide by, adhere to, keep, *with dat* 2.160; *with acc*, await, 3.505; attend, 9.299. (*rel to* μένω, remain).

Mānēs, ium *m* the deities of the lower world, 6.896; gods or powers below, 12.646; the spirits or souls of the dead in Hades; ghosts, shades, Manes, 3.63; penalties of the lower world, punishments, expiations, purgatory, 6.743; abode of the dead, 4.387; infernal regions, the world below, 10.820.

manica, ae *f* something connected with the hand; a sleeve reaching to the hand; a long sleeve; found only in the *pl* manicae, ārum, sleeves, 9.616; handcuffs, chains, cords, manacles, 2.146. (manus).

manifēstē *adv* manifestly; *compar* manifēstius, more plainly, evidently, clearly, 8.16. (manifēstus).

manifēstus, a, um *adj* made obvious; palpable, plain, clear, evident, 2.309; manifest, visible, 3.151 *et al.*

manīplus, ī *m* a handful, a bundle, bunch; the standard or ensign of a company of soldiers, bearing on the top originally a bundle of hay; hence, *metonym* a troop, a company, 11.463 *et al.* (manus and pleō).

Mānlius, iī *m m* Manlius Capitolinus, who saved the Capitol from the Gauls, and was afterwards condemned to be cast from the Tarpeian rock for alleged treason, 8.652.

mānō, āvī, ātus *1 v* to ooze forth, 3.175; distill, trickle, drop, 3.43; flow.

mantēle, is *n* a handcloth, a napkin, towel, 1.702.

Mantō, ūs *f* a nymph and prophetess, mother of Ocnus, founder of Mantua, 10.199.

Mantua, ae *f* a city of northern Italy, on the Mincius.

manus, ūs *f* the hand, 1.487; *freq*; *metonym* action, movement of the hand; work, art, handiwork, 3.486; prowess, heroic deed, action, 2.434; force, violence, 2.645; a collection of persons; a band, crew, troop; an army, 2.29; forces, 5.623; multitude, 6.660; *pl* manūs, workmen, 11.329; dare manūs, to yield, 11.558; extrēma manus, the finishing hand or touch, 7.572.

Mārcellus, ī *m* the name of a Roman family in which the most illustrious were Marcus Claudius Marcellus, the first successful opponent of Hannibal, and the conqueror of Syracuse (212, BC), 6.855; and his descendant, *c* Claudius Marcellus, a son of Gaius Claudius Marcellus and Octavia, sister of Augustus; who was adopted by that emperor and died in early youth, 23 BC, 6.883.

mare, is, *n* the sea, *freq*; ocean, 1.84; water, flood, 1.246.

Marīca, ae *f* a nymph of the river Liris, supposed to be the mother of the Latins, 7.47.

marīnus, a, um *adj* (mare), of the sea; sea-.

marītus, ī *m* a husband, 3.297; suitor, 4.35. (mās).

marmor, oris, *n* marble, 6.69; of the surface of the sea, 10.208.

marmoreus, a, um *adj* (marmor), of marble, marble, 4.392; like marble; smooth, marble-, 6.729; fair.

Marpēsius, a, um *adj* (Marpēsus), of Marpesus, a mountain in Paros; Marpesian, Parian, 6.471.

Marruvius, a, um *adj* (Marruvium), of Marruvium, the capital of the Marsi; Marsian, 7.750.

Mārs (*archaic form,* **Māvors**), **Mārtis** Mars, son of Jupiter and Juno; the patron of war and tutelar god of the Romans, 1.274 *et al.*; *metonym* martial spirit, courage, warlike fury, 6.165; battle, conflict, 2.335 *et al.*

Mārsī, ōrum *m* a tribe of the Apennines, among the most warlike of the Italians, 10.544 *et al.*

Mārsus, a, um *adj* (Mārsī), Marsian, 7.758.

mãssa, ae *f* a lump, mass, 8.453.

Massicus, a, um *adj* (Massicus), of Mount Massicus, in Campania; Massic; *subst* Massica, ōrum, *n* (*sc* iuga), the Massic hills, 7.726.

Massicus, ī *m* an Etruscan warrior, 10.166.

Massȳlī, ōrum or **um** *m* the Massyli, a people in the northern part of Numidia, 6.60.

Massȳlus, a, um *adj* (Massȳlī), Massylian, Libyan, 4.132.

māter, matris *f* a mother, matron, 1.314; 2.489; parent stem, trunk, plant, or tree, 12.209; native, motherland, 10.172; Māter Īdaea, Māter (māgna), the Idaean Mother, the Great Mother of the gods, Cybele, 9.619. (μήτηρ).

māteriēs, ēī *f* matter, stuff, material, 11.328. (*rel to* māter).

māternus, a, um *adj* (māter), pertaining to a mother; mother's, maternal, 4.144; maternal, on the mother's side, 4.258; of a mother's gift, 12.107.

mātrōna, ae *f* a matron, mother, 11.476. (māter).

mātūrō, āvī, ātus *1 v* to bring to maturity, ripen; *fig*; hasten, speed, 1.137. (mātūrus).

mātūrus, a, um *adj* ripe, mature; advanced, 5.73.

mātūtīnus, a, um *adj* (Mātūta), pertaining to Matuta, goddess of the morning; in the morning, early, morning, 8.456.

Maurūsius, a, um *adj* Moorish, Mauretanian, 4.206.

Māvortius, a, um or **Mārtius, a, um** *adj* (Māvors), pertaining to Mavors or Mars; ; warlike, martial; of Mars, 1.276; son of Mars, 6.777; received in

battle, honorable, 7.182;
sacred to Mars, 9.566.

Māximus, ī *m* a title of Fabius
Rullianus (cons. BC 322) and
his descendants, the most
illustrious of whom was
Fabius Cunctator, 6.845.

meātus, ūs *m* a going;
passage, course, movement,
motion, 6.849. (meō).

medeor 2 *dep v* to heal, cure;
(gerund *abl impers*), medendō,
by treatment, 12.46.

medicīna, ae *f* the healing art,
7.772; medicine, remedy.
(medicīnus, sc. ars).

medicō, āvī, ātus *1 v*, and
medicor, ātus sum *1 dep v*
to heal with drugs; heal,
7.756; mix with drugs or
poisons; medicate, drug,
6.420. (medicus).

medicus, a, um *adj*
(medeor), healing.

meditor, ātus sum *1 dep v*
to think upon; meditate,
10.455; design, purpose,
4.171; practice, play.

medium, iī, *n* medium, iī, *n*,
the middle, midst, 2.218; the
intervening space, 6.131; ad
medium, in the middle of
the body, 12.273; in medium,
into the midst, in public;
before them, 5.401; for the
common weal, 11.335.

medius, a, um *adj* mid, said of
an inner point or part of a
thing; midway, midst, 3.665
et al.; of one or of several
objects, 1.440 *et al.*; of the
location of a person or thing;

intervening, between, 6.634;
in the midst, 5.76; disturbing,
untimely, 1.682; discordant,
1.348; *subst* medius, iī,
m, a mediator, 7.536.

Medōn, ontis *m* one of the Trojan
leaders or allies of Troy, 6.483.

medulla, ae *f pl* medullae,
ārum, the marrow, 4.66.
(*rel to* medius).

Megaera, ae *f* one of the
Furies, 12.846.

Megarus, a, um *adj* (Megara),
of or belonging to Megara;
pertaining to the Sicilian
Megara; Megarean, 3.689.

meī *m pl* my kindred, friends,
countrymen, descendants,
etc., 2.587 *et al.*; mea,
ōrum, *n*, my possessions,
enjoyments, 12.882. (mē).

mel, mellis, *n*, *pl* mella,
abl, **mellibus** (no *gen*
or *dat*) honey, 6.420.

Melampus, odis *m* a companion
of Hercules, 10.320.

Meliboeus, a, um *adj* (Meliboea),
of Meliboea in Thessaly;
Meliboean, 3.401.

Melitē, ēs *f* Melite, a sea
nymph, 5.825.

membrum, ī, *n* a limb, joint,
part, member, 1.691 *et al.*

meminī, isse, *def v* (w. *acc,
gen*, or *inf*), to have in mind;
remember, be mindful,
recollect, 1.203; distinguish,
3.202. (*rel to* mēns).

Memmius, iī *m* Memmius,
a Roman gentile or
family name, 5.117.

Memnōn, onis *m* Memnon, son of Tithonus and Aurora, king of the Ethiopians, and slain by Achilles at Troy, 1.489.

memor, oris *adj* (*rel to* mēns and meminī), mindful, remembering, 1.23; heedful, 480; thankful, grateful, 4.539; not forgetting; relentless, 1.4; with nōn or nec, unmindful, regardless, 12.534.

memorābilis, e *adj* (memorō), deserving to be remembered; memorable, remarkable, famous, honorable, 2.583.

memorandus, a, um worthy of mention; famed, renowned, 10.793.

memorō, āvī, ātus *1 v* to call to memory; mention, rehearse, relate, 1.8; say, speak, 3.182; name, 1.327; mention proudly, boast of, 5.392. (memor).

mendāx, ācis *adj* (mentior), given to lying; false, deceitful, 2.80.

Menelāus, ī *m* son of Atreus, king of Sparta and husband of Helen; who joined his brother Agamemnon in the war against Troy, and after its capture returned with Helen to Sparta, 2.264 *et al.*

Menoetēs, ae *m* 1. A Trojan pilot, 5.161. 2. An Arcadian slain by Turnus, 12.517.

mēns, mentis *f* the thinking faculty; rational soul, 6.727; reason, intellect, mind, 2.736 *et al.*; sense, 10.640; disposition, 1.304; spirit, 10.629; heart, confidence, 12.609 *et al.*; a thought, design, purpose, plan, intention, will, 2.170 *et al.*

mēnsa, ae *f* a table, 1.640; dish, food, viands, 1.216; course of food, 1.723.

mēnsis, is *m* a month, 1.269.

mentior, ītus sum *4 dep v* to devise; falsify, lie, pretend, 2.540; feign, counterfeit; *part*, mentitus, a, um; *passive* 2.422. (mēns).

mentum, ī the chin, 4.250; the beard, 6.809. (minor, to project).

mephītis, is *f* a poisonous, pestilential vapor, gas, or exhalation, 7.84.

mercēs, mercēdis *f* that which goes for gain; reward; condition, consideration; cost, penalty, 7.317. (merx, merchandise, and cēdō).

mercor, ātus sum *1 dep v* to exchange merchandise; traffic, trade; buy, purchase, 1.367. (merx, merchandise).

Mercurius, iī *m* Mercury, an Italian god, identified with the Greek Hermes, son of Jupiter and Maia, and messenger of the gods, 4.222 *et al.*

mereō, uī, itus *2 v* to deserve, merit, 2.585; earn, gain, win, 11.224; deserve well, 6.664; bene merēre, to deserve well, 4.317.

mereō, uī, itus *2 v and n*, and **mereor, itus sum** *2 dep v* to deserve, merit, 2.585; earn, gain, win, 11.224; deserve well, 6.664; *with* ut, 2.434; bene merēre, to deserve well, 4.317.

mergō, mersī, mersus *3 v* to dip, immerse, plunge, *with abl alone or with prep*, 6.342; cover, 6.267; *figuratively* involve, overwhelm, 6.615.

mergus, ī *m* a sea bird, gull, diver, 5.128. (mergō).

meritō *adv* by desert, worthily, with justice, 11.392. (mereō).

meritum, ī, *n* a thing deserved; desert; service, favor, merit, 1.74. (mereō).

meritus, a, um having deserved, deserving, 3.667; *passive* deserved, merited, 4.611; due, 5.652. (mereō).

Merops, opis a Trojan, 9.702.

merus, a, um *adj* pure, unmixed, 5.77; *subst n*, merum (*sc* vīnum), unmixed wine; wine, 1.729.

Messāpus, ī *m* a Latin chief, allied with Turnus, 7.691 *et al.*

mēta, ae *f* a meta; one of the cone-shaped pillars, three of which terminated each end of the spina in the Roman circus, and marked the turning point of the course; a turning point, goal, 5.129; *figuratively* limit, extremity, end, bound, 1.278; 8.594; meridian, zenith, 5.835; mētae mortis, the bounds of death; i.e., fixed by death, 12.546. (mētior).

Metabus, ī *m* the father of Camilla, 11.540.

metallum, ī, *n* a mine; metal, 6.144.

mētior, mēnsus sum *4 dep v* to measure, 12.360; traverse.

Metiscus, ī *m* the charioteer of Turnus, 12.469 *et al.*

metō, messuī, messus *3 v* to reap, mow, cut, 4.513; of any harvest, gather, harvest.

Mettus, ī *m* Mettus Fuffetius, an Alban general, put to death by Tullius Hostilius for treachery, 8.642.

metuō, uī, ūtus *3 v* to fear, dread, be in terror of, be afraid of; to experience fear; fear, 6.733; *with dat* fear for, be careful for; *part*, metuēns, entis, apprehensive of, 5.716. (metus).

metus, ūs *m* fear, dread, terror, 1.218; awe, reverence, 7.60; *personif*, Metus, the demon of fear, Fear, 6.276.

meus, a, um (poss. *adj pron*), my, mine, my own, 1.664 *et al.*; mea, ōrum, *n*, my possessions, enjoyments, 12.882. (mē).

Mēzentius, iī *m* tyrant of Agylla or Caere, and ally of Latinus and Turnus, 7.648.

micō, micuī *1 v* to vibrate, dart, 2.475; flash, glitter, gleam, 1.90; tremble, quiver, 10.396.

migrō, āvī, ātus *1 v* to go or move from one place to another; migrate, go away, depart, 4.401.

mīles, itis *m* a soldier, 2.7; collectively, a body of soldiers; armed men, troops, soldiery, 2.20.

mīlitia, ae *f* warfare, war, 11.261; discipline, 8.516. (mīles).

mīlle (*num adj*, *indecl*), a thousand, 1.499; *subst pl* mīlia, ium, *n*, thousands, 1.491.

Mimās, antis *m* a Trojan slain by Mezentius, 10.702.

minae, ārum *f* the projecting parts; points, pinnacles, battlements, 4.88; threats, menaces, 4.44; perils, 6.113; curses, 3.265. (cf. -mineō in immineō, etc.).

mināx, ācis *adj* (minor), projecting; overhanging; threatening, 8.668; wrathful, 10.817.

Mincius, iī *m* the river Mincius, flowing by Mantua northerly into the Po.

Minerva, ae *f* an Italian goddess, understood to be the same as the Greek Athena; the goddess of wisdom, of the liberal and industrial arts, and of systematic or strategic warfare, 2.31 *et al.*; *metonym* wisdom, wit; household work, spinning, the loom, etc., 5.284 *et al.*

Miniō, ōnis *m* a small river in the southern part of Tuscany, 10.183.

minister, trī *m* a subordinate; an attendant, minister, waiter, servant, 1.705; helper, creature, tool, agent, 2.100. (cf. minus).

ministerium, iī, *n* service, attendance, office, 6.223. (minister).

ministra, ae *f* a female attendant; maid servant; counselor, attendant, 11.658. (minister).

ministrō, āvī, ātus *1 v* to serve, attend to, manage, 6.302; to minister, give, furnish, supply, 1.150. (minister).

minitō, āvī, ātus *1 v*, and **minitor, ātus sum** *1 dep v* to threaten, 12.762. (1. minor).

Mīnōius, a, um *adj* (Minōs), pertaining to Minos, king of Crete; of Minos, 6.14.

minor, ātus sum *1 dep v* to jut out, project; ascend, tower, 1.162; threaten, menace, 3.540. (minae).

Mīnōs, ōis *m* king of Crete, son of Jupiter and Europa, grandfather of Minos, the husband of Pasiphae; one of the judges of Hades, 6.432.

Mīnōtaurus, ī *m* the Minotaur; the offspring of Pasiphae, born with the head of a bull and body of a man, and confined by Minos in the Cretan Labyrinth, 6.26.

mīrābilis, e *adj* (mīror), wonderful, extraordinary, wondrous, admirable, 1.652 *et al.*; strange, 2.680.

mīrandus, a, um to be wondered at; wonderful, strange, 1.494. (mīror).

mīror, ātus sum *1 dep v* to wonder at, admire, 1.421; marvel, wonder, 6.317; *with gen*, 11.126.

mīrus, a, um *adj* (mīror), wonderful, wondrous, marvelous, 9.304; strange, 1.354; extraordinary, great, 7.57.

misceō, miscuī, mixtus or
mistus *2 v* to mix; mingle
(the object with which is in
dat, or in *abl alone or with
prep*), 1.440; unite, 4.112;
multiply, 12.720; assemble,
flock together, 7.704; confuse,
disturb, confound, agitate,
1.134; scatter, 1.191.

Mīsēnus, ī *m* son of Aeolus;
a skillful trumpeter, who
followed Hector in the Trojan
war, and afterwards Aeneas,
and was drowned on the
coast of Campania, 3.239.

miser, era, erum *adj* (cf.
maereō), wretched, miserable,
unfortunate, unhappy,
1.344; morbid; consuming,
passionate, deep, 5.655;
mean, paltry, wretched;
subst miser, erī, *m*, unhappy
one, 3.41; miserum, as
(*interj*), ah! cruel lot! *superl*,
miserrimus, a, um, 2.655 *et al*.

miserābile *adv* wretchedly,
pitiably, 12.338.

miserābilis, e *adj* (miseror),
that deserves to be pitied;
pitiable, miserable,
deplorable, wretched,
1.111; *adv* miserābile,
wretchedly, pitiably, 12.338.

miserandus, a, um to be pitied,
11.259; *part*, unhappy, 6.882;
wretched, 3.591; deplorable,
direful, 3.138. (miseror).

misereō, uī, itus *2 v*, and
misereor, itus sum *2
dep v* to pity, commiserate,
have compassion, 2.645;
impers, miseret (mē, tē,
etc.), *with gen* of the object

of pity, it grieves me for, I
pity, etc., 5.354. (miser).

miserēscō *3 inc v* to feel
pity, *alone or with gen*,
2.145; 8.573. (misereō).

miseror, ātus sum *1 dep v* to
express, manifest, or feel
pity for; compassionate,
pity, 1.597. (miser).

missilis, e *adj* (mittō), that is
sent or cast; missive, thrown,
hurled, 10.421; *subst* missilia,
ium, *n*, missile weapons,
darts, missiles, 10.802.

missus, ūs *m* a sending;
a dispatch, command,
7.752. (mittō).

mītēscō *3 inc v* to become
mellow; to become mild,
gentle, peaceful, 1.291. (mītis).

mītigō, āvī, ātus *1 v* to make soft
or mild; to soothe, appease,
5.783. (mītis and agō).

mītis, e *adj* mellow; ripe,
ripening; of a lake or pool,
mild, gentle; calm, still, 8.88.

mitra, ae *f* headband;
turban, cap, 4.216.

mittō, mīsī, missus *3 v* to send,
freq; dispatch, 2.115; conduct,
convey; bring, present, offer,
6.380; fling, throw, cast, 4.254;
figuratively put, bring, 4.231;
suggest, impart, 12.554; let
go, lay aside, dismiss, 1.203;
6.85; bring to an end, end,
5.545; pass over, omit, 11.256;
passive mittī, be conveyed;
arrive, reach, 3.440; sē
mittere, descend, 9.645; to
yield one's self or themselves,

12.191; sub iugum mittere, to subject, conquer, 8.148.

Mnestheus, and **Menestheus**, **eī** and **eos** *m* Mnestheus, one of the Trojan chiefs under Aeneas, 5.117; 10.129 *et al.*

Mnestheus, and **Menestheus**, **eī** and **eos** *m* Mnestheus, one of the Trojan chiefs under Aeneas, 5.117; 10.129 *et al.*

mōbilitās, **ātis** *f* movableness; swiftness, speed, velocity, 4.175. (mōbilis).

modo *adv* only, but, 1.389; lately, just now, 5.493; provided that, in case, 3.116; modo nōn, almost, 9.141. (*abl* of modus, with limit or qualification).

modulor, **ātus sum** *1 v* to measure; regulate, tune, sing, play. (modulus).

modus, **ī** *m* a method, 4.294; mode, manner, way, 1.354 *et al.*; a measure, of song, measure, strain, note, 7.701 *et al.*; bound, limit, end, 4.98 *et al.*; fashion, of building, 11.328; *abl*, modō, in the manner or fashion; like, 9.119.

moenia, **ium**, *n* fortified walls, city walls, ramparts, fortifications, walls, 1.7; battlements, 11.506; town, city, 1.410; prison house, 6.549.

mola, **ae** *f* a mill; *metonym* ground or cracked grain; cracked spelt or coarse meal, 4.517.

molāris, **is** *m* a millstone; *metonym* a huge stone, 8.250. (mola).

mōlēs, **is** *f* a cumbrous mass; a heavy pile or fabric; mound, rampart, 9.35; dike, 2.497; a mass of buildings, vast buildings, 1.421; structure, 11.130; frame or figure, 2.32; bulk, 5.118; weight, 7.589; pile, mass, 1.61; gigantic frame, 5.431; warlike engine, siege tower, 5.439; array, pomp, train, 12.161; body of soldiers, phalanx, 12.575; heavy storm, tempest, 5.790; toil, work, labor, 1.33.

mōlior, **ītus sum** *4 dep v* to pile up; build, erect, construct, 1.424; plan, undertake, attempt, 2.109; pursue, 6.477; cleave, 10.477; contrive, devise, 1.564; occasion, 1.414; prepare, equip, 4.309; arrange, adjust, 12.327; of missiles, discharge, hurl, 10.131. (mōlēs).

molliō, **īvī** or **iī**, **ītus** *4 v* to soften; to soothe, calm, assuage, appease, 1.57. (mollis).

mollis, **e** *adj* soft, tender, delicate; pliant, flexible, soft, 1.693; soft-cushioned, 8.666; subtle, 4.66; tamed, gentle; yielding, accessible, favorable, 4.293; haud mollia, things hard, difficult, harsh, unwelcome, 12.25.

molliter *adv compar* mollius (mollis), softly, gently, sweetly; delicately, skillfully, 6.847.

moneō, **uī**, **itus** *2 v* to remind; admonish, warn, instruct, 2.183; forewarn, foretell, 3.712; *with subj.*, 3.684. (*rel to* meminī *and* mēns).

monīle, **is**, *n* a necklace, collar, 1.654; a poitrel, 7.278.

monitum, ī, *n* an admonition; counsel; advice, warning, 4.331; command, 8.336; influence, 10.689. (moneō).

monitus, ūs *m* an admonition, warning, 4.282. (moneō).

Monoecus, ī *m* a promontory and harbor on the Ligurian coast west of Genoa, 6.830.

mōns, montis *m* a mountain, hill, mount, 3.105; rock, crag, cliff, 6.360; a mighty or huge rock, 12.687; a great wave, 1.105. (*rel to* -mineō, project).

mōnstrō, āvī, ātus *1 v* to show, point out, indicate, 1.444; inform, tell, 1.321; direct, incite, 9.44; ordain, appoint, prescribe, 4.636. (mōnstrum).

mōnstrum, ī, *n* the thing which warns; an omen, a portent, 3.26; supernatural token, sign, 12.246; a prodigy, marvel, wonder, terror, 3.583; monster, 2.245. (moneō).

montānus, a, um *adj* (mōns), pertaining to mountains; mountain-, 2.305.

montōsus, a, um *adj* (mōns), abounding in hills or mountains; hilly, mountainous, 7.744.

monumentum, ī, *n* a means of admonishing, reminding, or instructing; a memorial, 3.486; record, tradition, 3.102; memento, 12.945; token, 6.512. (cf. moneō).

mora, ae *f* delay, 3.453; cessation, pause, respite, stay, 5.458; hindrance, obstacle, 1.746; bulwark, 10.428.

morbus, ī *m* disease, sickness, malady, 6.275; plague, pestilence, 12.851; *personif*, Morbī, ōrum, *m*, Diseases, 6.275.

mordeō, momordī, morsus *2 v* to bite, 1.418; rub, bind, confine, 12.274.

moribundus, a, um *adj* (morior), in a dying condition; ready to die, dying, 4.323; lifeless, 10.341; mortal, 6.732.

Morinī, ōrum *m* a tribe dwelling on the northwestern coast of Gaul, 8.727.

morior, mortuus sum, morī, *3 and 4, dep v* to die, perish, 2.353 *et al.*; *fut part*, moritūrus, a, um, destined to die, 12.55; resolved to die, 4.519.

moror, ātus sum *1 dep v* to delay, linger, tarry, 2.102; retard, hinder, detain, delay, 2.373; think upon, 7.253; notice, regard, 2.287; nihil or nōn morārī, not to consider as important; to think nothing of, 11.365; not to value, 5.400. (mora).

mors, mortis *f* death, *freq*; deadly wound, 9.348; *pl* mortēs, various kinds of death, 10.854; *personif*, Mors, the goddess of death, daughter of Erebus and Nox, Death, 11.197. (cf. morior).

morsus, ūs *m* a biting; eating, 3.394; tooth, 7.112; fang, 2.215; gripe, hold, 12.782; fluke, 1.169. (mordeō).

mortālēs, ium, *c* mortals, men, mankind, 2.142.

mortālia, ium, *n* human affairs; fortunes, woes, 1.462.

mortālis, e *adj* (mors), subject to death, mortal, 10.375; of mortal nature, lineage, or descent; earthly, human, 1.328; made by man, mortal, 12.740; *subst* mortālēs, ium, *c*, mortals, men, mankind, 2.142; mortālia, ium, *n*, human affairs; fortunes, woes, 1.462.

mortifer, era, erum *adj* (mors and ferō), bringing death; deadly, 6.279.

mōs, mōris *m* a manner, way, custom; practice, wont, 1.336; form, 3.65; rule, law, condition, terms, 6.852; *pl* mōrēs, um, laws, 1.264; character, virtues, morals, 6.683; mōre, in the manner, like, 4.551; sine mōre, without restraint, violently, 5.694; in violation of right, wrongfully, 8.635; in mōrem, and dē or ex mōre, after or according to the custom, form, fashion, usage, 1.318; 5.244.556.

mōtus, ūs *m* a moving, motion, *freq*; swiftness, agility, 5.430; impetus, swift fury, 12.503; *pl* movements, 4.297. (moveō).

moveō, mōvī, mōtus *2 v* to set in motion; to move, *freq*; to wield, 8.565; break up, 3.519; shake, 3.91; remove, 5.349; take away, 3.700; *figuratively* affect, move, 1.714; influence, persuade, 3.187; excite, arouse, stir up, raise, 2.96; inspire, 7.641; disturb, trouble, 6.399; revolve, meditate, 3.34; unfold, rehearse, declare, 1.262; open up, enter upon, 7.45; sīgna

movēre, break up the camp, march, advance; arma movēre, to get ready for battle, 12.16.

mox *adv* soon, by and by, presently, afterwards, thereupon, then, 3.274 *et al.*

mūcrō, ōnis *m* a sharp point or edge, esp. of a weapon, 2.333; point of a spear, 11.817; a sword, blade, 2.449.

mūgiō, īvī or **iī** *4 v* to low, bellow, 8.218; *figuratively* of a trumpet, 8.526; of the tripod, 3.92; to make a roaring sound, rumble, of the ground, 4.490.

mūgītus, ūs *m* a lowing; bellowing, 2.223. (mūgiō).

mulceō, mulsī, mulsus or **mulctus** *2 v* to stroke; lick, 8.634; *figuratively* soothe, caress, comfort, 1.197; mitigate, soften, calm, 1.66; to make harmonious, charm, 7.34.

Mulciber, eris and **erī** *m* one who softens, Mulciber or Vulcan, the god of the forge, 8.724. (mulceō).

mulcō, āvī, ātus *1 v* to punish, 11.839.

muliebris, e of woman; women's; female, 11.687. (mulier).

mulier, eris *f* a woman, 7.661.

multa, ōrum, *n adv* much, greatly, exceedingly, 4.390 *et al.* (compar.), plūra, more, 5.381; (superl), plūrima, very much, 9.335.

multa, ōrum, *n* many things, fortunes, hardships, etc., 1.750; (compar.) plūra, more things, words; more, 1.385

et al.; (*superl*) plūrima, very
many, many things, 4.333.

multī, ōrum *m subst* many
men, many, 2.124 *et al.*

multiplex, plicis *adj* (multus
and plicō), having many folds,
5.264; manifold, various, 4.189.

multō *adv* much, by much,
by far, far, 2.199 *et al.*

multum *adv* much, greatly,
exceedingly, 3.348 *et al.*

multus, a, um *adj* much, *freq*;
abundant, abounding, great,
3.151; powerful, 3.372; many
a, 1.334; dense, thick, 1.412;
pl many, *freq*; (compar.) plūs,
plūris, *n*, more, *freq*; *pl* plūrēs,
plūra, more, *freq*; several,
many; (*superl*) plūrimus, a,
um, the most; most abundant,
greatest, 11.312; very much,
abundant, great, 6.299; very
large, high, 1.419; very many a,
many a, 2.369; countless, 2.364.

mundus, i *m* ornament;
figuratively the universe, world.

mūniō, īvī or **iī, ītus** *4 v* to inclose
with walls; fortify; construct,
build, 1.271. (moenia).

mūnus, eris *n* a charge, service,
office, employment, function,
duty, 5.846; attribute, 12.393;
aid, kindness, favor, 4.429;
gift, present, 1.636; prize,
5.109; libation, 3.177; festival,
5.652; an honor, 12.520.

mūrālis, e *adj* (mūrus),
pertaining to walls;
battering, 12.921.

mūrex, icis *m* the murex or
purple fish; a sharp-pointed
shellfish from which was

obtained the Tyrian purple;
metonym purple dye,
purple, 4.262; a pointed
or jagged rock, 5.205.

murmur, uris, *n* a murmur,
6.709; uproar, 1.124;
roaring, reverberation, 1.55;
acclamation, applause,
5.369; thunder, 4.160.

murmurō, āvī, ātus *1 v* to
murmur, mutter, roar,
10.212. (murmur).

murra, ae *f* the myrrh tree; gum of
the myrrh tree; myrrh, 12.100.

Murrānus, ī *m* a Latin slain
by Aeneas, 12.529.

mūrus, ī *m* a wall, artificial
or natural, 1.423; 3.535;
a rampart, 9.371. (*rel to*
mūniō and moenia).

Mūsa, ae *f* a muse; one of the
nine daughters of Jupiter and
Mnemosyne, goddesses who
preside over the liberal arts of
poetry, music, etc., 1.8 *et al.*;
metonym a poem or song.

Mūsaeus, ī *m* Musaeus, a
Greek poet contemporary
with Orpheus, 6.667.

mussō, āvī, ātus *1 intens v* to
speak low; mutter, complain,
11.454; whisper, hesitate,
or fear to speak out, 11.345;
waver, 12.657; to low faintly,
12.718. (mūtiō, mutter).

mūtābilis, e *adj* (mūtō),
changeable, unstable, fickle,
inconstant, 4.569; changeful,
that brings changes, 11.425.

mūtō, āvī, ātus *1 v* to change
the position or location
of anything; change,

alter, shift, 3.581; of form
or condition; change,
transform, 1.658; change one
thing for or with another,
with acc and abl; revolve,
5.702; unsettle, disturb,
distract, 4.595. (moveō).

mūtus, a, um adj speechless,
dumb, mute, 12.718;
not spoken or heard of;
unfamed, humble, 12.397.

Mutusca, ae f a city of
the Sabines, 7.711.

mūtuus, a, um adj (mūtō),
interchangeable, reciprocal; on
both sides, 10.755; per mūtua,
mutually, to each other, 7.66.

Mycēnae, ārum, and **Mycēna,
ae** f Mycenae, an ancient
city of Argolis; the abode
of Danaus, Pelops, and
Agamemnon, 1.284 et al.

Mycēnaeus, a, um adj (Mycēnae),
of Mycenae; the Mycenaean
(king); Agamemnon, 11.266.

Myconos, ī f Myconos, one of the
Cyclades, N.E. of Delos, 3.76.

Mygdonidēs, ae m Mygdonides
or Coroebus, a son of Mygdon,
king of Phrygia, and ally
of the Trojans, 2.342.

Myrmidones, um m the
Myrmidons, Thessalian
followers of Achilles, once
dwelling in Aegina, where they
had been transformed from
ants to men in answer to the
prayer of Aeacus, grandfather
of Achilles, 2.7 et al.

myrteus, a, um adj (myrtus),
of myrtle, myrtle-, 6.443.

myrtus, ī and **ūs** f a myrtle;
sacred to Venus, a myrtle shaft
or spear, 7.817; a myrtle grove,
3.23; myrtle wreath, 5.72.

nam (conj caus.), for, because,
1.731 et al.; beginning a
parenthesis, 3.374.

namque conj, for indeed,
since indeed, for, 4.633;
affirmative, indeed, 10.614.

nancīscor, nactus or **nanctus
sum** 3 dep v to obtain,
secure, get, 7.511; find,
overtake, 12.749.

Nār, Nāris m the Nar, a
river of Umbria, 7.517.

nāris, is f a nostril; pl nārēs, ium,
the nostrils; the nose, 6.497.

nārrō, āvī, ātus 1 v to
narrate, relate, describe,
express, tell, 2.549.

Nārycius, a, um adj (Nāryx or
Nāricium), of Naryx, a town
of the Locri; Narycian, 3.399.

nāscor, nātus sum 3 dep v to
be born, 1.286; be produced,
spring up, grow; rise, 10.275;
arise, 7.44; part, nāscēns,
entis, coming into the world,
new-born; new-foaled, 4.515;
part, nātus, a, um, born,
sprung, descended, 8.315; with
abl, nātus deā, goddess-born,
1.582; subst nātus, ī, m, a
son, 1.407; pl nātī, children,
sons, 5.285; young offspring,
8.45; nāta, f, a daughter,
1.256. (old form, gnāscor,
from rt. gen rel to genō).

nāta, ae a daughter,
1.256. (nascor).

nātō, āvī, ātus 1 v to swim, 5.181; float, 4.398; overflow, swim with, 3.625.

nātūra, ae f a being born; that which is fixed by birth; disposition, constitution, quality, nature, 10.366. (nāscor).

nātus, a, um born, sprung, descended, 8.315; with abl, nātus deā, goddess-born, 1.582. (nāscor).

nātus, ī m a son, 1.407; pl nātī, children, sons, 5.285; young offspring, 8.45 (nāscor).

nātus, ūs m used only in the abl, nātū, birth, age, see māgnus. (nāscor).

nauta, ae m a boatman, ferryman, 6.315; sailor, mariner, 3.207. (nāvis).

Nautēs, is m a Trojan soothsayer, 5.704.

nauticus, a, um adj of ships; pertaining to seamen or sailors; nautical, 3.128.

nāvālis, e adj (nāvis), pertaining to ships; naval, 5.493; subst nāvālia, ium, n, dock, docks, dockyard, naval arsenal, 4.593; naval equipments, 11.329.

nāvifragus, a, um adj (nāvis and frangō), shipwrecking, 3.553.

nāvigium, iī, n a boat, craft, ship, 5.753. (nāvigō).

nāvigō, āvī, ātus 1 v to sail; set sail, 4.237; with acc, sail over, sail upon, 1.67. (nāvis and agō).

nāvis, is f a ship, 1.120.

Naxos, ī f Naxos, one of the Cyclades, east of Paros, noted for its wine and the worship of Bacchus, 3.125.

-ne (interrog enclitic; in direct questions), 1.37; 4.32; (in indirect questions), whether, 5.703; followed by an or -ne, -ne — an, -ne — -ne, whether — or, 1.308; with apostrophe, 3.319.

nē adv not, in prohibitions, 3.160; 3.453; nē — quidem, not even; conj, in order that not, that not, lest, 2.187, freq.

Nealcēs, ae m a Latin, 10.753.

nebula, ae f a cloud, 10.82; mist, fog, 1.412.

nec or **neque** (adv and conj), and not; neither, nor, 1.643 et al.; in prohibition, 3.394 et al.; neque (nec) — neque (nec), neither — nor, 5.21 et al.; nec — et, or -que, may be rendered neither — nor, 12.801; 2.534; nec nōn, and also, nor less, 6.183; nec nōn et, and also, 1.707.

necdum adv nor yet; and not yet, 1.25.

necesse (**nom. and acc**) (indecl adj), necessary, unavoidable, inevitable, 3.478.

necō, āvī or **uī, ātus** 1 v to slay, kill, 8.488.

nectar, aris, n nectar, the drink of the gods; honey, 1.433.

nectō, nexuī, or **nexī, nexus** 3 v to tie, bind, fasten, 4.239; bind together or round, 1.448; join, unite, of soul and body, 4.695; figuratively of arguments, 9.219.

nefandus, a, um *adj* (nē and farī), not to be spoken; impious, execrable, accursed, abominable, 5.785; perfidious, 4.497; *subst* nefandum, ī, *n*, wrong, 1.543.

nefās, *indecl n* that which is contrary to divine law; sin, impiety, wrong, 2.719; wickedness, guilt, crime, 2.184; a ghastly deed, 10.497; impious or guilty word, 2.658; mischief, 7.386; dishonor, disgrace, shame, 8.688; (exclamatory), fearful sight! 7.73; fearful penalty! 7.596; (of a person), a monster, wretch, 2.585; *adj* horrible, 3.365; nefās est, it is unlawful, wicked, impious, 6.391.

negō, āvī, ātus *1 v* to say no; say that not or no; deny, refuse, 3.171. (perhaps nē and āiō).

Nemea, ae *f* Nemea, a town of Argolis, near which Hercules killed the Nemean lion, and established the Nemean games, 8.295.

nēmō, inis (*gen not used in class. Latin*), *c* no one, none, 5.305. (nē and homō).

nemorōsus, a, um *adj* (nemus), abounding in woods, woody, 3.270.

nemus, oris, *n* a wood, forest, or grove, 1.165 *et al.*

neō, nēvī, nētus *2 v* to spin; interweave, 10.818.

Neoptolemus, ī *m* Neoptolemus or Pyrrhus, the son of Achilles, 3.333. See also Pyrrhus.

nepōs, ōtis *m* a grandson, 2.702; *pl* nepōtēs, um, grandchildren; posterity, descendants, 2.194.

Neptūnius, a, um *adj* (Neptūnus), pertaining to Neptune, built by Neptune, Neptunian, 2.625; son or descendant of Neptune, 7.691.

Neptūnus, ī *m* Neptune, one of the sons of Saturn, and brother of Jupiter, Juno, and Pluto; identified by the Romans, as god of the sea, with the Greek Poseidon, 1.125.

nequeō, īvī or **iī, itus, īre** *irreg v* to be unable; can not, 1.713.

nēquīquam *adv* in vain, to no purpose, 2.515.

Nērēis, idis or **idos** *f* a Nereid, any one of the daughters of Nereus and Doris; a sea-nymph, 3.74. (Nēreus).

Nērēius, a, um *adj* (Nēreus), of Nereus; Nereian, 9.102.

Nēreus (*dissyll*), **eī** or **eos** *m* Nereus, a sea-god, son of Oceanus and Tethys, and father of the Nereids, 2.419 *et al.*; *metonym* the sea, 10.764.

Nēritos, ī *f* Neritos, a small island near Ithaca, 3.271.

Nersae, ārum *f* Nersae, a town of the Aequī, 7.744.

nervus, ī *m* a nerve; sinew, tendon, 10.341; bow-string, 5.502; string of the lyre, 9.776.

nesciō, īvī or **iī, ītus** *4 v* not to know, to be ignorant of, 1.565; *with* object clause, 2.735 *et al.* (nē and sciō).

nescius, a, um *adj* (nesciō),
not knowing, unaware,
ignorant, 1.299; that knows
not how, that can not.

nēve or **neu** *conj*, or not, and
not, nor, neither, *with* subj.
or *imperat*, 7.202; ne — neu
(nēve), that not — nor,
lest — or lest, 2.188.

nex, necis *f* murder, slaughter,
violent death, destruction,
death, 2.85 *et al.* (necō).

nī *conj*, not, lest, that not,
3.686; for nisi, if not,
unless, except, 5.356 *et al.*

nīdor, ōris *m* vapor, steam;
a smell, 12.301.

nīdus, ī *m* a nest; brood,
nestling, 5.214.

niger, gra, grum *adj* black; dark,
swarthy, dusky, 6.134; gloomy.

nigrāns, antis black, dusky,
dark, 5.97; cloud-covered,
8.353; gloomy, 9.87. (niger).

nigrēscō, uī 3 *inc v* to become
or turn black; grow
dark, 4.454. (niger).

nigrō, āvī, ātus 1 *v* to be or
make black; *part*, nigrāns,
antis, black, dusky, dark,
5.97; cloud-covered, 8.353;
gloomy, 9.87. (niger).

nihil (nīl), *n indecl* nothing,
2.287; *adv* not at all; by no
means, not, 2.402, and *freq*
(nē and hīlum, a trifle).

Nīlus, ī *m* the Nile, 6.800.

nimbōsus, a, um *adj* (nimbus),
full of storms; stormy, rainy,
1.535; cloud-covered, 3.274.

nimbus, ī *m* a violent rain;
storm, tempest, 1.51; a
black cloud, thunder-cloud,
cloud, 3.587; a bright cloud;
the nimbus surrounding a
god, 2.616; cloud of smoke,
5.666; a multitude, 7.793.

nīmīrum *adv* without wonder
or doubt; certainly,
undoubtedly, doubtless, 3.558.
(nī, for nē, and mīrum).

nimis *adv* too much,
overmuch; too well, 9.472.

nimium *adv* too; very
much; but too, 6.514.

nimius, a, um *adj* (nimis), too
great, too much, excessive.

Niphaeus, ī *m* a Rutulian
warrior, 10.570.

Nīsaeē, ēs *f* one of the Naiads.

nisi and **nī** *conj*, if not,
unless, 5.49 *et al.*

Nīsus, ī *m* a follower of
Aeneas, 5.294.

nīsus, ūs *m* a leaning,
pressing against; bracing;
position of resistance,
5.437; effort, exertion, 3.37;
descent, 11.852. (nītor).

nitēns, entis shining,
glittering, sparkling;
bright, 1.228; *figuratively*
sleek, well-fed, 3.20.

nitēscō, nituī 3 *inc v* to
become bright, to shine,
glisten, 5.135. (niteō).

nitidus, a, um *adj* (niteō),
shining, bright,
glittering, 2.473.

nītor, nīsus or **nīxus sum** 3 *dep v*
to lean or rest upon, *with abl*,
6.760; tread, walk upon, 2.380;
to be borne upon, poised or
balanced upon, 4.252; push,
press, struggle forward or
upward; ascend, 2.443.

nivālis, e *adj* (nix), snowy; snow-
covered, 7.675; snowy, 3.538.

niveus, a, um *adj* (nix), snowy,
of snow; snow-white, 1.469.

nix, nivis *f* snow, 4.250.

nīxor, ātus sum 1 *dep v intens*
(**nītor**) to lean upon with
the idea of effort; struggle
forward on, 5.279.

nō, nāvī, nātus 1 *v* to swim, 1.118.

nōbilis, e *adj* (nōscō),
well-known, illustrious,
famous, 7.564.

nōbilitās, ātis *f* renown;
high birth, noble lineage,
11.341. (nōbilis).

noceō, uī, itus 2 *v* to be
hurtful; to hurt, harm,
injure; do mischief, 5.618.

noctivagus, a, um *adj* (nox
and vagus, wandering),
night-wandering; nightly,
nocturnal, 10.216.

nocturnus, a, um *adj* (nox),
pertaining to the night;
nightly, nocturnal, in the
night, by night, 4.490.

nōdō, āvī, ātus 1 *v* to tie
with a knot; bind, fasten,
4.138. (nōdus).

nōdus, ī *m* a knot, 1.320 *et al.*;
of a tree, 11.553; bond, 1.296;
coil, 2.220; *figuratively* difficult
point; center of strife, 10.428.

Noēmōn, onis *m* a Trojan, 9.767.

nomas, adis, *c* a nomad;
pl Nomades, um, *m*, the
Numidians, 4.320.

nōmen, inis, *n* a name,
1.248 *et al.*; designation,
name, indicating attribute,
invention, gift for mischief,
7.337; word, 3.444; fame,
renown, 2.583 *et al.* (nōscō).

Nōmentum, ī, *n* Nomentum,
a town of Latium, 6.773.

nōn *adv* not, *freq*; sometimes
for nē in prohibitions, 12.78.

nōndum *adv* not yet, 3.109 *et al.*

nōnus, a, um *adj* (novem),
the ninth, 5.64.

nōscō, nōvī, nōtus 3 *v*
to get knowledge of,
become acquainted with;
recognize, 6.809; (in *perf*
and cognate tenses), know,
knew, etc., 4.423 *et al.*

noster, tra, trum (poss. *adj
pron*), our, ours, our own,
freq; of us, or me, given by
me, 12.51; favorable to us,
auspicious, 12.187 *et al.* (nōs).

nostrī, ōrum *m* our friends,
kindred, allies, etc.,
2.411. (noster).

nota, ae *f* a distinguishing
mark; mark, spot, 5.87; letter,
character, 3.444. (nōscō).

nothus, a, um *adj* illegitimate,
bastard; *subst* nothus, ī, *m*,
a bastard son, 9.697; a horse
of mixed breed, 7.283.

notō, āvī, ātus 1 *v* to
mark; to observe, note,
mark, 3.515. (nota).

nōtus, a, um known, 1.669;
wonted, usual, 2.773;
well-known, 3.657; famed,
renowned, distinguished,
celebrated, 1.379; familiar,
well proved, 12.759;
nōtum, *n*, (referring to
a following clause) the
knowledge, etc., 5.6.

Notus, ī *m* identical in meaning
with auster; the south-wind,
1.85; wind, 6.355; storm, 1.575.

novem (*num adj*, *indecl*),
nine, 1.245.

noverca, ae *f* a step-mother.

noviēns (**noviēs**) (*num adv*),
nine times, 6.439. (novem).

novitās, ātis *f* newness,
1.563. (novus).

novō, āvī, ātus *1 v* to make new,
renew, renovate, repair, 5.752;
change, 5.604; build, 4.260;
rēs novāre, to change one's
purpose or plans; take new
measures, 4.290. (novus).

novus, a, um *adj* new, *freq*;
recent, fresh, 2.98; unusual,
strange, unknown, 1.307;
superl, novissimus, a,
um, last, 4.650.

nox, noctis *f* night, *freq*;
darkness, 1.89; dark cloud,
black storm-cloud, 3.198;
sleep, 4.530; death, 12.310;
personif, Nox, Night, the
goddess of night, 3.512.

noxa, ae *f* hurt, harm;
offense, outrage, violence,
1.41. (noceō).

noxius, a, um *adj* (noxa),
hurtful, baneful, 6.731;
destructive, 7.326.

nūbēs, is *f* a cloud, 1.516
et al.; storm, 10.809; the
air, 12.856; *figuratively*
flock, multitude, 7.705.

nūbigenae, ārum, *c* the cloud-
born; a name of the Centaurs,
born of Ixion and a cloud,
8.293. (nūbēs and genō).

nūbilis, e *adj* (nūbō, marry),
marriageable; grown up, 7.53.

nūbilum, ī, *n* cloudy weather.

nūbilus, a, um *adj* (nūbēs),
cloudy; *subst* nūbilum, ī,
cloudy weather; *pl* nūbila,
ōrum, clouds, 3.586.

nūdō, āvī, ātus, *1. v* to make bare,
naked; lay open, bare, 1.211;
figuratively expose, 5.586; lay
open, disclose, 1.356. (nūdus).

nūdus, a, um *adj* naked,
bare, 1.320; open, 2.512;
unburied, 5.871.

nūllus, a, um (*gen* nūllīus, *dat*
nūllī, *adj*) no, not any, 1.184;
unobservant, regardless,
11.725; *subst* no one, nobody,
none, 4.456. (nē and ūllus).

num (*interrog adv*, in single
independent questions,
untranslated); (in dependent
questions), whether, 4.369.

Numa, ae *m* the name of
two Rutulian warriors,
9.454; 10.562.

Numānus, ī *m* Numanus or
Remulus, a Rutulian slain
by Ascanius, 9.592.

nūmen, inis, *n* a command;
will; espec. the divine will
or purpose, 1.8; divine
command, 7.385; divine

power, 1.666; authority, revelation, 3.363; impulse, 1.674; assistance, 5.56; divine keeping, protection, 2.703; divine regard, favor, 4.611; permission, 6.266; presence, 1.447; manifestation, 2.623; majesty, divinity, 1.48; divine attribute, 10.221; a deity, god, divinity, 2.735; sacred image, 2.178. (nuō, nod).

numerō, āvī, ātus 1 v to number, count, reckon. (numerus).

numerus, ī m a number, 1.193; multitude, 2.424; order, 3.446; in music or poetry, measure, number, 6.646; pl numbers, measures; melody, tune.

Numīcus, ī m a river of Latium near Lavinium, 7.150.

Numida, ae m a Nomad; a Numidian, 4.41.

Numitor, ōris m 1. Numitor, one of the kings of Alba, and father of Ilia or Rhea Silvia, 6.768. 2. A Rutulian warrior, 10.342.

numquam adv never, freq (nē and umquam).

nunc adv now, at this time, 4.283; even now; in our times, at the present time, 6.234.

nūntia, ae f a messenger, 4.188.

nūntiō, āvī, ātus 1 v to announce, report, make known, announce, declare, 1.391 et al. (nūntius).

nūntium, ī, n an announcement, message, news.

nūntius, a, um adj announcing.

nūntius, iī m a messenger, 3.310; a message, dispatch, tidings; injunction, command, 4.237.

nūper adv recently, not long since, lately, 6.338. (novus and -per).

Nursia, ae f a Sabine town, 7.716.

nurus, ūs f a daughter-in-law, 2.501.

nūsquam adv nowhere, 2.620; sometimes transf. to time; on no occasion; never, 5.853. (nē and ūsquam).

nūtō, āvī, ātus 1 intens v to nod; sway to and fro, 2.629; move, wave, 9.682. (nuō, nod).

nūtrīmentum, ī, n nourishment; fuel, 1.176. (nūtriō).

nūtriō, īvī or iī, ītus 4 v to nourish, suckle, 11.572; breed, rear, train, 7.485.

nūtrīx, īcis f a nurse, 1.275. (nūtriō).

nūtus, ūs m a nod, 9.106; will, decree, command, pleasure, 7.592. (nuō, nod).

nympha, ae f a bride, a maiden; a nymph, one of the inferior deities, presiding over fountains, woods, etc., 1.71 et al.

Nȳsa, ae f a city on Mount Meros in India, which, according to one of the myths, was the birthplace of Bacchus, 6.805.

ō (interj expressing joy, grief, astonishment, desire, or indignation), O! oh! ah! with voc., 2.281 et al.; with sī and the subj., oh that, 11.415;

sometimes placed after the word to which it relates, 2.281.

ob *prep* owing to, for, on account of, 1.4; for the sake of, 6.660,

obdūcō, dūxī, ductus 3 *v* to draw or lead towards; draw over, 2.604.

obeō, īvī or **iī, itus, īre** *irreg v* to go towards or to; meet; visit, travel over, traverse, 6.801; survey (with the eye), 10.447; surround, encircle, encompass, 6.58; enter, take part in, engage in, 6.167; undergo, suffer, 10.641.

ōbex, icis *m and f* an obstacle; a barrier, 10.377; a bolt, bar, 8.227. (ob and iaciō).

obiciō, iēcī, iectus 3 *v* to throw against or towards; throw to, 6.421; present, oppose, 2.444; bar against, shut, 9.45; cast upon, 7.480; subject, expose, 4.549; *passive* to be presented, appear, 5.522; *part,* obiectus, a, um, thrown towards or against; opposite, projecting, 3.534. (ob and iaciō).

obiectō, āvī, ātus 1 *intens v* to throw towards, before, or against; to expose to, 2.751. (obiciō).

obiectus, ūs *m* a throwing against; projection, opposition, 1.160. (obiciō).

obitus, ūs *m* a going to; an encountering one's time, day, or death; destruction, death, 4.694. (obeō).

oblīquō, āvī, ātus 1 *v* to bend, turn to one side, veer, 5.16. (oblīquus).

oblīquus, a, um *adj* turning sideways; slanting, lying across, 5.274; *figuratively* indirect, cowardly, dastardly, 11.337.

oblīvīscor, oblītus sum 3 *dep v* to forget, *with acc* or *gen* of object, 2.148; to be heedless, unmindful, forgetful of, 5.174; *part,* oblītus, a, um, having forgotten; forgetful, 4.528.

oblīvium, iī, *n* oblivion, forgetfulness, 6.715. (oblīvīscor).

obloquor, locūtus sum 3 *dep v* to speak to or against; sing or play in response, *with acc,* 6.646.

obluctor, ātus sum 1 *dep v* to strive, struggle, press against, 3.38.

obmūtēscō, mūtuī 3 *inc v* to become speechless or dumb; to be silent, hushed, mute, 4.279.

obnītor, nīxus or **nīsus sum** 3 *dep v* to press, push against, *with dat* 12.105; without an object, push, 4.406; struggle, resist, 4.332; bear up, 5.21; strive, strike against, 5.206.

obnūbō, nūpsī, nūptus 3 *v* to cover up, 11.77.

oborior, ortus sum 4 *dep v* to arise, spring up; gush, burst forth, 3.492.

obruō, uī, utus 3 *v* to cover over; bury; overwhelm, 1.69; overpower, 2.424; destroy, 5.692.

obscēnus, a, um *adj* (caenum), filthy, indecent, loathsome, foul, 3.241; horrible, 3.367.

obscūrō, āvī, ātus *1 v* to
darken, 12.253. (obscūrus).

obscūrus, a, um *adj* dim,
dark, dusky, obscure, 1.411;
uncertain; of persons, unseen,
2.135; in the darkness, 6.268;
pl obscūra, ōrum, dim places;
obscurity, uncertainty, 6.100.

obserō, sēvī, situs *3 v* to plant
upon or over; *part*, obsitus,
a, um, overgrown, covered
over, 7.790; hoary, 8.307.

observō, āvī, ātus *1 v* to note,
observe, mark, watch,
6.198; remember, 9.393;
observe, respect, revere.

obsideō, sēdī, sessus *2 v* to sit
in or on; abide; hold, occupy,
3.421; besiege, beset, 2.441;
throng, 12.133; obstruct, fill
up, choke. (ob and sedeō).

obsidiō, ōnis *f* a blockade or
siege, 3.52. (obsideō).

obsīdō *3 v* to set before, watch,
9.159; block up, beset, 11.516;
invade, occupy, 7.334.

obstipēscō, stipuī (stupuī) *3 inc
v* to become stupefied; to be
astonished, amazed, 1.613.

obstō, stitī, stātus *1 v* to stand
before or against; withstand,
oppose, hinder, restrain,
4.91; to be obnoxious, 6.64.

obstruō, strūxī, strūctus *3 v*
to build before or against;
to stop, close up, 4.440.

obtegō, tēxī, tēctus *3 v* to
cover up or over, 2.300.

obtendō, tendī, tentus *3 v*
to stretch before; draw,
spread, 10.82; spread over.

obtentus, ūs *m* a spreading over;
a covering, 11.66. (obtendō).

obtestor, ātus sum *1 dep v*
to call to witness; conjure,
implore, 7.576; beseech,
10.46; swear, 9.260.

obtexō, texuī, textus *3 v*
to weave over; cover,
cloud, darken, 11.611.

obtorqueō, torsī, tortus *2 v* to
turn round, twist, 5.559.

obtruncō, āvī, ātus *1 v* to
lop off; cut down; cut to
pieces, slay, 2.663.

obtūsus, a, um enfeebled,
blunted, unfeeling, 1.567.
(obtundō, tudī, tūsus/tunsus
3 v, to beat against; beat
up; to make blunt, dull).

obtūtus, ūs *m* a looking at;
look, gaze, 1.495. (obtueor).

obumbrō, āvī, ātus *1 v* to
overshadow; darken, 12.578;
screen, protect, shield, 11.223.

obuncus, a, um *adj* bent
in, hooked, 6.597.

obūstus, a, um *adj* (ob and
ūrō), burnt, hardened
in the fire, 7.506.

obvertō, vertī, versus *3 v*
to turn towards, 6.3; turn
round (towards the sea),
3.549; *part*, obversus, a,
um, turned or turning,
wheeling, 11.601; turning
against; directly opposite,
facing towards, 9.622.

obvius, a, um *adj* (ob and via),
in the way; presenting one's
self or itself; meeting, 1.314;
against, 6.880; opposing,

9.56; in the way of; exposed to, 3.499; obvius fierī, to encounter, meet, 10.380.

occāsus, ūs *m* a going down; setting; the west, 11.317; fall, ruin, destruction, 1.238. (1. occīdō).

occīdō, cīdī, cāsus *3 v* to go down; set; fall, perish, 2.581; die. (ob and cadō).

occīdō, cīdī, cīsus *3 v* to slay, kill, slaughter, 11.193. (ob and caedō).

occubō *1 v* to lie, rest (in death), 1.547.

occulō, culuī, cultus *3 v* to cover up; hide, conceal, 1.312; *part*, occultus, a, um, secret, hidden, 3.695.

occulō, culuī, cultus *3 v* to cover up; hide, conceal, 1.312; *part*, occultus, a, um, secret, hidden, 3.695.

occultē *adv* secretly, 12.418. (occultus).

occultō, āvī, ātus *1 intens v* to hide carefully; cover up; hide, conceal, secrete, 2.45. (occulō).

occumbō, cubuī, cubitus *3 v* to sink, fall upon; die, 1.97; meet, 2.62. (ob and cubō).

occupō, āvī, ātus *1 v* to take against or before; get beforehand; take possession; seize, 7.446; possess, cover, 4.499; fill, reach, 3.294; smite, 9.770; surprise, hit by surprise, 10.384; anticipate in striking, strike beforehand, 10.699; hit first, 12.300. (ob and capiō).

occurrō, currī or **cucurrī, cursus** *3 v* to run, hasten to, or to meet, 3.82; meet, 10.220; make an attack, encounter, 10.282; present one's self, intervene, appear, 1.682; meet in speech, respond, reply, 12.625. (ob and currō).

Ōceanus, ī *m* the god Oceanus; the waters encompassing the lands; the ocean, 1.287; distinguished as eastern and western, 7.101.

ōcior, ius *adj* comp. (superl, ōcissimus, a, um), swifter, more fleet, 5.319 *et al.*; *adv* ōcius, more swiftly; rapidly, speedily, quickly, swiftly, 12.681.

Ocnus, ī *m* founder of Mantua, 10.198.

ocrea, ae *f* a greave; a covering made of metal for the protection of the leg, 7.634 *et al.*

oculus, ī *m* an eye, 1.228 *et al.*; nūllīs oculis, with unconcerned, untroubled eyes (as if without sight), 11.726.

ōdī, ōdisse, *def v* (*perf* with present meaning), to hate, 2.158; curse, 10.505.

odium, iī, *n* hatred, 1.361; animosity, enmity, 2.96 *et al.* (ōdī).

odor, ōris *m* scent, smell, odor, fragrance, 1.403; disagreeable odor, stench, 3.228; foul fumes, 12.591.

odōrātus, a, um sweet-smelling, fragrant, 6.658.

odōrifer, era, erum adj (odor and ferō), bearing odor; sweet, sweet-scented, 12.419.

odōrus, a, um adj (odor), that emits a smell; having a keen sense of smell, keen-scented, 4.132.

Oebalus, ī m an Italian prince, ally of Turnus, 7.734.

Oechalia, ae f a city of Euboea, 8.291.

Oenōtrius, and **Oenōtrus, a, um** adj (Oenōtria), of Oenotria, an ancient name of Southern Italy; Italian, Oenotrian, 1.532 et al.

offa, ae f a mouthful, a bit, lump, morsel, 6.420.

offerō, obtulī, oblātus, ferre irreg v to bring towards; present, offer, oppose, 6.291; with reflex pron, present one's self or itself, 2.61; expose, 7.425; appear, 1.450. (ob and ferō).

officium, iī, n anything done for another; service, duty, favor, kindness, 1.548. (officiō, come in the way of).

offulgeō, fulsī 2 v to shine against, flash upon, 9.110. (ob and fulgeō).

Oīleus (trisyll), **eī, ī,** or **eos** patronymic, son of Oileus, the king of Locris, 1.41.

olea, ae f an olive, olive berry, olive tree.

Ōlearos, ī f one of the Cyclades, southwest of Paros, 3.126.

oleaster, trī m the wild olive. (olea).

oleō, uī 2 v to emit a smell; to smell of; part, olēns, entis, smelling; fragrant, 11.137; strong-scented.

oleum, ī, n olive oil, oil, 3.281.

ōlim adv some time ago; formerly, once, 1.653 et al.; at some future time; hereafter, some time, 1.20; at times, ofttimes, 5.125.

olīva, ae f an olive tree, 6.230; olive branch, olive wreath, 5.309.

olīvifer, fera, ferum adj (olīva and ferō), olive-bearing, abounding in olives, 7.711.

olīvum, ī, n olive oil, 6.225 et al. (olīva).

olor, ōris m a swan, 11.580.

olōrīnus, a, um adj (olor), of the swan; swan's, 10.187.

Olympus, ī m Olympus, the name of several mountains in Greece and Asia Minor, the most famous of which was Mount Olympus in the northeastern part of Thessaly; the home of the superior gods; heaven, Olympus, 1.374; referring to the gods, 8.533.

ōmen, inis, n a prognostic, token, sign, omen, 2.182; metonym evil, 2.190; auspicious beginning, 7.174; pl auspices; rites, 1.346; in ōmen, as or for a warning, 12.854.

omnigenus, a, um adj (gen pl omnigenum), of all sorts, of every kind, 8.698.

omnīno adv wholly, entirely, altogether, 4.330. (omnis).

omniparēns, entis *adj* (omnis and pariō), all-producing, parent, mother of all, 6.595.

omnipotēns, entis *adj* (omnis and potēns), all-powerful, almighty, 1.60; supreme, sovereign, 10.1; *subst* The Almighty, 4.220.

omnis, e *adj* all, the whole, 6.138; every, 1.160; universal, supreme, 1.236; *subst* omnēs, ium, *m*, all men; omnia, ium, *n*, all things, 6.33; everything, 1.91.

onerō, āvī, ātus *1 v* to load; the thing or material with which, usually in *abl* and rarely in *acc*, 1.706; stow, lade, store away, *with dat* of the thing receiving, 1.195; *figuratively* burden, overwhelm, 4.549. (onus).

onerōsus, a, um *adj* (onus), burdensome, heavy, 5.352.

Onītēs, ae *m* a Rutulian, 12.514.

onus, oneris, *n* a load, burden, 2.723.

onustus, a, um *adj* (onus), loaded, laden, 1.289.

opācō, āvī, ātus *1 v* to shade, 6.195. (opācus).

opācus, a, um *adj* shady, 6.283; obscure, dark, 3.619; *subst* opāca, ōrum, *n*, partitive; opāca viārum, dark pathways, roads, 6.633.

opera, ae *f* a working; work; pains, labor, duty, 7.332. (opus).

operiō, uī, tus *4 v* to cover up; cover, 4.352; *part,* opertus, a,

um, covered; *subst* opertum, ī, *n,* a covered or secret place; partitive, operta tellūris, hidden, unseen regions of the earth, 6.140. (cf. aperiō).

operor, ātus sum *1 dep v* to work; be occupied with, engaged in (w. *dat*), 3.136; of religious rites, to sacrifice. (opus).

opertum, ī a covered or secret place; partitive, operta tellūris, hidden, unseen regions of the earth, 6.140. (operiō).

Opheltēs, ae *m* the father of Euryalus, 9.201.

opīmus, a, um *adj* (ops), rich, fertile, 1.621; sumptuous, 3.224; spolia opīma, the arms taken by a general from a general slain in battle, 6.855.

Ōpis, is *f* one of Diana's nymphs, 11.532.

opperior, perītus or **pertus sum** *4 dep v* to wait for, await, 1.454.

oppetō, petīvī or **petiī, petītus** *3 v* to encounter; with or without mortem, to die, fall, perish, 1.96. (ob and petō).

oppidum, ī, *n* a walled town; town.

oppōnō, posuī, positus *3 v* to place or put before or against, 5.335; oppose, 7.300; present, expose, 2.127; *part,* oppositus, a, um, placed in the way, opposed, 12.292; opposing, 2.333. (ob and pōnō).

opportūnus, a, um *adj* (ob and portus, opposite to, or at the entrance of a harbor), convenient, fit, 8.235; proper.

opprimō, pressī, pressus *3 v* to press against; press down, overpower, overwhelm, 1.129; come upon suddenly; surprise, 9.398. (ob and premō).

oppūgnō, āvī, ātus *1 v* to fight against; attack, lay siege to, 5.439. (ob and pūgnō).

ops, opis *f* power, might, ability, 1.601; splendor, pomp, magnificence, 8.685; aid, assistance, 2.803; *pl* opēs, um, means, resources, strength, riches, wealth, 1.14; supplies, assistance, 1.571; power, dominion, 2.4. (in the *sing* only the *gen, acc,* and *abl* are used).

optātus, a, um desired, longed for, much desired, 1.172; *adv* optātō, according to one's wish; in good time, 10.405.

optō, āvī, ātus *1 v* to choose, *with acc*, 3.109; desire, wish, 1.76; *with inf,* 6.501; *part,* optātus, a, um, desired, longed for, much desired, 1.172; *adv,* optātō, according to one's wish; in good time, 10.405.

opulentia, ae *f* wealth, riches, 7.262. (opulēns, wealthy).

opulentus, a, um *adj* (ops), abounding in means; wealthy, rich, 1.447; mighty, 8.475.

opus, eris, *n* work, labor, 1.436; task, toil, 6.183; enterprise, 3.20; the thing produced by work; a work (of art), 1.455; of buildings, 5.119.

opus, indecl *n* need, necessity, *with abl* of the thing needed, 6.261.

ōra, ae *f* a margin, border, 12.924; coast, shore, 3.396; region, 2.91; rim, extremity, 10.477; *pl* outline, compass, 9.528.

ōrāculum (ōrāclum), ī, *n* a divine utterance; oracle, response, 3.456; *metonym* the place of the response; oracular shrine, oracle, 3.143. (ōrō).

ōrātor, ōris *m* a speaker; envoy, ambassador, 7.153. (ōrō).

orbis, is *m* a circle, ring; orb, disk, 2.227; coil, fold, 2.204; the globe, world, earth, 1.331; circular movement, revolving course, revolution, 1.269; orbit, 3.512; a winding, turning round, 12.743; of the eyes, 12.670.

orbus, a, um *adj* deprived, bereaved, *with abl*, 11.216.

Orcus, ī *m* Orcus, the lower world, Hades, 4.242; *personif,* the god of the lower world, Orcus, Dis, Pluto.

ōrdior, ōrsus sum *4 dep v* to weave, spin; to begin; begin to speak; begin, 1.325.

ōrdō, inis *m* an arranging; line, 1.395; train; order, rank of oars, 5.271; order, 5.349; train, procession, 6.754; series, succession, course of events, 3.376; estimate, class, position, 2.102; *abl,* ōrdine, in due course, properly, 3.548; in historical order, in detail, 3.179; ex ōrdine, in succession, 5.773. (*rel to* ōrdior).

Orēas, adis *f* an Oread, a mountain nymph, 1.500.

Orestēs, ae or **is** *m* son
of Agamemnon and
Clytemnestra, pursued by the
Furies for the murder of his
mother until he was acquitted
by the Areopagus under the
direction of Athena, 4.471.

orgia, ōrum, *n* the rites
of Bacchus, 4.303.

orichalcum, ī, *n* mountain
copper; brass, 12.87.

Ōricius, a, um *adj* (Ōricus), of
Oricus or Oricum, a seaport
of Epirus; Orician; 10.136.

Oriēns, entis *m* the rising;
morning, morn, 5.42; the east,
1.289; the rising sun, 5.739.

orīgō, inis *f* a source, origin,
beginning, 1.372; descent,
lineage, birth, 1.286; source,
root, founder, 12.166. (orior).

Ōrīōn, ōnis *m* a fabulous giant,
celebrated as a hunter; the
constellation Orion, 1.535 *et al.*

orior, ortus sum, 4 (pres. **oritur,**
3 conj) to rise, spring up;
appear, occur, 2.680; arise,
2.411; be born of, spring,
descend, 1.626; *part,* oriēns,
rising, 7.138; *part,* ortus, a,
um, sprung, risen, 7.149.

Ōrīthyīa (*quadrisyll*), **ae** *f*
daughter of Erectheus, king of
Athens, and wife of Boreas.

ōrnātus, ūs *m* an equipping,
fitting out; adornment,
attire, 1.650. (ōrnō).

ōrnō, āvī, ātus *1 v* to
adorn, equip, 10.638.

ornus, ī *f* a mountain-
ash, 2.626 *et al.*

Ornȳtus, ī *m* an Etruscan
slain by Camilla, 11.677.

ōrō, āvī, ātus *1 v* to use the
mouth in utterance; to speak,
7.446; *with acc,* argue, plead,
6.849; beg, pray, implore,
entreat, beseech, 1.525; ask,
pray, beg for, 4.451; *with
two acc,* 11.111; *with subj.,*
6.76; *with inf,* 6.313. (1. ōs).

Orōdēs, is *m* an Etruscan slain
by Mezentius, 10.732.

Orontēs, is, ī, or **ae** a leader of
the Lycians and companion
of Aeneas, 6.334.

Orpheus (*dissyll*), **eī** *m* an
ancient bard and prophet
of Thrace, son of Onagrus
and Calliope, and husband
of Eurydice, 6.119 *et al.*

ōrsa, ōrum, *n* words, speech,
7.435; beginnings,
undertakings, purposes,
designs, 10.632. (ōrdior).

Orsēs, ae *m* a Trojan, 10.748.

Orsilochus, ī *m* a Trojan, 11.636.

Ortīnus, a, um *adj* (Orta), of Orta,
a Tuscan city; Ortine, 7.716.

ortus, ūs *m* a rising, 4.118. (orior).

Ortygia, ae *f* quail-island. 1.
Ortygia, an ancient name of
Delos, 3.124. 2. Ortygia, an
island forming part of the
city of Syracuse, 3.694.

Ortygius, iī *m* a Rutulian
killed by Caeneus, 9.573.

ōs, ōris, *n* the mouth, 1.559;
visage, face, countenance,
12.101; language, speech,
words, 2.423; an entrance,
door, 6.53; opening, 2.482;

ōs summum, the lips, 1.737; *pl* ōra, features, face, visage, form, countenance, 4.499; images, 4.62; ante ōra, before one's face, 12.82.

os, ossis, *n* a bone, 2.121.

Oscī, ōrum *m* the Oscans, an ancient people of Campania, 7.730.

ōsculum, ī, *n* the lip, 1.256; kiss, 1.687. (1. ōs).

Osīnius, iī *m* king of Clusium, 10.655.

Osīris, is or **idis** *m* a Latin, 12.458.

ostendō, tendī, tēnsus or **tentus** *3 v* to hold out towards; point out, show, 6.368; offer, promise, 1.206; sē ostendere, appear, 6.188.

ostentō, āvī, ātus *1 intens v* to hold out to view; display, disclose, 3.703; point out, show, 6.678; make a show of, display, 5.521. (ostendō).

ōstium, iī, *n* a mouth; entrance, gate, door, 6.81; *pl* ōstia, ōrum, harbor, port, 5.281; mouth of a river, 1.14. (1. ōs).

ostrum, ī, *n* the purple fluid of the murex; purple dye, purple, 5.111; purple cloth, covering or drapery, 1.700; purple decoration, 10.722; purple trappings, housings, 7.277.

Ōthryadēs, ae *m* Othryades, son of Othrys; Panthus, 2.319.

Ōthrys, yos *m* a mountain in Thessaly, 7.675.

ōtium, iī, *n* leisure, idleness, peace, quiet, retirement, inaction, 4.271.

ovīle, is, *n* a sheepcote, sheepfold. (ovis).

ovis, is *f* a sheep, 3.660.

ovō, ātus *1 v* to shout, rejoice, 3.544; triumph, 6.589; *part*, ovāns, antis, exulting, joyous, shouting, triumphant, 4.543; of things, 10.409.

pābulum, ī, *n* feeding material; food, pasturage, pasture, 1.473. (pāscō).

Pachўnum, ī, *n* Pachynum or Pachynus, the southeastern promontory of Sicily, 3.429.

pācifer, era, erum *adj* (pāx and ferō), peace-bringing; symbolical of peace; peaceful, 8.116.

pacīscor, pactus sum *3 dep v* to make a bargain; to agree upon, stipulate, contract, 4.99; purchase, 12.49; hazard, stake, 5.230; plight, betroth, 10.722.

pācō, āvī, ātus *1 v* to render peaceful; to quiet, 6.803. (pāx).

pacta, ae *f* one contracted for; a bride, 10.79. (pacīscor).

Pactōlus, ī *m* a river of Lydia which was said to wash down golden sand, 10.142.

Padus, ī *m* the river Po, the mythical Eridanus, 9.680 *et al.*

Padūsa, ae *f* a branch of the Po, 11.457.

Paeān, ānis *m* (*acc* paeāna and **-em**) originally Paean, the god of healing; later applied to Apollo; hence, a hymn in honor of Apollo, or of other deities; a triumphal chant; a paean, 6.657; song or shout of victory, 10.738.

paenitet, uit 2 *impers* or *v lit.* it repents one; one repents, regrets, 1.549 *et al.*

Paeonius, a, um *adj* pertaining to Paeon, god of medicine; medicinal, healing, 7.769.

Pagasus, ī *m* an Etruscan, 11.670.

Palaemōn, onis *m* Palaemon, a sea-god, son of Athamas and Ino; also called Melicerta, 5.823.

palaestra, ae *f* a place for wrestling or exercize, 6.642; *pl* wrestling, gymnastic, or palaestric games, 3.281.

palam *adv* openly, 9.153; plainly, 7.428.

Palamēdēs, is *m* Palamedes, son of the Euboean king Nauplius, who derived his lineage from the Egyptian king Belus, and one of the Greek chiefs at Troy; killed through the intrigues of Ulysses, 2.82.

Palātīnus, a, um *adj* (Palātium), belonging to, dwelling on the Palatine hill, 9.9.

Palīcī, ōrum *m* the Palici; two sons of Jupiter and the nymph Thalia or Aetna, 9.585.

Palinūrus, ī *m* 1. The pilot of Aeneas, 3.202 *et al.* 2. Promontory said to have been named from him, Palinurus, now Palinuro, 6.381.

palla, ae *f* a long and ample robe; mantle, 1.648.

Palladius, a, um *adj* (Pallas), pertaining to Pallas or Minerva, Palladian; *subst* Palladium, iī, *n*, the Palladium or image of Pallas, supposed to have been sent from heaven as a gift to the Trojans, and as a pledge of the safety of Troy so long as it should be preserved within the city, 2.166 *et al.*

Pallantēum, ī, *n* the city of Evander on the Palatine, 8.54 *et al.*

Pallantēus, a, um *adj* (Pallantēum), pertaining to Pallanteum or the city of Evander; Pallantean, 9.241.

Pallas, adis *f* Pallas Athena, identified by the Romans with Minerva, 1.39; rāmus Palladis, the bough sacred to Pallas, the olive, 7.154.

Pallās, antis *m* 1. A king of Arcadia, great-grandfather of Evander, 8.51. 2. Pallas, son of Evander, 8.104 *et al.*

palleō, uī 2 *v* to be pale; *part*, pallēns, entis, pallid, wan, pale, 4.26.

pallidus, a, um *adj* (palleō), pale, pallid, 3.217; ghastly, 8.197.

pallor, ōris *m* paleness, pallor, 4.499. (palleō).

palma, ae *f* the palm of the hand, 8.69; the hand, 1.93; palm branch, 5.111; a palm branch or wreath as the symbol of victory; reward, prize, 5.349; victory; a victor, 5.339.

palmōsus, a, um *adj* (palma), full of palm trees; palmy, 3.705.

palmula, ae *f* a small palm; an oar-blade, 5.163. (palma).

Palmus, ī *m* a Trojan, 10.697.

pālor, ātus sum 1 *dep v* to wander about, wander, 9.21; go astray; straggle, retreat, flee, 5.265.

palūs, ūdis *f* a marsh, swamp, moor, fen, 6.107; water, 6.414; pond, lake, 8.88.

pampineus, a, um *adj* (pampinus), covered with vine tendrils; entwined with vines, vine-wreathed, 6.804.

Pān, Pānos (*acc* **Pāna**) *m* the god of fields and woods, 8.344 *et al.*

panacēa, ae *f* an herb which cured all diseases; all-heal, 12.419.

Pandarus, ī *m* Pandarus, a Mysian chief, allied with the Trojans, who broke the truce at Troy by wounding Menelaus with his arrow, 5.496 *et al.*

pandō, pandī, passus or **pānsus** 3 *v* to spread out or open, 7.641; unfurl, 3.520; extend, expose, 6.740; break through, open, 2.234; unbind, dishevel, 1.480; *figuratively* disclose, declare, explain, reveal, 3.179.

pangō, pēgī or **pepigī, pāctus** 3 *v* to fasten; strike, covenant, agree to, contract, 10.902; appoint, 11.133; devise, attempt, undertake, 8.144.

Panopēa, ae *f* Panopea, a sea-nymph, daughter of Nereus, 5.240.

Panopēs, is *m* Panopes, a Sicilian youth, companion of Achates, 5.300.

Pantagiās, ae *m* Pantagias, a river on the east coast of Sicily, 3.689.

panthēra, ae *f* a panther, 8.460.

Panthūs (Panthous), ī *m* Panthus, son of Othrys and father of Euphorbus, slain at the capture of Troy, 2.318 *et al.*

papāver, eris, *n* the poppy, 4.486.

Paphos (-us), ī *f* Paphos, a town in the western part of Cyprus, devoted to the worship of Venus, 1.415.

papilla, ae *f* a nipple; the breast, 11.803.

pār, paris *adj* equal, 1.705; like, 2.794; equal, well-poised, steady, 4.252; side by side, 5.580; well-matched, 5.114.

Parca, ae *f* more *freq pl* Parcae, ārum, *f*, the Fates (Clotho, the spinner, Lachesis, the allotter, and Atropos, the unaverted), 1.22 *et al.*

parcō, pepercī, parcitus 3 *v* to spare, *with dat*; refrain from using, save, 8.317; spare, forbear to hurt or persecute, 1.526; cease, abstain, refrain from, 1.257; regard, yield to, 10.880; *with inf*, beware, forbear. (*rel to* parcus, scanty).

parēns, entis, *c* a parent; father, sire, 1.75 *et al.*; mother, 2.591; ancestor, 2.448 *et al.* (pariō).

pāreō, uī, itus 2 *v* to appear; to present one's self; to obey, 1.689; to be subject,

under command; to follow,
10.179; answer, reveal
signs or omens, 10.176.

pariēs, etis *m* a wall, whether
partition or external
wall, 5.589; 2.442.

pariō, peperī, partus *3 v* to
bring forth, bear, 6.89;
procure, 6.435; win, 2.578;
secure, 3.495; *part*, partus,
a, um, born; produced,
prepared, 2.784; won, 5.229.

Paris, idis *m* Paris, son of Priam
and Hecuba, who occasioned
the Trojan war by carrying off
Helen from Sparta; slain by the
arrow of Philoctetes, 4.215 *et al.*

pariter *adv* equally, 2.729; also,
in like manner, in the same
manner, on equal terms,
1.572; side by side, 2.205;
at the same time, 10.865;
pariter — pariter, 8.545. (pār).

Parius, a, um *adj* (Paros),
of Paros; Parian, 1.593.

parma, ae *f* a small round shield
or buckler, usually carried
by light troops, 11.693 *et al.*;
in *gen*, a shield, 2.175.

parō, āvī, ātus *1 v* to make ready,
prepare, build, 3.160; (w.
inf), begin, get ready, 1.179;
undertake, 6.369; *n*, 2.121.

Paros, ī *f* Paros, an island
in the Aegean, one of the
Cyclades, celebrated for its
statuary marble, 3.126.

Parrhasius, a, um *adj*
(Parrhasia), of Parrhasia
in Arcadia; Parrhasian
or Arcadian, 11.31.

pars, partis *f* a part, *freq*;
share, portion, 3.223; side, part,
4.153; way, 8.21; quarter,
direction, 12.521; partnership,
share, 12.145; *with* ellipsis
of first pars, 5.108.

Parthenius, īī *m* a Trojan, 10.748.

Parthenopaeus, ī *m*
Parthenopaeus, son of
Meleager and Atalanta, and
one of the seven chiefs who
fought against Thebes, 6.480.

Parthī, ōrum *m* the Parthi, a
nation occupying the country
of the Medes and Persians.

partim *adv* in part; partly,
10.330 *et al.* (pars).

partior, ītus sum *4 dep v* to
share, divide, distribute,
1.194; separate, 5.562. (pars).

partus, ūs *m* a bringing forth;
birth, 1.274; offspring;
son, 7.321. (pariō)

parum *adv* only a little, too little;
little; not, 6.862. (comp.)
minus, less; otherwise, 3.561;
(*superl*) minimē, least; very
little; in the least degree; not
at all, 6.97. (cf. parvus).

parumper *adv* a little while;
for a short time, 6.382.
(parum and -per).

parvulus, a, um *adj* (parvus),
very little; small, little, 4.328.

parvum, ī, *n*, a small estate,
6.843; small property, little,
9.607; *pl* small affairs, 1.24.

parvus, a, um (*compar* minor,
us; *sup*, minimus, a, um)
adj small, little, 2.677 *et al.*;
a child, infant, 10.317; *subst*

parvum, ī, *n*, a small estate, 6.843; small property, little, 9.607; *pl* small affairs, 1.24; *abl*, parvō, at small expense, 10.494; *compar* minor, us, less, smaller; younger, 9.593; inferior, 10.129; *pl* minōrēs, um, *m*, descendants, posterity, 1.532.

pāscō, pāvī, pāstus 3 *v* to furnish with food; to feed; rear, breed, 6.655; nourish, 1.608; *figuratively* 1.464; let grow, 7.391; cherish, indulge, nourish, 10.627; *pass* as *dep*, pāscor, pāstus sum 3 *v* and *n*, to graze, 1.186; feed upon, eat, 2.471; use for pasture, to pasture, 11.319.

Pāsiphaē, ēs *f* Pasiphaë, daughter of Helios, wife of Minos, and mother of Androgeos, Phaedra, Ariadne, and the Minotaur, 6.25.

passim *adv* here and there, in all directions; everywhere, 2.364 *et al.* (passus).

passus, ūs *m* a spreading or stretching; a step, pace, 2.724. (pandō.)

pāstor, ōris *m* one who feeds; herdsman, shepherd, 2.58. (pāscō.)

pāstōrālis, e *adj* (pāstor), pertaining to shepherds; country, rustic, 7.513.

pāstus, ūs *m* a pasturing, feeding; pasture, 11.494. (pāscō.)

Patavium, iī, *n* Patavium, now Padua, an ancient town in northern Italy, 1.247.

patefaciō, fēcī, factus (pass, patefierī) 3 *v* to open, 2.259. (pateō and faciō).

patēns, entis open; broad, gaping, 11.40.

pateō, uī 2 *v* to be or stand open, 1.298; fly open, open, 6.81; to lie open, to open, extend, 12.710; stretch, 6.578; stand exposed or ready, 11.644; *figuratively* be evident, patent, clear, manifest, 1.405.

pater, tris *m* a father, 1.60 *et al.*; sire, ancestor, forefather, 1.641; often for Jupiter, 1.60; applied to many of the gods, 5.241, et al; often to rivers and lakes; *pl* parents, 2.579; elders, senators, fathers, chiefs, 4.682; pater Rōmānus, Augustus (or, perhaps, the Roman citizen), 9.449. (πατήρ).

patera, ae *f* a broad, saucer-shaped dish, used in making libations; a libation cup, patera, 1.729. (pateō.)

paternus, a, um *adj* (pater), pertaining to a father; a father's, of a father, 5.81; derived from a father; paternal, ancestral, 3.121.

patēscō, patuī 3 *inc v* to begin to be open; to be open to view, stand open, 2.483; open, 3.530; become evident, manifest, 2.309. (pateō.)

patiēns, entis submissive, patiently, 5.390; *with gen*, yielding, submitting, 6.77. (patior.)

patior, passus sum 3 *dep v* to suffer, permit, allow,

1.644; submit to, bear, undergo, endure, 1.219.

patria, ae *f* (*sc* terra), father or native land; one's country, 2.291 *et al.*; ancestral land, 1.380; a country, land, 1.540.

patrius, a, um *adj* (pater), pertaining to one's father or ancestors; a father's, 2.658; paternal, natural to a father, 1.643; exacted by a father, 7.766; due to, felt for a father or parent, 9.294; ancestral, hereditary, 3.249; of one's country, native, 3.281; belonging to the nation, of the country, 11.374.

Patrōn, ōnis *m* Patron, a follower of Aeneas, 5.298.

patruus, ī *m* a father's brother, paternal uncle, uncle, 6.402. (pater).

patulus, a, um *adj* (pateō), opening, wide; wide, broad.

pauca, ōrum, *n* a few things; few words, 3.313 *et al.*

paucī, ōrum *m pl* few, a few (persons), 1.538 *et al.*

paucus, a, um *adj* small, little; *pl* paucī, ae, a, few, a few.

paulātim *adv* little by little; gradually, 1.720. (paulum).

paulisper *adv* for a short time, a little while, 5.846. (paulum and –per).

paulum *adv* a little, 3.597. (paulus, small).

pauper, eris *adj* of small means; dependent, poor, 2.87; little, lowly, humble, 6.811.

pauperiēs, ēī *f* narrow or straitened circumstances; poverty, 6.437. (pauper).

pavidus, a, um *adj* (paveō, fear), trembling, alarmed, terror-stricken, 2.489; solicitous, trembling with expectation, eager, 5.575.

pavitō, āvī, ātus *1 intens v* to be much agitated; tremble, quake with fear; be terrified, 2.107. (paveō).

pavor, ōris *m* a trembling, panic, fear, terror, 2.229; throbbing; eager, trembling, anxiety, 5.138. (paveō).

pāx, pācis *f* peace, 1.249; alliance, friendship, 7.266; indulgence, favor, pardon, 3.261; favor, assistance, 3.370. (cf. pacīscor).

peccātum, ī, *n* a fault, error, delinquency, sin, crime, 10.32. (peccō).

peccō, āvī, ātus *1 v* to commit a fault, sin, transgress, offend, 9.140.

pecten, inis *m* a comb; a weaver's sley; an instrument for striking the strings of the lyre; a plectrum, 6.647. (pectō).

pectō, pexī, pexus *3 v* to comb, 12.86.

pectus, oris, *n* the breast, 1.44; stomach, 5.182; *figuratively* mind, 1.227; thought, 5.7; breast, heart, soul, feeling, *freq*; spirit, courage, 6.261 *et al.*; *personif*; person, soul, spirit, 2.349.

pecus, oris, *n* a flock or herd, *freq*; cattle; brood, 1.435.

pecus, udis *f* one animal of a flock or herd; an animal, 1.743; a sheep, 3.120; victim for sacrifices, 4.63.

pedes, itis *m* one who goes on foot; as a footman; on foot, 12.510; a foot-soldier; collectively, infantry, soldiery, 6.516. (pēs).

pedestris, e *adj* (pedes), pedestrian; unmounted; on foot, 10.364.

pelagus, ī, *n* the sea; open sea, main, 1.138; flood, 1.246.

Pelasgī, ōrum *m* the Pelasgians, supposed to have been the original inhabitants of Greece and of several other countries and islands of the Mediterranean; in general for Greeks, 1.624 *et al.*

Pelasgus, a, um *adj* (Pelasgī), Pelasgian; Greek, 6.503.

Peliās, ae *m* a Trojan, 2.436.

Pēlīdēs, ae *m* 1. The son of Peleus, Achilles, 2.548. 2. Neoptolemus or Pyrrhus, grandson of Peleus, 2.263 *et al.*

pellāx, ācis *adj* (pelliciō), leading into error; wily, deceitful, artful, 2.90.

pellis, is *f* a skin, hide, 2.722 *et al.*

pellō, pepulī, pulsus *3 v* to drive; impel, throw, shoot, 12.320; slay, 11.56; drive away, expel, banish, 1.385; repel, 10.277; dismiss, 5.812; strike with sound, cause to echo, 7.702; to clash, reverberate, 8.529.

Pelopēus, a, um *adj* (Pelops), of Pelops; Pelopeian, Argive, Greek, 2.193.

Pelōrus, ī, *m*, and **Pelōrum, ī,** *n* the northeastern cape of Sicily, 3.411.

pelta, ae *f* a light crescent-shaped shield, 1.490.

Penātēs, ium *m* gods of the household; hearth-, fireside gods, 2.514 *et al.*; tutelary gods of the state as a national family, 1.68; *figuratively* fireside, hearth, dwelling-house, abode, 1.527. (penus).

pendeō, pependī *2 v* to hang, foll. by *abl* alone *or* with *prep*, 2.546 *et al.*; 5.511; be suspended, 1.106; cling, 9.562; bend, stoop forward, 5.147; *metonym* linger, delay, 6.151; listen, hang upon, 4.79.

pendō, pependī, pēnsus *3 v* to hold suspended; to hang, balance, weigh; weigh out money; hence, *figuratively* to pay or suffer punishment or penalty, 6.20.

Pēneleus (*trisyll*) **eī** or **eos** *m* Peneleus, a Greek warrior, said to have been one of the suitors of Helen, 2.425.

penes (*prep with acc*), within one's power or possession, 12.59.

penetrābilis, e *adj* (penetrō), that can be pierced; in an active sense, piercing, 10.481.

penetrālis, e *adj* (penetrō), innermost, inner, 2.297; *subst* penetrālia, ium, *n*, the interior of a house; sanctuary, shrine, chapel (of a dwelling or temple), 2.484 *et al.*

penetrō, āvī, ātus *1 v* to penetrate, reach, 1.243; attain to, go as far as, penetrate to, 7.207. (*rel to* penitus).

penitus *adv* (cf. penes), inwardly, far within, deep, deeply, 1.200; wholly, entirely, 6.737; afar, 11.623; far away, 1.512.

penna (**pinna**), ae *f* a feather, 12.750; wing, pinion, 3.258; in the form pinna, a pinnacle, battlement, palisade, 7.159.

pennātus, a, um *adj* (penna), winged, 9.473.

pēnsum, ī, *n* that which is weighed out or assigned for a day's spinning; a day's work; task, 8.412; a web, 9.476. (pendō).

Penthesilēa, ae *f* Penthesilea; the queen of the Amazons slain by Achilles at Troy, 1.491.

Pentheus (*dissyll*), eī or **eos** *m* Pentheus, king of Thebes, grandson of Cadmus, and son of Echion and Agave; torn to pieces by his mother and her Bacchanalian companions for mocking at the orgies of Bacchus, 4.469.

pēnūria, ae *f* want, destitution, need, 7.113.

penus, ūs and ī *m and f* also penus, oris, *n* (*rel to* penes, Penātēs, penetrō), that which is stored within; the household store of provisions; stores, provisions, viands, 1.704.

peplum, ī, *n* a mantle, robe, or shawl worn over the other garments; the mantle used for draping the statues of Athena, 1.480.

per (*prep with acc*), through, (of place, time, agency, instrumentality, medium, and manner), 4.357 *et al.*; along, 1.576; over, 1.498; on, 5.335; by, at, 4.56; through, throughout, during, 1.31; in, 9.31; in entreaties, adjurations, and oaths, by, 2.141 *et al.*

peragō, ēgī, āctus *3 v* to drive through; carry through; execute, achieve, accomplish, finish, perform, 4.653; pursue, 6.384; fulfill, achieve, 3.493; go through with, distribute, 5.362; go through mentally, 6.105.

peragrō, āvī, ātus *1 v* to go through fields or lands; to roam, travel; traverse, 1.384. (per and ager).

percellō, culī, culsus *3 v* to strike, smite vehemently; strike down, 5.374; overthrow, 11.310.

percipiō, cēpī, ceptus *3 v* to take in completely; perceive; feel, 7.356; understand, 9.190. (per and capiō).

percurrō, cucurrī or currī, cursus *3 v* to run through or over, 8.392; *figuratively* run over in narration, relate briefly, 6.627.

percutiō, cussī, cussus *3 v* to smite through; strike, smite, 4.589; *part*, percussus, a, um, struck, smitten, 7.503; of the effect of sound, reverberating, echoing, penetrated, filled, 1.513; 8.121. (per and quatiō).

perdō, didī, ditus *3 v* to put through completely; ruin, undo, kill, destroy, 7.304; to abandon; lose, 11.58.

peredō, ēdī, ēsus 3 v to eat through or completely; eat up; consume, 6.442.

peregrīnus, a, um adj (peregre from per and ager), of foreign lands; foreign, barbarian, 11.772.

perennis, e adj (per and annus), throughout the year; lasting, continual, perpetual, endless, 9.79.

pereō, iī, itus, īre irreg v to go out of sight; to be lost, undone, 4.497; perish, 2.660; die, 2.408.

pererrō, āvī, ātus 1 v to wander through or over, 2.295; survey, 4.363; explore, try, 5.441; pervade, 7.375.

perferō, tulī, lātus, ferre irreg v to carry or bear through; carry, restore, return, 11.717; report, 5.665; convey completely, carry home, 10.786; reach the mark, 12.907; undergo, endure, suffer, 3.323; (w. *reflex pron*), betake one's self, go, 1.389; *part*, perlātus, a, um, carried to the mark; striking, 11.803.

perficiō, fēcī, fectus 3 v to make completely; finish, complete, 6.745; perform, 3.178; *part*, perfectus, a, um, worked, wrought, executed, 5.267; fulfilled, 3.548. (per and faciō).

perfidus, a, um adj (per and fidēs), violating one's faith; faithless, perfidious, treacherous, 4.305; of things, disappointing; deceptive, treacherous, 12.731.

perflō, āvī, ātus 1 v to blew through or over; sweep over, 1.83.

perfodiō, fōdī, fossus 3 v to dig or pierce through, transfix, 11.10.

perforō, āvī, ātus 1 v to bore or pierce through, 10.485.

perfringō, frēgī, frāctus 3 v to break through; break completely; dash or break in pieces, crush, 10.279; break, dash, 11.614. (per and frangō).

perfundō, fūdī, fūsus 3 v to pour over or along; wash, 3.397; overspread, overflow, 11.626; spot, stain, 2.221; anoint, 5.135; besprinkle, 12.611.

perfurō, uī 3 v to rage wildly; rave, 9.343.

Pergama, ōrum, n, **Pergamum, ī,** n, and **Pergamus (-os), ī** f 1. The citadel or walls of Troy, 3.87; Troy, 4.344 et al. 2. The Trojan citadel of Helenus in Epirus, 3.336.

Pergameus, a, um adj (Pergamus), of Pergamus, Pergamean; Trojan, 3.110. Pergamea (sc urbs), the city built by Aeneas in Crete, 3.133.

pergō, perrēxī, perrēctus 3 v to direct one's course right onward; go on, 1.389; march, 11.521; continue, 6.198; *figuratively* of narration, 1.372. (per and regō).

perhibeō, uī, itus 2 v to hold persistently; maintain, assert; say, report, 4.179. (per and habeō).

perīculum (perīclum), ī, *n* a trial; risk, hazard, danger, peril, 1.615 *et al.*

Perīdīa, ae *f* the mother of Onites, 12.515.

perimō, ēmī, ēmptus *3 v* to take away completely; annihilate, destroy, 5.787; slay, kill, 6.163. (per and emō).

Periphās, antis *m* Periphas, a Greek warrior, companion of Pyrrhus, 2.476.

periūrium, iī, *n* a false oath; perjury, perfidy, treachery, 4.542. (periūrus).

periūrus, a, um *adj* (per and iūs), violating one's oath; perjured, forsworn, 2.195.

perlābor, lāpsus sum *3 dep v* to glide through or over, 1.147; reach, come down in tradition, 7.646.

perlegō, lēgī, lēctus *3 v* to scan narrowly; survey, examine, 6.34.

permētior, mēnsus sum *4 dep v* to measure completely; traverse, 3.157.

permisceō, miscuī, mistus or **mixtus** *2 v* to mix completely; mix, mingle, 1.488; *figuratively* disturb, confound, 7.348.

permittō, mīsī, missus *3 v* to let go without hindrance; allow, permit, 1.540; give up, commit, consign, 4.640; surrender, 4.104.

permulceō, mulsī, mulsus or **mulctus** *2 v* to stroke; calm, soothe, cheer, 5.816.

permūtō, āvī, ātus *1 v* to exchange, 9.307.

pernīx, īcis *adj* nimble, fleet, swift, agile, 4.180 *et al.*

pērō, ōnis *m* a boot or high shoe made of rawhide, 7.690.

perōdī, ōdisse, ōsus sum, *def v* to hate, abhor, loathe, 6.435. (per and ōdī).

perpetior, pessus sum *3 dep v* to bear completely; suffer, endure, 9.60; permit, 12.644. (per and patior).

perpetuus, a, um *adj* (per and petō), continuing through; perpetual, continual, 4.32; stretching out, long extending or reaching, 8.183.

perplexus, a, um *adj* much entangled; puzzling, intricate, 9.391.

perrumpō, rūpī, ruptus *3 v* to break, burst through, 2.480.

persentiō, sēnsī, sēnsus *4 v* to feel deeply; feel, 4.448; perceive, 4.90.

persequor, secūtus sum *3 dep v* to follow continually; follow, 9.218; pursue, follow closely, 10.562.

persolvō, solvī, solūtus *3 v* to loosen completely; set free; free one's self from obligation; pay, render, give, return, 1.600 *et al.*; sacrifice, offer, 5.484.

personō, sonuī, sonitus *1 v* to sound loudly; sing, play, 1.741; cause to or make resound, 6.171.

perstō, stitī, stātus *1 v* to continue standing; remain fixed, 5.812; persist, 2.650.

perstringō, strīnxī, strīctus *3 v* to bind tightly; graze, 10.344.

pertaedet, taesum est *2 impers* (with mē, tē, etc.), it much wearies me, you, etc.; one is weary, disgusted; *with gen* of the thing, 4.18; 5.714.

pertēmptō, āvī, ātus *1 intens v* to handle completely; test, prove; to search through; thrill, penetrate, pervade, fill, 1.502 *et al.*

perterreō, uī, itus *2 v* to fill with terror; to affright, dismay, 10.426.

perveniō, vēnī, ventus *4 v* to come to the end; arrive, reach, 2.81.

perversus, a, um turned the wrong way; contrary, adverse, 7.584. (pervertō).

pervius, a, um *adj* (per and via), that can be passed through; unobstructed, free; common, 2.453.

pervolitō, āvī, ātus *1 intens v* to fly about; flit around, 8.24.(pervolō).

pervolō, āvī, ātus *1 v* to fly through or over, 12.474.

pēs, pedis *m* the foot; claw, talon, paw, hoof, *freq*; of the current of a river, 9.125; the footrope at the lower corner of a sail, the sheet; hence, facere pedem, to manage the sheet, shift the sail; tack, 5.830; pedem reprimere, to retreat, draw back, 2.378;

ferre pedem, go, 2.756; efferre pedem, go out, depart, 2.657; pedem advertere, approach, draw near, 6.386; aequō pede, in equal combat, 12.465. (πους, ποδός).

pestifer, era, erum *adj* (pestis and ferō), pest-bringing; pestilential, 7.570.

pestis, is *f* destruction, 5.699; plague, pest, scourge, 3.215; death, 9.328; infection, pollution, 6.737; fatal, baneful passion, 1.712. (perdō).

Petēlia, ae *f* Petelia, a town on the eastern coast of Bruttium, 3.402.

petō, īvī or **iī, ītus** *3 v* to fall upon, attack, assail, 3.603; seek, 1.181; strike, 11.9; advance towards, 2.213; follow up, pursue, 5.226; make for, 1.158; repair to, 1.519; hasten, approach to, 1.717; greet, 1.611; aim at, 5.508; *figuratively* assail, try, 4.675; purpose, intend, 2.151; apply to, solicit, entreat, beg, beseech, crave, ask, seek, 4.433 *et al.*; *with inf*, 7.96; petere terram, fall prostrate upon the ground, 3.93.

Phaeāces, um, *m, pl* the Phaeacians, the Homeric name of the inhabitants of Corcyra, the modern Corfu, 3.291.

Phaedra, ae *f* one of the daughters of Minos, king of Crete, and wife of Theseus, king of Athens, 6.445.

Phaëthōn, ontis *m* Phaëthon, the son of Helios and Clymene; for the sun-god, the sun, 5.105.

phalanx, ngis f a body of troops in compact array; a battalion, army, host, 6.489; of a fleet, 2.254.

phalārica, ae f a heavy spear wound with combustibles; fiery dart, 9.705.

phalerae, ārum f bosses of metal worn on the corselet; trappings, 9.458; trappings or caparisons for the heads, necks, and breasts of horses, 5.310.

Phaleris, is m (acc -im) a Trojan, 9.762.

pharetra, ae f a quiver, 1.323 et al.

pharetrātus, a, um adj (pharetra), bearing the quiver, 11.649.

Pharus, ī, and **Pharō, ōnis** m a Rutulian, 10.322.

Phēgeus (dissyll), **ī** or **eos** m 1. A follower of Aeneas, 5.263. 2. Another follower of Aeneas, 12.371.

Pheneos (-us), eī f a town of Arcadia, 8.165.

Pherēs, ētis m an Arcadian, follower of Pallas, 10.413.

Philoctētēs, ae m son of the Thessalian king Poeas of Meliboea, companion of Hercules, from whom he inherited the bow and arrows with which he killed Paris, 3.402.

Phīnēius, a, um adj (Phineus), pertaining to Phineus, king of Salmydessus, who was smitten by the gods with blindness and tormented by the Harpies, for putting out the eyes of his sons, 3.212.

Phlegethōn, ontis m a river of Tartarus, 6.551.

Phlegyās, ae m a son of Mars and king of the Lapithae, 6.618.

Phoebē, ēs f the sister of Apollo; Diana, Luna.

Phoebēus, a, um adj (Phoebus), pertaining to Phoebus or the sun; Phoebean, 3.637.

Phoebigena, ae m the son of Phoebus, Aesculapius, 7.773. (Phoebus and genō).

Phoebus, ī m Phoebus or Apollo, 1.329 et al.

Phoenīces, um m the Phoenicians, 1.344.

Phoenissus, a, um adj Phoenician, 1.670; subst Phoenissa, ae, f, a Phoenician woman; Dido, 1.714 et al.

Phoenīx, īcis m Phoenix, son of Amyntor, and companion of Achilles, 2.762.

Pholoē, ēs f a Cretan woman, slave of Aeneas, 5.285.

Pholus, ī m a centaur, son of Ixion; a Trojan warrior, 12.341.

Phorbās, antis m Phorbas, a son of Priam, killed at the siege of Troy, 5.842.

Phorcus, ī m a sea-god, son of Neptune or Pontus and Gaia, 5.240; a Latin patriarch, 10.328.

Phryges, um m Phrygians; the inhabitants of Phrygia, which originally included the Troad; hence, also, Trojans, 1.468

et al.; *sing* Phryx, ygis, *m*, a Phrygian or Trojan, 12.99.

Phrygia, ae *f* Phrygia, the Troad, 7.207. (Phryx).

Phrygius, a, um Phrygian, Trojan, 1.381; *subst* Phrygiae, ārum, *f*, Phrygian or Trojan women, 518. (Phryx).

Phryx, ygis Phrygian; of the inhabitants of Phrygia, which originally included the Troad; hence, also, Trojans, 1.468 *et al.*; *sing* Phryx, ygis, *m*, a Phrygian or Trojan, 12.99.

Phthīa, ae *f* Phthia, the native town of Achilles in Thessaly, 1.284.

piāculum, ī, *n* an expiation; expiatory, sacrifice, offering, 4.636; purifying sacrifice; lustration, 6.153; *metonym* that which requires such expiation; sin, crime, 6.569. (piō).

picea, ae *f* the pitch-pine; the pine, 6.180. (pix).

piceus, a, um *adj* (pix), of pitch; smoking with pitch, pitchy, 9.75; pitch-black, 3.573.

pictūra, ae *f* the art of painting; painting, 1.464. (pingō).

pictūrātus, a, um adorned with painting; embroidered, 3.483. (pictūra).

pictus, a, um embroidered, 1.708; many-colored, speckled, spotted, variegated, 4.525.

Pīcus, ī *m* the son of Saturn, grandfather of Latinus, king of the aborigines, changed by Circe into a woodpecker, 7.48 *et al.*

pietās, ātis *f* piety, reverence, devotion, love with respect to gods or parents, 1.10; in other relations, dutiful affection; fidelity, regard; righteousness; pity for the injured, just retribution, justice, 2.536; pity, compassion, mercy, 5.688; patria pietās, affection for a parent, 9.294. (pius).

piget, uit 2 *impers v* to cause disgust, vexation, irksomeness; with mē, tē, etc., I am, you are ... vexed, displeased, annoyed; regret, 4.335 *et al.*

pīgnus, oris, *n* a pledge, stake, token, assurance, 3.611. (*rel to* pangō *and* paciscor).

pīla, ae *f* a pier; mole, 9.711.

pīlātus, a, um *adj* (pīlum), armed with the pilum, javelin, or dart, 12.121.

pīlentum, ī, *n* a chariot, carriage, 8.666.

pīlum, ī, *n* the heavy javelin used by the Roman legionary soldier; the pilum.

Pīlumnus, ī *m* a Latin deity, ancestor of Turnus, 10.619 *et al.*

Pīnārius, a, um *adj* (Pīnārius), of Pinarius, head of a family devoted to the rites of Hercules; Pinarian, 8.270.

pīneus, a, um *adj* (pīnus), of pine, made of pine, produced from pine, piny, 11.786; pine-, 2.258; piny, pine-growing, 11.320.

pingō, pīnxī, pīctus 3 *v* to paint, 5.663; color, stain, dye, 7.252; tattoo, 4.146.

pinguis, e *adj* fat, 1.215; well-fed, 1.635; fertile; reeking, 4.62; fat or rich with victims, 9.585.

pīnifer, era, erum *adj* (pinus and ferō), pine-bearing, pine-covered, 4.249.

pīnus, ūs or **ī** a pine tree, pine, 3.659 *et al.*; *metonym* a ship, 5.153; a torch, 7.397; a pine brand or torch, 9.522.

piō, āvī, ātus *1 v* to atone for, expiate, 2.184; appease, 6.379; avenge, punish, 2.140. (pius).

Pīrithous, ī *m* son of Ixion and king of the Lapithae; chained in Hades for attempting, with the aid of Theseus, to carry away Proserpina from the abode of Pluto, 6.393 *et al.*

Pīsae, ārum *f* a city of Etruria, now Pisa, 10.179.

piscis, is *m* a fish.

piscōsus, a, um *adj* (piscis), abounding in fish; haunt of fish, 4.255.

pistrīx, īcis *f* a sea monster, 3.427. (cf. pristis).

pius, a, um *adj* dutiful, pious, especially to gods and parents, 1.220 *et al.*; pious, reverent, devout, 1.526; sacred, holy, 4.637; righteous, good, 1.603; pure, 3.42; blessed, 5.734; of the gods, righteous, just, 4.382 *et al.*

pix, picis *f* pitch.

plācābilis, e *adj* (plācō), that can be appeased; placable, propitious, 7.764.

placeō, uī or **placitus sum** *2 v* to be agreeable, pleasing;

to please, 4.38; (*impers*), placet, placuit or placitum est, it pleases (me, you etc.); I resolve, decree, will, 1.283.

placidē *adv* gently, softly, quietly, calmly, 5.86.

placidus, a, um *adj* (placeō), gentle, calm, tranquil, peaceful, serene, 5.848; inactive, idle, 9.187; friendly, propitious, 3.266; *adv* placidē, gently, softly, quietly, calmly, 5.86.

placitus, a, um, agreeable, pleasing, 4.38. (placeō).

plācō, āvī, ātus *1 v* to appease, 2.116; calm, quiet, still, 1.142; subdue, quell, 6.803. (*rel to* placeō).

plaga, ae *f* a tract, region, 1.394; zone, 7.226.

plaga, ae *f* a net, hunter's net; a snare, a trap, 4.131.

plāga, ae *f* a blow, wound; lash, whip, 7.383.

plangō, plānxī, planctus *3 v* to beat, strike, smite the breast; hence, intransitive, lament, wail, 11.145. (cf. 1. plāga).

plangor, ōris *m* lamentation by beating the breast; lamentation, wailing, cry of grief, 2.487. (plangō).

plānitiēs, ēī *f* a level surface, plain, 11.527. (plānus, flat).

planta, ae *f* the sole of the foot, 4.259. (cf. plānus, flat).

plaudō, plausī, plausus *3 v* to beat, slap, stroke, 12.86; clap, flutter, 5.516;

of the dance, perform by beating, beat, 6.644.

plaustrum, ī, *n* a cart, car, wain.

plausus, ūs *m* a beating, clapping, flapping; fluttering sound, 5.215; plaudit, applause, 5.148. (plaudō).

plēbs (plēbēs), is (eī and ī) *f* the multitude, throng, 9.343; mass, common people.

Plēmyrium, iī, *n* Plemyrium, a promontory in Sicily, near Syracuse, 3.693.

plēnus, a, um *adj* full, 1.460; mature, 7.53; swelling, 1.400; overflowing, 1.739. (cf. -pleō in compleō, impleō, etc.).

plicō, cāvī or **cuī, cātus** or **citus** *1 v* to wind together, fold, coil, 5.279.

plūma, ae *f* the soft under-feather; a soft feather; plume, feather, 3.242; plumage, 11.771.

plumbum, ī, *n* lead, 5.405; a leaden bullet, 9.588.

pluō, uī or **ūvī** *3 v pers* and *impers* to rain, 10.807.

Plūtōn, ōnis *m* Pluto, son of Saturn, king of Hades, 7.327.

pluvia, ae (*sc* **aqua**) *f* rain (pluvius).

pluviālis, e *adj* (pluvia), causing rain; rainy, 9.668.

pluvius, a, um *adj* (pluō), causing rain or attended by rain; rainy, 1.744.

pōculum, ī, *n* a drinking-cup; goblet, 1.706; draught, drink. (cf. pōtō, drink).

Podalīrius, iī *m* a Trojan follower of Aeneas, 12.304.

poena, ae *f* penalty, punishment, 1.136; pain, torture, torment, 6.543; revenge, vengeance, 2.572; 7.766.

Poenī, ōrum *m* the Carthaginians, 1.302; Africans, 12.4.

poliō, īvī or **iī, ītus** *4 v* to smooth, furbish, polish; finish, 8.426; make bright, adorn, 8.436.

Polītēs, ae *m* Polites, a son of Priam and Hecuba, killed by Pyrrhus, 2.526.

pollex, icis *m* the thumb, 11.68. (polleō).

polliceor, licitus sum *2 dep v* to promise, 1.237.

polluō, uī, ūtus *3 v* to soil, pollute, defile, 3.234; break, violate, 3.61.

Pollūx, ūcis *m* son of Tyndarus and Leda, and twin brother of Castor, 6.121.

polus, ī *m* the terminating point of an axis; the celestial pole; *metonym* the heavens, sky, 1.90; air, 1.398.

Polyboetēs, ae *m* a Trojan priest of Ceres, 6.484.

Polydōrus, ī *m* son of Priam and Hecuba, 3.49.

Polyphēmus, ī *m* a cyclops, son of Neptune, 3.657.

Pōmetiī, ōrum, *m,* and **Pōmetia, ae** *f* Pometia, a city of the Volsci, called also Suessa Pometia, 6.775.

pompa, ae *f* a solemn procession or ceremonial, a funeral procession, 5.53.

pōmum, ī, *n* any kind of tree fruit; an apple, pear, fig, etc., *freq.*

pondus, eris, *n* weight, 5.447; burden, load, 6.413; a stone, a shot, 11.616. (pendō).

pōne (*adv* of place), behind, after, 2.208.

pōnō, posuī, positus *3 v* to put, set, place, 1.706 *et al.*; lay, stretch, 1.173; level, 12.569; deposit, 6.73; plant, settle, fix, 3.88; set up, establish, make, 1.264; assign, appoint, 1.278; dispose, determine, 10.623; bestow, 6.611; put to rest or sleep, 4.527; bury, 6.508; for dēpōnō, lay down or aside, *figuratively* 1.302; 9.687; give up for another, change, 8.329; give up, 11.309; lose, 12.209; *n* (*sc* sē), to subside, be hushed, sink to rest, 7.27; 10.103.

pōns, pontis *m* a bridge; a bridge connecting battlements and towers, 9.530; gangway, bridge for embarking, 10.288.

pontus, ī *m* the sea; the deep, 2.295; wave, billow, 1.114.

poples, itis *m* the hinder part of the knee; hamstring, 9.762; knee, 12.492.

populāris, e *adj* (populus), pertaining to the people or nation; popular, 6.816.

pōpuleus, a, um *adj* (pōpulus), of the poplar tree; poplar-, 5.134.

Populōnia, ae *f* a town on the coast of Etruria near the modern Piombino, 10.172.

populor, ātus sum *1 dep v,* and **populō, āvī, ātus** *1 v* to lay waste; ravage; ransack, 4.403; devastate, plunder, 1.527; rob, deprive, 6.496; of things, 12.525. (populus).

pōpulus, ī *f* a poplar tree; a wreath of poplar, 8.276.

populus, ī *m* a people; state, nation, 1.21; canton, clan, tribe, 7.716; multitude, throng, 1.148; the common people as opposed to the senate, commons, people, 9.192.

porca, ae *f* a sow, 8.641. (porcus).

porrigō (*contract form* **pōrgō**, 8.274), **rēxī, rēctus** *3 v* to stretch forth, hold forth, lift, 8.274; *passive* to be stretched out, extend, 6.597. (prō and regō).

porrō *adv* forward, of space, time, or of mental operations, far off, 6.711; afterwards, in process of time, then, 5.600; further, 9.190.

Porsenna, ae *m* an Etruscan lars or king allied with the banished Tarquins against Rome, 8.646.

porta, ae *f* a gate, 1.294 *et al.*; passage, avenue, door, 1.83.

portendō, tendī, tentus *3 v* to stretch, hold forth; to foretell, portend, presage; to 3.184. (prō and tendō),.

portentum, ī *n* an omen, portent, prodigy, 8.533. (portendō).

porticus, ūs *f* a portico, porch, gallery, pillared hall, colonnade, hall, 3.353. (porta).

portitor, ōris *m* a carrier; ferryman, boatman. (portō).

portō, āvī, ātus 1 *v* to bring, convey, carry, 1.68; carry away, 1.363; announce, declare, 3.539.

Portūnus, ī *m* Portunus, the Roman god of harbors or seaports; identified with the Greek Palaemon or Meliecrtes, 5.241. (portus).

portus, ūs *m* a port, harbor, haven, 1.159, et al; *figuratively* 7.598.

poscō, poposcī 3 *v* to demand, require, 11.901; 1.414; ask, inquire, 3.59; request, call, ask for, 1.728; seek, summon, 10.661; entreat, supplicate, 1.666; claim, 5.342; *with* two accusatives, 4.50.

possum, potuī, posse *irreg v* to be able; can, 1.242 *et al.*; to avail, have influence, power, 4.382. (potis and sum).

post (*prep with acc*, and *adv* of place and time); *prep*, behind, 1.296; next to, 7.655; after, 5.626; *adv* afterwards, then, next, 1.612; hereafter, 1.136.

posterus, a, um *adj* (post), the next, following, 3.588; *superl*, postrēmus or postumus, a, um, last, 11.664; the last, lowest, 3.427; latest-born, youngest, 6.763; *subst* postrēma, ōrum, *n*, the rear, 9.27.

posthabeō, uī, itus 2 *v* to hold next; esteem less, 1.16.

postis, is *m* a post; doorpost, jamb, 3.287; door, 2.480. (*rel to* pōnō).

postquam (*adv* referring the time of one action or event to that of another), after that, as soon as, *with perf*, 3.463; 1.520; from the time that, 4.17.

potēns, entis able, powerful, mighty, 2.296; potent, great, 1.531; rich, 6.843; of medicines, 12.402; sovereign, ruler, lord, master of, *with gen*, 1.80; factus, facta potēns, *with gen*, having obtained, 7.541; *subst* potentēs, ium or um, the great, 12.519.

potentia, ae *f* power, force, potency, might, 1.664 *et al.* (potēns).

potestās, ātis *f* ability, power, physical or moral, 9.97; 9.739; virtue, efficacy, 12.396; possibility, opportunity, 3.670; authority, 10.100; *metonym* the possessor of power, sovereign, 10.18. (possum).

potior, ītus sum 4 *dep v* to become master or possessor of; get, take possession, *with abl*, 3.56; enjoy, 4.217; seize, 12.642; win, 9.363; achieve, execute, 6.624; gain, reach, 1.172. (potitur, 3.56; 4.217) (potis).

potis, e *adj* able, 3.671; compar., potior, ius, better, preferable, 4.287.

Potītius, iī *m* the founder of one of the families charged with the sacred rites of Hercules, 8.269.

potius *adv* preferably; rather, 3.654. (potis).

pōtō, āvī, ātus or pōtus 1 *v* to drink, 6.715.

prae (*prep with abl*), before; prae sē portāre, to carry, 11.544; prae sē iactāre, to pretend, 9.134. (*rel to* prō).

praebeō, uī, itus 2 *v* to hold before, afford, offer, 9.693. (prae and habeō).

praecēdō, cessī, **cessus** 3 *v* to go before, 9.47.

praecelsus, a, um *adj* very high, lofty, 3.245.

praeceps, cipitis *adj* (prae and caput), head foremost; headlong, 2.307; deep, 11.888; hurried, hasty, quick, speedy, 4.573; flying, running swiftly, 2.516; 3.598; rash, impetuous, fiery, 9.685; prolept., ready to sink, 10.232; *subst* praeceps, *n*, a steep, precipice, verge, 2.460; in praeceps, headlong; downwards, 6.578.

praeceptum, ī, *n* an injunction, direction, order, command, 6.236; warning, 2.345; rule, precept, maxim. (praeceptus).

praecipiō, cēpī, ceptus 3 *v* to take, get beforehand, 10.277; *figuratively* anticipate, 6.105; await, 11.491; instruct, direct, order, 9.40; teach, prescribe, 11.329. (prae and capiō).

praecipitō, āvī, ātus 1 *v* to cast headlong, hurl, plunge, 2.37; urge, hurry, hasten; impel, incite, 2.317; break off, end swiftly, 12.699; hasten away, 4.565; *n* (*sc* sē), fall headlong, 6.351; descend swiftly, 2.9; run down, 4.251. (praeceps).

praecipuē *adv* chiefly, especially, particularly, most of all, 1.220. (praecipuus).

praecipuus, a, um *adj* (praecipiō), taken first; foremost, chief, 11.214; distinguished, 5.249; most distinguished, 8.177.

praecīsus, a, um abrupt, ragged, 8.233. (prae and caedō).

praeclārus, a, um *adj* very clear or bright; illustrious, splendid, 4.655.

praecō, ōnis *m* a herald, 5.245.

praecordia, ōrum, *n* the diaphragm or midriff; the vital parts; the heart, 9.413; the heart as the seat of courage, 2.367; spirit, heart, 9.596. (prae and cor).

praeda, ae *f* booty, spoil, 1.528; prey, game, 1.210; often in the *pl* as 7.749.

praedīcō, dīxī, dictus 3 *v* to say beforehand; foretell, prophesy, predict, 3.252; forewarn, 3.436; *part*, praedictus, a, um, foretold.

praedictum, ī, *n* a thing foretold; a prediction, prophecy, 4.464. (praedīcō).

praedīves, itis *adj* very rich, opulent, wealthy, 11.213.

praedō, ōnis *m* a robber, 10.774. (cf. praedor, rob).

praedulcis, e *adj* very sweet; pleasing, dear, 11.155.

praedūrus, a, um *adj* very hard; hardy, sturdy, powerful, 10.748.

praeeō, īvī, or iī, itus, īre *irreg v* to go before; *part*, praeiēns, euntis, going before, preceding, 5.186.

praeferō, tulī, lātus, ferre *irreg v*
to carry before, bear, 7.237;
offer, 11.249; present, exhibit,
10.211; put before or first,
5.541; choose rather, prefer.

praeficiō, fēcī, fectus 3 *v* to put
at the head or in command; to
place or set over, *with acc and
dat* 6.118. (prae and faciō).

praefīgō, fīxī, fīxus 3 *v* to fasten
before, in front of, *with acc and
dat* 11.778; on the end, 9.466;
to tip, head, point, 5.557.

praefodiō, fōdī, fossus 3 *v* to dig
before or in front of, 11.473.

praefor, fātus sum 1 *dep v*
to address first, 11.301.

praefulgeō, fulsī 2 *v* to shine
or glitter at the end, 8.553.

praegnāns, antis with
young, pregnant, 7.320.
(prae and genō).

praemetuō 3 *v* to fear
beforehand, dread, 2.573.

praemittō, mīsī, missus 3 *v* to
send before, in advance, or
forward; dispatch, 6.34.

praemium, iī, *n* that which
is taken first or as the
best; prize, 5.70; reward,
recompense, 1.461; gift,
blessing, 4.33. (prae and emō).

praenatō 1 *v* to swim in front
of or by; *figuratively* flow
by, along by, 6.705.

Praeneste, is, *n and f* a town in
Latium on a lofty hill about
twenty miles southeast of
Rome; now Palestrina, 7.682.

Praenestīnus, a, um
adj (Praeneste), of
Praeneste, 7.678.

praenūntia, ae *f* a harbinger,
forerunner, 11.139.

praepes, etis *adj* hastening
before, swift, fleet,
3.361; winged, 5.254.

praepes, etis *adj* hastening
before, swift, fleet,
3.361; winged, 5.254.

praepinguis, e *adj* very
fat; rich, 3.698.

praeripiō, ripuī, reptus 3 *v* to
snatch, seize before another;
seize quickly; snatch away,
4.516. (prae and rapiō).

praerumpō, rūpī, ruptus 3 *v* to
burst or break off in front;
part, praeruptus, a, um,
broken or torn off; precipitous,
abrupt, steep, 1.105.

praesaepe, is, *n* an inclosure,
fold, stall, stable, pen, 7.17;
hive, 1.435.(*rel* to praesaepio).

praesāgus, a, um *adj*
(praesāgiō), divining,
prophetic, 10.177; foreboding,
with gen, 10.843 *et al.*

praescius, a, um *adj*
foreknowing, prescient, 6.66;
foreboding, ill-boding, 12.452.

praesēns, entis *adj* being before,
present in person; present
before one, 3.174; propitious,
9.404; immediate, instant,
1.91; prompt, 12.152; urgent,
powerful, 12.245. (praesum).

praesentia, ae *f* a being present;
presence, 9.73. (praesēns).

praesentiō, sēnsī, sēnsus
4 v to feel, perceive
beforehand, 4.297.

praeses, idis, c one presiding;
an arbiter; arbitress,
11.483. (praesideō).

praesideō, sēdī 2 v to sit before;
preside over, rule over, *with
dat* 3.35. (prae and sedeō).

praesidium, iī, n protection,
11.58. (praesideō).

praestāns, antis, *compar*
praestantior, ius excellent,
superior, distinguished,
5.361; *with gen*, 12.19.

praestō, stitī, stātus or **stitus**
1 v to stand before; surpass;
represent, 11.438; (*impers*),
praesta, praestitit, it is,
was better, preferable, more
fitting, important, 1.135.

praesūmō, sūmpsī, sūmptus
3 v to take beforehand;
anticipate, 11.18.

praetendō, tendī, tentus 3 v
to hold out before; stretch
forth, extend, wave, 8.116;
stretch, extend before, 3.692;
oppose, 9.599; *figuratively*
pretend, promise, 4.339.

praeter (*prep with acc*),
beyond, 7.24. (prae).

praeter *adv* besides, along
by, past, 10.399.

praetereā *adv* besides,
moreover, *freq*; then too,
1.647; hereafter, 1.49.

praetereō, īvī, or **iī, itus, īre**
irreg v to pass by, to come
to an end; to go, pass by,

5.156; outstrip, 4.157; *part*,
praeteritus, a, um, past, 8.560.

praeterlābor, lāpsus sum 3
dep v to glide, flow along by,
6.874; sail past or by, 3.478.

praetervehor, vectus sum 3 *pass
of praetervehō, as* *dep v* to
go by; pass, sail by, 3.688.

praetexō, texuī, textus 3 v to
weave in front; to fringe, 6.5;
figuratively palliate, cloak,
4.172; conceal, 4.500.

praeūrō, ussī, ūstus 3 v to
burn at the point, 7.524.

praevehor, vectus sum 3 *dep* to
ride before, ride up, 7.166.

praevertō, vertī, versus 3 v to
turn before; to preoccupy,
prepossess, 1.721; surpass,
7.807; *pass* as *dep* (only
in pres.), praevertor, to
surpass, outstrip, 1.317.

praevideō, vīdī, vīsus 2 v to see
beforehand; foresee, 5.445.

prātum, ī, n a meadow, 6.674.

prāvus, a, um *adj* crooked; *subst*
prāvum, ī, n, perverseness,
wrong, evil, falsehood, 4.188.

precor, ātus sum 1 *dep v* to
pray; entreat, invoke,
implore, beseech, supplicate,
4.521; pray for, 3.144; *with
dat* 8.127; *part*, precāns,
antis, suppliant, 7.237.

prehendō (prēndō), ī, ēnsus
3 v to lay hold of; seize,
2.592; catch, 3.450; seize,
hold for defense, 2.322;
overtake, reach, 6.61.

premō, pressī, pressus 3 v
to press, *freq*; tread upon,

2.380; trample, 5.331; press together, close, 6.155; press after, pursue, 1.324; overflow, overwhelm, 1.246; press upon, 2.530; follow up in speech, 7.119; stab, slay, 9.330; hem in, 11.545; suppress, keep down, conceal, 1.209; 12.322; obscure, withdraw, 4.81; restrain, curb, 1.63; check, discourage, 11.402; repress, 4.332; subject, reduce, oppress, 1.285; premere vestīgia, arrest the footsteps, 6.197; plant one's footsteps on, tread on (with *abl* of place), 11.788.

prēnsō, **āvī**, **ātus** *1 intens v* to grasp, 2.444. (prēndō).

pressō, **āvī**, **ātus** *1 intens v* to press hard; squeeze, press; milk.

pretium, **iī**, *n* price, 4.212; value, worth, 9.232; money; bribe, 6.622; reward, punishment, 12.352; prize, 5.292; ransom, 9.213.

(prex), **precēs** *f* (not used in *nom* and *gen sing*), a prayer, supplication, entreaty, 2.689. (precor).

Priamēius, **a**, **um** *adj* (Priamus), of Priam, 2.403; Priam's, 7.252.

Priamidēs, **ae** *m* son of Priam, 3.295.

Priamus, **ī** *m* 1. Priam, son of Laomedon, king of Troy, 1.458 *et al.* 2. A Trojan youth, son of Polites and grandson of King Priam, 5.564.

prīmaevus, **a**, **um** *adj* (primus and aevum), first in age; eldest born, 9.545; youthful, 10.345; early, 7.162.

prīmitiae, **ārum** *f* the first fruits; first offerings, 11.16; beginnings, first essays, 11.156. (primus).

prīmōris, **e** *adj* (primus), first; *subst* prīmōrēs, um, the chiefs, princes, nobles, 9.309.

prīmus, **a**, **um** (*num adj*, *superl* of prior), first in space, time, order, degree, or dignity (usually referring to three or more); first, foremost, 5.151; front, fore-, 5.566; nearest, 2.32; first part of, 1.541; edge, border, outskirt of, 9.244; chief, 9.785; earliest, first, 1.345; for the first time, 11.573; as an *adv*, 1.442; 6.810 *et al.*; in the earliest times, 1.1; prīma proelia, the beginning of battle, 12.103; *subst* prīmum, ī, *n*, the chief concern, affair, work, 8.408; prīmī, ōrum, *m*, foremost, first, 2.494; prīma, ōrum, *n*, the first place, front, van, 10.157; first prize, 5.194; *adv*, prīmum, first, 2.375; ut prīmum, as soon as, 1.306; prīmō, at first, in the beginning, 4.176; in prīmīs, or imprīmīs, especially, chiefly, 1.303.

prīnceps, **ipis** *adj* (primus and capiō), first; chief; foremost, 5.160; *subst m*, a chief, leader, commander, prince, 1.488; progenitor, founder, ancestor, 3.168.

prīncipium, **iī**, *n* a beginning, commencement; *abl* adverbially, prīncipiō, in the beginning, at first, in the first place, 2.752. (prīnceps).

prior, ius, ōris (*superl*, **prīmus,
wh. see**) first or foremost,
of two, first in order of
time, 1.581; earlier, former,
first, 3.213; beforehand,
anticipating, 11.760; superior,
11.292; (subst.), priōrēs,
m, ancestors, 3.693.

prīscus, a, um *adj* old, former,
ancient, 7.706; Prīscī
Latīnī, the ancient Latins,
occupying Latium prior to the
foundation of Rome, 5.598.

prīstinus, a, um *adj* primitive,
pristine, former, 6.473; recent,
10.143; *subst* prīstina, ōrum, *n*,
former, first condition, 12.424.

pristis, is *f* 1. A sea-monster,
10.211. 2. Pristis, the
Pristis, one of the ships
of Aeneas, 5.154. (another
form for pistrīx).

prius *adv* before, sooner
rather, 2.190. (prior).

priusquam *adv* before
that, before, 1.472.

Prīvernum, ī a city of
Latium, 11.540.

Prīvernus, ī *m* a Rutulian
warrior, 9.576.

prō (*prep with abl*), before, in
front of, 12.661; on the front
of an elevated place; on,
9.575; in defense of, 8.653;
on account of, for the sake
of, 6.821; in place of, instead
of, for, 1.659; for, in return
for, 3.604; in preference
to, 5.483; prō sē, according
to his strength, 5.501.

prō (**prōh**) (*interj*) denoting
wonder, surprise,

lamentation, distress,
agony). O! ah! alas! 4.590.

proavus, ī *m* a great-grandfather;
sire, ancestor, 3.129.

probō, āvī, ātus *1 v* to try, put to
proof; approve, 5.418; permit,
allow, 4.112. (probus, upright).

Procās, ae *m* one of the Alban
kings, and father of Numitor
and Amulius, 6.767.

procāx, ācis *adj* bold, insolent;
figuratively wild, raging, 1.536.

prōcēdō, cessī, cessus *3 v* to
go or come forth or forward;
advance, proceed, go on,
2.760; move, 4.587; elapse,
pass by, 3.356; continue, 5.461.

procella, ae *f* a gale, storm,
squall, tempest, 1.102.

procer, eris *m* a chief, noble; *pl*
procerēs, um, elders, nobles,
princes, 1.740. (in the *sing*
found only in the *acc*).

Prochyta, ae *f* an island
near the Bay of Naples,
now Procida, 9.715.

prōclāmō, āvī, ātus *1 v* to cry
out; declare, announce,
proclaim, 5.345.

Procris, idis *f* Procris, a daughter
of Erectheus, married to
Cephalus, king of Phocis, by
whom she was accidentally
killed in a forest, whither
she had followed him
out of jealousy, 6.445.

procul *adv* far off, at a distance,
2.42; far hence, away, 6.258;
from a distance, from far,
10.401; high, aloft, 5.642.

prōculcō, āvī, ātus *1 v* to tread down, trample upon, 12.534. (prō and calcō).

prōcumbō, cubuī, cubitus *3 v* to lie down; to bend, lean forward, lie along, 8.83; bend down, lie prostrate; fall upon, 11.150; bend to, ply the oars, 5.198; to fall in death or battle, 2.426; fall down, sink in ruins, 2.505.

prōcūrō, āvī, ātus *1 v* to care for; attend to; refresh, 9.158.

prōcurrō, cucurrī or **currī, cursus** *3 v* to run forth or forward, 12.267; advance, sally forth, 9.690; roll, rush along, 11.624; jut, run out, project, 5.204.

prōcursus, ūs *m* a running forward, onward course, career, 12.379; charge, onset, 12.711. (prōcurrō).

prōcurvus, a, um *adj* curved forward; curving, 5.765.

procus, ī *m* one who asks, a wooer, suitor, 4.534. (procor, ask).

prōdeō, īvī or **iī, itus, īre** *irreg v* to go forth; move forward or along, 6.199; advance, project, 10.693.

prōdigium, iī *n* a prognostic, sign, prodigy, wonder, portent, 3.366; monster, 8.295.

prōditiō, ōnis *f* a giving forth, betrayal; treachery, treason; allegation or charge of treason, 2.83. (prōdō).

prōdō, didī, ditus *3 v* to put, bring, give forth; propagate, 4.231; give up, desert, betray, 1.252; expose, 12.42; discover, 9.374; give over, sentence, 2.127; announce, disclose, make known, 10.99.

prōdūcō, dūxī, ductus *3 v* to lead, draw forth, carry, bring, conduct, lead forth, 9.487; breed, produce, 12.900; prolong, protract, 2.637.

proelium, iī, *n* a battle, conflict, contest, combat, fight, 5.375 *et al.*; charge, 11.631. (in Virgil always *pl*).

profānus, a, um *adj* (prō and fānum, shrine), in front or outside of the sacred inclosure; not sacred; profānōs facere, to desecrate, 12.779; *subst* profānī, ōrum, *m*, the unconsecrated; uninitiated, profane, 6.258.

profectō *adv* as a fact; in truth, truly, indeed, surely, certainly, 8.532. (prō and factum).

prōferō, tulī, lātus, ferre *irreg v* to carry forward or forth; extend, 6.795; postpone, delay, 12.395.

proficīscor, profectus sum *3 dep v* to put one's self forward; set out, depart, 1.340; proceed, spring from, 8.51.

prōflō, flāvī, flātus *1 v* to blow; breathe forth noisily, by snoring, 9.326.

profor, fātus sum *1 dep v* to speak out; say; speak, 1.561.

profugus, a, um *adj* (profugiō, flee), fleeing forth; fugitive, exiled, 1.2.

profundō, fūdī, fūsus *3 v* to pour forth; pour, shed, 12.154.

profundus, a, um *adj* deep, 5.614; lofty, deep-vaulted, 1.58; *subst* profundum, ī, *n*, the deep, the sea, 12.263.

prōgeniēs, ēī *f* lineage, progeny, race, 1.19; offspring, 5.565; son, 7.97. (prōgignō).

prōgignō, genuī, genitus *3 v* to beget; bear, bring forth, 4.180.

prōgredior, gressus sum, *3 dep v* to go, come forward or forth, 4.136; advance, 3.300; move on, 12.219. (prō and gradior).

prohibeō, uī, itus *2 v* to hold before or off, prohibit; to keep, ward off, 1.525; withhold, debar, 7.313; prevent, hinder, forbid, 5.631. (prō and habeō).

prōiciō, lēci, iectus *3 v* to throw or cast forth; to throw or cast down, as an offering; to throw or fling down, 5.402; throw away, 6.835; plunge, 5.859; expose, 11.361; *with dat* 12.256. (prō and iaciō).

prōiectus, a, um projecting, jutting, 3.699. (prōiciō).

proinde (*dissyll* in poetry) just so; then, therefore, 11.383.

prōlābor, lāpsus sum *3 dep* to slip forward, tumble down; *part*, prōlāpsus, a, um, fallen, in ruins, 2.555.

prōlēs, is *f* that which springs forth; offspring, race, progeny, 1.75; lineage, 3.180.

prōlūdō, lūsī, lūsus *3 v* to play or practice beforehand; prepare for, 12.106.

prōluō, luī, lūtus *3 v* to wash forth or out, cast out; wash away, 12.686; wet, drench, fill, 1.739.

prōluviēs, ēī *f* a flowing forth; excrement, discharge, 3.217. (prōluō).

prōmereor, meritus sum *2 dep* to merit for one's self by favors given; deserve, merit, put under obligation, 4.335.

prōmissum, ī, *n* a promise, 2.160; a thing promised; prize, 5.386.

prōmittō, mīsī, missus *3 v* to let go, send forth or down; promise, 4.228; vow, pledge, 2.96; *part*, prōmissus, a, um, promised, betrothed, 12.31.

prōmō, prōmpsī, prōmptus *3 v* to take, give, bring forth, exhibit, put forth, 5.191; with sē, come forth, 2.260. (prō and emō).

Promolus, ī *m* a Trojan, 9.574.

prōmoveō, mōvī, mōtus *2 v* to move forward; push forward, 10.195.

prōnuba, ae *f* aiding in marriage rites; presiding over marriage; bridal-, 4.166; bridesmaid, 7.319. (prō and nūbō, marry).

prōnus, a, um *adj* inclined, stooping or bending forward, 3.668; leaning 8.236; descending, falling, 11.485; going down, 9.713; favorable, safe, 5.212.

propāgō, inis *f* that which is fastened forward or along; the layer of a vine; offspring, progeny, race, lineage, 6.870; 12.827. (prō and pangō).

prope *adv* near; *compar* propius, more nearly, closely, plainly,

12.218; more attentively, more propitiously, favorably, 1.526.

properē *adv* hastily, in haste, speedily, 6.236.

properō, āvī, ātus 1 *v* to hurry forward, get ready, prepare promptly, make in season or in haste; to hasten; make haste, 1.745; be eager for, desire much, 7.57; (*impers*), properārī, one hastens, they are hastening, stirring, 4.416.

properus, a, um *adj* forward; prompt, active, 12.85; *adv* properē, hastily, in haste, speedily, 6.236.

prōpexus, a, um *adj* (prō and pectō), combed out; hanging down, long, 10.838.

propinquō, āvī, ātus 1 *v* to bring near; render favorable, 10.254; to draw near, approach, *with dat* 2.730 *et al.* (propinquus).

propinquus, a, um *adj* (prope), near, neighboring, near at hand, 3.381; not remote, 11.156; near of kin, related, 2.86.

propior, ius *adj comp.* (prope), nearer, 3.531; *subst* propiōra, ōrum, *n*, nearer places; the inner course or track, 5.168; *adv* propius, see prope; *superl*, proximus, a, um, the nearest in place, time, or rank; next, 1.157.

prōpōnō, posuī, positus 3 *v* to place before; place in view; offer, 5.365.

proprius, a, um *adj* peculiar to any one; one's own, 1.73; fitting, proper; lasting, permanent, enduring, 6.871.

propter (*adv and prep with acc*), near to, by the side of; on account of, for the sake of, 4.320; after its case, 12.177. (prope).

prōpūgnāculum, ī, *n* a defense, rampart, fortification, bulwark, 4.87. (prōpūgnō, defend).

prōra, ae *f* the extreme forward part of a ship; the prow, 1.104.

prōripiō, ripuī, reptus 3 *v* to snatch forth; *with pers pron* expressed or understood, rush forth, hasten away, 5.741. (prō and rapiō).

prōrumpō, rūpī, ruptus 3 *v* to cause to burst forth; cast forth, 3.572; spring forth, 10.796; rush, run, burst into, 7.32; *part*, prōruptus, a, um, breaking, starting out, 7.459; dashing, rushing, broken, 1.246.

prōsequor, secūtus sum 3 *dep v* to follow on after; follow, pursue, 6.476; attend, 3.130; greet, 11.107; without an object, go on, 2.107.

Prōserpina, ae *f* Proserpina, daughter of Jupiter and Ceres, carried away by Pluto from Enna in Sicily, and made queen of Hades, 4.698 *et al.*

prōsiliō, uī, īvī or **iī** 4 *v* to leap or spring forth, 5.140. (prō and saliō).

prōspectō, āvī, ātus 1 *intens v* to look forth; look forth upon; gaze at, 7.813; behold, look for, await, 10.741. (prōspiciō).

prōspectus, ūs *m* a looking forth, view, 9.168; sight,

prospect, view, *with dat* of
the object, 1.181. (prōspiciō).

prōsper, *or, more frequently,*
prōsperus, a, um *adj* (prō
and spēs), favorable to
one's hope; propitious,
favorable, auspicious, 3.362.

prōspiciō, spexī, spectus 3 *v*
to look forth, forward; to see
afar, in the distance, descry,
see, 3.648; to look forth or
out upon, *with dat* 1.127.
(prō and speciō, look).

prōsum, prōfuī, prōdesse
irreg v to be advantageous,
useful, profitable; to benefit,
profit, avail, 5.684.

prōtegō, tēxī, tēctus 3 *v* to cover
in front; shelter, protect, 2.444.

prōtendō, tendī, tēnsus or
tentus 3 *v* to stretch forth
or out; extend, 5.377.

prōterō, trīvī, trītus 3 *v* to rub
before; trample upon or down,
crush to pieces, 12.330.

prōterreō, terruī, territus 2 *v*
to frighten forth or away;
put to flight, 12.291.

Prōteus (*dissyll*), **eī** or **eos** *m* a
sea-god who often changed
his form; Prōteī Columnae,
the island of Pharos, the
boundary of Egypt, 11.262.

prōtinus *adv* forward in
space, before one; right
on, continuously, 3.416;
(in time) continuously,
in order, 6.33; forthwith,
2.437; suddenly, 10.340;
right on, thenceforward,
7.601. (prō and tenus).

prōtrahō, trāxī, trāctus 3 *v* to
draw, drag, bring forth, 2.123.

prōturbō, āvī, ātus 1 *v*
to push, thrust away,
9.441; repel, 10.801.

prōvehō, vexī, vectus 3 *v* to
carry forward or forth; *passive*
provehor, vectus sum, to be
borne, ride, sail forth or away,
3.72; proceed, continue, 3.481.

prōveniō, vēnī, ventus 4 *v*
to come forth, proceed
from, 12.428.

prōvolvō, volvī, volūtus 3 *v* to roll
forward or along, 10.556; roll,
whirl over or along, 12.533.

prūdentia, ae *f* a foreseeing; wise
foresight, prudence, wisdom,
3.433. (prūdēns, foreseeing).

prūna, ae *f* a live coal, 5.103.

Prytanis, is *m* a Trojan, 9.767.

pūbēns, entis *adj* pubescent;
full of vigor; full of
sap, juicy, 4.514.

pūbēs, eris *adj* grown up,
pubescent; of plants,
mature, full grown, 12.413.

pūbēs, is *f* the groin, middle,
3.427; the youthful
population; youth, young
men; youthful band, 1.399;
brood, offspring, 6.580.

pūbēscō, pūbuī 3 *inc v* to be
growing up, 3.491. (pūbēs).

pudendus, a, um that one
should be ashamed of;
shameful, inglorious, 11.55.

pudeō, uī, itus 2 *v* to be
ashamed; to make ashamed;
impers, pudet, puditum est,

with acc of person, it shames one; one is ashamed, 5.196.

pudor, ōris *m* shame; feeling or fear of shame, 5.455; modesty; purity, virtue, honor, 4.27. (pudeō).

puella, ae *f* a girl, maiden, 2.238. (cf. puer).

puer, erī *m* a boy, 1.267; youth, 1.475; son, child, boy, 4.94; infant, 8.632.

puerīlis, e *adj* (puer), pertaining to a boy; a boy's, 11.578; boyish, 5.548.

pūgna, ae *f* a fight, battle, struggle, combat, contest, conflict, *freq*; war, 12.241.

pūgnātor, ōris *m* a fighter; adjectively, fighting, fierce, 11.680. (pūgnō).

pūgnō, āvī, ātus *1 v* to battle, fight, contend, war, *freq*; with cognate *acc*, 8.629; pull against, resist, *with dat* struggle with, resist, 4.38; 11.600; *impers*, pūgnātur, they contend, 7.553. (pūgna).

pūgnus, ī *m* a fist, hand, 4.673.

pulcher, chra, chrum *adj* (*compar* pulchrior, ius; *superl*, pulcherrimus, a, um), beautiful, fair, lovely, 1.75; splendid, 4.266; excellent, wise, 5.728; illustrious, 1.286; warlike, valiant, 7.657.

pullulō, āvī, ātus *inc* to spring out; sprout, shoot, bristle, 7.329. (pullus, young animal).

pulmō, ōnis *m* a lung; lungs, 9.701.

pulsō, āvī, ātus *1 intens v* to beat much; batter, buffet, 5.460; strike, 6.647; lash, 3.555; beat with the hoofs, dash along, 11.660; violate, insult, 12.286; pulsate, throb, 5.138; rebound, 4.313. (pellō).

pulsus, ūs *m* a striking or beating; tramp, reverberation, 6.591. (pellō).

pulvereus, a, um *adj* (pulvis), full of dust, dusty; of dust, 8.593.

pulverulentus, a, um *adj* (pulvis), full of dust; covered with dust, dusty, 4.155.

pulvis, eris, *m, rarely f* dust, 2.273; soil, ground, earth; dusty plain, 7.163.

pūmex, icis *m* pumice stone; rock abounding in crevices; pumice stone, porous, hollow rock, 5.214.

Pūniceus, a, um *adj* (cf. Poenī), of Punic or Phoenician color; reddish, red, rosy, crimson, 12.77; purple-colored, purple, 5.269.

Pūnicus, a, um *adj* (cf. Poenī), Punic, Carthaginian, 1.338.

puppis, is *f* the hinder part of a ship; the stern, 5.12; (by synecdoche), a vessel, boat, ship, 1.69; *metonym* crew, 8.497.

pūrgō, āvī, ātus *1 v* to render pure, clean, or clear; sē pūrgāre, to dissolve, disappear, 1.587. (pūrus and agō).

purpura, ae *f* purple color, purple; purple border or fringe, 5.251. (πορφύρα, the purple-fish).

purpureus, a, um *adj* (purpura), of purple; purple-colored, scarlet, red, purple, 1.337; of blood, 9.349; ruddy, glowing, brilliant, 1.591.

pūrus, a, um *adj* free from stain, pure, 7.489; clear, serene, 2.590; open, unobstructed, 12.771; unmixed, 6.746; pointless, 6.760; unmarked, without symbol, or device, 11.711.

puter, pūtris, e *adj* (puteō, to be foul-smelling), fetid, foul-smelling; putrid, crumbling, dusty, 8.596.

putō, āvī, ātus *1 v* to make clean; make clear, trim, dress, prune; to consider, ponder, 6.332; think, imagine, believe, suppose, 2.43.

Pygmaliōn, ōnis *m* Pygmalion, son of Belus, brother of Dido, and king of Phoenicia, 1.347 *et al.*

pyra, ae *f* a funeral pile, pyre, 4.494.

Pyracmōn, onis *m* a Cyclops, servant of Vulcan, 8.425.

Pyrgī, ōrum *m* a tower on the coast of Etruria, 10.184.

Pyrgō, ūs *f* a Trojan woman, nurse of the children of Priam, 5.645.

Pyrrhus, ī *m* Pyrrhus Neoptolemus, son of Achilles, killed by Orestes, 3.296 *et al.*

quā *adv interrog, relat,* and *indef* (*ablat* of quī), in, by, what way? how? 1.676; where, which way, side, direction, 2.463; for quācumque, any way, anywhere; in any way, by any means; where, in whatever way; so far as, 12.147; sī quā, if in any way, 1.18.

quācumque *adv* by whatever way, wherever; by whatever means, by all means, wherever; separated by tmesis, 11.762.

quadra, ae *f* anything quadriform; one of the equal quarters of a wheaten loaf or cake, 7.115. (cf. quattuor).

quadrifidus, a, um *adj* (quattuor and findō), four-cleft, split into four parts, 7.509.

quadrīgae, ārum *f* a yoke or team of four horses, 8.642; a four-horse chariot, chariot, 6.535. (quadriiugae fr. quattuor and iugum).

quadriiugis, e *adj* (quadrīgae), pertaining to a team of four; four-yoked, 10.571.

quadriiugus, a, um *adj* (quadrīgae), pertaining to a team of four; four-horse-, 12.162.

quadrupedāns, antis *adj* going on four feet; galloping, 8.596; *subst gen pl* horses, 11.614.

quadrupēs, edis *adj* (quattuor and pēs), four-footed; *subst c,* a quadruped, animal, beast, 3.542; courser, steed, 11.875.

quaerō, quaesīvī or **quaesiī, quaesītus** *3 v* to seek, search, look for, 1.380; inquire, ask, demand, 1.370; ask as a gift, 4.647; desire, 7.449; miss, 10.395.

quaesītor, ōris *m* an investigator; examiner; judge, 6.432. (quaerō).

quaesō 3 *v* to seek; ask, beg, beseech, 3.358. (*archaic form* of quaerō).

quālis, e (*adj interrog* and *rel*), of what sort? what? of what aspect? 2.274; of such kind as; such as, as, 1.430; such as = many of which, 7.200; *with* ubi, 2.471.

quam (*adv interrog* and *rel*) how, *freq*; as, answering to tam, expressed or understood, even as, just as, so far as, 6.96; quam māgnus, so great as, 10.763; with a *superl*, to denote the highest degree possible; quam prīmum, as soon as possible, instantly, 4.631; after the comparative, than, *freq*; antequam, priusquam (often separated by tmesis), before that, before, 4.27, *freq*; postquam, often separated, after that, after, as soon as, 3.463 *et al.*

quamquam *conj*, though, although, 2.12; *freq*; corrective, but, 11.415.

quamvīs (*adv* and *conj*), as much as you will; however much; however, although, albeit; *with* subj., 3.454; *freq with* an *adj* (quam and volō).

quandō (*adv interrog* and *rel*, and *conj*), when; (*indef*), at any time, 3.500; (*conj* of cause), when, since, 6.50; as, since, because, 1.261; 4.291 *et al.*; sometimes joined *with* sī as one word.

quandōquidem *conj*, since indeed; inasmuch as, because.

quantum (interrogative adverb) how much, how, 2.274.

quantum (relative pronoun or adverb) as much as, however much, to the extent that.

quantus, a, um (relative adjective, with or without tantus preceding) as, so great as, as much as, such as, in respect to quantity, 3.641.

quantus, a, um (interrogative adjective) how great; what, 1.719 *et al.*

quārē (*adv interrog* and *rel*), on account of what thing? why? wherefore? on account of which thing, for which reason, wherefore, 1.627. (*abl* of quī and rēs).

quārtus, a, um *num adj* (quattuor), the fourth, 3.205.

quassō, āvī, ātus 1 *intens v* to shake violently; shatter, 1.551; 4.53; shake, 5.855; brandish, 9.521. (quatiō).

quater (*num adv*), four times. (quattuor).

quaternī, ae, a (*adj num* distr.), by fours, four by four; of four kinds, 10.202. (quattuor).

quatiō, no perf, quassus 3 *v* to shake, *freq*; brandish, 11.767; flap, 3.226; shatter, 2.611; make tremble, 5.200; thrill, penetrate, 3.30; ransack, beat up, search, scour, 11.513; torment, 6.571; assault, 9.608; spur, 12.338.

quattuor (*num adj indecl*),
four, 3.537, *freq.*

-que (*conj* enclit.), and, *freq*; and
indeed, 7.51; as an adversative,
4.96; -que — que, et — que,
both — and, *freq*; sometimes
irregularly placed, 5.47 *et al.*;
-que — et, both — and.

queō, quīvī or **quiī, quitus, quīre**
irreg v to be able, can, 6.463.

Quercēns, entis *m* a Rutulian
warrior, 9.684.

quercus, ūs *f* an oak tree,
3.680; *metonym* an oak
leaf crown, 6.772.

querēla, ae *f* a complaining;
complaint, 4.360; lowing,
8.215. (queror).

quernus, a, um *adj*
(quercus), oaken, 11.65.

queror, questus sum *3 dep v*
to complain of, bemoan,
complain, 1.385; moan, 4.463.

questus, ūs *m* a complaining;
moaning; groans, 7.501;
mournful sound. (queror).

quī, quae, quod (*dat pl* **quīs** for
quibus, 1.95 *et al.*) (*interrog*
and *rel pron*; *interrog*), who,
which, what? (*rel*), who,
which, what, that; ex quō,
from which, from what time;
after, 2.163 *et al.*; *abl*, quī,
m, *f*, and *n*, sometimes used
for the regular *abl*; hence,
quīcum, with whom, 11.822.

quia *conj*, because, 4.696 *et al.*;
because, forsooth, 4.538.

quianam (*interrog adv*), why?
ah! why? wherefore? 5.13.

**quīcumque, quaecumque,
quodcumque** (*indef rel*),
whoever, whatever, whosoever,
whatsoever, 1.610; no matter
who; who, 12.143. (quī and
indef adv -cumque).

quidem *adv* indeed, truly, at
least, yet, 3.628 *et al.*

quiēs, ētis *f* rest, repose,
3.495; sleep, 2.268; respite,
intermission, 1.723.

quiēscō, quiēvī, quiētus *3 v* to
rest, 7.6; repose, rest in death,
1.249; be hushed, still, quiet,
4.523; cease from action, 5.784;
lie, 10.836; *part*, quiētus,
a, um, at rest, quiet, 5.848;
still, calm, tranquil, 5.216;
peaceful, in repose, 4.379;
gentle, friendly, 1.303. (quiēs).

quīn *conj*, why not, wherefore
not? nay but, 1.279; nay
even, 2.768; that not, 5.456.

quīngentī, ae, a *num adj*
(quīnque and centum),
five hundred, 10.204.

quīnī, ae, a distr. *num*
(quīnque), five each; as
cardinal, five, 2.126.

quīnquāgintā *num adj indecl*
(quīnque), fifty, 1.703.

quīnque (*num adj indecl*), five.

quippe (*conj* and *adv*), because
indeed, for indeed, for;
because forsooth, 1.39;
forsooth, while indeed, 4.218;
surely, truly, indeed, 12.422.

Quirīnālis, ae *adj* (Quirīnus),
pertaining to Quirinus or
Romulus; Quirinal, 7.187.

Quirīnus, **ī** *m* Quirinus, the name of the deified Romulus, 1.292.

Quirītēs, **ium** *m* ancient Sabines, especially of the city of Cures, 7.710; Sabines amalgamated with the Romans; Roman citizens.

quis, **qua** or **quae**, **quid** or **quod** (*indef pron*, *adj*, and *subst*), any, some, 2.94 *et al.*; some one, any one, any body, anything, something, 1.413 *et al.*; sī quis, nē quis, etc., if any, lest any, etc., *freq*; *adv* quid, as to anything, in anything, at all, *freq*; sī quid, if at all, *freq*.

quis, **quae**, **quid** (*interrog pron*), who? what? which? 2.42 *et al.*; quid, elliptical, what then? what is it? 10.77; quid, *adv* as to what? how? why? 2.101 *et al.*; with num, whether any, any? nescio quis, — quid, I know not who, — what; often equivalent to some one, something, denoting doubt, 2.735.

quisnam (**quīnam**), **quaenam**, **quidnam** (emphatic *interrog pron*), who, pray? what, pray? who? what? 3.338.

quisquam, **quaequam**, **quidquam**, or **quicquam** (*indef pron subst*), any one, any, anything, in negative sentences, *freq*; *adj*, any, 6.875 *et al.*; *adv* quāquam, in any way.

quisque, **quaeque**, **quodque** or (**subst.**) **quidque** or **quicque** (*indef pron*), each, every; each one, every one, everything, 2.130 *et al.*; in apposition *with pl* 6.743.

quisquis, **quaequae**, **quidquid** or **quicquid** (*indef pron*), whoever, whosoever, whatever, whatsoever, 1.387 *et al.* (quis).

quīvīs, **quaevīs**, **quodvīs**, or (**subst.**) **quidvīs** (*indef pron*), who or what thou pleasest; any whatever, any, 8.577.

quō (*interrog*) where? to what place? whither? whereto? 5.29; wherefore? 12.879; whither? 6.43.

quō (*indef*) wheresoever, 2.337.

quō (final *conj*) that, to the end that, in order that, 4.106; quō magis, by how much more, that the more, 4.452.

quōcircā *adv* for which reason, wherefore, and therefore, 1.673.

quōcumque *adv indef*, to whatever place, whithersoever, wherever; however, 12.203; separated by tmesis, 2.709.

quod *conj*, as to which thing; in that, that, indeed that, because; but, moreover, however, *freq*; quod sī, but if, indeed if, if however, 6.133.

quōmodō, *or, separately*, **quō modō** in what way, manner? how? 6.892; in the same manner as; just as; as, 5.599.

quōnam (emphatic *interrog adv*), whither, pray? whither? where? 2.595.

quondam *adv* some time or other; once; formerly, 4.307; lately, just now, 11.819; at

times, 2.367; ever, 6.876.
(quom = cum and -dam).

quoniam *conj*, since now;
forasmuch as, since, seeing
that, because, 4.324.

quoque *conj*, also, too, as
well, even, 1.407.

quot (*interrog* and *rel adj
indecl*), how many? so or
as many as, 4.181 *et al*.

quotannīs (*or* **quot annīs**)
adv every year, yearly, 5.59.

quotiēns (*interrog* and *rel
adv*), how often? so or
as often as. (quot).

quoūsque *adv* how long
(separated by tmesis),
5.384. (quō and ūsque).

rabidus, a, um *adj* raving,
savage, mad, raging, 6.421;
frenzied; frantic, raving, 6.80.

rabiēs, em, ē *f* madness, frenzy,
fury, fierceness, 2.357 *et al*.; of
inanimate things, 5.802 *et al*.

radiō, āvī, ātus *1 v* to emit rays
of light; flash, beam, be
radiant, 8.616. (radius).

radius, iī *m* a staff, rod; spoke
of a wheel, 6.616; beam,
ray, 5.65; a shuttle, 9.476;
the representation of rays
on a crown, 12.163.

rādīx, īcis *f* a root, 3.27 *et al*.

rādō, rāsī, rāsus *3 v* to rub,
scrape, graze; skim along
or over, 5.170; coast along,
sail near to, 3.700.

rāmus, ī *m* a branch,
bough, 4.485 *et al*.; limb,
8.318; wreath, 5.71.

rapidus, a, um *adj* (rapiō), that
tears away; violent, fierce;
swiftly moving, rapid, 1.42;
speedy, quick, prompt, 5.513.

rapīna, ae *f* a plundering;
booty, prey, 8.263. (rapiō).

rapiō, rapuī, raptus *3 v* to seize,
snatch, *freq*; carry off, bear
away, 1.28; tear off, 6.496; take,
2.675; kindle by rapid motion,
1.176; rescue, 1.378; plunder,
pillage, 2.374; hurry, speed,
4.286; swiftly lead on, 12.450;
hasten into, penetrate, range,
6.8; ravish, violate, 4.198.

Rapō, ōnis *m* an Etruscan, 10.748.

raptō, āvī, ātus *1 intens v* to seize
violently; drag, 1.483; hurry
away, transport. (rapiō).

raptor, ōris *m* a plunderer,
robber; adjectively,
plundering, 2.356. (rapiō).

raptum, ī, *n* plunder,
prey, spoil, 4.217.

rārēscō *3 inc v* to become thin;
to part or begin to stand
open; to open, 3.411. (rārus).

rārus, a, um *adj* the opposite
of dense; thin; straying,
scattered, 1.118; wide-meshed,
distended, 4.131; standing
far apart, infrequent, here
and there = few; broken,
interrupted, faltering, 3.314;
rarely lighted, seen now and
then, uncertain, 9.383.

rāstrum, ī, *n*, usually *pl* **rāstrī,
ōrum** *m* a heavy pronged
hoe, rake, mattock. (rādō).

ratiō, ōnis *f* a reckoning,
calculation; deliberation,
purpose, 2.314; plan, method,

way, means, manner, 4.115; reason, prudence, judgment, 8.299. (reor).

ratis, is *f* a raft, float; bark, boat, ship, 1.43 *et al.*

raucus, a, um *adj* rough-sounding, hoarse; screaming, 7.705; roaring, resounding, 2.545; *adv* rauca, hoarsely, 9.125.

rebellis, e *adj* (re- and bellum), warring or making war again, 12.185; rebellious, insurgent, 6.858.

recaleō 2 *v* to be warm or hot, 12.35.

recēdō, cessī, cessus 3 *v* to go back, retire, withdraw, 12.129; recede, retreat, 2.633; stand apart, retire, 2.300; depart, 2.595; disappear, 3.72; vanish, 5.526.

recēns, entis *adj* new, recent, fresh, 1.417; pure, 6.635; newly wrought or finished, 8.654; foll. by ab, just from, 6.450.

recēnseō, uī, us or **itus** 2 *v* estimate from the beginning; reckon, review, survey, 6.682.

receptō, āvī, ātus 1 *intens* *v* to take back or out; recover, 10.383. (recipiō).

recessus, ūs *m* recess, cavity, 8.193; retreat, ambush, 11.527. (recēdō).

recidīvus, a, um falling back; returning; rebuilt, restored, 4.344. (recidō, to fall back).

recīdō, cīdī, cīsus to cut away; lop off, 12.208. (re- and caedō).

recingō, cīnxī, cīnctus 3 *v* to ungird, loosen; *part*, recinctus, a, um, ungirded, loosely hanging, 4.518.

recipiō, cēpī, ceptus 3 *v* to take back; receive, take, 2.524; take, draw back or out, 9.348; take in, let in, admit, 9.780; recover, save, 1.178; rescue, 6.111; take from, inflict on, 4.656; win back, recover, secure, 6.818; recipere gressum, to return, 11.29; sē recipere, to resort, withdraw, betake one's self. (re- and capiō).

reclīnō, āvī, ātus 1 *v* recline; rest, lay back or down, 12.130.

reclūdō, clūsī, clūsus 3 *v* to unclose; to open, *freq*; throw open, 3.92; reveal, disclose, 1.358; unsheathe, 4.646; cut or lay open, 4.63. (re- and claudō).

recognōscō, cognōvī, cognitus 3 *v* look over; survey, review, 8.721.

recolō, coluī, cultus 3 *v* to till again; *figuratively* think over, reflect, consider, 6.681.

recondō, didī, ditus 3 *v* to place again; put back, up, or away; hide, conceal, 1.681; bury, 10.387; bury in oblivion, 5.302.

recoquō, coxī, coctus 3 *v* to boil again; recast, forge anew, 7.636; purify, refine, 8.624.

recordor, ātus sum 1 *dep* *v* to call to mind; remember, 3.107. (re- and cor).

rēctor, ōris *m* a director, leader, ruler, 8.572; general, commander, 9.173; guide; helmsman, pilot, 5.161. (regō).

rēctum, ī, *n* (subst.), right, 1.604. (regō).

rēctus, a, um straight, direct, directly along, 6.900; straight forward, 8.209; rēctō lītore, flūmine, directly along the shore, along the stream, 6.900.8.57. (regō).

recubō 1 *v* to be lying back or down; recline; be extended; lie, 3.392.

recumbō, cubuī 3 *v* to lie down again; sink down, 9.713; depend, rest, 12.59. (re- and cubō, lie down).

recurrō, currī, cursus 3 *v* to run back; return, revolve, 7.100.

recursō 1 *intens v* to rush back; come back, recur to the mind, 4.3; return, 1.662.

recursus, ūs *m* a running back; return; retreat, 5.583; a receding, an ebbing, 10.288. (recurrō).

recurvus, a, um *adj* curving back or round; bending, crooked, rounding, 7.513.

recūsō, āvī, ātus 1 *v* to bring a reason against; object; reject, decline, 5.417; refuse, 2.607; shrink back, recoil, 5.406. (re- and causa).

recutiō, cussī, cussus 3 *v* to strike back; cause to resound; *part*, recussus, a, um, resounding, reverberating, 2.52. (re- and quatiō).

redarguō, uī 3 *v* disprove, confute, 11.688.

reddō, didī, ditus 3 *v* to give back; put back, restore, 12.785 *et al.*; deliver, 2.543; pour forth, 9.700; return, 1.409; render, pay; answer, 2.323; reproduce, bring back, 6.768; render, make, 5.705; sē reddere, emerge, 9.121; *part*, redditus, a, um, being conveyed back; brought back to the land or earth; alighting, 6.18.

redeō, īvī or **iī, itus, īre** *irreg v* to go, come back, return; retreat, 9.794.

redimīculum, ī, *n* something bound round; a chaplet, fillet, ribbon, 9.616. (redimiō).

redimiō, iī, ītus (imperf., redimībat, 10.538) 4 *v* to bind round; wreathe, crown, 3.81.

redimō, ēmī, ēmptus 3 *v* to buy back; ransom, redeem, 6.121. (re- and emō).

reditus, ūs *m* a return, 2.17. (redeō).

redoleō, uī 2 *v* to give forth a smell; to be redolent of, fragrant with, 1.436.

redūcō, dūxī, ductus 3 *v* to lead, bring back; restore, 1.143; return, 9.257; draw back, 5.478; rescue, 4.375.

reductus, a, um reductus, a, um, retired, remote, solitary, 6.703; receding, 1.161. (redūcō).

redux, ucis *adj* (redūcō), led back, brought back, returning, 1.390.

refellō, fellī 3 *v* to prove that one is in error; refute, gainsay, 4.380. (re- and fallō).

referō, rettulī, relātus, referre *irreg v* to bear, carry, bring back, 4.392; bear again, 5.564; cast up, vomit, 9.350; turn, 12.657; of solemn rites, render, pay, 5.605; bring back as a prize, win, get, 4.93; put back, stay, 11.290; repeat, 5.598; claim, 7.49; answer, reply, 4.31; report, relate, announce, 1.309; reproduce, resemble, 4.329; imitate, 10.281; turn, change, 11.426; 1.281; render, make, 8.343; vōce referre, speak, utter, exclaim, 1.94; referre pedem, return; *passive* referrī, go back, recede, 2.169; return, revert, 12.37.

rēficiō, fēcī, fectus *3 v* to make again; restore, 10.234; repair, amend, recruit, refresh, reanimate, encourage, 11.731. (re- and faciō).

refīgō, fīxī, fīxus *3 v* to unfasten, loosen, 5.527; take down, 5.360; unfasten or take down the tablets of the laws, render null, annul, abolish, 6.622; refixus, a, um, loosened, falling, 5.527.

reflectō, flexī, flexus *3 v* to bend back; bend, 11.622; twist back, 10.535; change, 10.632; animum reflectere, to turn one's thoughts to any object; think of, recollect, 2.741.

refluō *3 v* to flow back, 8.240.

refringō, frēgī, frāctus *3 v* to break back; break off, 6.210. (re- and frangō).

refugiō, fūgī *3 v* to fly, 3.258; flee away, 6.472; recede, stand distant, 3.536; shrink, 2.12; *with acc*, start back from, 2.380; shrink from, refuse, 7.618; fugere, refugere, to fly to and fro, 12.753.

refulgeō, fulsī, fulsus *2 v* to flash back; shine forth, flash, be radiant, 1.402; glitter, glisten, 6.204.

refundō, fūdī, fūsus *3 v* to pour back or up; cast, throw up, 7.590; boil up, 1.126; flow back, overflow, 6.107; *part*, refūsus, a, um, thrown back, beaten back; poured back, flowing back upon itself, encircling, 7.225.

refūtō, āvī, ātus *1 v* to repel; disprove, refute, falsify, disappoint, 12.41.

rēgālis, e *adj* (rēx), belonging to a king; regal, kingly, royal, 1.673.

rēgia a palace, 7.171. (rēgius, a, um, sc. domus).

rēgificus, a, um *adj* (rēx and faciō), made meet for a king; magnificent, royal, 6.605.

rēgīna, ae *f* a queen, 1.9; princess, 1.273. (rēx).

regiō, ōnis *f* a direction, 2.737; region, territory, country, 1.460; quarter, tract, place, 9.390; regiō viārum, the beaten track, open road or path, 11.530. (regō).

rēgius, a, um *adj* (rēx), pertaining or belonging to a king or queen, 1.696; the king's, 1.677; royal, 1.443; *subst* rēgia (sc domus), a palace, 7.171.

rēgnātor, ōris *m* one who reigns; sovereign, lord, 2.779 *et al.* (rēgnō).

rēgnō, āvī, ātus *1 v* to exercise sovereignty; to be king, to reign, 1.141; rule, govern, 3.14; *impers*, rēgnātur, etc., there is kingly rule, 1.272. (rēgnum).

rēgnum, ī, *n* kingly sway; royal power or glory, 1.268; dominion, rule, sovereignty, 1.78; the territory of a king; realm, kingdom, dominion, 3.333; royal seat, 1.270; *pl* realms, kingdom, 11.461; royal power, 4.591; royal abode, 12.567. (rēx).

regō, rēxī, rēctus *3 v* to rule, govern, guide, control, direct *et al.*; help, prosper, 12.405.

regressus, ūs *m* a going back; *figuratively* turn, change, retrieve, 11.413. (regredior).

rēiciō, iēcī, iectus *3 v* to throw back or off, 5.421; drive back, rout, 11.630; put or turn behind, 11.619; of the eyes, turn from, avert, 10.473. (re- and iaciō).

relābor, lāpsus sum *3 dep v* to slip back; retreat, 10.307.

relēgō, āvī, ātus *1 v* to send away, remove; consign, give in charge, 7.775.

relegō, lēgī, lēctus *3 v* to gather again; pass by, survey again; coast again, 3.690.

religiō, ōnis *f* reverence for divine things; piety, devotion, 2.715; sanctity, 8.349; worship, sacred ceremonial, observance, 3.409; sacred thing, symbol, token, 2.151; object of worship; divinity, 12.182; augury, 3.363.

religiōsus, a, um *adj* (religiō) devout; sacred, holy, 2.365.

religō, āvī, ātus *1 v* to lie back or up; to picket, 9.352; moor, 7.106.

relinquō, līquī, līctus *3 v* to leave behind, 3.190; commit, 7.123; spare, leave, 2.659; give up, relinquish, 4.432; desert, abandon, 2.28; leave out of sight, unnoticed, 2.454.

rēliquiae, ārum *f* the things left; remnant, 1.30; relics, remains, 4.343. (relinquō).

relūceō, lūxī *2 v* to shine back or again, or brightly; glow, flash, 2.312; to take fire, 12.300.

remeō, āvī, ātus *1 v* to go back, return, 2.95.

remētior, mēnsus sum *4 dep v* to measure again, retrace, recross, 2.181; survey, observe again, 5.25.

rēmex, igis *m* an oarsman, a rower, 4.588; a band of oarsmen, crew, oarsmen, 5.116. (rēmus and agō).

rēmigium, iī, *n* a rowing; oarage, rowing movement, 1.301; body of rowers, oarsmen; a crew, 3.471; rēmigium ālārum = ālae, wings, 6.19. (rēmex).

reminīscor *3 dep v* to call to mind; recall, remember, think of, 10.782. (re- and rt. men, *cf.* meminī).

remittō, mīsī, missus *3 v* to let go back; send back, 2.543

et al.; send up, 5.99; repay, 4.436; yield up, resign, 10.828; give up, 11.346; forego, lay aside, 5.419; give back, reëcho, 12.929; sē remittere, to submit, yield, 12.833.

remordeō, *no perf*, **morsus** 2 *v* to bite again and again; *figuratively* harass, torment, vex, afflict, 1.261; disturb, concern, 7.402.

removeō, **mōvī**, **mōtus** 2 *v* to move away; remove, take away, 1.723.

remūgiō 4 *v* to bellow again or loudly; resound, reëcho, 6.99 *et al.*

remulceō, **mulsī**, **mulsus** 2 *v* to stroke back; fondle; hide, 11.812.

Remulus, **ī** *m* 1. A Rutulian, brother-in-law of Turnus, 9.593. 2. Remulus, a Tiburtine, 9.360. 3. A second Rutulian, 11.636.

remurmurō 1 *v* to give back a murmur; resound, 10.291.

Remus, **ī** *m* a Rutulian warrior, 9.330; the twin brother of Romulus, by whom, tradition says, he was murdered for leaping over the new walls of Rome in mockery, 1.292.

rēmus, **ī** *m* originally steering-oar; an oar, 1.104.

renārrō 1 *v* to relate again; recount, 3.717.

renāscor, **nātus sum** 3 *dep v* to be born again; to be reproduced; grow again, 6.600.

renovō, **āvī**, **ātus** 1 *v* to renew; revive, suffer again, 2.3; brave, risk, dare again, 2.750.

reor, **ratus sum** 2 *dep v* to reason; reckon; think, believe, 3.381; *part*, ratus, a, um, active, having thought, believing, 11.712; *passive* determined by reckoning, settled, fixed, 9.104; 10.629.

repellō, **reppulī**, **repulsus** 3 *v* to push or drive back; repel, 2.13; reject, refuse, disdain, 4.214.

rependō, **pendī**, **pēnsus** 3 *v* to weigh again or in return; to compensate for, balance, 1.239; repay, requite, return, 2.161.

repēns, **entis** *adj* sudden, 12.313.

repēns, **entis** *adv* suddenly, unexpectedly, 1.594.

repercutiō, **cussī**, **cussus** 3 *v* to strike back; reflect, 8.23.

reperiō, **repperī**, **repertus** 4 *v* to find again; find by searching, discover, find out, detect, 4.128; find, 6.343; *part*, repertus, a, um, found, 6.343; acquired, 6.610.

repertor, **ōris** *m* a finder; inventor, 7.772; author, creator; father, 12.829. (reperiō).

repetō, **petīvī** or **petiī**, **petītus** 3 *v* to seek again; return to, 2.749; call back, 7.241; renew, 2.178; trace back, 7.371; retrace, call to mind, recollect, 3.184; speak of again, mention, 10.36; repeat, 3.436.

repleō, **plēvī**, **plētus** 2 *v* to fill again; fill up, fill, 2.679 *et al.*

repōnō, posuī, positus (postus)
3 v to lay, place, put back,
replace, 3.231; lay aside or
down, 5.484; put, lay up, store
away, *with abl*, 4.403; lay,
deposit, place, 6.220; *with dat*
11.594; restore, *with* in and *acc*,
1.253; return, repay, 12.878.

reportō, āvī, ātus *1 v* to carry
back, announce, report, 2.115.

reposcō *3 v* to demand back,
demand again; require,
11.240; demand in return,
2.139; ask, 6.530; summon,
10.374; reassert, 12.573;
with two accusatives,
demand back from, 7.606.

repositus, (repostus), a, um
replaced; treasured up,
cherished, 1.26; buried, 6.655;
remote, 3.364. (repōnō).

reprimō, pressī, pressus *3 v*
to press back; stop, restrain,
withhold, check, arrest,
2.378. (re- and premō).

repūgnō, āvī, ātus *1 v* to fight
against, resist, 11.749.

requiēs, ētis or **ēī** *f* repose,
rest, 3.393; respite, 4.433;
support, comfort, 9.482;
cessation, 12.241.

requiēscō, quiēvī, quiētus
3 v to be completely at
rest; rest, cease, 2.100.

requīrō, quīsīvī or **quīsiī,
quīsītus** *3 v* to seek much or
earnestly; seek out, search
for, 3.170; demand; ask,
question, 2.390; inquire, 2.506;
speak with regret of, mourn,
1.217. (re- and quaerō).

rēs, reī *f* a thing, in the most
general sense; object, 1.450;
treasure, store, 12.589; state,
situation, condition, 1.563;
circumstance; fortune, 1.204;
affair, business, interest,
9.227; a side, party, cause,
3.54; 11.400; conflict, 9.154;
misfortune, calamity, 1.462;
commonwealth, state,
empire, dominion, power,
1.268; action, deed, exploit,
achievement, 1.641; adventure,
fortune, 4.290; *pl* the universe,
10.40; the world, 1.282; nature,
creation, 9.131; rēs summa, the
public interest, common weal,
11.302; the chief conflict, 2.322.

rescindō, scidī, scissus *3 v* to
tear off or away, rase, tear
down, 6.583; lay open, 12.390.

reserō, āvī, ātus *1 v*
unbolt; open, 7.613.

reservō, āvī, ātus *1 v* to keep
back or in reserve; save, keep,
reserve, 4.368; keep in store
for, bring back upon, 8.484.

reses, idis *adj* (resideō), that
remains seated; *figuratively*
inactive, slothful, quiet,
6.813; sluggish, torpid,
dormant, 1.722.

resideō, sēdī *2 v* to be or remain
seated; remain behind, 2.739;
encamp, 8.503. (re- and sedeō).

resīdō, sēdī *3 v* to sit or settle
down; seat one's self, 1.506;
settle, take up one's abode,
5.702; retreat, 9.539; sink,
subside, 7.27; come to an end,
9.643; of passion, become
quiet, calm, subside, 6.407.

resīgnō, āvī, ātus to unseal; *figuratively* to open, of the eyes, 4.244.

resistō, stitī 3 *v* to remain standing; stand revealed, 1.588; oppose, withstand, resist, 2.335; interpose, 2.599; halt, stop, falter, 4.76.

resolvō, solvī, solūtus 3 *v* to untie, loosen, unbind, 3.370; break apart, 9.517; dispel, 8.591; of the lips, open, 3.457; of the body, relax, unbend, extend, 6.422; of separation of body and spirit, dissolve, separate, release, 4.695; unravel, disclose, 6.29; break, violate, 2.157.

resonō, āvī 1 *v* to sound again or loudly; reëcho, resound, 4.668; (w. *acc*), make resound, fill, 7.12.

resorbeō 2 *v* to suck back, draw back, 11.627.

respectō, *freq* 1, *v* to look back or again; look behind, 11.630; regard, care for, 1.603. (respiciō).

respergō, spersī, spersus 3 *v* to sprinkle over; besprinkle, stain, 7.547. (re- and spargō).

respiciō, spexī, spectus 3 *v* to look back, again, or around, 2.564; behold, 2.615; look back upon, 5.3; look back and observe or notice, 2.741; 9.389; look at again and again, 3.593; consider, 12.43; regard, care for, be mindful of, 4.225. (re- and speciō, look).

respīrō, āvī, ātus 1 *v* to breathe again; to breathe, 9.813.

resplendeō 2 *v* to shine brightly; glitter, 12.741.

respondeō, spondī, spōnsus 2 *v* to promise in return; answer, respond, 6.474; to be in accord with, correspond, agree, 1.585; to correspond in position, stand opposite, 6.23; meet the desire.

respōnsō 1 *intens v* to make answer; echo, reply, 12.757. (respondeō).

respōnsum, ī, *n* an answer, reply, 2.376; oracular answer, response, 6.799. (respondeō).

restinguō, stīnxī, stīnctus 3 *v* to put out, quench, 2.686.

restituō, stituī, stitūtus 3 *v* to place again; reëstablish, restore, 6.846. (re- and statuō).

restō, restitī 1 *v* to remain in place; to stand, stop; to be left, 2.142; remain, 1.556; remain for infliction, wait to be repeated, be in reserve, 10.29; *with abl*, 1.679.

resultō, *no perf, ātus* 1 *intens v* to leap back or again, rebound, 10.330; reëcho, reverberate, resound, 5.150. (resiliō, leap back).

resupīnus, a, um *adj* bent back; lying extended on the back; supine, thrown backwards, 1.476; stretched out, 3.624.

resurgō, surrēxī, surrēctus 3 *v* to rise again, 1.206; revive, return, 4.531.

rēte, is, *n* a net, 4.131.

retegō, tēxī, tēctus 3 *v* to uncover; leave uncovered,

retentō, **āvī**, **ātus** 1 *intens*
v to hold back; restrain,
retard, 5.278. (retineō).

retexō, **texuī**, **textus** 3 *v* to weave
again; *figuratively* compass
again, repeat, 12.762.

retinaculum, **ī**, *n* that which
holds back; a halter, rein;
cable, rope, 4.580. (retineō).

retineō, **tinuī**, **tentus**
2 *v* to hold back; hold,
retain, restrain, 5.669.

retorqueō, **torsī**, **tortus** 2 *v*
to twist back; throw, fold
or double back, 12.400;
turn or hurl back, or away,
12.485; change, 12.841.

retrāctō, **āvī**, **ātus** 1 *freq v* to
handle again; gripe or grasp
again, 10.396; take up again,
resume, 7.694; recall, 12.11; *n*,
hesitate, hold back, 12.889.

retrahō, **trāxī**, **trāctus** 3 *v* to
draw back, 10.307; lead
back, recall, 5.709.

retrō *adv* back, backwards,
2.753. (re-).

retrōrsus *adv* backwards,
back; again, 3.690. (retrō
and versus from vertō).

reus, **ī** *m* a defendant; the
accused; hence, *figuratively*
reus vōtī, liable in respect
to a vow; bound by one's
vow, 5.237. (rēs).

revehō, **vexī**, **vectus** 3 *v* to carry,
convey or bring back, 8.37.

revellō, **vellī**, **vulsus** 3 *v* to
pull back; pluck out, tear
out or off, 4.515; rend, rip,
tear open, 12.98; snatch,
bring away, rescue, 4.545;
disturb, violate, 4.427.

revertō 3 *v*, and **revertor**, **versus
sum** 3 *dep v* to turn back; go,
come back, return, 3.101.

revinciō, **vinxī**, **vinctus** 4 *v*
to bind back, 2.57; bind
fast, 3.76; bind around,
wreathe, festoon, 4.459.

revīsō 3 *v* to look at again; visit
again, return to see; return
to, 2.760; revisit, 3.318.

revocō, **āvī**, **ātus** 1 *v* to call
back, summon back; order
back, 5.167; rehearse, 7.40;
recall, 1.202; restore, 1.235;
save, 5.476; recover, renew,
revive, 1.214; retrace, 6.128.

revolvō, **volvī**, **volūtus** 3 *v* to
roll back, 5.336; *figuratively*
bring back, recall, repeat,
2.101; retrace, 9.391; go over
again, suffer again, 10.61;
turn, change again, 6.449;
passive revolvor, fall back, fall
down, 9.476; *part*, revolūtus,
a, um, rolling, 10.660;
returning, following, 10.256.

revomō, **vomuī** 3 *v* to vomit
back or up; vomit, 5.182.

rēx, **rēgis** *m* a king, *freq*;
chief, ruler, sovereign,
1.65; prince, 9.223.

Rhadamanthus, **ī** *m* son of
Jupiter and Europa, and one
of the judges in Hades, 6.566.

Rhaebus, **ī** *m* the name of the
warhorse of Mezentius, 10.861.

Rhamnes, ētis *m* a Rutulian chief, 9.325 *et al.*

Rhēa, ae *f* a priestess, mother of Aventinus, 7.659 *et al.*

Rhēnus, ī *m* the river Rhine, 8.727.

Rhēsus, ī *m* a Thracian king allied with the Trojans, 1.469.

Rhoeteus (*dissyll*), **eos** *m* a Rutulian slain by Pallas, 10.399.

Rhoetēus, a, um *adj* of Rhoeteum, a promontory on the coast of the Troad; Rhoetean, 6.505; Trojan, 12.456.

Rhoetus, ī *m* a Centaur, 9.345; a Rutulian slain by Euryalus, 9.344; king of the Marrubii, and father of Anchemolus, 10.388.

rīdeō, rīsī, rīsus 2 *v* to laugh or smile, 5.358; laugh at, deride, 5.181.

rigeō, riguī 2 *v* to be stiff, 4.251; *part*, rigēns, entis, stiff, 1.648.

rigidus, a, um *adj* (rigeō), stiff, inflexible, unbending; of iron weapons, 12.304.

rigō, āvī, ātus 1 *v* to moisten, wet, bedew, 6.699; bespatter, stain, 12.308.

rīma, ae *f* a cleft; crack, chink, fissure, 1.123.

rīmor, ātus sum 1 *dep v* to force open in cracks or chinks; *figuratively* to ransack, explore, search, 6.599. (rīma).

rīmōsus, a, um *adj* (rīma), full of cracks or crevices; leaky, 6.414.

rīpa, ae *f* the shore, border, or bank of a stream, 6.314; for flūmen, 7.106.

Rīpheus (*dissyll*), **eī** *m* a Trojan slain in the sack of Troy, 2.339.

rīte *adv* properly, fitly, rightly, 6.145; justly, meetly, 3.36; well, 3.107. (rītus).

rītus, ūs *m* a farm of religious ceremonial; a form, rite, 12.836; custom, manner, 7.741; *abl*, rītū, in the manner of, like, 11.611.

rīvus, ī *m* a small stream; a rill, brook, rivulet, stream, 3.350.

rōbur, oris, *n* hard oak or wood, 6.181; a tree, 8.315; *metonym* timber, a wooden structure; fabric, 2.260; *figuratively* sturdiness, strength, firmness, courage, vigor, 2.639; *pl* rōbora, wood, timber, 4.399; vigor, flower, 8.518.

rogitō, āvī, ātus 1 *freq v* to ask again and again; question, 1.750. (rogō).

rogō, āvī, ātus 1 *v* to ask, inquire, 2.149; desire, request, 7.229.

rogus, ī *m* a funeral pile, 4.640.

Rōma, ae *f* Rome, 1.7 *et al.*

Rōmānus, a, um *adj* (Rōma), belonging to Rome; Roman, 1.33; *subst* Rōmānus, ī, *m*, a Roman, 1.234.

Rōmānus, ī *m* a Roman, 1.234.

Rōmuleus, a, um *adj* (Rōmulus), of Romulus; Romulean, 8.654.

Rōmulidae, ārum *m* descendants or people of Romulus; Romans, 8.638. (Rōmulus).

Rōmulus, a, um *adj* (Rōmulus), of Romulus; Romulean, 6.876.

Rōmulus, ī *m* Romulus, the eponymous founder of Rome, son of Mars and Rhea Silvia or Ilia, 1.276 *et al.* (cf. Rōma).

rōrō, āvī, ātus *1 v* to be moist with dew; *figuratively* to drop, drip, 8.645. (rōs).

rōs, rōris *m* dew, *freq*; moisture, 5.854; rōrēs, drops of blood, 12.339.

rosa, ae *f* a rose, 12.69.

rōscidus, a, um *adj* (rōs), covered with dew; dewy, 4.700; wet, 7.683.

roseus, a, um *adj* (rosa), pertaining to roses; rose-colored; rosy, 1.402.

Rōseus, a, um *adj* (Rōsea), of Rosea, a region or district near Reate; Rosean, 7.712.

rōstrātus, a, um *adj* (rōstrum), beaked; adorned with beaks, 8.684.

rōstrum, ī a bill, beak, 6.597; the beak of a ship, 5.143; *pl* Rōstra, ōrum, *n*, the platform or tribunal for magistrates and orators in the Roman forum, so called because adorned with the beaks of the captured ships of Antium; the Rostra. (rōdō, gnaw).

rota, ae *f* a wheel, 1.147; *figuratively* circle or orbit of time, 6.748.

rotō, āvī, ātus *1 v* to move like a wheel; whirl about, 10.362; to brandish, 10.577. (rota).

rubeō, rubuī *2 v* to be red, blush; glow, redden, 12.77.

ruber, bra, brum *adj* (rubeō), red, ruddy, 12.247; litore rubrō, shore of the Mare Rubrum or Persian Gulf, 8.686.

rubēscō, rubuī *3 inc v* to grow or turn red; begin to glow, redden, 3.521. (rubeō).

rubor, ōris *m* redness; glow, 12.66. (rubeō).

rudēns, entis *m* a rope; cord; *pl* rudentēs, um or ium, cordage, 1.87.

rudīmentum, ī, *n* a beginning; first lesson, 11.157. (*rel* to rudis).

rudis, e *adj* uncultivated; rough.

rudō, īvī, ītus *3 v* to send forth a loud, rough sound; bellow, roar, of men, 8.248; of beasts, 7.16; of the roaring sound of the rushing water, 3.561. (p. *gen pl* rudentum, 7.16).

Rufrae, ārum *f* a town of Campania, 7.739.

rūga, ae *f* a wrinkle, 7.417.

ruīna, ae *f* a falling down; fall, overthrow; convulsion, commotion, destructive force, 1.129; onset, shock, 11.613; *pl* ruin, overthrow, destruction, 1.238; dare, trahere ruīnam, to fall in ruins, 2.310; bring destruction, 12.454. (ruō).

rūmor, ōris *m* report, rumor, 4.203; a cheer, shout, 8.90.

rumpō, rūpī, ruptus *3 v* to break, burst; tear, sever, *freq*; break through, open, force, 2.494; rend, sever, cut, tear, 3.640;

dash, 11.615; *figuratively* break off, end, 4.569; interrupt, 8.110; violate, 4.292; utter with fury, shout or shriek forth, 3.246; *part*, ruptus, a, um, breaking forth, bursting forth, 2.416; darting, flashing, 8.391;. sē rumpere, to dart forth; to burst, 11.549; rumpere vōcem, to break silence, 2.129.

ruō, ruī, rutus *3 v* to fall with violence; tumble down, fall, *freq*; fall in battle, 10.756; of the sun, go down, set, 3.508; rush forward, 2.64; of the chariot of Nox, hasten up; ascend, rise, 2.250; advance, 10.256; plunge, rush, 2.353; flee, 12.505; tremble, quake, 8.525; hasten, pass away, 6.539; cause to fall; cast down, 9.516; plow, 1.35; cast, throw up, 1.85; throw up or together, 11.211.

rūpēs, is *f* a rock, cliff, crag, ledge, *freq*; quarry, 1.429. (rumpō).

rūrsus or **rūrsum** *adv* backward; again, anew, 2.401; in turn, 4.534. (for reversum from revertō).

rūs, rūris, *n* the country as opposed to the town; land, a farm, field, *freq*; *pl* rūra, the fields, 1.430 *et al.*

rutilō, āvī, ātus *1 v* to redden; gleam, 8.529.

rutilus, a, um *adj* (*rel to* rubeō), of a red and gold color or flame color; red, glowing.

Rutulī, ōrum *m* the Rutulians, an ancient tribe of Latium dwelling south of the Tiber, 1.266 *et al.*

Rutulus, ī *m* a Rutulian; Turnus, 7.409; for the *pl* the Rutulians, 8.474.

Sabaeī, ōrum *m* the Sabaeans or people of Arabia Felix. (Saba).

Sabaeus, a, um *adj* (Saba), Sabaean, Arabian, 1.416; *pl* Sabaeī, ōrum, *m*, the Sabaeans or people of Arabia Felix.

Sabellus, a, um *adj* (Sabellī), of the Sabelli or Sabines; Sabine.

Sabīnae, ārum *m* the Sabine women, an ancient people occupying the hill country on the border of Latium, from whom were derived a part of the Roman people or Quirites, 8.635.

Sabīnī, ōrum *m* the Sabines, an ancient people occupying the hill country on the border of Latium, from whom were derived a part of the Roman people or Quirites, 7.706.

Sabīnus, ī *m* Sabinus or Sabus, the founder of the race of Sabines, 7.138.

sacer, sacra, sacrum *adj* set apart, consecrated, holy, sacred, 2.167 *et al.*; consecrated to, priest of, 6.484; devoted to the infernal gods; damned, accursed, 5.57.

sacerdōs, ōtis, *c* a priest or priestess, 2.201; 1.273; a poet or bard (as priest of the Muses), 6.645. (sacer).

Sacēs, is *m* a Latin, 12.651.

Sācrānus, a, um *adj* pertaining to the Sacrani, a Latin people; Sacranian, 7.796.

sacrārium, iī (sacrum) sanctuary; sacred court, 12.199.

Sacrātor, ōris m an Etruscan, 10.747.

sacrātus, a, um holy, 3.371. (sacrō).

sacrilegus, a, um adj (sacer and legō), impious, 7.595.

sacrō, āvī, ātus 1 v to set apart to the gods; devote, consecrate, 2.502; with acc and dat devote, 10.419. (sacer).

sacrum, ī, n a holy thing; pl sacra, ōrum, n, sacred symbols, rites, 12.13; sacred rites, ceremonies, sacrifices, 2.132; sacred things, utensils, symbols, 2.293; mysteries, 3.112.

saeculum and saeclum, ī, n a generation, race; century, period, age, time, 1.291 et al.

saepe adv (compar saepius), often, frequently, 2.108 et al.; cum saepe, when, as often happens, 1.148.

saepiō, saepsī, saeptus 4 v to fence in; inclose, surround, 1.506; envelop, 1.411. (saepēs, inclosure).

saeta, ae f a bristle; a stiff hair, 6.245; fur.

saetiger, era, erum adj (saeta and gerō), bristle-bearing, bristly, 7.17.

saeviō, iī, ītus 4 v to be fierce; to be furious, rage; be angry, 6.544. (saevus).

saevus, a, um adj fierce, fell, wrathful, of men, animals, and things; cruel, 1.458; dreadful, direful, fearful, 2.559; furious, 9.792; stern, bloody, 6.824; formidable, valiant, warlike, 1.99; relentless, 12.849; maddening, angering; bitter, 1.25; mortal, 12.857.

Sagaris, is m Sagaris, a slave of Aeneas, 5.263.

sagitta, ae f an arrow, 1.187 et al.

sagittifer, a, um adj (sagitta and ferō), arrow-bearing, 8.725.

sagulum, ī, n a soldier's cloak, 8.660. (sagum, a military cloak).

sāl, salis m salt; brine, salt water, 1.173; metonym the sea, 1.35.

Salamīs, īnis (acc **Salamīna**) f an island opposite Eleusis, 8.158.

salīgnus, a, um adj (salix, willow), made of willow; willow-, 7.632.

Saliī, ōrum the Salii, or priests of Mars who had charge of the sacred shields called ancilia, which they bore once a year in solemn procession through the city, with hymns and dances, 8.285. (saliō).

saliō, uī, saltus 4 v to leap, spring, jump, dance, bound.

Salius, iī m Salius, an Acarnanian, 5.298 et al.

Sallentīnus, a, um adj pertaining to the Sallentini, a people in Iapygia, southeast of Tarentum; Salentine, 3.400.

Salmōneus (trisyll), eī m Salmoneus, king, of Elis, son of Aeolus and brother of Sisyphus; for attempting to imitate the thunder of

Jupiter, cast into Tartarus
by a thunderbolt, 6.585.

salsus, a, um *adj* (cf. sal),
made salty; salted, 2.133;
salt-, briny, 2.173.

saltem *adv* at any rate,
at least, 1.557.

saltus, ūs *m* a leap,
bound, spring, 2.565; an
ascending, 6.515. (saliō).

saltus, ūs *m* woodland pasture,
glade, forest, 4.72 *et al.*

**salūbris (also salūber,
m), e** *adj* (salūs), health-
bringing; healing, 12.418.

salum, ī, *n* the tossing or
heaving swell of the sea; the
open sea, the main, 1.537.

salūs, ūtis *f* the state of
being well; safety, 1.555;
preservation, means of safety,
remedy, relief, deliverance,
1.451. (*rel to* salvus, safe).

salūtō, āvī, ātus *1 v* to wish safe
or well; greet, salute, 3.524;
welcome, hail, 12.257. (salūs).

salveō *2 v* to be well;
imperative, all hail! hail!
5.80. (salvus, safe).

Samē, ēs *f* Same, a name
of Cephallenia, in the
Ionian sea, west of the
Gulf of Corinth, 3.271.

Sāmos (-us), ī *f* Samos, an island
southwest of Ephesus, near
the coast of Ionia, 1.16.

Samothrācia, ae *f* Thracian
Samos, a small island about
thirty-eight miles south of the
Thracian coast, supposed by

some to have been colonized
from Samos, 7.208.

sanciō, sānxī, sānctus *4 v*
to make sacred; sanction,
ratify, 12.200. (sacer).

sānctus, a, um sacred, holy,
2.700; sacred, venerable, 1.426;
unstained, with untarnished
honor, 12.648. (sanciō).

sānē *adv* truly, indeed,
10.48 *et al.* (sānus).

sanguineus, a, um *adj* (sanguis),
of blood; bloodshot, 4.643;
of bloody color or aspect,
bloody, 2.207; fiery, bloody,
10.273; ruddy, burnished,
8.622; bloodthirsty, 12.332.

sanguis, inis *m* blood, 3.30 *et al.*;
parentage, lineage, descent,
race, 1.19; offspring, son, 6.835.

saniēs, em, ē *f* putrid, corrupt
blood; bloody matter; gore,
3.618. (*rel to* sanguis).

sānus, a, um *adj* sound in
body or mind; male sānus,
diseased, morbid with
love, love-sick, 4.8.

Sarnus, ī *m* a river running
into the Bay of Naples
near Pompeii, 7.738.

Sarpēdōn, onis *m* Sarpedon,
son of Jupiter and Europa,
killed at the siege of Troy
by Patroclus, 1.100 *et al.*

Sarrastēs, um *m* the Sarrastes,
a people dwelling near
the Sarnus, 7.738.

sata, ōrum, *n* things sown or
planted; grain, growing
grain; crops, 3.139. (serō,
serere, sēvī, satus).

Satīculus, ī *m* a Saticulan; of Saticula, a Campanian town, 7.729. (Satīcula).

satiō, āvī, ātus *1 v* to satisfy; appease, 2.587. (satis).

satis or **sat** (*adj* and *adv*), sufficient, enough; *with gen*, 2.314; alone as subject, 2.291; as predicate, 2.642; *compar* satius, better, preferable, 10.59.

sator, ōris *m* a planter; sire, father, 1.254. (1. serō).

Satura, ae *f* a place in Latium, probably on the Pontine marshes, 7.801.

Sāturnius, a, um *adj* (Sāturnus), belonging to Saturn; Saturnian; sprung from Saturn; Saturnian, 4.372; *subst* Sāturnius, iī, *m*, the son of Saturn, 5.799; Sāturnia, ae, *f*, 1. Daughter of Saturn, Juno, 1.23; 2. The city of Saturnia, built by Saturn on the Capitoline hill, 8.358.

Sāturnus, ī *m* a deified king of Latium, whose reign was the golden age; identified by the Romans with the Greek Cronos, 8.319 *et al.*

saturō, āvī, ātus *1 v* to fill; glut, cloy, appease, 5.608. (satur, full).

satus, a, um begotten of, born of, sprung from, *with abl* 2.540; offspring, son of, 5.244; daughter of, 7.331. (serō, serere, sēvī, satus).

saucius, a, um *adj* wounded, 2.223; pierced, 4.1.

saxeus, a, um *adj* (saxum), rocky, stony, 9.711.

saxum, ī, *n* a large rough stone, rock, *frequently* cliff, crag, stone, 1.150; 3.699.

Scaea, ae *adj* western; Scaea Porta, and *pl* Scaeae Portae, the Scaean or western gate of Troy, 2.612.

scaena, ae *f* the stage of a theatre, 4.471; a sylvan scene, view, 1.164.

scālae, ārum *f* a ladder; scaling ladder, 2.442. (scandō).

scandō, scandī, scānsus *3 v* to climb, 2.401; ascend, 2.237.

scelerō, *no perf*, ātus *1 v* to make impious; desecrate, pollute, 3.42; *part*, scelerātus, a, um, foul with crime; polluted, impious, wicked, 2.231; accursed, 6.563; pertaining to the guilty or to guilt, due to wickedness, 2.576; sacrilegious, 9.137. (scelus).

scelus, eris, *n* an evil or atrocious deed; a crime, *freq*; wickedness, 6.742; *metonym* punishment, 7.307; like nefās for wretch, imp; hence, scelus artificis = artifex scelestus, the accursed deceiver, 11.407.

scēptrum, ī, *n* a royal staff; scepter, 1.653; *freq*; *metonym* rule, sway, power, royal court, realm, 9.9; 1.253; authority, 11.238.

scīlicet *adv* one may know or understand; be assured; certainly, in sooth, doubtless; for this purpose, 6.750; ironical, forsooth, 2.577 *et al.* (sciō and licet).

scindō, scidī, scissus *3 v* to cut asunder; split, 6.182; part, separate, divide, 1.161; tear, 9.478; *figuratively* divide, 2.39.

scintilla, ae *f* a spark, 1.174.

sciō, īvī or **iī, ītus** *4 v* to know, understand, 1.63 *et al.*; know how, be able, can.

Scīpiadēs, ae *m* one of the Scipios, a Scipio, 6.843. (Scīpiō)

scītor, ātus sum *1 dep intens v* to seek to know; ascertain; inquire, 2.105; *part*, scītāns, antis, consulting, to consult, 2.114. (sciō).

scopulus, ī *m* a projecting ledge of rock; a high cliff or rock, 1.180; crag, 1.45; ledge, reef, 1.145; detached rock, fragment of rock, 12.531.

scrūpeus, a, um *adj* (scrūpus, a sharp stone), consisting of jagged stones; flinty, 6.238.

scūtātus, a, um *adj* (scūtum), equipped or armed with a shield, 9.370.

scūtum, ī, *n* an oblong shield carried by the Roman legionary; a shield in general, 1.101 *et al.* (σκύτος, hide).

Scylacēum, ī, *n* a town on the Bruttian coast, 3.553.

Scylla, ae *f* 1. A dangerous rock on the Italian side of the Straits of Messana opposite Charybdis, 3.420; personified as a monster, half woman and half fish, 3.424. 2. The name of one of the ships of Aeneas, 5.122.

Scyllaeus, a, um *adj* (Scylla), pertaining to Scylla; Scyllaean, 1.200.

scyphus, ī *m* a cup, goblet, bowl, 8.278.

Scȳrius, a, um *adj* (Scȳros), of Scyros, an island in the Aegean northeast of Euboea; Scyrian, 2.477.

Sēbēthis, idis or **idos** *f* the daughter of Sebethus, a river or river-god of Campania, 7.734.

sēcernō, crēvī, crētus *3 v* to separate.

sēcessus, ūs *m* a going apart; a retreat, retirement; a recess, 1.159. (sēcēdō).

sēclūdō, clūsī, clūsus *3 v* to shut apart, off, out; shut up, 3.446; shut out, dismiss, 1.562. (se- and claudō).

sēclūsus, a, um sequestered, retired, 6.704. (sēclūdō).

secō, secuī, sectus *1 v* to cut, *freq*; cut off, 4.704; engrave, carve, 3.464; cut through, cleave, 5.218 *et al.*; of the channel of a river, 8.63; sail through, pass, 8.96; speed, 6.899; shape out mentally, form, 10.107.

sēcrētum, ī, *n* anything apart; a solitary place, recess, cave; *pl* sēcrēta, ōrum, solitude, chamber, 8.403; secret abode, 6.10. (sēcernō).

sēcrētus, a, um separated, apart, retired, solitary, 2.299; secret; unnoticed, 4.494. (sēcernō).

secundō 1 v to direct favorably; aid, favor, prosper; make auspicious, 3.36. (secundus).

secundus, a, um adj (sequor), the following; second, 5.258; inferior, 11.441; favorable, fair, 4.562; swiftly flying, 1.156; fortunate, prosperous, 1.207; successful, 2.617; joyful, 8.90; 10.266; auspicious, propitious, 4.45; of a river, easily flowing, downwards.

secūris, is f an ax, 2.224 et al. (secō).

sēcūrus, a, um adj (sē- and cūra), free from anxiety; untroubled, no longer fearing, 1.290; tranquil, undisturbed; peace-giving, peaceful, 6.715;. with gen, reckless, regardless, 1.350; safe from, 7.304.

secus following, late; otherwise, differently; nōn or haud secus, not otherwise, not less; likewise, even so, 2.382 et al.; none the less, nevertheless, 5.862; haud secus ac, nor otherwise than, just as. (comp. adv), sētius, less, the less; haud sētius, not the less, 7.781.

sed conj, except that; but, yet, freq; sed enim, but indeed, however, 1.19 et al.; sed autem, but yet, 2.101.

sēdātus, a, um composed, calm, quiet, 9.30; of the mind, 9.740. (sēdō).

sedeō, sēdī, sessus 2 v to sit, 1.56; sit inactive, 9.4; alight, 6.192; figuratively to be fixed, settled, resolved, 4.15; to suit, be pleasing, 5.418; circum sedēre, to encamp about; to besiege.

sēdēs, is f a seat of any kind, freq; metonym an habitation, abode, dwelling (pl for sing), 2.634; destined or proper place, 2.232; foundation, 2.465; of the sea, bottom, 1.84; temple, shrine, 2.742; palace, 2.760; final resting-place, grave, tomb, 6.328; realm, 7.52. (sedeō).

sedīle, is n a bench, seat, 1.167. (sedeō).

sēditiō, ōnis f a mutiny; faction, 11.340; uprising, riot; outbreak, tumult, 1.149. (sēd- and eō).

sēdō, āvī, ātus 1 v to cause to sit, to render quiet. (sedeō).

sēdūcō, dūxī, ductus 3 v to lead apart or away; to separate, 4.385.

seges, etis f a field of grain; standing corn, 2.304; crop, harvest, growth of spears, 3.46; pasture land, 4.129.

sēgnis, e adj tardy, sluggish; dilatory, backward, 11.736; slothful, inactive, 3.513; mean-spirited, cowardly, 9.787; helpless, 10.700; figuratively idle, exhausted; compar sēgnior, less glorious, less divine, 4.149; less rapid, 7.383.

sēgniter adv sluggishly; compar sēgnius, more backward, less furiously; less impetuously, 12.525. (sēgnis).

sēgnitiēs, ēī f sloth, tardiness, delay, 2.374. (sēgnis).

Selīnūs, ūntis f Selinus, a town on the southwestern coast of Sicily, 3.705.

sella, ae f a seat; chair; chair of state, 11.334. (sedeō).

semel adv once, even once, 3.431; once for all, finally, 11.418.

sēmen, inis, n seed; figuratively a spark, an element, 6.6; pl sēmina, seeds of things, vital germs, elements, 6.731. (1. serō).

sēmēsus, a, um adj (sēmi- and edō), half eaten, 3.244.

sēmianimis (in hexam. poetry pron **semyanimis), e** adj half alive; dying, 4.686.

sēmifer, fera, ferum adj half wild; savage; half brute, 10.212; subst sēmifer, ferī m (sc homō), half beast, 8.267.

sēmihomō, inis m a half man, 8.194. (in hexam. poetry the oblique cases are pronounced semyomin-).

sēminex (nom. not in use), ecis adj (semi- and nex), half slain, half dead, 5.275.

sēminō, āvī, ātus 1 v to plant, sow; produce, 6.206. (sēmen).

sēmita, ae f a byway, lane, 9.383; path, 1.418. (sē- and cf. meō, to go).

sēmivir, virī, adj m half man, effeminate, unmanly, 4.215.

semper adv always, ever, 2.97 et al.

sēmustus, a, um adj (sēmi- and ūrō), half burned, half consumed, 3.578.

senātus, ūs m the council of elders; a senate, 1.426. (senex).

senecta, ae f old age, 5.395. (senex).

senectūs, ūtis f old age, 5.416; personified, 6.275. (senex).

senex, senis adj old, aged, hoary, 7.180; (comp.) senior, ōris, older; very aged, 5.179; hoary, 5.704.

senex, senis (gen pl senum, 9.309) an old man, 4.251; (comp.) senior, ōris, a very aged person; old man, 5.469; sire, 2.509.

sēnī, ae, a distrib. num adj (sex), six by six, six each; as a cardinal, six, 1.393 et al.

sēnsus, ūs m feeling; emotion, 4.408; faculty of sense; sense, 7.355; inclination, affection, 4.22; spirit, soul, 6.747; thought, purpose, 12.914. (sentiō).

sententia, ae f a feeling or thinking; opinion; resolution, design, purpose, 1.237; 11.21; judgment, 2.35; plan, 4.287; idea, thought, 1.582. (sentiō).

sentiō, sēnsī, sēnsus 4 v to perceive by the senses; hear, 3.669; see, 4.588; perceive, 1.125; of the intellect and moral faculties, understand, know, 3.360; think, 10.534; will, desire, 10.623; (w. acc of person), know, 7.434.

sentis, is m and f a thorn, brier, bramble, 2.379.

sentus, a, um adj (sentis), thorny; rugged; squalid, 6.462.

sepeliō, pelīvī or **pelīī, pultus**
4 *v* to perform the rites of
sepulture, whether by interring
(humāre), or cremation
(cremāre); to bury, 3.41; *part*,
sepultus, a, um, buried, 4.34;
of slumber, 6.424 *et al.*

septem (*num adj*), seven, *freq.*

septemgeminus, a, um *adj*
sevenfold, said of the
Nile on account of its
seven mouths, 6.800.

septemplex, icis *adj* sevenfold,
12.925. (septem and plicō),.

septēnī, ae, a distrib. *num
adj* (septem), seven by
seven, seven each; as a
cardinal, seven, 5.85.

septimus, a, um (ordin. *num adj*),
the seventh, 1.755. (septem).

sepulcrum, ī, *n* a place of burial;
tomb, sepulchre, grave; burial,
sepulture, 2.542. (sepeliō).

sequāx, ācis *adj* (sequor), prone
to follow; following, pursuing,
swiftly pursuing; darting,
lambent, 8.432; rapid, 5.193.

sequestra, ae *f* one with whom
something is placed in trust;
sequestrā pāce, a mediatory
peace; a truce, 11.133. (sequor).

sequor, secūtus sum 3 *dep v* to
follow, 1.185; follow closely,
pursue, 5.227; seek after,
pursue, 3.327; seek to reach,
seek, 4.381; 10.193; pursue a
plan or course, 3.368; compass,
attain, find, 6.457; follow
in narrative, recount, 1.342;
follow; of words responding
to the will, 12.912; yield to the
hand, 6.146; attend, favor, 8.15.

serēnō, āvī, ātus 1 *v* to make
clear or calm, 1.255; spem
serēnāre, to exhibit the
calm or cheerful look of
hope, 4.477. (serēnus).

serēnum, ī, *n* (*sc* caelum),
a clear sky. (serenus, clear,
calm, tranquil, serene).

serēnus, a, um *adj* clear, calm,
tranquil, serene, 3.518 *et al.*;
fair, 2.285; *subst* serēnum, ī,
n (*sc* caelum), a clear sky.

Serestus, ī *m* a companion
of Aeneas, 1.611 *et al.*

Sergestus, ī *m* commander
of one of the ships of
Aeneas, 1.510 *et al.*

Sergius, a, um *adj* (Sergius), of
Sergius, founder of the Roman
gens Sergia; Sergian, 5.121.

seriēs, em, ē *f* a chain of things,
train, row, succession,
series, 1.641. (2. serō).

sermō, ōnis *m* the joining
of words; language,
conversation, talk, discourse,
1.217; report, rumor, 4.189;
speech, words, 12.223; a
language, 12.834. (2. serō).

serō (seruī), sertus 3 *v* to
join together; interweave,
plait; interchange words;
multa serere, to interweave
many things, talk,
commune much, 6.160.

serō, sēvī, satus 3 *v* to sow or
plant; with indefinite object
omitted, 6.844; scatter,
spread, disseminate, 12.228.

serpēns, entis (*gen pl*
serpentum, 8.436) *m* and

f a creeping thing; snake, serpent, 2.214 *et al.* (serpō).

serpō, serpsī, serptus 3 *v* to creep, glide, 5.91; steal on or over, 2.269.

Serrānus, ī *m* 1. Serranus, a surname in the Atilian gens, 6.844. 2. A Rutulian, 9.335.

serta, ōrum, *n* things entwined; garlands, festoons, wreaths, 1.417 *et al.* (sero, serere, serui, sertus).

sērus, a, um *adj* late, *freq*; late in life, 6.764; slow, tardy, 2.373; too late, 5.524; *adv* sērum, late, 12.864.

serva, ae *f* a female slave, slave, 5.284.

servāns, antis (*superl*, **servantissimus, a, um**) observant, *with gen*, 2.427.

serviō, īvī or **iī, ītus** 4 *v* to be a slave; *dat*, to serve, obey, 2.786. (servus, slave).

servitium, iī, *n* slavery, bondage, 3.327. (servus, slave).

servō, āvī, ātus 1 *v* to save, 3.86 *et al.*; reserve, 1.207; retain, keep, 6.200; hold, 7.179; continue, maintain, 10.340; guard, 2.450; keep, cherish, 1.36; preserve, inherit, 7.52; sit by, 2.568; dwell, abide by, 6.402; give heed to, watch, observe, 6.338; 11.200.

sēscentī, ae, a *num adj* (sex and centum), six hundred, 10.172.

seu *conj*, or if, *freq*; or, 5.69; elliptical, 11.327; sīve (seu) — sīve (seu),

whether — or, 1.569.570; either — or, 4.240.241.

sevērus, a, um *adj* stern, strict, exacting; controlled by inflexible laws or fate; fatal, dreadful, 6.374.

Sevērus, ī *m* a mountain in the Sabine country, 7.713.

sex six, 9.272 *et al.* (*num indecl adj*).

sī *conj*, if, *freq*; causal, if, indeed, since, 2.102; equivalent to cum, 5.64 *et al.*; whether, *with* subj., 4.110; *with* indic., 1.578; for Ō sī, would that, *with* subj., 6.187.

sībilō 1 *v* to hiss, 7.447. (sībilus, a hissing).

sībilus, a, um *adj* hissing, 2.211 *et al.*

Sibylla, ae *f* a prophetess, a sibyl; the Cumaean sibyl, Deiphobe, 3.452 *et al.*

sīc *adv* in this manner; in such a manner; so, thus; explanatory, 2.440 *et al.*; referring to a preceding participle, 1.225.

Sicānī, ōrum *m* the Sicanians or Sicilians, 5.293 *et al.*

Sicānia, ae *f* Sicily, 1.557.

Sicānus (Sicānius), a, um *adj* (Sicānī), Sicilian, Sicanian, 5.24 *et al.*

siccō, āvī, ātus 1 *v* to make dry, drain, suck; dry up, wipe away, 4.687; wash, 10.834. (siccus).

siccum, ī, *n* dry ground, sand, or land, 10.301.

siccus, a, um *adj* dry, 3.135; thirsty, dry, hungry, fasting,

2.358; nearly equivalent to
carēns or prīvātus, with *abl*
foll., drained of blood, 8.261;
hence, thirsting for blood,
9.64; *subst* siccum, ī, *n*, dry
ground, sand, or land, 10.301.

sīcubi *adv* if anywhere, 5.677.

Siculus, a, um *adj* (Siculī),
pertaining to the Siculi, an
ancient race, part of which
migrated from Latium to
Sicily; Sicilian, 1.34 *et al*.

sīcut (sīcutī) *adv* so as,
just as, even as, 8.22.

sīdereus, a, um *adj* (sīdus),
abounding in stars, starry,
10.3; star-lighted, 3.586;
glittering, flashing, 12.167.

Sidicīnus, a, um *adj* (Sidicīnī),
pertaining to the Sidicini,
or people of Teanum and its
territory in the northern part of
Campania; Sidicinian, 7.727.

sīdō, sīdī 3 *v* to seat one's
self; perch, alight, 6.203.

Sīdōn, ōnis *f* one of the capitals
of Phoenicia, 1.619.

Sīdōnius, a, um *adj* of Sidon;
Sidonian; Phoenician,
Tyrian, 1.678 *et al*.

sīdus, eris, *n* a constellation;
figuratively season, 4.309;
star, 6.338; bright aspect;
weather; storm, 12.451;
pl sīdera, um, weather,
vicissitudes of weather, 5.628.

Sīgēus, a, um *adj* (Sīgēum),
pertaining to Sigeum, a
promontory and town in
the Troad, at the mouth
of the Dardanelles, about

five miles northwest of
Troy; Sigean, 2.312.

sīgnificō, āvī, ātus 1 *v* to make
a sign, signal, beckon,
12.692. (sīgnum *and* faciō).

sīgnō, āvī, ātus 1 *v* to distinguish
by a mark or symbol,
6.780; mark, mark out;
indicate, designate, 2.697;
inscribe, record, 3.287; of
the mind, observe, mark,
notice, 2.423. (sīgnum).

sīgnum, ī, *n* a sign, mark,
impress; token, 1.443; sign,
3.388; signal, of games,
5.315; of battle, 10.310; goal,
5.130; figure, 1.648; standard,
7.628; *metonym* a body of
men following a standard,
troop, battalion, 11.517.

Sīla, ae *f* an extensive forest
in the country of the Bruttii
in Southern Italy, 12.715.

silēns, entis (*gen pl* -tum,
6.432) still, silent, noiseless,
voiceless, 6.264.

silentium, iī, *n* of the
absence of any kind of
sound; noiselessness,
silence, stillness, 1.730;
pl 2.255. (silēns).

sileō, uī 2 *v* to be, keep, remain
silent, 2.126; be hushed,
calm, still, 1.164; *with acc*,
to pass over in silence; leave
unmentioned, unsung, 10.793.

silēscō 3 *inc v* to become
still, 10.101. (sileō).

silex, icis *m and f* a hard
stone, flint, 1.174; rock,
6.602; crag, 6.471.

silva, ae *f* a forest, wood, or grove, 6.444 *et al.*; stubble, 10.406; *figuratively* forest or mass of spears, 10.887.

Silvānus, ī *m* Silvanus, the god who presides over woods. (silva).

silvestris, e *adj* (silva), pertaining to the woods and fields; sylvan, pastoral; living in the forest, 9.673.

Silvia, ae *f* daughter of Tyrrheus, 7.487. (silva).

silvicola, ae, *c* an inhabitant of the woods, 10.551. (silva and colō).

Silvius, iī *m* the name of several of the descendants of Aeneas, who were kings of Alba, 6.763.

similis, e *adj* (*compar* similior, ius; *superl* simillimus, a, um), like, similar, 1.136 *et al.*

Simoïs, Simoentis *m* a river which falls into the Scamander near Troy, 1.100 *et al.*

simplex, plicis *adj* uncompounded, simple; unmixed, 6.747; single, one, the same.

simul *adv* at once, together, at the same time, 1.144 *et al.*; *with abl* (cum being omitted), 5.357; simul ac or atque, as soon as, 4.90; without ac, as soon as, when; *with* et, 1.144; simul — simul, and at the same time — and, 1.631; both — and, 1.513 *et al.*; as soon as — then, no sooner — than, 12.268.

simulācrum, ī, *n* an effigy, an image, 2.172; phantom, specter, ghost, apparition, 2.772; representation, image, 5.585. (simulō).

simulō, āvī, ātus *1 v* to make similar; imitate, 6.591; pretend, 2.17; to make a false show of, feign, 1.209; *part*, simulātus, a, um, made to imitate, counterfeiting, 4.512; dissembling, 4.105; imitating, resembling, 3.349. (similis).

sīn *conj*, but if, if on the contrary, 1.555 *et al.*

sine (*prep with abl*), without, 1.133 *et al.*; (connecting substantives), 6.292; 10.636. For sē- or sēd- in composition, see sē-.

singulī, ae, a (distrib. *num adj*), one by one; one each; separate, single, 3.348 *et al.*; *subst* singula, ōrum, *n*, all things individually, 1.453; everything, every object or part, 8.618.

singultō, no perf, ātus *1 v* to sob, rattle in the throat, gulp, 9.333.

singultus, ūs *m* a gasp.

sinister, tra, trum *adj* left, 7.689; on the left side or left hand, 6.548; *figuratively* wrong-headed, perverse, 11.347; adverse, inauspicious, unlucky, ill-boding.

sinistra, ae *f* (*sc* **manus**) the left hand, 2.443 *et al.*

sinō, sīvī, situs *3 v* to allow, permit, suffer, 1.18; leave off, forbear, 10.15; (with *inf* or subj. following), suffer, let, 10.433; 5.163; spare, 10.598; leave, (w. *acc* and *dat*), 9.620.

Sinōn, ōnis *m* a Greek, son of Aesimus, 2.79 *et al.*

sinuō, āvī, ātus *1 v* to make into a fold or folds; to coil, wind, 2.208. (sinus).

sinuōsus, a, um *adj* (sinus), winding, tortuous, 11.753.

sinus, ūs *m* a fold, 1.320; *figuratively* sail, canvas, 5.16; bosom, 4.686; a gulf or bay, 1.243; winding stream, a winding, 6.132; a winding, curvature, depth, 1.16l; curving billow, 11.626.

Sīrēnes, um *f* the Sirens, fabulous beings, in the form of birds with the faces of virgins, dwelling on dangerous rocks near the coast of Campania, to which they attracted mariners by their songs, 5.864.

Sīrius, a, um *adj* (Sīrius), of the dog-star; Sirian, 10.273.

Sīrius, iī *m* Sirius or Canicula, the dog-star, 3.141.

sistō, stitī, status *3 v* to cause to stand, put, set, place, *with abl* of place, 2.245 *et al.*; place before one, bring, 4.634; fix, plant, 10.323; stop, 12.355; arrest, stay, 6.465; support, sustain, maintain, 6.858; set, place, 6.676; *n*, stand still, to stop, remain, abide, 3.7; stand in fight, 11.873.

sīstrum, ī, *n* a metallic rattle, consisting of a small frame of horseshoe form with sliding cross-bars, used by the priests of Isis, 8.696.

sitis, is *f* thirst; dryness, drought, 4.42.

situs, ūs *m* position; order, 3.451; being let alone; neglect, roughness, squalor, mold, 6.462; rust, decrepitude, dotage, 7.440. (sinō).

sīve or **seu** *conj*, or if, *freq*; or, 5.69; elliptical, 11.327; sīve (seu) — sīve (seu), whether — or, 1.569.570; either — or, 4.240.241.

sīve or **seu** *conj*, or if, *freq*; or, 5.69; elliptical, 11.327; sīve (seu) — sīve (seu), whether — or, 1.569.570; either — or, 4.240.241.

socer, erī *m* a father-in-law, 6.830 *et al.*; *pl* socerī, ōrum, parents-in-law, parents, 2.457.

sociō, āvī, ātus *1 v* to make one a socius; to share, unite, associate, 1.600; join in marriage, 12.27. (socius).

socius, a, um *adj* (socius), allied, friendly, 3.15; confederate, 2.613; of one's country or countrymen, 5.36; kindred, 3.352.

socius, iī *m* an associate, ally, 9.150; companion, friend, comrade, 1.198 *et al.*

sodālis, e, *c* a comrade, companion, 10.386.

sōl, sōlis *m* the sun, 1.431 *et al.*; a day, 3.203; sunlight, 2.475; as a god, Sōl, 1.568 *et al.*; *pl* sōlēs, days, 3.203.

sōlācium, iī, *n* a soothing; solace, consolation, 5.367. (sōlor).

sōlāmen, inis, *n* a means of consoling; a solace, 3.661; consolation, 10. (sōlor).

soleō, solitus sum *2 v* to be wont, accustomed, 2.456.

solidum, ī, *n* solid ground; *fig*; 11.427.

solidus, a, um *adj* the whole, whole, entire, 6.253; massive, 2.765; solid, hard, 6.552; sound, unimpaired, 2.639.

solitus, a, um having been accustomed, wont, 9.591; *part*, wonted, usual, habitual, 7.357 *et al*.

solium, iī, *n* a seat, 8.178; throne, 1.506.

sollemnis, e *adj* (sollus, whole, and annus), coming at the completion of a year; annual; stated; ceremonial; religious, solemn, 5.53; festive, 2.202; customary, 12.193; *subst* sollemne, is, *n*, *pl* sollemnia, ium, solemnities, sacrificial rites, offerings, 5.605.

sollicitō, āvī, ātus *1 v* to stir up, agitate; try to pull out, 12.404; make anxious, disquiet, disturb, 4.380. (sollicitus).

sollicitus, a, um *adj* (sollus, whole, and cieō), wholly excited; of the mind, solicitous, troubled, burdened with care, anxious, 3.389.

sōlor, ātus sum *1 dep v* to solace, console, 5.770; assuage, comfort, aid, relieve, 5.41; console one's self for, 1.239.

solum, ī, *n* the bottom or ground of anything; soil, earth, ground, 1.367 *et al.*; land, 3.698; foundation, 10.102; the water beneath a ship, as its support; the water, sea, 5.199; support, table, 7.111.

sōlus, a, um *adj* alone, sole, only, 1.664 *et al.*; solitary, 4.82; lonely, 4.462; remote, solitary, 11.545; one only, an only, 7.52; *adv* sōlum, only.

solvō, solvī, solūtus *3 v* to unbind, loosen, 6.652 *et al.*; unfurl, 4.574; unfasten, cast off, 5.773; unyoke, unharness; of the hair, undo, dishevel, 3.65 *et al.*; dissolve, confound, mix, 12.205; separate, divide, 5.581; *figuratively* set free, release, disenthrall, 4.487; exempt, release, 10.111; break, 10.91; pay, fulfill, perform, 3.404; dispel, cast off, banish, 4.55; 1.463; paralyze, 1.92; 12.951; of sleep or drunkenness, relax, 5.856; drown, 9.189; *passive* solvor, sink, 4.530. (2. sē- and luō).

somnifer, era, erum *adj* (somnus and ferō), sleep-bringing; soothing, 7.758.

somnium, iī, *n* a dream, 5.840; personified, 6.283. (somnus).

somnus, ī *m* sleep, slumber, 1.680 *et al.*; a dream, 1.353; night, 1.470 *et al.*; *personif*, Somnus, the god of sleep, 5.838 *et al.*

sonāns, antis sounding, resounding, murmuring, rustling, rattling, *freq* (sonō).

sonipēs, edis *adj* (sonus and pēs), noisy-hoofed; *subst m*, horse, courser, steed, 4.135.

sonitus, ūs *m* a sounding; noise, 2.732 *et al.*; roaring, 2.209; thunder, 6.586. (sonō).

sonō, sonuī, sonitus *1 v* to sound, resound, *freq*; murmur, 3.442 *et al.*; chirp, 12.477; rattle, 4.149; roar, 1.246; thunder, 2.113; (w. *acc*) indicate by sound, betray, reveal, 1.328; boast, 12.529.

sonor, ōris *m* a noise, sound; clash, clang, din, 9.651. (sonō).

sonōrus, a, um *adj* (sonor), loud-sounding; roaring, 1.53; ringing, resounding, 12.712.

sōns, sontis *adj* hurtful; guilty, 6.570.

sonus, ī *m* a sound, noise, 2.728. (sonō).

sōpiō, īvī or **iī, ītus** *4 v* to put to sleep; *part*, sōpītus, a, um, lulled to sleep, 1.680; slumbering, 5.743. (sopor).

sopor, ōris *m* sleep; sound, deep slumber, 2.253; personified, 6.278.

sopōrifer, era, erum *adj* (sopor and ferō), somniferous, sleep-bringing, 4.486.

sopōrō, no perf, ātus *1 v* to cause to sleep or to render sleepy; to make soporific; to drug, 5.855. (sopor).

sopōrus, a, um *adj* (sopor), sleep-bringing, drowsy, 6.390.

Sōracte, is, *n* Soracte, in Etruria, northeast of Rome, on which in ancient times was a temple of Apollo, 7.696.

sorbeō, uī *2 v* to suck; absorb, draw on, 3.422.

sordidus, a, um *adj* (sordēs, filth), unclean, filthy, unsightly, squalid, 6.301.

soror, ōris *f* a sister, 1.322; sorōrēs Tartareae, the Furies, 7.327.

sors, sortis *f* a lot, 5.490 *et al.*; fate, lot, destiny, fortune, condition, 6.114; hazard, 12.54; luck, success, victory, 12.932; oracular response, oracle, 4.346; 7.254; allotment, designation, 6.431; division, part, 10.40.

sortior, ītus sum *4 dep v* to cast lots; obtain, get, take by lot, 3.634; share, 8.445; distribute, 3.510; assign, allot, appoint, 3.376; select, choose, 2.18; 12.920. (sors).

sortītus, ūs *m* a drawing of lots; allotment, 3.323. (sortior).

sōspes, itis *adj* saved; safe, 11.56; alive, 8.470.

spargō, sparsī, sparsus *3 v* to scatter, strew; cast in fragments, 3.605; disperse, 1.602; shower, hurl, 12.51; sprinkle, 4.512; besprinkle, bedew, stain, 8.645; infuse, 4.486; *figuratively* spread abroad, disseminate, 2.98; bring over or upon, diffuse, 7.754.

Sparta, ae *f* Sparta, or Lacedaemon, in Laconia.

Spartānus, a, um *adj* (Sparta), Spartan, 1.316.

sparus, ī *m* a rustic weapon having an iron head with projecting hook or blade, something like a halberd; a hunting spear, 11.682.

spatior, ātus sum *1 dep v* to walk about or to and fro; move about, 4.62. (spatium).

spatium, iī, *n* room, space, distance, 5.321 *et al.*; course, voyage, 10.219; place, direction, 5.584; respite, time, 4.433; *pl* spatia, ōrum, course, track, 5.316.

speciēs, ēī *f* aspect, appearance, 6.208; sight, 2.407; form; in a moral sense, reputation, propriety, honor, 4.170. (speciō, look).

specimen, inis, *n* a means of seeing or knowing; token, symbol, emblem, 12.164. (speciō, look).

spectāculum, ī, *n* a striking object of sight; a sight, show, spectacle, 6.37. (spectō).

spectātor, ōris *m* a beholder, 10.443. (spectō).

spectō, āvī, ātus *1 intens v* to look at, view, gaze at, 5.655; *figuratively* examine, prove, try, test, approve, 8.151; estimate, 9.235; *n*, look on, 10.760. (speciō, look).

specula, ae *f* a lookout; watch-tower, 4.586; eminence, hill, 3.239; a height, 11.526. (speciō, look).

speculātor, ōris *m* a lookout; scout, spy, 12.349. (speculor).

speculor, ātus sum *1 dep v* to look out, mark, survey, behold, espy, 7.477; watch, consider, observe, 1.516. (specula).

specus, ūs *m f,* a cave, cavern; cavity, deep wound, 9.700.

spēlunca, ae *f* a cavern, 1.60; retreat, 5.213.

spernō, sprēvī, sprētus *3 v* to sever, remove; *figuratively* reject, despise, scorn, disdain, 4.678; insult, 1.27.

spērō, āvī, ātus *1 v* to hope, with *acc*; hope for, 1.451; expect, fear, 1.543; look for, expect, 4.419; *with acc and inf* 9.158; *with inf fut,* 4.382; *with inf pres.,* 4.338. (spēs).

spēs, speī *f* hope, expectation, prospect, *freq.*

spīculum, ī, *n* a sharp point; *metonym* an arrow, a dart, javelin, spear, 5.307.

spīna, ae *f* a thorn, 3.594 *et al.*; the vertebrae, spine, backbone, 10.383.

Spīō, ūs *f* Spio, one of the Nereids, 5.826.

spīra, ae *f* a fold, coil, especially of serpents, 2.217 *et al.*

spīrābilis, e *adj* (spīrō), that may be breathed; vital, 3.600.

spīrāculum, ī, *n* a breathing-place; *figuratively* of Hades, breathing vent, mouth, 7.568. (spīrō).

spīrāmentum, ī, *n* a means of breathing; of the lungs, breathing-cell, air-duct, channel, 9.580. (spīrō).

spīritus, ūs *m* a breathing; breath; air; blast, 12.365; life, soul, spirit, 4.336; divine air, mien, 5.648. (spīrō).

spīrō, āvī, ātus *1 v* to breathe, blow, 5.844; palpitate, 4.64; pant; breathe heavily, 7.510; heave, boil, 10.291; of odors, breathe forth, exhale, emit;

with *acc*, 1.404; *part*, spīrāns, antis, lifelike, breathing, 6.847.

spissus, a, um *adj* compact, thick, dense, 2.621; hardened, 5.336.

splendeō, uī 2 *v* to shine, gleam, 7.6.

splendidus, a, um *adj* (splendeō), gleaming, shining, bright, brilliant; splendid, sumptuous, stately, 1.637.

spoliō, āvī, ātus 1 *v* to take the spoils; to strip; despoil, 12.297; plunder, rob, 5.661; *with acc* and *abl*, strip, deprive, despoil of, 5.224 *et al.* (spolium).

spolium, ī, *n* that which is taken from the body of a slain man or beast; spoil, trophy, 1.289; spolia opīma, the arms or spoils taken by a victorious general from the body of a hostile commander slain in battle, 6.855.

sponda, ae *f* the frame of a bedstead or couch; a couch, 1.698.

spondeō, spopondī, spōnsus 2 *v* to promise, pledge, give assurance, 5.18 *et al.*

spōnsa, ae *f* one promised as a bride; the betrothed, 2.345. (spondeō).

sponte *f abl of obs* spōns, of which only the *gen*, spontis, and *abl* occur, by or of one's own will, of their own will, 4.341; of one's self, of itself, of themselves, 6.82; freely, voluntarily, spontaneously; nōn sponte, helplessly, 11.828.

spūma, ae *f* froth, foam, spray, 1.35; *pl* spray, 3.208. (spuō, spit).

spūmeus, a, um *adj* (spūma), foamy, frothy, foaming, 2.419.

spūmō, āvī, ātus 1 *v* to foam, 3.534 *et al.* (spūma).

spūmō, āvī, ātus 1 *v* to foam, 3.534 *et al.* (spūma).

spūmōsus, a, um *adj* (spūma), full of foam; foaming, 6.174.

squāleō, uī 2 *v* to be rough, foul, neglected, waste; *part*, squālēns, entis, foul, filthy, neglected, squalid, 2.277; of armor, scaly, covered with work of scales, embossed, 10.314.

squālor, ōris *m* foulness, roughness, filth, squalor, 6.299. (squāleō).

squāma, ae *f* a scale of fishes, serpents, etc.; of the small plates or scales of armor, 11.488; singular as a collective, scales, 5.88 *et al.*

squāmeus, a, um *adj* (squāma), covered with scales; scaly, 2.218.

stabilis, e *adj* (stō), steadfast, lasting, permanent, 1.73.

stabulō 1 *v* to be in a stall or standing-place; to stay, harbor, dwell, 6.286. (stabulum).

stabulum, ī, *n* stable, stall, 2.499; a shepherd's dwelling, grange, 7.512; den, haunt, 6.179; cattle-camp, 8.207. (stō).

stāgnō, āvī, ātus 1 *v* to be stagnant, to form a standing pool; to overflow, so as to form standing pools or lakes; overflow, 3.698. (stāgnum).

stăgnum, **ī**, *n* a collection of standing water; a pond, pool, lake; sluggish water or stream, 6.323; *pl* stāgna, ōrum, deep waters of the sea, 1.126; waters, 6.330. (stō).

statiō, **ōnis** *f* a standing; place of standing; station, post, 9.183; anchorage, 2.23; resting-place, haunt, 5.128. (stō).

statuō, **statuī**, **statūtus** *3 v* to station, place, set, 1.724; to place at or on the altar; found, build, 1.573; set up, 8.271; restore, stay, 12.506; of the mind, resolve, determine, decide, 11.302. (status).

status, **ūs** *m* a standing; position, state, condition, 7.38. (stō).

stella, **ae** *f* a star, *freq*; a meteor, 2.694.

stellō, *no perf*, **ātus** *1 v* to cover over with stars; to stud with stars; *part*, stellāns, antis, starry, 7.210; *part*, stellātus, a, um, set with stars; *figuratively* glittering, gleaming, 4.261. (stella).

sterilis, **e** *adj* unproductive, unfruitful, 3.141; barren, 6.251.

sternāx, **ācis** *adj* (sternō), throwing flat; throwing the rider; plunging, 12.364.

sternō, **strāvī**, **strātus** *3 v* to spread out, spread, 1.700; stretch on the ground, strike down, slay, 1.190; cast down, prostrate, devastate, 2.306; make level, smooth, calm, 5.763; spread, cover, 8.719;

strew, litter; overthrow, conquer, 6.858; *pass* (in middle sense), sternor, ī, to stretch one's self, lie down, 3.509.

Steropēs, **is** *m* a lightning-forger; a cyclops at the forge of Vulcan, 8.425.

Sthenelus, **ī** *m* 1. Sthenelus, an Argive chief, charioteer of Diomedes, 2.261. 2. A Trojan slain by Turnus, 12.341.

Sthenius, **iī** *m* a Rutulian slain by Pallas, 10.388.

stimulō, **āvī**, **ātus** *1 v* to spur; to rouse, urge, 4.576; infuriate, incite, 4.302. (stimulus).

stimulus, **ī** *m* a prick; spur, *figuratively* 6.101 *et al.*; incentive, sting.

stīpātus, **a**, **um** pressing on, charging together, 10.328; surrounded, 4.544. (stīpō).

stīpes, **itis** *m* a log or post, stem, trunk of a tree, 3.43; club, 7.524.

stīpō, **āvī**, **ātus** *1 v* to tread down, compress; pack together, store up, 1.433; load, *with acc and dat* 3.465; throng around, attend, 4.136.

stirps, **stirpis** *f* the lower part of the trunk together with the roots of plants and trees; the extremity, end; root; trunk, tree, 12.770; *figuratively* origin, descent, lineage, stock, race, 1.626 *et al.*

stō, **stetī**, **status** *1 v* to stand; stand up or erect, 2.774; remain standing, remain, 1.268; rise, 6.554; stand one's ground, fight, 5.414; of blood,

to be stanched, 12.422; stand
complete, be built, 3.110;
stand at anchor, be moored,
3.277.403; to be situated, lie,
3.210; remain firm, persistent,
7.374; to stand out with, be
filled with, 6.300; to be thick
with, 12.408; emphatic for
esse, to be, 6.471 *et al.*; of
the mind, to be fixed, 1.646;
to depend, 2.163; (*impers*),
stat, it is fixed, determined,
resolved, 2.750 *et al.*; stāre
prō, to defend, 8; 653.

stomachus, ī *m* the gullet;
chest, stomach, 9.699.

strāgēs, is *f* a prostrating;
slaughter, havoc, carnage,
6.829 *et al.*; ēdere strāgem, to
make havoc, 9.784. (cf. sternō).

strāmen, inis, *n* something
spread out; a couch,
litter, 11.67. (sternō).

strātum, ī, *n* that which
is spread out; a layer,
cover; bed, couch, 3.513;
pavement, 1.422. (sternō).

strepitus, ūs *m* a noise; an
uproar; din, 6.559; stir, noise
of festivity, 1.725; confused
noise, 1.422. (strepō).

strepō, uī, itus 3 *v* to make a
noise; murmur, 6.709; of
music, resound, 8.2; of arms,
ring, rattle, clash, 10.568.

strīctūra, ae *f* a mass or bar of
hot iron, 8.421. (stringō).

strīdeō 2 *v*, and **strīdō, strīdī,** 3
to produce a grating or shrill
sound; to creak, 1.449; gurgle,
4.689; rustle, 1.397; whiz, roar,
1.102; hiss, 8.420; twang, 5.502.

strīdor, ōris *m* a harsh,
grating, or whizzing sound;
a creaking, whistling, 1.87;
din, clank, rattling, 6.558;
humming, 7.65. (strīdō).

strīdulus, a, um *adj* (strīdō),
hissing, whizzing,
twanging, 12.267.

stringō, strīnxī, strīctus 3 *v* to
draw tight, bind; of a sword,
draw out, draw, 2.334; graze,
touch lightly, go near, 5.163;
trim up, cut, 1.552; *figuratively*
touch the mind, 9.294.

Strophades, um *f* the Strophades,
two small islands in the
Ionian Sea off the coast of
Messenia, where the Harpies
were allowed to remain,
and where Zetes and Calais
turned back from the pursuit
of them. Hence the name,
from στρέφειν, to turn; the
islands of turning, 3.210.

struō, strūxī, strūctus 3 *v* to
place side by side or upon;
to pile up; build, erect, 3.84;
cover, load, 5.54; arrange,
1.704; like instruō, to form or
draw out a line of battle, 9.42;
figuratively to plan, purpose,
intend, 4.271; bring about,
effect, 2.60. (*rel to* sternō).

Strȳmonius, a, um *adj*
(Strȳmon, a river of Thrace),
Strymonian, Thracian, 10.265.

Strȳmonius, iī *m* an Arcadian
follower of Pallas, 10.414.

studium, iī, *n* earnest feeling or
effort; eager or deep anxiety,
12.131; desire, impatience,
4.400; emulous zeal, rival
acclamation, applause, 5.148;

desire, purpose, 2.39; pursuit, study, sympathy, interest, 5.450; delight, 11.739; *abl* studiō, with zeal, earnestly, thoughtfully, 6.681 *et al.* (studeō, to be zealous).

stupefaciō, fēcī, factus 3 *v* to amaze, stupefy, astound, bewilder, 5.643; surprise, 7.119. (stupeō and faciō).

stupeō, uī 2 *v* to be amazed or dazed; to be bewildered, confounded, lost in wonder, 1.495; wonder at, 2.31.

stūppa, ae *f* the coarse part of flax; the calking of a ship; tow, 5.682.

stūppeus, a, um *adj* (stūppa) made of tow or flax; flaxen, 2.236.

Stygius, a, um *adj* (Styx), pertaining to the Styx; of Hades; Stygian, 4.638 *et al.*

Styx, Stygis *f* the Styx, the river of Hades which encompassed the final abode of the dead, 6.439 *et al.* (the hateful).

suādeō, suāsī, suāsus 2 *v* to advise, warn, urge, exhort, 1.357 *et al.*; invite, 2.9; impel, prompt, 11.254; compel, force, 10.367.

sub (*prep* with *abl* and *acc*); (with *abl*), under, (denoting situation); beneath, under, *freq*; at the foot of, 3.5; in the lower part of a thing, in, 1.453; down in, deep in, 1.36; by, close, to, 5.837; (of time), in, 4.560; (of rank or order), just behind, next after, 5.323; close to, in subjection to, subordinate to, under, 9.643;

by reason of, under, 2.83; (with *acc*), denoting tendency, down to, 4.243; down under, into, 4.654; down before, 6.191; near to, 5.327; in the midst of, 12.811; (of approaching the foot of some high object), up to or close to, 2.442; to or towards, 6.541; (of some object situated above or on high), up to, towards, 3.422 *et al.*; of time, just before or after; following after, in reply to, 5.394; coming under, subject to, under, 4.618; sub noctem, at nightfall, 1.662.

subdō, didī, ditus 3 *v* to put under; place or fasten under, 12.675; bury, 7.347.

subdūcō, dūxī, ductus 3 *v* to haul, draw up, 1.573; *with abl* of place, 3.135; (w. *acc* and *dat*), draw, rescue from, 10.81; draw or take away stealthily, withdraw, 6.524; draw from beneath, 3.565.

subeō, iī, itus (p. subiēns, euntis) 4 *v* to go or come under, into, or up to; *alone or with acc* and *prep, or with dat*; without a case, come up, 2.216; go under, bend, stoop down under, 10.522; come after; follow, 2.725; take one's place, 12.471; enter, 1.171; come into or upon the mind, suggest itself, occur, 2.560; *with acc* and *prep*, go, advance towards, 8.359; *with dat* come or go up to, down to, into, 5.203; succeed to, 5.176; come after, follow, 10.371; *with acc* approach, enter, 1.400; go under a burden, bear, with *abl* of instrument, 2.708; go under the yoke, draw, 3.113;

enter the mind of, strike,
occur to, 9.757; approach,
reach, 3.512; approach,
7.22; meet, encounter,
10.798; attack, 9.344.

sūber, eris, *n* the cork tree, 7.742.

subiciō, iēcī, iectus *3 v* to cast,
throw, place or put under,
2.236; *figuratively* to excite,
kindle, 12.66; to subjoin,
utter in reply, answer, 3.314;
part, subiectus, a, um, cast
under, put under, 6.223;
situated under, bowed,
bending, 2.721; put down,
subdued, conquered,
6.853. (sub and iaciō).

subigō, ēgī, āctus *3 v* to drive
under or up; drive, push, force,
drive on, urge, compel, 5.794;
subdue, subject, conquer,
1.266; urge on, exasperate,
12.494. (sub and agō).

subitō *adv* suddenly, 1.88 *et al.*

subitus, a, um having come
up suddenly; unexpected,
sudden, 2.692; suddenly,
3.225. (subeō).

subiungō, iūnxī, iūnctus *3 v* to
join under or to; fasten, 10.157;
figuratively conquer, 8.502.

sublābor, lāpsus sum *3 dep v* to
slip or glide beneath, 7.354;
sink down, decline, ebb, wane,
2.169; pass silently by, 2.686.

sublevō, āvī, ātus *1 v* to lift from
beneath; uplift, raise, 10.831.

subligō, āvī, ātus *1 v* to bind
under; bind, gird on, 8.459;
attach, fasten, 11.11.

sublīme *adv* loftily, aloft,
on high, 10.664.

sublīmis, e *adj* raised up,
elevated, uplifted, 11.602;
aloft; on high, 1.259; through
the air, 1.415; on high, 6.720;
to heaven, 5.255; of lofty soul,
12.788; *adv* sublime, loftily,
aloft, on high, 10.664.

sublūstris, e *adj* (sub
and *cf.* lūx), faintly
gleaming, lurid, 9.373.

subnectō, nexuī, nexus *3 v* to
tie beneath; to bind under,
1.492; bind, fasten, 4.139;
tie or bind up, 10.138.

subnīxus, a, um resting or
seated on, 1.506; sustained,
defended by, 3.402; held up
by or bound under, 4.217.

subolēs, is *f* a shoot;
twig, sprout; offspring,
of men, 4.328.

subrēmigō *1 v* to row lightly,
swim along, 10.227.

subrīdeō, rīsī *2 v* to smile,
1.254; 10.742.

subrigō *3 v* to raise up, erect,
4.183; *cf.* surgō. (sub and regō).

subsidium, iī, *n* that which
remains behind; a reserve;
support; relief, 10.214; aid,
12.733. (sub and *cf.* sedeō).

subsīdō, sēdī, sessus *3 v* to
sit or settle down, 12.492;
to sink down, fall, subside,
5.820; remain, 5.498; subside,
remain below, be lost or
disappear, 12.836; (w. *acc*),
to lie in wait for, remain, or
watch for the spoils of, 11.268.

subsistō, stitī *3 v* to stand
after; halt, stand still,
2.243; wait, remain, 11.506;

tarry, remain behind, 2.739; stop, 12.491; withstand, resist, hold out, 9.806.

subtēmen, inis, *n* that which is woven under or passed under or across the warp in weaving; the cross thread, weft, woof or filling; thread; 3.483. (subtexō).

subter (*prep with acc and abl*), below, beneath, under, 3.695; beneath, 4.182. (sub).

subtexō, texuī, textus *3 v* to weave beneath; to veil or cover from below; cover, veil, 3.582.

subtrahō, trāxī, trāctus *3 v* to draw from beneath; withdraw, 6.465; sweep away, 5.199.

suburgeō *2 v* to push up to, 5.202.

subvectō *1 freq v* to carry up often, carry up, bring up, 11.474; transport, convey, 11.131; carry across, 6.303.

subvehō, vexī, vectus *3 v* to carry up; *passive* ride up, ascend, 11.478; 5.721; sail, float up, 8.58.

subveniō, vēnī, ventus *4 v* to come up to; relieve, succor, 12.406.

subvolvō, volvī, volūtus *3 v* to roll up, 1.424.

succēdō, cessī, cessus *3 v* to go, come up to or under, *with dat or acc and prep*, or without a case, to go up to, visit, 8.507; ascend, 12.235; come up to, advance to, 2.478; approach, 7.214; encounter, 10.847; enter, 1.627; creep under, disappear beneath, 5.93; to descend into the earth, to be buried, 11.103;

take up, take upon one's self, 2.723; go under, be yoked to, 3.541; to follow, 11.481; to turn out well; succeed, come to pass, 11.794. (sub and cēdō).

succendō, cendī, cēnsus *3 v* to set on fire from beneath; *figuratively* inflame, incite, 7.496. (*sub and obs* candō; *cf.* incendō).

successus, ūs *m* a going up, an advance; success, good fortune, 2.386; speed, 12.616. (succēdō).

succidō *3 v* to fall down; sink down, 12.911. (sub and cadō).

succīdō, cīdī, cīsus *3 v* to cut beneath; cut, sever, 9.762. (sub and caedō).

succingō, cīnxī, cīnctus *3 v* to gird beneath; gird up; wrap, 10.634; gird, 1.323. (sub and cingō).

succumbō, cubuī, cubitus *3 v* to fall down; succumb, yield, 4.19. (sub and cubō).

succurrō, currī, cursus *3 v* to run up; run to assist; *with dat* to aid, succor, relieve, help, 1.630; *impers,* succurrit, it comes into the mind, occurs, seems, 2.317. (sub and currō).

Sūcrō, ōnis a Rutulian, 12.505.

sūcus, ī *m* juice.

sudēs, is *f* a stake; a palisade, 11.473.

sūdō, āvī, ātus *1 v* to sweat, *with abl,* 2.582 *et al.*; ooze out, distill.

sūdor, ōris *m* sweat, 2.174. (sūdō).

sūdus, a, um *adj* (se- and udus), dry; *subst* sūdum, ī, *n*, clear weather; clear sky, 8.529.

suēscō, suēvī, suētus 3 *v* to become accustomed, to be wont, used, accustomed, 3.541.

sufferō, sustulī, sublātus, ferre *irreg v* to carry from beneath, bear up, sustain; resist; withstand, 2.492. For the tenses of the perfect stem and participle in the sense of lift up, take away, etc., see tollō. (sub and ferō).

sufficiō, fēcī, fectus 3 *v* to make or produce underneath or within anything; dye; tinge, suffuse, 2.210; raise up, produce; supply, lend, afford, 2.618; to be adequate to, sufficient for; strong enough, able, 5.22. (sub and faciō).

suffundō, fūdī, fūsus 3 *v* to pour from below; pour through; overspread, suffuse, 1.228. (sub and fundō).

suggerō, gessī, gestus 3 *v* to bring or put under or up to; supply, reach, 10.333; place beneath, apply to, 7.463. (sub and gerō).

suī (*gen*), **sibi** (*dat*), **sē** or, emphasized, **sēsē** (*acc* and *abl*) (*reflex pron, sing* and *pl*), of himself, herself, itself, themselves, etc., *freq*; (*abl* with cum), sēcum, with one's self, 4.29.

suī, ōrum *m* one's friends, kinsmen, countrymen, followers, etc., 6.611 *et al.* (suus).

sulcō, āvī, ātus 1 *v* to plow, 5.158. (sulcus).

sulcus, ī *m* a furrow, 6.844; furrow, 1.425; track, train, 2.697.

Sulmō, ōnis *m* a Latin, 9.412.

sulphur, uris, *n* sulphur, 2.698.

sulphureus, a, um *adj* (sulphur), sulphureous, 7.517.

sum, fuī, esse *irreg v* to be, as the copula between subject and predicate, *freq*; to exist, be, 2.325 *et al.*; to pertain, belong to; one has or possesses, 3.433 *et al.*; (*impers*), to be possible, one can, one may, 6.596; (*imperat*), estō, be it so, grant, 4.35; archaic forms, pres, subj., fuam, ās, at, -ant, from fuō, 10.108; imperf. subj., forem, ēs, et, -ent, *inf*, fore, 1.235; rēs est alicui cum aliquō, one has a contest with one, 9.155.

summa, ae *f* the chief thing; chief point, 12.572; the sum and substance; all, the whole, 4.237; summa bellī, the command or direction of the war, 10.70. (f. of summus, sc. rēs).

summergō, mersī, mersus 3 *v* to plunge beneath; submerge, sink, 1.40. (sub and mergō).

summittō, mīsī, missus 3 *v* to send or put under; yield, 4.414; *part*, summissus, a, um, let down; bowing down, kneeling, prostrate, 3.93; submissive, 10.611; humble, 12.807. (sub and mittō).

summoveō, mōvī, mōtus 2 *v* to move from beneath; remove, drive away, 6.316; separate, 7.226. (sub and moveō).

summum, ī, *n* the top. (superus).

sūmō, sūmpsī, sūmptus to take up, 2.518; to take, accept, receive; to exact, take, inflict, 2.576; adopt, select, choose, 4.284; assume, put on. (sub and emō).

suō, suī, sūtus 3 *v* to sew or stitch; fasten, form compactly; *part,* sūtus, a, um; *part subst* sūtum, ī, *n,* texture, plate, or scale of a coat of mail, 10.313.

super (*prep with acc and abl*); (with *acc*), over, above, 1.379; beyond, 6.794; upon, on, 1.295.680; besides; super ūsque, even beyond, beyond, 11.317; (with *abl*), upon, 1.700; over (him or his body), 5.482; about, of, concerning, 1.750 *et al.*; for, for the sake of, 4.233 *et al.*

super *adv* above, 4.684 *et al.*; above, from above, 10.384; moreover, 4.606; besides, 1.29; more than enough, 2.642; remaining, surviving, left (with ellipsis of esse), 3.489 *et al.*; still (or above), 4.684; of time, in, during, 9.61.

superbia, ae. *f* haughtiness, pride, arrogance, audacity, insolence, 1.529. (superbus).

superbus, a, um *adj* (super), overbearing, haughty, proud, insolent, fierce, 1.523; superior, mighty, 1.21; audacious, 12.326; hard, cruel, 12.877; stately, superb, magnificent, splendid, 1.639.

superēmineō 2 *v* to rise above, tower above, 1.501.

superī, ōrum *m* those of the upper world, the living as opposed to the dead, 6.481; the gods above, or gods of Olympus as opposed to the infernal gods, 1.4.2.302 *et al.*

superiaciō, iēcī, iectus 3 *v* to throw above or over; overcast, overtop, 11.625.

superimmineō, 2 to overhang, press upon, 12.306.

superincumbo, -ere lay or cast oneself upon.

superīnfundō, *no perf,* **fūsus,** 3 *v* to pour out upon (by tmesis), 6.254.

supernē *adv* from above, out above, above, 6.658. (supernus).

superō, āvī, ātus 1 *v* surmount; go over, 6.676; rise above, 2.219; pass by or beyond, 1.244; make one's way through, 8.95; overpower, slay, 1.350; overcome, conquer, 2.311; prevail, 5.22; surmount, 3.368; remain, survive, be still living, 3.339; be left; remain, 12.873; be proud, elated, rejoice, 5.473; superāre ascēnsū, to mount, ascend, 2.303. (super).

superstes, itis *adj* (superstō), remaining over, surviving, 11.160.

superstitiō, ōnis *f* religious awe; superstition, 8.187; sacred oath, fear-inspiring oath, 12.817. (superstō).

superstō, *no perf nor sup* 1 *v* to stand over, 10.540.

supersum, fuī, esse, *irreg, n*
to be over; to be left, remain
(separated by tmesis),
2.567; survive, 8.399.

superus, a, um *adj* (super),
above, upper, supreme,
3.20; of the upper world
as opposed to Hades, 2.91;
10.40; superae sēdēs, the sky,
Olympus, 11.532; supera, the
upper world, 7.562; the sky,
heaven, 6.787; *subst* superī,
ōrum, *m*, those of the upper
world, the living as opposed
to the dead, 6.481; the gods
above, or gods of Olympus as
opposed to the infernal gods,
1.4; *superl*, suprēmus, a, um,
the highest; most exalted,
10.350; illustrious, 7.220;
extreme, 3.590; last, final,
2.11; *subst* suprēmum, ī, *n*, the
end, 12.803; *pl* suprēma, ōrum,
the last honors, rites, 6.213;
adv suprēmum, for the last
time, 3.68; *superl*, summus, a,
um, the uppermost, topmost,
highest, 2.463; situated on a
height; high, 2.166; the highest
part of, summit of, top of, 2.302
et al.; surface of, 5.819 *et al.*;
main, chief, 1.342; utmost,
greatest, 5.197; supreme, 1.665;
most important, 9.227; latest,
last, 2.324 *et al.*; summa rēs,
the chief or common interest,
common weal, 11.302; the
chief conflict, 2.322; *subst*
summum, ī, *n*, the top.

superveniō, vēnī, ventus 4
v to come over or upon;
come unexpectedly;
fall upon, 12.356.

supervolō, āvī, ātus 1 *v* to fly
over or above, 10.522.

supīnus, a, um *adj* (sub), on
the back; bent backward;
of the hands bent back in
supplication, suppliant, 3.176.

suppleō, plēvī, plētus 2 *v* to
fill up; to supply, furnish,
3.471. (sub and pleō, fill).

supplex, icis *adj* (supplicō,
beseech), kneeling,
entreating, suppliant,
3.439; *subst* supplex, icis,
c, a suppliant, 2.542.

supplex, icis, *c* a suppliant,
2.542. (supplicō, beseech).

suppliciter *adv* in a suppliant
manner; suppliantly; as a
suppliant or suppliants,
1.481. (supplex).

supplicium, iī, *n* a kneeling to
receive blows; punishment,
4.383; penalty, 6.740; hurt,
wound, 6.499. (supplex).

suppōnō, posuī, positus 3 *v* to
put, place under, 6.24; put
to the throat, thrust under,
6.248. (sub and pōnō).

suprā (*prep with acc* and *adv*),
over, 3.194; above, 12.839;
upon, 9.553; after its case,
4.240; *adv* above, 7.32.

suprēmum *adv* for the last
time, 3.68. (superus).

suprēmum, ī, *n* the end, 12.803;
pl suprēma, ōrum, the last
honors, rites, 6.213. (superus).

sūra, ae *f* the calf of the
leg; the leg, 1.337.

surgō, surrēxī, surrēctus 3 *v* to
raise, prick up, 4.183; rise,
spring up, arise, 3.513 *et al.*;
as an enemy, 10.28; to swell,

9.30; to tower up, 10.725; increase, grow, rise, 4.274; impend, threaten, 4.43. *cf.* subrigō. (sub and regō).

sūs, suis, *c* a hog, swine, 1.635; sow, 3.390.

suscipiō, cēpī (succēpī, 1.175), **ceptus** 3 *v* to take up, 4.391; receive, catch, 1.175; conceive, beget, 4.327; undertake, 6.629; reply, 6.723; to take up the new-born child; *passive* to be born, 4.327. (sub and capiō).

suscitō, āvī, ātus 1 *v* to stir up, turn up; to rekindle, 5.743; rouse, incite, 2.618; call forth, 8.455.

suspectus, a, um suspected, conjectured, guessed at; in suspicion, suspicious, mistrusted, 2.36; causing suspicion, fear, apprehension; distrusted, 3.550. (suspiciō).

suspectus, ūs *m* a looking up; upward views; distance upward, height, 6.579; elevation, 9.530. (suspiciō).

suspendō, pendī, pēnsus 3 *v* to hang up, 6.859; hang, 1.318; *part,* suspēnsus, a, um, suspended, scarcely touching the ground or water, 7.810; hanging, 8.190; as *adj,* in suspense, uncertain, doubtful, in doubt, 6.722; anxious, 2.729; filled with awe, 3.372.

suspēnsus, a, um in suspense, uncertain, wavering, in doubt, 6.722; anxious, 2.729; filled with awe, 3.372.

suspiciō, spexī, spectus 3 *v* to look up to, 6.668; behold, see; look upon with wonder; admire; survey, 1.438. (sub and speciō, look).

suspīrō, āvī, ātus 1 *v* to breathe from beneath or deeply; to sigh, 1.371.

sustentō, āvī, ātus 1 *intens v* to uphold; hold up, support, sustain, 10.339; poise, 10.304; second, support, 11.224; maintain, 12.662; bear up against, withstand, 11.873. (sustineō).

sustineō, tinuī, tentus 2 *v* to hold up; sustain, bear, 7.786; hold up, poise, 12.726; hold, wave, 7.398; check, withstand, 10.799; keep off, 11.750; repel, 9.708; maintain, support. (sub and teneō).

sūtilis, e *adj* (suō), stitched together, sewed; made of stitched hides or skins, 6.414.

suus, a, um his, her, its, their; his own, etc., 6.641 *et al.*; proper, appropriate, peculiar; fitting, 5.54; favorable, friendly, propitious, 5.832; emphatic for ēius, 4.633. (suī).

Sybaris, is *m* a Trojan warrior, 12.363.

syrtis, is *f* a sand-bank or shoal in the sea; esp., Syrtis Maior and Syrtis Minor, on the northern coast of Africa, 4.41; a sand-bank, shoal, 1.111.

Sychaeus, a, um *adj* (Sychaeus), pertaining to Sychaeus, of Sychaeus, 4.552.

Sychaeus, ī *m* a Tyrian prince, the husband of Dido, 1.343 *et al.*

Sȳmaethius, a, um *adj* (Sȳmaethum), of Symaethum, a river and town on the eastern coast of Sicily; Symaethian, 9.584.

tābeō *2 v* to melt; drip, be drenched, 1.173; to waste away, be wan, 12.221.

tābēs, is *f* a melting, wasting away; repining, woe, grief, 6.442. (tābeō)

tābidus, a, um *adj* (tābeō), melting away; wasting, consuming, 3.137.

tabula, ae *f* a board, plank, 1.119.

tabulātum, ī, *n* a planking; floor, platform, story, 2.464. (tabula).

tābum, ī, *n* corrupt matter; putrid blood; gore, 3.29. (tābeō).

Taburnus, ī *m* a ridge of the Apennines south of Caudium, 12.715.

taceō, uī, itus *3 v* to be silent, not to speak, 2.94; to be still, quiet, hushed, 4.525; leave unmentioned; *part,* tacēns, entis, noiseless, silent, 6.265.

tacitus, a, um passed over in silence, unmentioned, 6.841; unobserved, 2.568; unexpressed, secret, hidden, 4.67; silent, in silence, 2.125; silent, speechless, 4.364; still, noiseless, 6.386; calm, 1.502; quiet, solitary, in the night, 7.343; per tacitum, in silence, quietly, 9.31. (taceō).

tāctus, ūs *m* a touching; touch, 2.683. (tangō).

taeda, ae *f* pitch-pine, 4.505; a brand, 7.71; torch, nuptial torch, 4.18; marriage, 4.339.

taedet, taeduit or **taesum est** *2 impers v* it irks, wearies, disgusts me, thee, etc.; I (thou, he, etc.) am wearied, tired, 4.451.

taenia, ae *f* a band, fillet; hairband; ribbon, braid, forming the ends of the vitta, 5.269.

taeter, tra, trum *adj* disagreeable; foul, loathsome, 3.228.

Tagus, ī *m* a Rutulian, 9.418.

tālāria, ium, *n* sandals; winged sandals, 4.239. (tālus, ankle).

talentum, ī, *n* a monetary weight or sum, varying in different periods and countries, but around 60-70 lb., usually gold or silver; a large sum, weight, or amount, 5.112 *et al.*

tālis, e *adj* such, in kind or nature; correlative to quālis, such, 1.503; such, of such sort or kind, 1.74; without quālis, such as has been said, 1.50; such as follows; this, 1.131; so distinguished, so great, 1.335; so critical, 11.303; introducing a comparison, 9.710.

Talos, ī *m* a Rutulian, 12.513.

tam correlative to quam, so much, by so much, 7.787; without quam, so as, so much, in such a manner, to such a degree, *freq.*

tamen *conj,* however, notwithstanding, nevertheless, still, yet.

Tanais, is *m* a Rutulian, 12.513.

tandem *adv* at length, at last, finally, 2.76 *et al.*; pray then, now, 1.369. (tam).

tangō, tetigī, tāctus 3 *v* to touch, 3.324 *et al.*; of lightning, strike, blast; of touching a shore, reach, enter, arrive at, 4.612; *figuratively* affect, move, 1.462; encounter, experience, 4.551; overtake, come home to, 4.596.

tantō by so much, so much, 6.79. (tantus).

tantum *adv* so much, 6.877; just so much; only, 2.23; in tantum, to such a degree or height, so high, 6.876; tantum — quantum, so great (such, so much) — as.

tantus, a, um *adj* so great, such, regularly *followed by* quantus; *alone* 1.606 *et al.*; explanatory, so great, such, 1.33 *et al.*; *followed by* quam, so great as, 6.352 *et al.*; in tantum, to such a degree or height, so high, 6.876; tantum — quantum, so great (such, so much) — as.

tapēte, is, *n* and **tapēs, ētis** (*acc pl* **tapētas**) *m* a coverlet; tapestry, hanging; a carpet, 9.358; *abl pl* tapētis (perhaps from tapētum, ī), with housings, 7.277.

Tarchō, ōnis or **ontis** *m* an Etrurian prince, ally of Aeneas, 11.727 *et al.*

tardō, āvī, ātus 1 *v* to render slow; hinder, cripple, delay, 5.453; impede, enfeeble, 6.731; hold back, detain, retard, 11.21. (tardus).

tardus, a, um *adj* slow, sluggish, tardy, 5.154; backward, lingering, coming on late, 1.746; sluggish, gross, carnal, 6.720.

Tarentum, ī, *n* Tarentum, a city of Greek origin on the coast of lower Italy, 3.551.

Tarpēia (*trisyll*), **ae** *f* a follower of Camilla, 11.656.

Tarpēius (*trisyll*), **a, um** *adj* pertaining to the Tarpeian rock or precipitous part of the Capitoline Hill at Rome; Tarpeian, 8.347.

Tarquinius, a, um *adj* Tarquinian; the designation of the Roman gens to which belonged Tarquinius Priscus and Tarquinius Superbus, 6.817; *subst* Tarquinius, iī, Tarquinius or Tarquin, 8.646.

Tarquitus, ī *m* a Rutulian slain by Aeneas, 10.550.

Tartareus, a, um *adj* (Tartarus), pertaining to Tartarus; Tartarean, 6.551; in a general sense, infernal, Tartarean, 6.295.

Tartarus, ī, *m, pl* **Tartara, ōrum,** *n* the lower world, Hades; especially that portion which was set apart for the wicked; Tartarus, 5.734 *et al.*

Tatius, iī *m* Titus Tatius, a Sabine king, at first hostile to Romulus, but at last joint king with him over Romans and Sabines, 8.638.

taureus, a, um *adj* (taurus), of bulls; bull's-, 9.706.

taurīnus, a, um *adj* (taurus), of a bull or bull's, 1.368.

taurus, ī *m* a bull, steer, ox, bullock, 2.202 *et al.*

tēctum, ī, *n* a covering; roof, 2.302; a house, 1.425; building, 3.134; 6.29; palace, 1.632; habitation, dwelling, abode, 6.211; shelter, haunt, covert, 6.8; battlement, 9.558. (tegō).

Tegeaeus, a, um *adj* (Tegea), of Tegea, a town in Arcadia; Tegean, Arcadian, 5.299.

tegmen (tegumen), inis, *n* a means of covering; skin, hide, 1.275; clothing, 3.594; shield, 9.577; tegmen crūrum, close-fitting trousers worn by Phrygians, 11.777. (tegō).

tegō, tēxī, tēctus 3 *v* to cover, 3.25 *et al.*; cover in the funeral urn, inclose, 6.228; surround, encompass, 11.12; protect, defend, shield, 2.430; shelter, 3.583; hide, conceal, 3.236; shut up, 2.126; overshadow, 8.95.

tēla, ae *f* a web; the long thread of a woven fabric; the warp; web, 4.264. (texō).

Tēleboae, ārum (um) *m* a people of Acarnania, a part of whom migrated to the island of Capreae in the Bay of Naples, 7.735.

tellūs, ūris *f* the earth, 6.140; ground, soil, earth, 1.358; land, 1.171; a land (of an island), 1.34; a country, territory, state, kingdom, 11.245; personified, Tellūs, the goddess Tellus or Earth, 4.166.

Telōn, ōnis *m* king of the Teleboans in the island of Capreae, 7.734.

tēlum, ī, *n* a missile weapon, *freq*, 1.665; a bolt, 1.665; shaft, arrow, 1.191; spear, lance, javelin, 1.99; weapon, 2.447; point, 12.387; blow or caestus, 5.438.

temerē *adv* by chance; promiscuously, 9.329; in vain, 9.375.

temerō, āvī, ātus 1 *v* to treat recklessly; outrage; desecrate, defile, profane, 6.840.

temnō 3 *v* to despise, disdain, scorn, defy, 1.665; *part*, temnendus, a, um, to be despised; insignificant, small, 10.737.

tēmō, ōnis *m* the tongue or pole of a plow or cart; wagon, chariot, 12.470.

temperō, āvī, ātus 1 *v* to attemper; combine in due proportions; *with acc* regulate, adjust; refresh; allay, moderate, calm, 1.146; restrain, 1.57; with *abl* or *dat*, abstain from, 2.8. (tempus).

tempestās, ātis *f* a portion of time; a season; weather; flashing light; radiance, 9.20; a storm, tempest, 1.53; cloud, tempest of missiles, 12.284; storm of war, 7.223; calamity, 11.423; cloud, *personif*, Tempestātēs, um, demons of storms, storms, 5.772. (tempus).

templum, ī, *n* a portion of the heavens marked out or cut off for auguries; a place set apart as holy; holy ground; a shrine, fane, chapel, temple, 1.416 *et al.*(cf. τέμνω, cut off).

temptāmentum, ī, *n* a trial; essay; experiment; approach, 8.144. (temptō).

temptō, āvī, ātus *1 freq v* to hold much; handle, feel; make trial in any way; examine, investigate, search out, test, sound, explore, 2.38; seek for, attempt to find, seek, 3.146; seek to win the mind, approach, conciliate, gain, 4.113; attempt, try, essay, 2.334; assail, attack, 11.350; stir up, provoke, 10.87. (teneō).

tempus, oris, *n* 1. Time in general, a period, time, 1.278; interval or space of time, 4.433; crisis, circumstance, juncture, 7.37; season, fitting time, opportunity, proper moment, 4.294; ex longō (tempore), in or for a long time, 9.64. 2. The temple of the forehead, 9.418; commonly *pl* 2.684; of animals, 12.173.

tenāx, ācis *adj* (teneō), holding on or fast; tenacious; adhering to, persistent in, *with gen,* 4.188.

tendō, tetendī, tentus or **tēnsus** *3 v* to stretch; stretch forth or out, 6.314; strain, lift, raise, 2.405; hold, reach out or up, 2.674; direct, 1.410; aim, 5.489; strain, bend, 7.164; shoot, 9.606; stretch, fill, 3.268; *n,* reach, extend, descend, 4.446; hold, direct one's course, go to, proceed, 5.286 *et al.*; advance, 12.917; 9.795; hasten, 2.321; make for, advance, 2.205; hold one's flight, fly, 6.198;

make one's way to, visit (ad omitted), 6.696; maintain, keep one's course, 5.21; stretch the tents; encamp, 2.29; tend, lead, 6.541; struggle, endeavor, strive, 5.155; contend, 12.553; design, purpose, intend, 1.18; essay, try to answer, 9.377; quō tenditis, what is your purpose? 5.670.

tenebrae, ārum *f* darkness, 9.425; gloom, 6.238; 2.92; dark abode, 6.545.

tenebrōsus, a, um *adj* (tenebrae), dark, dusky, murky, 5.839.

Tenedos, ī *f* an island in the Aegean about five miles from shore in sight of Troy, 2.21.

teneō, uī, tentus *2 v* to hold, in every sense, *freq*; hold fast, grasp, 2.530; 12.754; cling to, 2.490; keep, hold, 1.482; inhabit, 1.12; gain, reach, 1.400; seize upon, 12.673; hold one's course through, traverse, 7.287; hold, direct one's way, 1.370; retain, 6.235; to have, inherit, 5.121; preserve, maintain, observe, 3.408; govern, rule, 1.236; detain, 1.670; withhold, forbid, 12.819; bind, control, 2.159; fill, possess, 1.132; keep in mind or memory; *n,* have possession, be master, 2.505; prīma tenēre, to take the lead, 10.157; sē tenēre, stand fast, 7.589. (*rel to* tendō).

tener, era, erum *adj* tender, 2.406; young, 11.578; light, delicate, 3.449; thin, 9.699.

tenor, ōris *m* a holding on; a continuous course; course. (teneō).

tentōrium, iī, *n* a tent,
1.469. (tendō).

tenuis, e *adj* (cf. tendō),
stretched out; slender, thin,
4.278; light, 3.448; little, 10.511;
airy, ethereal, 6.292; delicate,
fine, 4.264; scanty, yielding
a scanty livelihood, 8.409;
reduced, perishing, sinking,
5.690; simple, trivial, humble.

tenus (*prep with gen* or *abl*,
placed after its case), as far as;
up to, 2.553; down to, to, 3.427;
to, 1.737; hāc tenus, separated
by tmesis, thus far, 5.603.

tepefaciō, fēcī, factus *3 v*
to make tepid or warm;
passive to reek, 9.333.

tepeō *2 v* to be moderately
warm; to reek, 8.196.

tepēscō, uī *3 inc v* to grow
warm, 9.701. (tepeō).

tepidus, a, um *adj* (tepeō),
lukewarm, tepid; warm, 3.66;
smoking, reeking, 9.455.

ter (*num adv*), thrice, three
times, 1.94 *et al.* (trēs).

terebinthus, ī *f* the turpentine
tree; a kind of ebony, 10.136.

terebrō, āvī, ātus *1 v* to bore
through; pierce, penetrate,
2.38; take out by boring,
bore out, 3.635. (terebra, an
instrument for boring).

teres, etis *adj* (terō), rubbed or
rounded off smooth; tapering,
7.665; polished, 5.313; well
twisted, strong, 11.579.

Tēreus, eī or **eos** *m* a
Trojan, 11.675.

tergeminus, a, um *adj* of
threefold birth; threefold,
having three bodies,
8.202; of three forms or
names; triple, 4.511.

tergeō, tersī, tersus *2 v*,
and **tergō** *3 v* to wipe;
clean, polish, 7.626.

tergum, ī, and **tergus, oris**
(1.211; 9.764), *n* the back of
men or animals, 1.296 *et al.*;
the stern of a ship, 5.168;
skin, hide, 1.211; gauntlet,
hide, 5.403; form, frame,
body, 2.231; carcass, body,
1.635; length, long body,
2.208; a layer, plate, 10.482;
pl terga, ōrum, members,
frame, 6.422; gauntlets, 5.419;
ā tergō, behind, 1.186; in
tergum, to the rear, 11.653;
vertere or dare terga, to run
away, retreat, 6.491; 9.794.

terminō, āvī, ātus *1 v* to
put bounds to; limit,
1.287. (terminus).

terminus, ī *m* a boundary line;
limit, end, destiny, 4.614.

ternī, ae, *v distrib. num adj*
(trēs), three each, 5.247; as a
cardinal, three, 1.266; once in
the *sing* ternō ōrdine, in triple
rank, in three tiers, 5.120.

terō, trīvī, trītus *3 v* to rub;
wear, clash, strike, 5.324;
of time, spend, pass,
9.609; waste, 4.271.

terra, ae *f* the earth; a land,
country, 3.13; land as opposed
to sea or water, 1.598 *et al.*; to
air, sky, 4.184 *et al.*; ground,
1.395; an estate, a farm, 6.811;
pl terrae, ārum, lands, for

the *sing* 6.18; the world, all lands, 4.607; orbis terrārum, the world, the whole earth, 1.233; sub terrās, to the lower world, 4.654; terram petere, to fall upon the ground prostrate in awe and fear, 3.93; in death, 10.489.

terrēnus, a, um *adj* (terra), made of earth; earthen, of earth, 11.850; earthly, earth-born, 6.732.

terreō, uī, itus 2 *v* to frighten, alarm, appall, terrify, *freq*; threaten, seek to terrify, 10.879.

terribilis, e *adj* (terreō), frightful, appalling, terrible, fearful, 6.299 *et al.*

terrificō, āvī, ātus 1 *v* to affright, terrify, 4.210. (terrificus).

terrificus, a, um *adj* (terreō and faciō), causing terror; dread-inspiring, alarming, terrifying, dreadful, dread, 5.524.

territō 1 *freq v* to fill with alarm; affright, alarm, 4.187. (terreō).

terror, ōris *m* fright, fear, dread, alarm, 7.552 *et al.* (terreō).

tertius, a, um (ordin. *num adj*), the third, 1.265 *et al.* (trēs).

tessera, ae *f* a square tablet; a ticket inscribed with the watchword; the watchword or password, 7.637.

testis, is, *c* a witness, 5.789.

testor, ātus sum 1 *dep v* to testify, bear witness to, *with acc* of object witnessed, 3.487; to call to witness, appeal to, *with acc* of witness called upon, 2.155; invoke, 12.496; *with object*

omitted, adjure, implore, 3.599; declare, proclaim, 6.619; beseech (call to witness the offering), 11.559. (testis).

testūdō, inis *f* a tortoise; a vaulted roof, vault, 1.505; a testudo, formed of the shields of soldiers held over their heads, 2.441.

Tetrica, ae *m* a mountain in the Sabine country, 7.713.

Teucer (Teucrus), crī *m* 1. Teucer, first king of Troy, son of the river-god Scamander, and father-in-law of Dardanus, 1.235. 2. Teucer, son of Telamon and Hesione, half-brother of Ajax, and founder of Salamis in Cyprus, 1.619.

Teucrī, ōrum *m* the Trojans, descendants of Teucer, 1.38 *et al.*; *adj*, Teucrian, Trojan, 9.779 *et al.* (Teucer).

Teucria, ae *f* the Trojan land; Troy, 2.26. (Teucer).

Teuthrās, antis *m* an Arcadian follower of Pallas, 10.402.

Teutonicus, a, um *adj* (Teutonī), of the Teutons, Teutonic, Germanic, 7.741.

texō, texuī, textus 3 *v* to weave; to build cunningly; form, fashion, fabricate, construct, 2.186; make intricate movements, interweave, 5.593; *part*, textus, a, um, woven, constructed, made, 5.589.

textilis, e *adj* (texō), woven, embroidered, 3.485.

textum, ī, *n* that which is woven or plaited; a texture, 8.625. (texō).

Thaemōn, ŏnis *m* a Lycian, follower of Aeneas, 10.126.

thalamus, ī *m* a bedchamber; chamber, 2.503; couch, 6.280; marriage, 4.18; bridals, the bride, 7.388; *pl* thalamī, ōrum, nuptials, wedlock, marriage, 6.94.

Thalīa, ae *f* Thalia, an Oceanid or sea-nymph, 5.826.

Thamyrus, ī *m* a Trojan, 12.341.

Thapsus, ī *f* Thapsus, a city and peninsula of the eastern coast of Sicily, 3.689.

Thaumantias, adis *f* the daughter of Thaumas, Iris, 9.5. (Thaumas).

Theānō, ūs *f* the wife of the Trojan Amycus, 10.703.

theātrum, ī, *n* a place for seeing; a theater, 1.427; any place suited for public spectacles; theatrī circus, the curving area of a theater, formed by nature, 5.288.

Thēbae, ārum *f* Thebes, the capital of Boeotia, 4.470.

Thēbānus, a, um *adj* (Thēbē), of Thebe, in Mysia; Theban, 9.697.

Themillās, ae *m* a Trojan, 9.576.

Thermōdōn, ontis *m* a river of Pontus, in the country of the Amazons, 11.659.

Thērōn, ōnis *m* a Latin warrior slain by Aeneas, 10.312.

Thersilochus, ī *m* 1. A Paeonian allied with the Trojans, and slain by Achilles, 6.483. 2. A Trojan.

thēsaurus, ī *m* a treasure, 1.359.

Thēseus (*dissyll*), **eī** or **eos** *m* Theseus, son of Aegeus, and king of Athens, who descended with Peirithous into Hades to aid him in his attempt to carry away Proserpina, 6.121 *et al.*

Thessandrus, ī *m* Thessandrus, a Greek chief, 2.261.

Thetis, idis or **idos** *f* Thetis, daughter of Nereus and Doris, married to Peleus, of Thessaly, by whom she became the mother of Achilles, 5.825.

thiasus, ī *m* a dance in honor of Bacchus; a wild dance, 7.581.

Thoās, antis *m* 1. Thoas, a Greek chief, 2.262. 2. An Arcadian, follower of Pallas, 10.415.

tholus, ī *m* a cupola, dome, the vault of a temple, vaulted shrine, 9.408.

thōrāx, ācis, *acc pl* -ācas *m* a corselet, breastplate, cuirass, 7.633.

Thrāca, ae *f* Thrace, 12.335.

Thrācius, a, um *adj* Thracian, 5.536 *et al.*

Thrāx, ācis *adj* Thracian; *subst pl* Thrāces, um, Thracians, 3.14 *et al.*

Thrēicius, a, um *adj* Thracian, 3.51 *et al.*; Thracian in character, northern, 11.659.

Thrēissus, a, um *adj* Thracian, 1.316 *et al.*; *subst* Thrēissa, a huntress, 11.858.

Thronius, iī *m* a Latin, 10.753.

Thymber, brī *m* a Rutulian, son of Daucus, 10.391.

Thymbraeus, a, um *adj* (Thymbra), of Thymbra, a town in the Troad, in which was a temple of Apollo; hence, Thymbraean, an epithet of Apollo, 3.85.

Thymbraeus, ī *m* a Trojan warrior, 12.458.

Thymbris, idis *m* a Trojan, 10.124.

Thymoetēs, ae *m* a Trojan, 2.32 *et al.*

thymum, ī, *n* the herb thyme, 1.436 *et al.*

thyrsus, ī *m* the stalk of a plant; a staff wreathed with ivy and vine-leaves, and borne by Bacchus and his worshipers; the thyrsus, 7.390.

Thȳbris, idis *m* an ancient king of Latium, 8.330.

Thȳias (*dissyll*), **adis** *f* a female worshiper of Bacchus; a Bacchante, Bacchanal, or Thyiad, 4.302.

tiāra, ae *f,* and **tiārās, ae** *m* a headband or crown worn by the Asiatics; a tiara, 7.247.

Tiberīnus (Thȳbrinus, 12.35), **a, um** *adj* (Tiberis), pertaining to the Tiber; Tiberine, 1.13 *et al.*; *subst* Tiberīnus, *m,* the river-god, Tiber; the Tiber, 6.873.

Tiberis, is (Thȳbris, 2.782 *et al.,* **idis,** *acc* **-brim,** *voc.* **-brī)** the river Tiber.

tībia, ae *f* the larger of the shinbones; a pipe or flute, as this bone was used for a musical pipe.

Tībur, uris, *n* a city on the eastern border of Latium, 7.630.

Tīburs, tis *adj* (Tibur), of Tibur, 9.360; *n pl* Tiburtia, 7.670; *subst* Tīburtēs, um, *m,* the people of Tibur; the Tiburtines, 11.757.

Tīburtus, ī *m* the founder of Tibur, 7.671.

tigris, is or **idis,** *c* a tiger or tigress, 4.367 *et al.*

Tigris, is or **idis** *f* the name of a ship, 10.166.

Timāvus, ī *m* the Timavus, a river at the head of the Adriatic, northwest of Trieste, 1.244 *et al.*

timeō, uī 2 *v* to fear, dread, 1.661 *et al.*; show fear or terror; to tremble, 5.505.

timidus, a, um *adj* (timeō), subject to fear; fearful, cowardly, trembling, timid, 6.263 *et al.*

timor, ōris *m* fear, apprehension, dread, anxiety, 1.202; personified, Fear, 9.719. (timeō).

tingō, tīnxī, tīnctus 3 *v* to wet; moisten, 3.665; wash, dip, bathe, 1.745; imbrue, 12.358.

tinnītus, ūs *m* a jingling, rattling, jingle, clinking, 9.809. (tinniō, jingle).

Tīrynthius, a, um *adj* (Tiryns), of Tiryns, a town in Argolis, where Hercules was brought up; Tirynthian; *subst* Tirynthius, iī, *m,* the Tirynthian; Hercules, 7.662.

Tīsiphonē, ēs *f* one of the three Furies, 6.571 *et al.*

Tītān, ānis *m* a Titan, one of the six sons of Caelus and Terra; any descendant of a Titan; the Sun (son of Hyperion), 4.119.

Tītānius, a, um *adj* (Tītān), Titanian, consisting of Titans, 6.580; of Titanian origin, 6.725.

Tīthōnius, a, um *adj* (Tīthōnus), of Tithonus; Tīthōnia coniūnx, Aurora, 8.384.

Tīthōnus, ī *m* brother of Priam, lover of Aurora, by whom he became father of Memnon, 4.585 *et al.*

titubō, āvī, ātus *1 v* to totter; *part*, titubātus, a, um, made to totter; tottering, unsteady, 5.332.

Tityos, ī *m* a giant, son of Jupiter and Elara, who was slain by Apollo for offering violence to Latona, 6.595.

Tmarius, a, um *adj* (Tmaros), of Tmaros, a mountain in Epirus; Tmarian, 5.620.

Tmarus, ī *m* a Rutulian warrior, 9.685.

togātus, a, um *adj* (toga), wearing the toga; of the toga, 1.282.

tolerābilis, e *adj* (tolerō), that can be borne; endurable, 5.768.

tolerō, āvī, ātus *1 v* to sustain; support, maintain, 8.409; endure, 8.515. (cf. tollō).

tollō, sustulī, sublātus *3 v* to lift up, raise, rear, 1.66 *et al.*; carry, bear, 1.692; bear off, 5.390; remove, 8.175; take or carry away, 3.601; lift, impel, 10.295; remove, take away; end, cause to cease, 12.39; destroy, cut down, 12.771; rouse, excite, 9.127; exalt, praise, extol, 3.158; *part*, sublātus, a, um, lifted up in spirit; haughty, proud, 10.502.

Tolumnius, iī *m* a Latin chief and soothsayer, 11.429 *et al.*

tondeō, totondī, tōnsus *2 v* to shear; finish, 1.702; clip, trim, 5.556; browse, feed upon, graze upon.

tonitrus, ūs *m* thunder, 4.122 *et al.*; thunderbolt, 8.391. (tonō).

tonō, uī *1 v* to thunder, 3.571 *et al.*; of speech, 11.383; (with *acc*) utter, invoke with a loud voice, thunder forth, 4.510.

tōnsa, ae *f* an oar, 7.28.

tormentum, ī, *n* an engine for hurling missiles by means of twisted ropes; a catapult or ballista, 11.616; punishment by the rack, torture, 8.487. (torqueō).

torpeō, uī *2 v* to be numb, torpid; unmoved, 9.499.

torpor, ōris *m* numbness; *figuratively* dread, 12.867. (torpeō).

Torquātus, ī *m* a surname of Titus Manlius, who wore the collar or torques of a Gallic champion whom he had slain in single combat, 6.825. (torquēs, a twisted collar).

torqueō, torsī, tortus *2 v* to wind, turn, twist, 4.575; roll along, 6.551; whirl, hurl, 3.208; shoot, 5.497; cast, dash, 1.108; direct, 4.220; turn away, 6.547; turn, cause to revolve, 4.269; control, 12.180; *part*, tortus, a, um, whirled, whirling, impetuous, 7.567.

torreō, uī, tostus *2 v* to burn, scorch, roast, parch, 1.179; rush, roll, 6.550; of a river bank, 9.105; *part*, torrēns, entis, *subst* a torrent, 7.567.

torris, is *m* a firebrand; brand, 7.506. (torreō).

tortilis, e *adj* (torqueō), of twisted work, winding, 7.351.

tortus, ūs *m* a twisting, coil, 5.276. (torqueō).

torus, ī *m* a bed, couch, 1.708; seat, 5.388; royal seat, throne, 8.177; bank, 6.674; the swelling part of flesh; a brawny muscle.

torvus, a, um stern, grim, wild; savage, lowering, 3.677; fierce, 6.571; shaggy, 3.636; *adv*, torvum and torva, sternly, wildly, 7.399; 6.467.

tot (*num adj pron, indecl*), so many, 4.182 *et al.*

totidem (*num adj pron, indecl*), just, even so many; as many, 4.183 *et al.*

totiēns (**totiēs**) *num adj* (tot), so many times, so often, 1.407 *et al.*

tōtus, a, um *adj* the whole, total, entire, 1.128 *et al.*; tōtō corpore, with all one's strength, 12.920.

trabālis, e *adj* (trabs, a beam), of beams; like a beam, 12.294.

trabea, ae *f* a toga of purple cloth, or one of white cloth with horizontal purple stripes, worn by Roman dignitaries, and ascribed to the primitive Latin kings, 7.612.

trabs, trabis *f* a beam; timber, 1.552; post, jamb, 1.449; trunk, 6.181; tree, 9.87; ship, 3.191.

trāctābilis, e *adj* (trāctō, handle), that can be handled; indulgent, yielding, flexible, 4.439; nōn trāctābilis, unfavorable, inclement, 4.53.

trāctus, ūs *m* a dragging, drawing, an extending; stretch of space, tract, region of land, sea, or sky, 3.138. (trahō).

trādō, didī, ditus *3 v* to give over; give up, submit, 4.619; intrust, consign, 5.713.

trahō, trāxī, trāctus *3 v* (*inf*, trāxe *for* trāxisse, 5.786) to draw, pull; draw along, drag, 1.477; tear, 9.340; carry, sweep along, away, 2.307; bring, conduct, 6.753; lead, conduct, 2.457; draw, catch, 4.701; draw in, drink, of passion, 4.101; derive, 8.511; draw out; extend, protract, 1.748; spend, 6.537; trahere sorte, draw or assign by lot, distribute, 1.508.

trāiciō, iēcī, iectus *3 v* to throw across, over; pass over, cross, 6.536; pierce, 2.273; transfix, 1.355; *part*, trāiectus, a, um, drawn or passed through, 5.488; transfixed, pierced, 9.419. (trāns and iaciō).

trāmes, itis *m* a crossway; by-path or narrow way; a pass, 11.515; course, line, track, 5.610.

trānō, āvī, ātus *1 v* to swim or sail across, 6.671; fly across or through, 4.245. (trāns and nō).

tranquillus, a, um *adj* calm, still, 2.203; *subst* tranquillum, ī, *n*, a calm; calm weather, 5.127.

trāns (*prep with acc*), across, with verbs of motion, over, beyond, across; through, athwart, 7.65; of rest, on the other side of, beyond, 3.403.

trānsadigō, adēgī, adāctus *3 v* to drive through, thrust, 12.508; of the object which is stabbed, pierce, 12.276.

trānscrībō, scrīpsī, scrīptus *3 v* to transfer by writing; enroll, 5.750; transfer, convey, 7.422.

trānscurrō, currī or **cucurrī, cursus** *3 v* to run across; flash or shoot across, 5.528; traverse, 9.111.

trānseō, iī, itus, īre *irreg v* to go across; go through, pass, 12.926; pass by, 5.326; pass away, 1.266; run over, 5.274; pass through, 9.413.

trānsferō, tulī, lātus, ferre *irreg v* to carry over; transfer, remove, 1.271; give over, 2.327.

trānsfīgō, fīxī, fīxus *3 v* to pierce, transfix, 1.44.

trānsfodiō, fōdī, fossus *3 v* to dig through; run through, transfix, 9.544.

trānsfōrmō, āvī, ātus *1 v* to change the form, transform, 7.416.

trānsiliō, īvī, iī or **uī** *4 v* to leap over; pass over, 10.658; fly through, 12.859. (trāns and saliō).

trānsmittō, mīsī, missus *3 v* to send across; bear or convey across or over, 3.403; give over, 3.329; to cross, pass over, fly over, *with acc* of the space crossed over, 4.154; to make across, of a passage or voyage, 6.313.

trānsportō, āvī, ātus *1 v* to carry across or over, governing the *acc* of the space crossed, 6.328.

trānstrum, ī, *n* a cross-timber; a thwart, transom, or bench for rowers; bench, 3.289. (trāns).

trānsverberō, āvī, ātus *1 v* to beat or strike through; pierce through, 10.484.

trānsversus, a, um across the path or course, 5.19; crosswise.

trecentī, ae, a *num adj* (trēs and centum), three hundred, 10.173 *et al.*

tremebundus, a, um *adj* (tremō), quivering, 10.522.

tremefaciō, fēcī, factus *3 v* to cause to tremble or quake; to shake, 9.106; make to tremble with fear; cause to tremble, 6.803; *part*, tremefactus, a, um, trembling, 2.382; 10.102; quivering, 2.629. (tremō and faciō).

tremendus, a, um to be trembled at; dreadful, fearful, terrible, 2.199. (tremō).

tremēscō *3 v* to begin to tremble; to tremble, quake, 5.694; to tremble at, 3.648. (tremō).

tremō, uī *3 v* to tremble, quake, shake, quiver, 5.198; tremble at, fear, dread, 8.296.

tremor, ōris *m* a trembling; quaking; tremor, a shudder, horror, 2.121. (tremō).

tremulus, a, um tremulous, quivering, 7.395. (tremō).

trepidō, āvī, ātus *1 v* to be in trepidation, alarm or panic, 10.788; to hurry, hasten to and fro or about, 2.685; to hasten (with *inf*), 9.114; to strive nervously, make trembling effort, 12.403. (trepidus).

trepidus, a, um *adj* agitated, uneasy, disturbed, trembling, affrighted, 2.380; excited, tumultuous, 11.300; confused, in disorder, 10.283; alarmed, fearful of, anxious for, *with gen*, 12.589; panic-stricken, 12.583.

trēs, tria, *gen* **trium,** *acc* **trēs** *adj* three, 1.108 *et al.*

tribus, ūs *f* one of three original grand divisions of the Roman people; and retained as the designation of similar bodies of the people when they were multiplied; a (Roman) tribe, 7.708.

tricorpor, oris *adj* (trēs and corpus), three-bodied, 6.289.

tridēns, entis *adj* (trēs and dēns), three-pronged, trident, 5.143; *subst* tridēns, entis, *m*, a triple-pointed spear; trident, 1.138.

trietēricus, a, um *adj* triennial, 4.302.

trifaux, faucis *adj* found only once (trēs and faux), three-throated., three-voiced, triple, 6.417.

trīgintā (*num adj, indecl*), thirty, 1.269.

trilīx, īcis *adj* (trēs and līcium, thread), of three threads or leashes; of three layers of thread; three-ply; triple, 3.467.

Trīnacria, ae *f* the three-cornered land; Sicily, Trinacria, 3.440. (Τρινακρία, with three promontories).

Trīnacrius, a, um *adj* (Trīnacria), Sicilian, 3.384.

triō, ōnis *m* an ox as the breaker of the sod in plowing; the Team or Wain; *pl* Triōnēs, um, *m*, the constellation of the greater and lesser bear, 1.744.

triplex, icis *adj* (trēs and plicō), threefold, triple, 10.784 *et al.*

tripus, odis *m* a three-footed vessel or seat; a tripod, 5.110; the seat of the priestess of Apollo; an oracle, 3.360.

trīstis, e *adj* sad, sorrowful, 1.228 *et al.*; melancholy, woeful, mournful; dismal, gloomy, 4.243 *et al.*; grim, stern, 6.315; dire, 2.337; inauspicious, 11.259; fearful, 3.366; fatal, 5.411.

trisulcus, a, um *adj* (trēs and sulcus), three-furrowed; three-forked, 2.475.

Trītōn, ōnis *m* Triton, a son of Neptune, 1.144; *pl* Trītōnēs, um, *m*, sea-gods of the form of Triton, 5.824.

Trītōnis, idis *f* Pallas or Minerva, so called from Lake Triton near the Lesser Syrtis in Africa, near which, according to an Egyptian fable, she was said to have been born, 2.226. (Trītōn).

Trītōnius, a, um *adj* (Trītōn), pertaining to the lake Triton (see Trītōnis); Tritonian, an epithet of Pallas, 2.615 *et al.*; *subst* Trītōnia, ae, Minerva, Tritonia, 2.171.

triumphō, āvī, ātus *1 v* to have the honor of a triumph; *with acc* of the country over which the triumph is held, to triumph over, conquer, 6.836. (triumphus).

triumphus, ī *m* the grand procession at Rome awarded to a victorious general; a victory, 2.578.

Trivia, ae *f* an epithet of Hecate or Diana, whose images were placed at the forks of roads, 6.13 *et al.* (trivium).

trivium, iī, *n* the intersection of three roads; a road-crossing; a public place, 4.609. (trēs and via).

Trōas, adis or **ados** *f* A Trojan woman, 5.613.

Trōes *m* (subst.), the Trojans, 1.30 *et al.* (Tros, one of the kings of Troy).

Trōia, ae *f* 1. Troy, the capital of the Troad, 2.625 *et al.* 2. A city built by Helenus in Epirus, 3.349. 3. A part of the city of Acesta in Sicily, 5.756. 4. The name of an equestrian game of Roman boys, 5.602.

Trōiānus, a, um *adj* (Trōia), Trojan, 1.19; *subst* Trōiānus, ī, *m*, a Trojan, 1.286; *pl* Trōiānī, ōrum, *m*, the Trojans, 5.688.

Trōilus, ī *m* one of the sons of Priam, 1.474.

Trōiugena, ae, *c* of Trojan descent; Trojan, 3.359; Trōiugenae, ārum, *c*, Trojans, 8.117. (Trōia and *cf.* gignō).

Trōius, a, um *adj* of Troy, Trojan, 1.119.

tropaeum, ī, *n* a memorial of the turning (cf. τρέπειν, to turn) or rout of an enemy; the trunk of a tree on which were hung the arms or spoils of an enemy slain; any memento of victory; a trophy.

Trōs, ōis *m* Trojan, 6.52 *et al.* (Tros, one of the kings of Troy).

trucīdō, āvī, ātus *1 v* to slaughter, kill, slay, 2.494. (trux and caedō).

trudis, is *f* a pole, boathook, pike, 5.208. (trūdō).

trūdō, sī, sus *3 v* to thrust, shove, push, 4.405.

truncus, a, um *adj* (truncus), stripped of its branches, 3.659; mutilated, maimed, mangled, 6.497; broken, shattered, 11.9.

truncus, ī *m* the stem, stock, or trunk of a tree; stem, trunk, 6.207; trunk of the human body, 2.557.

trux, trucis *adj* ferocious, grim, stern, fierce, 10.447.

tū, *pers pron pl* **vōs** you, *freq*; *abl* with cum, tēcum, vōbīscum, with you; vōsmet, yourself, yourselves, 1.207.

tuba, ae *f* a trumpet, 2.313 *et al.*; trumpet-signal, 11.424.

tueor, tuitus or **tūtus sum** 2 *dep v* to look at, gaze upon, behold, regard, 4.451 *et al.*; watch, guard, defend, maintain, protect, 1.564 *et al.*; *part*, tūtus, a, um, secure, safe; in safety, 1.243; sure, 4.373; *subst* tūtum, ī, *n*, safety, place of safety, 1.391; *pl* tūta, ōrum, safe places, safety, security, 11.882; *adv*, tūtō, with safety, safely, without danger, 11.381.

tuī, ōrum *m* your friends, kinsmen, countrymen, descendants, etc., 3.488; *freq* (tuus).

Tulla, ae *f* a follower of Camilla, 11.656.

Tullus, ī *m* Tullus Hostilius, the third king of Rome, 6.814.

tum *adv* then, *freq*; then too; at the same time, moreover, 4.250 *et al.*; referring to a *perf part*, 5.719; answering to, cum, cum — tum, while — at the same time; both — and, not only — but; opposed to nunc, 10.14.

tumeō, uī 2 *v* to swell, 2.381; to be puffed up, boastful, 11.854; *part*, tumēns, entis, swollen, 2.381.

tumidus, a, um *adj* (tumeō), swollen, 1.142; distended, 10.387; elated, 9.596; incensed, angry, 6.407; causing to swell, swelling, 3.357.

tumor, ōris *m* a swelling; of the mind, passion, indignation, resentment, 8.40. (tumeō).

tumultus, ūs *m* commotion; uproar; outcry, 9.397; shouting, cries, 3.99; haste, 11.447; uprising, 6.857. (tumeō).

tumulus, ī *m* a rising ground; a low hill, 9.195; a mound, 2.713; sepulchral mound, sepulcher, tomb, 3.304; 11.103. (tumeō).

tunc *adv* then, at that time; then, thereupon, afterwards, 11.208. (tum-ce).

tundō, tutudī, tūnsus or **tūsus** 3 *v* to beat, pound, bruise, strike, smite, 1.481; lash, 5.125; *figuratively* importune, assail, 4.448.

tunica, ae *f* the under-garment of men and women; vest, tunic, 9.616; cuirass, corselet, 10.314.

turba, ae *f* confusion, uproar, tumult, 5.152; a crowd, throng, 2.580; multitude, 6.305; herd, 1.191; flock, 3.233.

turbidus, a, um *adj* (turbō), confused; mingled, foul, 6.296; dismal, dark, 6.534; whirling, 5.696; of the mind, sad, troubled, 4.353; startled, in alarm, 11.814; furious, 11.742.

turbō, āvī, ātus 1 *v* to stir up, confuse, disturb, 3.449; scatter, 1.395; overthrow, 11.796; agitate, 4.566; perplex, 1.515; enrage, anger, 8.435; madden, 7.767; without obj. *acc*, to make disturbance, uproar, 6.857, et a1.; *reflex*, to be troubled, 6.800. (turba).

turbō, inis *m* a tornado, whirlwind; storm, tempest, 1.442; whirling cloud, 3.573; wind accompanying the lightning; lightning-blast, 1.45;

6.594; whirling or stormy force, 11.284 *et al.*; a whirling top, a child's top, 7.378. (cf. turba).

tūreus, a, um *adj* (tūs), of frankincense, 6.225.

tūricremus, a, um *adj* (tūs and cremō), incense-burning, 4.453.

turma, ae *f* a squadron or troop, properly of Roman cavalry; in general, a troop, squadron, 5.560; host, army, 11.503; in turmās, into or in squadrons, 11.599.

Turnus, ī *m* the chief of the Rutulians, 7.56 *et al.*

turpis, e *adj* unsightly, unseemly, *freq*; squalid, 6.276; foul; besmeared, covered, 5.358; shameful, base, dishonorable, disgraceful, 2.400.

turpō, āvī, ātus *1 v* to make indecent; to soil, disfigure, defile, 12.611. (turpis).

turriger, gera, gerum *adj* (turris and gerō), turret-bearing, tower-crowned, 7.631; 10.253.

turris, is *f* a tower, 2.445 *et al.*

turrītus, a, um *adj* (turris), turreted, 8.693; crowned with turrets; with crown of towers, 6.785; tower-like, towering, lofty, 3.536.

tūs, tūris, *n* incense, 1.417 *et al.*

Tuscī, ōrum *m* the people of Etruria; Etruscans, Etrurians, Tuscans, 11.629 *et al.*

Tuscus, a, um *adj* Etrurian, Tuscan.

tūtāmen, inis, *n* a means of protection; a defense, 5.262. (tūtor).

tūtor, āvī, ātus sum *1 dep intens v* to protect, defend, 2.677; befriend, 5.343. (tueor).

tūtum, ī, *n* safety, place of safety, 1.391; *pl* tūta, ōrum, safe places, safety, security, 11.882.

tūtus, a, um secure, safe; in safety, 1.243; sure, 4.373; *adv* tūtō, with safety, safely, without danger, 11.381. (tueor).

tuus, a, um your, yours. (tū).

tympanum, ī, *n* a drum, timbrel, tambourine, 9.619.

Tyndaris, idis *f* a daughter of Tyndarus; Helen, 2.569.

Typhōeus (*trisyll*), **eī** or **eos** *m* Typhoeus or Typhon, a giant struck down to Hades by the thunderbolt of Jupiter.

Typhōeus, a, um *adj* (Typhōeus), pertaining to the giant Typhoeus; Typhoian, 1.665.

tyrannus, ī *m* a sovereign prince, chief, ruler, 4.320; in a bad sense, a despot, tyrant, 1.361.

Tyrēs, ae *m* an Arcadian follower of Pallas, 10.403.

Tyrius, a, um *adj* (Tyrus), of Tyre; Tyrian or Phoenician, 1.12; *subst* Tyrius, iī, *m*, a Tyrian, 1.574; *pl* 1.747.

Tyros (**Tyrus**), **ī** *f* Tyre, the ancient maritime capital of Phoenicia, 1.346.

Tyrrhēnī, ōrum *m* the Tyrrheni, a branch of the Pelasgic race who are said

to have settled in Etruria;
Etrurians, Tuscans, 8.603.

Tyrrhēnus, a, um *adj* (Tyrrhēnī),
Tyrrhenian; Etruscan,
Tuscan, 1.67; *subst* Tyrrhēnus,
ī, *m*, a Tuscan, 10.787.

Tyrrhēnus, ī *m* the name of an
Etruscan ally of Aeneas, 11.612.

Tyrrheus (*dissyll*), **eī**, *m*, and
Tyrrhus, ī *m* a shepherd
of Latium, in the service
of Latinus, 7.532 *et al.*

Tyrrhīdae, ārum *m* the sons of
Tyrrheus, 7.484. (Tyrrheus).

Tȳdeus (*dissyll*), **eī** or **eos** *m* son
of Oeneus and Periboea, and
father of Diomed, 6.479.

Tȳdīdēs, ae *m* the son of Tydeus,
Diomedes or Diomed, 1.97 *et al.*

ūber, eris *adj* fruitful, fertile,
3.106. (compar., ūberior;
superl, ūberrimus), (ūber).

ūber, eris, *n* a teat, an udder,
3.392; the breast, 5.285;
breast, bosom, 3.95; *metonym*
richness, fertility, fruitfulness,
productiveness, 1.531.

ubī (*adv* of place and time;
relat), where; (indefinite),
wheresoever, 7.400; (*interrog*),
where, 3.312 *et al.*; (of time),
when; whenever, 4.143
et al.; as soon as, 1.81; in
comparison, 2.471; 7.719 *et al.*

ubīque (*adv* of place),
wheresoever; anywhere,
1.601; everywhere, 2.368.

Ūcalegōn, ontis *m* a Trojan;
metonym the house of
Ucalegon, 2.312.

ūdus, a, um *adj* (ūvidus,
moist), wet, moist, 5.357.

Ūfēns, entis *m* 1. A river of
Latium flowing into the sea
west of Terracina, 7.802. 2. A
chief of the Aequi, 7.745 *et al.*

ulcīscor, ultus sum 3
dep v to take revenge
for, to avenge, 2.576.

Ulixēs, is, eī or **ī** *m* Ulysses, son
of Laertes, king of Ithaca, and
one of the Greek chiefs at Troy,
distinguished for shrewdness
and cunning, 2.44 *et al.*

ūllus, a, um (*gen* ūllīus, *dat*
ūllī) *adj* any, any one,
in clauses expressing or
implying a negative; (*subst*
m), any one, any, 1.440 *et al.*
(for ūnulus from ūnus).

ulmus, ī *f* an elm tree, elm, 6.283.

ulterior, ius *adj* that is
beyond; farther, 6.314; *adv*
ulterius, farther, 12.806;
superl, ultimus, a, um.

ultima, ōrum the end, goal,
5.317; the last, the final hour;
the end, 2.446. (ulterior).

ultimus, a, um (of space), the
farthest, uttermost; remotest,
utmost, 4.481; (of time), the
last, 2.248; the remotest, 7.49;
(of order), the last, 5.347;
(of quality), worst, most
humiliating, most degrading,
4.537. (*superl* of ulterior).

ultor, ōris *m* an avenger,
2.96; translated adjectively,
avenging, 6.818. (ulcīscor).

ultrā (*prep with acc*),
beyond, 6.114; *adv* longer,
beyond, farther, 3.480.

ultrīx, īcis *adj* (ulcīscor), avenging, 2.587.

ultrō *adv* to the farther side; furthermore, over and above, moreover, 2.145 *et al.*; even, 9.127; beyond the limit of necessity; uncompelled, unasked, unimpelled; apart from all external influences, of one's self, of one's own accord or motion, voluntarily, willingly; unprompted by any words on another's part, first, 2.372; 4.304; unaddressed, 10.606; promptly, 10.282; impetuously, 12.3. (cf. ulterior).

ululātus, ūs *m* a yelling, howling, 7.395; wailing, shrieking, 4.667. (ululō).

ululō, āvī, ātus *1 v* to howl, 6.257; wail, shriek, 4.168; to utter wild cries of triumph, 11.662; shriek the name of; invoke with cries, 4.609.

ulva, ae *f* water-grass, sedge, 2.135.

Umber, bra, brum *adj* Umbrian; *subst* Umber, brī, *m*, an Umbrian dog or hound, 12.753.

umbō, ōnis *m* the boss of a shield, 2.546; a shield, 7.633.

umbra, ae *f* shade, shadow, 1.165 *et al.*; darkness, night, 2.693 *et al.*; a shade of doubt, 12.669; the shade of the dead, *freq*; a ghost, 4.386; a phantom, 10.636; *pl* umbrae, ārum, the Manes, shades, 3.638; *freq*; sub umbrās, to the abode of the dead, 4.660.

umbrifer, era, erum *adj* (umbra and ferō), shady, 6.473.

umbrō, āvī, ātus *1 v* to shade, 6.772; *passive* to be thrown into shadow; to be darkened, grow dark, 3.508. (umbra).

Umbrō, ōnis *m* a soothsayer of the Marsi, 7.752.

umbrōsus, a, um *adj* (umbra), shady; dark, shadowy, 8.242.

ūmectō, āvī, ātus *1 v* to moisten, bedew, bathe, 1.465.

ūmeō *2 v* to be moist; *part*, ūmēns, entis, wet, dewy, humid, 7.763. (ūmor).

umerus, ī *m* the upper bone of the arm; the shoulder, 1.501, and *freq*.

ūmidus, a, um *adj* (ūmeō), moist, wet, damp, dewy, 2.8 *et al.*; liquid, 4.486.

umquam *adv* even at any time, ever, 6.770; at all, 12.649.

ūnā *adv* in one place or at one time, together with, at once, at the same time, 3.634 *et al.*; with -que following, 11.864.

ūnanimus, a, um *adj* (ūnus and animus), of one mind or heart; sympathizing, loving, 4.8; with one heart, 12.264.

uncus, a, um *adj* hooked, crooked, 1.169; talon-shaped, hooked, 3.217.

unda, ae *f* a wave, billow, 1.161; *freq*; the sea, 3.202; water, river, stream, 9.22.

unde *adv* whence, of place; *relat*, 2.458; *interrog*, from what place, point, or quarter; of other relations, from which event, 1.6; on which account, 6.242; from whom, 5.123.

undique *adv* from or on every side or all sides; all around, everywhere, 3.193 *et al.* (unde and -que).

undō, āvī, ātus *1 v* to rise in waves; of flame, smoke, dust, etc., surge, 2.609; overflow, stream forth, burst forth, gush, 10.908; boil, seethe, 6.218; of lines or reins, hang free, flow, 5.146. (unda).

undōsus, a, um *adj* (unda), billowy, stormy, 4.313; sea-washed, 3.693.

unguis, is *m* a finger-nail, 4.673; talon, 12.255; claw, 5.352; in unguem, (polished) to the nail.

ungula, ae *f* a hoof, 8.596. (unguis).

unguō (ungō), ūnxī, ūnctus *3 v* to anoint, cover with oil, 6.219; envenom, 9.773; *part*, ūnctus, a, um, oiled over, oiled; of the bottoms of ships, covered with pitch, pitchy, 4.398.

ūnus, a, um (*gen* ūnīus, *dat* ūnī) (*num adj*), one, 2.527 *et al.*; one alone, a single one (*emphatically*), 1.47; only, alone, 9.544; one in particular, 5.704; with a comparative, 1.15; with a *superl*, 2.426; with ante aliōs, 3.321; common, 5.308; one and the same, at once, 10.871; *pl* one, 2.642; ad ūnum, to a man, without exception, utterly, 5.687; in ūnum, in one, together, 12.714; *adv* ūnā, in one place or at one time, together with, at once, at the same time, 3.634 *et al.*; with -que following, 11.864.

urbs, urbis *f* a city, especially a walled city, 1.12 *et al.*

urgeō, ursī *2 v* to drive, impel, press forward, 1.111; ply, hasten, 9.489; press, oppress, crush, bear down, 3.579; press around, inclose, surround, hem in, 11.524; weigh upon, oppress, close, 10.745; overpower, 2.653; attack, 10.375; punish, torture, 6.561.

urna, ae *f* a water-vessel, an urn, 7.792; an urn for casting lots, 6.22; of judges, 6.432.

ūrō, ussī, ūstus *3 v* to burn; burn up, 2.37; inflame with love, 4.68; trouble, disturb, torment, 1.662.

ursa, ae *f* a she-bear; a bear, 5.37. (ursus).

ursus, ī *m* a bear.

ūsquam *adv* anywhere, 1.604; by any means, at all, 8.568.

ūsque *adv* all the way; all along; continuously, constantly, 2.628; quō ūsque, how long, 5.384; ūsque adeō, so far, so much, to such a degree, so, 12.646; ūsque ad or adūsque, quite to, 11.262; ab ūsque, even from, 7.289; super ūsque, even beyond, 11.317; ūsque dum, even while, as long as, 10.321.

ūsus, ūs *m* a using; use, usage, employment, purpose, 4.647; experience, practice, communication, 2.453; profit, use, advantage, foll. by *abl*, use for, need of, necessity of, 8.441. (ūtor).

ut (**utī**) (*conj*, denoting result), so that, 6.553 *et al.*; purpose;

in order that, that, 1.685
et al.; with subj. for *inf*
and *acc*, that, 11.269.

ut (**utī**) (*relat adv* of manner),
as, just as, *freq*; in oaths, so
truly as, 12.206; of time, as
soon as, when, 8.1 *et al.*; ut
prīmum, as soon as, 1.306.

ut (**utī**) (*adv*, *interrog*), in
what manner, how? 1.466
et al.; sometimes with indic.
in a dependent question,
6.855; how gladly, 8.154.

utcumque *adv* in whatever way,
however, howsoever, 6.822.

uterque, utraque, utrumque
each (of two); both, 2.214;
subst utrumque, *n*, each,
either thing or alternative,
2.61; *adv* utrōque, to or on both
sides; on either side, 5.469.

uterus, ī *m* the womb, belly,
11.813; cavity, 2.38.

utinam (*interj*), O that! would
that! with subj., 1.575.

ūtor, ūsus sum 3 *dep v* to use,
foll. by the *abl*; employ,
show, display, 5.192; address,
1.64; experience, enjoy,
prove, meet with, 6.546.

utrimque *adv* on or from either
side; on both sides; on every
side, 7.566. (uterque).

uxōrius, a, um *adj* (uxor, wife),
pertaining to a wife; enslaved
to one's wife, uxorious,
slave of a wife, 4.266.

vacca, ae *f* cow, 6.251; heifer, 4.61.

vacō, āvī, ātus 1 *v* to be empty;
to be open, 11.179; to be free
from, unoccupied by, *with abl*

3.123; (*impers*), vacat, there is
leisure, one has time, 1.373.

vacuus, a, um *adj* (vacō),
empty, void, 12.592; open,
5.515; deserted, 2.528;
solitary, 2.761; 4.82; without
employment, unoccupied;
subst vacuum, ī, *n*, emptiness,
void space, 12.906.

vādō 3 *v* to go, walk, advance,
go on, 2.396 *et al.*; rush,
2.359; move, speed on,
8.702; *imperat*, vāde,
away, go on! 3.462.

vadōsus, a, um *adj* (vadum),
that can be forded;
fordable, shallow, 7.728.

vadum, ī, *n* a ford; a shallow,
shoal, 1.112; sand-bank, 10.303;
shallow water, 11.628; bottom,
depth, 1.126; water, tide,
stream, 6.320; water of the
sea, 5.158; wave, sea, 7.198.

vāgīna, ae *f* a scabbard,
sheath, 4.579.

vāgītus, ūs *m* a wailing,
6.426. (vāgiō).

vagor, ātus sum 1 *dep v* to
wander about, 6.886; ride to
and fro, career about, 5.560;
to be rumored round, spread,
2.17. (vagus, wandering).

valēns, entis strong, vigorous,
powerful, 5.431. (valeō).

valeō, uī, itus 2 *v* to be strong
physically; to be well,
vigorous, powerful; to
excel, 5.67; to have power,
be able; can, 2.492; to avail;
can do, 12.798; *imperat*,
vale, farewell! 2.789.

Valerus, ī *m* a Latin warrior, 10.752.

validus, a, um *adj* (valeō), strong, 1.120; vigorous, powerful, 5.15; mighty, 2.50; heavy, massive.

vallēs, is *f* a valley, dell, dale, ravine, vale, 1.186 *et al.*

vāllō, āvī, ātus *1 v* to surround with a rampart; to encamp around, 11.915. (vāllum).

vāllum, ī a rampart, breastwork, or fort with palisades, 9.524.

vānus, a, um *adj* containing nothing, empty; devoid of truth, deceitful, false, 1.352; unavailing, 8.259; groundless, 4.12; ignorant, 10.631; *subst* vāna, ōrum, *n*, useless things, 2.287; *adv* vāna, vainly, 11.854.

vānus, a, um *adj* containing nothing, empty; devoid of truth, deceitful, false, 1.352; unavailing, 8.259; groundless, 4.12; ignorant, 10.631; *subst* vāna, ōrum, *n*, useless things, 2.287; *adv* vāna, vainly, 11.854.

vapor, ōris *m* vapor, steam, 7.466; fiery vapor; fire, 5.683.

vapōrō, āvī, ātus *1 v* to send out steam; to fumigate; perfume, 11.481. (vapor).

variō, āvī, ātus *1 v*, to diversify; exchange, relieve, 9.164; *n*, change, waver, 12.223. (varius).

varius, a, um *adj* diversified, manifold, various, 5.605 *et al.*; different, 4.286; mingled, 11.475; varying, 1.748; changing, 4.564; *subst* varium, iī, *n*, a changeable, fickle, inconstant thing, 4.569.

vāstātor, ōris *m* ravager, destroyer, 9.772. (vāstō).

vāstō, āvī, ātus *1 v* to make void or empty; to desolate, lay waste, ravage, devastate, 1.471 *et al.*; deprive of, strip, rob, *with acc* and *abl*, 8.8. (vāstus).

vāstus, a, um *adj* empty, void, wild, waste, 9.323; vast, unbounded, 1.118; huge, enormous, immense, 3.647; deep-, vast-, sounding, 1.245.

vātēs, is *c* a prophet, soothsayer, augur, seer, 3.433; prophetess, 3.187; poet, bard, 6.662; priest, 11.774.

-ve (*conj* enclit.), usually appended to the first word in the clause or phrase, or *freq*; ve — ve, either — or, both — and, 10.150.

vectis, is *m* a pole, lever, bar, bolt, 7.609. (vehō).

vectō, āvī, ātus *1 intens v* to convey, 6.391. (vehō).

vehō, vexī, vectus *3 v* to carry, 1.113 *et al.*; bring, usher in, 5.105; *passive* vehor, vectus sum, to be carried, fly, 7.65; with or without equō, nāvibus, etc., to ride, go, sail, 1.121; 12.162; *with acc* sail over, 1.524.

vel *conj*, or implying indifference as to the alternative or choice, or, *freq*; even, or whether, and, 6.769; vel — vel, either — or, 4.24.25 *et al.*

vēlāmen, inis, *n* a veil, 1.649; a covering, garment, vestment, 6.221. (vēlō).

Velīnus, a, um *adj* (Velia), of
Velia, a town on the western
coast of Lucania; Velian, 6.366.

Velīnus, ī *m* a lake in the country
of the Sabines, 7.517.

vēlivolus, a, um *adj* (vēlum
and volō), sail-flying,
sail-covered, 1.224.

vellō, vellī or **vulsī, vulsus** *3 v* to
pluck; pull up, 3.28; wrench,
tear away, 2.480; tear down,
9.506; move, 11.19; seize, lift,
10.381; vellere sīgna, pluck up
the standards from the ground;
move the camp, depart.

vellus, eris, *n* a fleece,
6.249; woolen band or
fillet, 4.459; skin, 7.95.

vēlō, āvī, ātus *1 v* to veil,
3.405; cover, clothe; bind
around, wreathe, crown,
5.72; festoon, adorn, 2.249;
to shade by bearing in the
hand, 7.154; 11.101. (vēlum).

vēlōx, ōcis *adj* swift, fleet,
4.174; quick, ready, 5.444.

vēlum, ī, *n* a cloth; sail,
1.103 *et al.*; a curtain,
canvas, covering, 1.469.

velut (velutī) *adv* even as, like,
as it were, as, just as, as if,
1.82 *et al.* (vel and ut).

vēna, ae *f* a vein, 4.2.

vēnābulum, ī, *n* a hunting-
spear, 4.131. (vēnor).

vēnātor, ōris *m* a huntsman,
11.678; vēnātor canis, a
hunting-dog, 12.751. (vēnor).

vēnātrīx, īcis *f* a huntress,
1.319; *adj*, 11.780. (vēnor).

vēnātus, ūs *m* a hunting, the
chase, 7.747; the spoils of
the chase, 9.407. (vēnor).

vēndō, didī, ditus *3 v* to offer
for sale; to sell, 1.484; betray,
6.621.(vēnum, sale, and dō).

venēnum, ī, *n* a poisonous
drug; poison, venom,
2.221; a charm, drug, 7.190;
poison of love, 1.688.

venerābilis, e *adj* (veneror),
deserving of respect;
venerable, venerated, revered,
6.408; sacred; 12.767.

veneror, ātus sum *1 dep v* to
venerate, reverence, revere,
3.79; adore, worship, 5.745;
bow before, kneel at, 12.220;
part, venerātus, a, um, *passive*
supplicated, entreated, 3.460.

venia, ae *f* favor, 4.50; mercy,
kindness, 4.435; forbearance,
indulgence, concession,
10.626; grace, favor, 11.101;
relief, help, 1.519.

Venīlia, ae *f* a nymph,
mother of Turnus, 10.76.

veniō, vēnī, ventus to come,
freq; come forth; approach,
6.755; rise, appear, 1.353;
dawn, 10.241; to present
one's self or itself, 5.344;
descend, spring from, 5.373;
impers, ventum est, we, they
came or have come, 4.151.

vēnor, ātus sum *1 dep v*
to hunt, 4.117.

venter, tris *m* the belly, 3.216;
figuratively hunger, 2.356.

ventōsus, a, um *adj* (ventus),
windy, stormy, 6.335;
fleeting, unreal, inflated,

windy, noisy, 11.390; empty, vain boasting, 11.708; fleet as the wind, 12.848.

ventūrum, ī, *n* that which is to come, the future, futurity, 6.66. (veniō).

ventus, ī *m* wind, 1.43 *et al.*; blast, 2.649.

Venulus, ī *m* a Latin messenger, 8.9.

Venus, eris *f* Venus, goddess of love and beauty, identified by the Romans with Aphrodite, daughter of Jupiter and Dione, 1.411 *et al.*; *metonym* love, lust, 6.26.

vepres, is *m* a thorn, brier, bramble, 8.645.

verbēna, ae *f* laurel, olive, or myrtle boughs for the altar; sacred boughs. (usually in the plural).

verber, eris, *n* a lash, whip; a stripe, blow, 6.558 *et al.*; flapping, beating, 12.876.

verberō, āvī, ātus *1 v* to lash, beat, strike, 3.423 *et al.* (verber).

verbum, ī, *n* a word, 1.710 *et al.*

vērē *adv* truly, correctly, 6.188. (vērus).

vereor, itus sum *2 dep v* to fear.

vergō *3 v* to incline; go down, sink, 12.727.

vērō *adv* in truth; in fact, but in fact, but, 2.438 *et al.* (vērus).

verrō, no perf, versus *3 v* to sweep; snatch, bear, sweep away, 1.59; sweep over, 3.208.

versicolor, ōris *adj* (versō and color), of various colors, particolored, 10.181.

versō, āvī, ātus *1 freq v* to turn much; writhe, 11.753; turn, 5.408; handle, wield, 9.747; to buffet, drive, beat round and round, 5.460; drive to and fro, 12.664; toss about, 6.362; turn, hurry, 4.286; involve in or distract with, 7.336; with or without mente, pectore, etc., revolve, meditate, devise, consider, 1.657. (vertō).

versus, ūs *m* a turning; a verse or line of poetry; a rank, row, tier of oars, 5.119. (vertō).

vertex, icis *m* a whirl; whirlpool, 7.567; vortex, 1.117; whirling column of flame, 12.673; the top, crown of the head, the head, 1.403; summit, top, 1.163; mountain summit, height, 3.679; ā vertice, from on high, from above, 1.114. (vertō).

vertō, vertī, versus *3 v,* to turn, *freq*; turn round, 12.462; turn back, put to flight, 10.512; turn toward, send to, 11.798; direct, 3.146; transfer, 11.282; reverse, 8.210; upturn, invert, 1.478; turn out, empty, drain, 9.165; overthrow, destroy, 1.20; subvert, 11.264; change, 1.237; transform, 12.891; sē vertere, to change; to be directed, to result, issue, tend, 1.671; *passive* vertī, of the heavens, to turn round, revolve, 2.250; of the year or seasons, to come round, revolve, return, 5.526; to move about, career about, 11.683; to turn upon, depend on, 10.529; to move,

verū, *ūs*, *n* a spit, 1.212; a slender, tapering lance; spit-dart, 7.665.

vērum but indeed, but yet, yet, but, 3.670 *et al.*

vērum *adv* in truth; truly.

vērum, *ī*, *n* that which is true; truth, justice, right, 2.141.

vērus, **a**, **um** *adj* true, *freq*; real, 1.405; vērius est, it is or would be more just, 12.694.

vēsānus, **a**, **um** insane, mad, furious, 9.340.

vescor *3 dep v* (*with abl* or absolute); to feed upon, 3.622; breathe, 1.546; banquet, feast, 6.657.

vesper, **eris** or **erī** *m* the evening; the evening star; the west, 5.19; *personif*, Vesper, Hesperus, 1.374 *et al.*

Vesta, **ae** *f* Vesta, daughter of Saturn, and granddaughter of Vesta, wife of Coelus; goddess of the hearth and household, 2.296 *et al.*; *metonym* the hearth, the fire.

vester, **tra**, **trum** possessive *pron* (vōs), your, yours, 1.573 *et al.*

vestibulum, **ī**, *n* entrance, porch, portal, vestibule, 2.469 *et al.*

vestīgium, **iī**, *n* a footstep; step, 2.711; footprint, track, 8.209; course, 5.592; footprint or foot; foot or hoof, 5.566; trace, 3.244; sign, vestige, 4.23. (vestīgō).

vestīgō *1 v* to track; trace, explore, search; seek

out, hunt, 12.467; 6.145; descry, 12.588.

vestiō, **īvī** or **īī**, **ītus** *4 v* to clothe; *figuratively* deck, array, cover, clothe, 6.640 *et al.* (vestis).

vestis, **is** *f* a garment, *freq*; robe, 6.645; vestment, 1.404; clothing, 6.359; covering, drapery, tapestry, 1.639.

Vesulus, **ī** *m* a mountain in the Maritime Alps, west of Liguria, 10.708.

vetitum, **ī**, *n* that which is forbidden; a prohibition, 10.9. (vetō).

vetō, **uī**, **itus** *1 v* to prohibit, 1.39; with *infin*, to forbid, 1.541; (with *acc*), oppose, 2.84.

vetus, **eris** *adj* old, aged, *freq*; ancient, early, former, 1.23 *et al.*

vetustās, **ātis** *f* oldness; age, antiquity; length of time, duration, continuance, 3.415; period, length of time, 10.792. (vetus),.

vetustus, **a**, **um** old, ancient, 2.713. (vetus).

vexō, **āvī**, **ātus** *1 intens v* harass, 4.615. (vehō).

via, **ae** *f* a highway, road, path, 1.401 *et al.*; limit, tropic, zodiac, 6.796; course, 5.28; voyage, wandering, 3.714; passage, entrance, 2.494; method, way, means, 12.405. (vehō).

viātor, **ōris** *m* a wayfarer, traveler, 5.275. (via).

vibrō, **āvī**, **ātus** *1 v*, to cause to move tremulously; to dart, flash, 8.524; to move to and fro, brandish, 11.606; curl, 12.100; *n*, vibrate, 2.211; quiver, 10.484; glitter, flash, 9.769.

vīcīnus, a, um *adj* (vīcus, village), of the same district or village; neighboring, near, 3.382.

vicis, *gen f* a change, turn in affairs; stage, interchange, 6.535; vicissitude, event, 3.376; combat, encounter, peril, 2.433, part, place, post, 3.634; watch, guard, 9.175. (nom. *sing* wanting).

vicissim *adv* in turn, 4.80; in one's turn, on one's part, 6.531. (vicis).

victima, ae *f* an animal offered in sacrifice; a victim, 12.296.

victor, ōris *m* a conqueror, victor, *freq*; as *adj*, successful, 3.439; in triumph, 2.329; with success, 8.50; victorious, 1.192. (vincō).

victōria, ae *f* victory, 2.584; personified, Victory, 11.436. (victor).

victrīx, īcis *f* a female conqueror; in triumph, 7.544; as *adj*, victorious, 3.54. (vincō).

vīctus, ūs *m* a living; nourishment, sustenance, food, 1.214. (vīvō).

videō, vīdī, vīsus (*interrog* **viden'** for **vidēsne**, 6.779) 2 *v* to see or perceive, in all senses of the words, *freq*; see to it, look to it; determine, 10.744; *passive* vidērī, to be seen, 2.461 *et al.*; to seem, appear, 1.396 *et al.*; (*impers*), vidētur, vīsum est, it seems to one, seems good, proper, is the will of; one thinks, judges, 2.428 *et al.*

viduō, āvī, ātus 1 *v* to bereave, *with acc* and *abl*, 8.571. (viduus).

vigeō 2 *v* to be active, lively, vigorous; to flourish, be strong, 2.88; excel, 4.175.

vigil, ilis *adj* (vigeō), awake, on the watch; sleepless, 4.182; perpetual, 4.200; *subst* vigil, ilis, *m*, a watchman, guard, sentinel, 2.266 *et al.*

vigilō, āvī, ātus 1 *v*, to be awake, watch, 10.228; wake up, awake, 4.573; to watch against, look out for, guard against; *part*, vigilāns, antis, watchful, 5.438. (vigil).

vīgintī (*num adj indecl*), twenty, 1.634.

vigor, ōris *m* activity, force, vigor, energy, 6.730. (vigeō).

vīlis, e *adj* of small value; cheap, worthless, insignificant, base, inferior, 11.372.

villōsus, a, um *adj* (villus), shaggy, hairy, 8.177.

villus, ī *m* shaggy hair, 5.352; nap, 1.702.

vīmen, inis, *n* a flexible twig; osier, sprout, shoot, sprig, stem, 3.31.

vinciō, vinxī, vinctus 4 *v* to bind, 11.81; bind round, 1.337; wreathe, bind round, 12.120.

vincō, vīcī, victus 3 *v*, to conquer, 1.529 *et al.*; slay, 10.842; overcome, overpower, overwhelm, 1.122; dispel, 1.727; win, possess, 6.148; persuade,

2.699; *n*, to be victorious, gain the victory, conquer, 11.712.

vinculum (**vinclum**), **ī**, *n* that which serves for binding; a chain, 6.395; fetter, bond, 1.54; a rope, cable, 1.168; 2.236; cord, 5.510; a halter, 11.492; morally, a bond, tie, 4.16; *pl* vincula or vincla, ōrum, *n*, gauntlets, 5.408; a sandal, 4.518; *figuratively* constraint, compulsion, 7.203. (vinciō).

vindicō, **āvī**, **ātus** *1 v* to claim or get by legal process; claim; rescue, save, 4.228. (vindex, defender).

vīnum, **ī**, *n* wine, 1.195 *et al*.

viola, **ae** *f* a violet, 11.69.

violābilis, **e** *adj* (violō), that may be violated; violable; nōn violābile, inviolable, 2.154.

violentia, **ae** *f* violence, 11.354; fierceness, impetuosity, fire, passion, fury, rage, 12.9. (violentus).

violentus, **a**, **um** *adj* (vīs), having much or excessive force; violent, impetuous, 6.356.

violō, **āvī**, **ātus** *1 v* to exercise force upon; hurt, wound, 11.277; break, 7.114; devastate, 11.255; desecrate, profane, 2.189; stain, 12.67. (vīs).

vīpereus, **a**, **um** *adj* (vīpera, viper), pertaining to vipers or snakes; viperous, snaky, 6.281.

vir, **virī** *m* a man as distinguished by sex, 9.479, and *freq*; husband, 2.744; hero, 6.415; *pl* virī, ōrum, comrades, friends, 2.668; citizens, 1.264; people in general, 1.532.

virāgō, **inis** *f* a woman of masculine spirit; a heroine, warlike maid, 12.468. (cf. vir).

Virbius, **iī** *m* a Latin hero, son of Hippolytus and Aricia, 7.762.

virectum, **ī**, *n* a green or grassy spot; a lawn or meadow, 6.638. (vireō).

vireō, **uī** *2 v* to be green, 6.206 *et al*.; *part*, virēns, entis, green, 6.679.

virga, **ae** *f* a twig, bough, branch, 6.144; a wand (the caduceus of Mercury), 4.242. (vireō).

virgātus, **a**, **um** *adj* (virga), made of twigs; of basketwork; checkered or striped; plaid-, 8.660.

virgeus, **a**, **um** *adj* (virga), of twigs, rods, osiers; of brushwood, 7.463.

virgineus, **a**, **um** *adj* (virgō), pertaining to a virgin; of a virgin, of virgins; a maiden's, 11.68; maiden-, virgin-, 2.168.

virginitās, **ātis** *f* virginity, 12.141. (virgo).

virgō, **inis** *f* a maiden, virgin, *freq*; virgin daughter, 2.403; virgin child, 11.565; the transformed virgin, Io, 7.791.

virgultum, **ī**, *n* (used only in the plural) a growth of brambles; a thicket, grove, 12.522; shrubs, 3.23; shoots or sprigs, 12.207. (virga).

viridāns, **antis** green, grassy, verdant, 5.388; mossy, 8.630. (viridō).

viridis, **e** *adj* (vireō), verdant, green, 3.24; green wood-,

7.677; fresh, blooming, 5.295; vigorous, 6.304.

viridō *1 v* to be green, verdant. (viridis).

virīlis, e *adj* (vir), pertaining to a man; male, 7.50; manly, 3.342; of manhood, 9.311.

virtūs, ūtis *f* manhood; valor, courage, 2.367 *et al*.; prowess, 1.566; moral worth, virtue, 5.344; greatness, glory, 6.806; heroism, 4.3; heroic effort, struggle, 12.913. (vir).

vīs, vīs, *pl* **vīrēs, vīrium** strength, force; persistence, industry, force, power, 2.452; keenness of scent, 4.132; might, 7.432; violence, fury, 1.69; hurt, injury, 3.242; *pl* vīrēs, ium, physical power, strength, 2.639; military strength, power, resources, 2.170; natural power, 7.258; personal power, influence, 8.404.

vīscum, ī, *n* the mistletoe, 6.205.

vīscus, eris, *n* an inner part of the body; *pl* vīscera, um, the entrails, vitals, 6.599; the flesh, 1.211; heart, bosom, 6.833.

vīsō, vīsī, vīsus *3 intens v* to look at much; look at carefully, observe, see, 2.63; visit, 8.157. (videō).

vīsum, ī, *n* anything seen; a vision, 3.172; portent, prodigy, 4.456. (videō).

vīsus, ūs *m* a seeing; vision, sight, 4.277; a phenomenon, spectacle, appearance, sight, 2.212; aspect, 11.271; prodigy, 3.36. (videō).

vīta, ae *f* life, 2.92; of society or nations, 6.663; the living spirit, a soul or spirit, 4.705. (vīvō).

vītālis, e *adj* (vīta), pertaining to life; essential to life, vital, 1.388.

vītisator, ōris *m* a vine-planter, 7.179. (vītis, a vine, and 1. serō).

vītō, āvī, ātus *1 v* to shun, avoid, 2.433.

vitreus, a, um *adj* (vitrum), of or like glass, clear, shining, crystal, 7.759.

vitta, ae *f* a fillet, band, or chaplet for the head, especially for religious occasions, 5.366 *et al.*

vitulus, ī *m* a young bullock, steer, calf, 5.772.

vīvidus, a, um *adj* (vīvō), full of life; lively, vigorous, ardent, 5.754; quick, swift, 12.753.

vīvō, vīxī, vīctus *3 v* to live, 3.311, and *freq*; to survive, remain, be still living, 1.218; to support life, live, 7.749; exist, prosper, flourish, 1.445; of inanimate things, live; grow, increase; vīvite, live and be happy; farewell.

vīvus, a, um *adj* (vīvō), alive, living, 6.531; lifelike, 6.848; immortal, 12.235; of water, living, running, pure, 2.719; of rock, natural, unquarried, living, 1.167.

vix *adv* hardly, scarcely, with difficulty, 5.263, and *freq*.

vocātus, ūs *m* a calling; summons; *pl* a call, 12.95. (vocō).

vōciferor, ātus sum *1 dep v* to raise the voice; cry out, exclaim; utter with loud cries, 2.679. (vōx and ferō).

vocō, āvī, ātus *1 v* to call, name, 3.133; mention, speak of, 3.185; invoke, implore, 3.264; propitiate, 3.253; invite, 3.70; summon, 2.668; challenge, 6.172; incite, 7.614; assemble, rally, 7.508.

volāns, antis *f* a winged creature; a bird, 6.239. (volo -are).

volātilis, e flying; winged, 4.71. (volō).

Volcēns, entis *m* a Latin chief, 9.370.

volēns, entis willing, ready, unresisting, spontaneously, 6.146.

volitō, āvī, ātus *1 freq n* to fly about, whirl about, hover, flit, 6.329; ride or gallop around, 12.126; circulate, pass rapidly, fly. (1. volō).

volō, āvī, ātus *1 v* to fly, 1.300 *et al.*; of rumor, to be spread rapidly, noised or spread abroad, 3.121.

volō, voluī, velle, *irreg* and *def v* to will, wish, desire, intend, purpose, *freq*; *followed by the infin*, with or without subject *acc*, by the subj., or by a noun in the *acc*; wish, desire, 2.104 *et al.*; of the gods, order, decree, 5.50 *et al.*; be willing, 1.733; think

of, intend, mean; of things, to signify, mean, 6.318.

Volscī, ōrum the Volsci or Volscians, a warlike tribe of Latium.

Volscus, a, um *adj* Volscian, 7.803.

volūbilis, e *adj* (volvō), turning, whirling, spinning, 7.382.

volucer, cris, cre *adj* (1. volō), having the power to fly; of birds or winged creatures, swift-winged, 5.488; of things, winged, fleeting, 2.794; swift, 1.317; *subst* volucris, is, *f*, a bird, 3.262.

volūmen, inis, *n* a roll; fold, coil, 2.208. (volvō).

voluntās, ātis *f* a willing; will, wish, desire, 6.675; consent, 4.125. (2. volō).

voluptās, ātis *f* satisfaction, delight, pleasure, 3.660. (2. volō).

Volusus, ī *m* a follower of Turnus, 11.463.

volūtō, āvī, ātus *1 intens v* to roll about; to roll back, reëcho, 5.149; roll or send through, make resound, 1.725; of thought, turn over, ponder, think over; meditate, 1.50; with ellipsis of the *acc*, 4.533; *n*, fall prostrate, 3.607. (volvō).

volvō, volvī, volūtus *3 v* to roll, 1.86; roll along or down, 1.101; roll or cast up, 3.206; toss, hurl, 12.906; roll over, roll in the dust, 12.329; cast, hurl down, 1.116; 9.512; roll, wheel, 1.163; of books, open, unroll, 1.262; of the

Fates, fix the circle of events, decree, ordain, dispose, 1.22; 3.376; of the mind, revolve, meditate, reflect upon, 1.305; pass, continue, live through, experience, endure, suffer, 1.9; rotam volvere, to complete a cycle, period; *passive* volvī, roll over, roll, 10.590; turn or wind about, 7.350; to be shed, to flow, 4.449; roll on, revolve, 1.269.

vōmer, eris *m* a plowshare, plow, 7.635.

vomō, uī, itus *3 v* to vomit; belch, vomit forth, 5.682.

vorāgō, inis *f* a chasm, abyss, gulf, whirlpool, 6.296; torrent, 9.105. (vorō).

vorō, āvī, ātus *1 v* to swallow up, 1.117.

vōs and vōsmet you, *pl*; *abl* with cum, vōbīscum, with you; vōsmet, yourself, yourselves, 1.207.

vōtum, ī, *n* a thing vowed; a conditional pledge made to some deity, a vow, 5.234, prayer, 4.65; votive offering, 2.17; sacrifice, 3.279. (voveō).

voveō, vōvī, vōtus *2 v* to make a pledge or vow to a deity; vow, 10.774; consecrate, devote, 11.558.

vōx, vōcis *f* a voice, 1.328; note, tone, 6.646; language, 12.825; response, answer, 2.119; sound, 3.556.

Vulcānius, a, um *adj* (Vulcānus), pertaining to Vulcan; forged or wrought by Vulcan, 12.739 *et al.*; of fire or flame, 10.408.

Vulcānus, ī *m* the god of fire and of the forge, son of Jupiter and Juno, 8.422; *metonym* fire, 2.311 *et al.*

vulgō *adv* in the multitude; in common, generally, 6.283; all around, everywhere, 3.643.

vulgō, āvī, ātus *1 v* to make common or commonly known; spread abroad, 1.457; divulge, disclose, 10.64. (vulgus).

vulgus, ī, *n, rarely m* the common people; populace, people, 2.39; multitude, 2.798; common soldiery, 2.99; rabble, throng, 1.149; of animals, the herd, 1.190.

vulnerō, āvī, ātus *1 v* to wound; offend, hurt, wound, 8.583. (vulnus).

vulnificus, a, um *adj* (vulnus and faciō), wound-making; hurtful, deadly, 8.446.

vulnus, eris, *n* a wound, 2.436, and *freq*; blow, 5.433; aim, thrust, 2.529; of the mind, distress, 12.160; heart-wound, passion, 4.2; of revenge, 1.36.

vultur, uris *m* a vulture, 6.597.

Vulturnus, ī *m* a river of Campania, 7.729.

vultus, ūs *m* the look or expression of the face; face, visage, countenance, 1.209; features, 4.556; appearance, aspect, 5.848; eyes, sight, 2.539.

Xanthus, ī *m* 1. The Xanthus or Scamander, a river near Troy, 5.808 *et al.* 2. A small river in Epirus named by Helenus after

the Trojan Xanthus, 3.350.
3. A river in Lycia, 4.143.

Zacynthus, ī *f* an island in the
Ionian sea opposite Elis, 3.270.

Zephyrus, ī *m* Zephyrus or
Favonius, the god of the
west wind, 2.417 *et al.*; west
wind, 4.562; wind, 10.103.

CPSIA information can be obtained
at www.ICGtesting.com
Printed in the USA
LVHW090931310822
727260LV00005B/810